ANNUAL EDITIONS

Mass Media 10/11

Sixteenth Edition

EDITOR

Joan Gorham
West Virginia University

Joan Gorham completed her undergraduate work at the University of Wisconsin and received master's and doctoral degrees from Northern Illinois University. She is currently associate dean for academic affairs in the Eberly College of Arts and Sciences and a professor of communication studies at West Virginia University. Dr. Gorham is the author of *Commercial Media and Classroom Teaching* and has published numerous articles on communication in instruction. She has taught classes dealing with mass media and media literacy at the high school and college levels, as well as for teachers throughout the state of West Virginia.

ANNUAL EDITIONS: MASS MEDIA, SIXTEENTH EDITION

Published by McGraw-Hill, a business unit of The McGraw-Hill Companies, Inc., 1221 Avenue of the Americas, New York, NY 10020. Copyright © 2011 by The McGraw-Hill Companies, Inc. All rights reserved. Previous edition(s) 2005, 2007, 2008. No part of this publication may be reproduced or distributed in any form or by any means, or stored in a database or retrieval system, without the prior written consent of The McGraw-Hill Companies, Inc., including, but not limited to, in any network or other electronic storage or transmission, or broadcast for distance learning.

Some ancillaries, including electronic and print components, may not be available to customers outside the United States.

Annual Editions® is a registered trademark of The McGraw-Hill Companies, Inc.

Annual Editions is published by the **Contemporary Learning Series** group within the McGraw-Hill Higher Education division.

1 2 3 4 5 6 7 8 9 0 WDQ/WDQ 1 0 9 8 7 6 5 4 3 2 1 0

ISBN 978–0–07–805061–9
MHID 0–07–805061–8
ISSN 1092–0439

Managing Editor: *Larry Loeppke*
Developmental Editor: *Dave Welsh*
Editorial Coordinator: *Mary Foust*
Editorial Assistant: *Cindy Hedley*
Production Service Assistant: *Rita Hingtgen*
Permissions Coordinator: *Rita Hingtgen*
Senior Marketing Manager: *Julie Keck*
Senior Marketing Communications Specialist: *Mary Klein*
Marketing Coordinator: *Alice Link*
Director Specialized Production: *Faye Schilling*
Senior Project Manager: *Joyce Watters*
Design Coordinator: *Margarite Reynolds*
Production Supervisor: *Sue Culbertson*
Cover Graphics: *Kristine Jubeck*

Compositor: Laserwords Private Limited
Cover Image: © The McGraw-Hill Companies, Inc./John Flournoy, photographer (inset);
© The McGraw-Hill Companies, Inc./Lars A. Niki, photographer (background)

Library in Congress Cataloging-in-Publication Data
Main entry under title: Annual Editions: Mass Media. 2010/2011.
  1. Mass Media—Periodicals. I. Gorham, Joan, *comp.* II. Title: Mass Media.
658'.05

www.mhhe.com

Editors/Academic Advisory Board

Members of the Academic Advisory Board are instrumental in the final selection of articles for each edition of ANNUAL EDITIONS. Their review of articles for content, level, and appropriateness provides critical direction to the editors and staff. We think that you will find their careful consideration well reflected in this volume.

ANNUAL EDITIONS: Mass Media 10/11
16th Edition

EDITOR

Joan Gorham
West Virginia University

ACADEMIC ADVISORY BOARD MEMBERS

Editors/Academic Advisory Board continued

Preface

In publishing ANNUAL EDITIONS we recognize the enormous role played by the magazines, newspapers, and journals of the public press in providing current, first-rate educational information in a broad spectrum of interest areas. Many of these articles are appropriate for students, researchers, and professionals seeking accurate, current material to help bridge the gap between principles and theories and the real world. These articles, however, become more useful for study when those of lasting value are carefully collected, organized, indexed, and reproduced in a low-cost format, which provides easy and permanent access when the material is needed. That is the role played by ANNUAL EDITIONS.

The mass media are a part of the fabric of American society. Learning how to evaluate media messages critically—asking, Who created this message? What is its intent? How objective is it? How does what I am seeing or hearing reflect and/or shape real-world realities?—is a part of being literate in today's world. The organization of articles in this collection reflects this media literacy perspective. Unit 1 offers commentary on mass media use and content and its impact on individuals and society. Unit 2 explores media as sources of news and information. Unit 3 introduces perspectives on media access, ownership, regulation, and ethics. Unit 4 addresses relationships between the content and financial sides of media enterprises.

The articles selected for inclusion in this sixteenth edition of *Annual Editions: Mass Media* reflect the firm entrenchment of "new media" into the traditional media landscape. Issues of access, liberal versus conservative bias, changing interest in and definition of "news," and media effects on children continue. However, where the "mass" in mass media was traditionally about selected messages reaching large audiences through few channels—narrow on the head end, wide on the receiving end—it is increasingly about mass channels and messages. Articles reviewed over the past year for inclusion in this edition focused overwhelmingly on business models, on changing organizational and financial structures within which media messages are produced, as opposed to message effects.

The eminent media theorist Marshall McLuhan proposed four questions that help predict how new media invariably affect the form and content of old media: (1) What does a new medium enhance or amplify in the culture? (2) What does it make obsolete or push out of a position of prominence? (3) What does it retrieve from the past? and (4) What does a medium "reverse into" or "flip into" when it reaches the limits of its potential? Early adopters of new media tend to use them like old media. Network television, for example, started out with actors reading scripts. It took a while for producers to fully understand how television could tell stories differently from radio, but once they did, folks who had been listening to serial dramas, comedies, and soap operas on radio came to prefer watching them on TV. Radio, in turn, flipped into talk and music programming. DVD players have flipped the way movies are made

and marketed. Outtakes and special features such as alternative endings and camera angles became part of the filmmaking craft, saved for the DVD release where "active viewers" can fiddle with them. In return, movie theatres added stadium seating and enhanced sound systems, a return to the grand cinema experience of earlier years, with hopes of making moviegoing a bigger and more sensual, if more passive, experience than watching DVDs at home.

Technology is the conduit through which mass media messages move between senders and receivers. Its development is a scientific experiment, but its use is a social endeavor. Mass media shape the form and content of what is communicated, of who communicates with whom, with what intent and to what effect.

Most of the articles in this collection, even those that are primarily descriptive, include an editorial viewpoint and draw conclusions or make recommendations with which you may disagree. These editorial viewpoints are more frequently critical than they are complimentary. They are not necessarily my opinions and should not necessarily become yours. I encourage you to debate these issues, drawing from the information and insights provided in the readings as well as from your own experiences as a media consumer. If you are an "average" American, you have spent a great deal of time with mass media. Your own observations have as much value as those of the writers whose work is included in these pages.

As always, those involved in producing this anthology are sincerely committed to including articles that are timely, informative, and interesting. We value your feedback and encourage you to complete and return the postage-paid *article rating form* on the last page of the book, to share your suggestions and let us know your opinions.

B Gorham

Joan Gorham
Editor

Contents

UNIT 1
Living with Media

The concepts in bold italics are developed in the article. For further expansion, please refer to the Topic Guide.

UNIT 2
Telling Stories

The concepts in bold italics are developed in the article. For further expansion, please refer to the Topic Guide.

UNIT 3
Players and Guides

The concepts in bold italics are developed in the article. For further expansion, please refer to the Topic Guide.

UNIT 4
A Word from Our Sponsor

The concepts in bold italics are developed in the article. For further expansion, please refer to the Topic Guide.

The concepts in bold italics are developed in the article. For further expansion, please refer to the Topic Guide.

Correlation Guide

The *Annual Editions* series provides students with convenient, inexpensive access to current, carefully selected articles from the public press. **Annual Editions: Mass Media 10/11** is an easy-to-use reader that presents articles on important topics such as *the coverage of war, catastrophes, advertising, the Internet,* and many more. For more information on *Annual Editions* and other *McGraw-Hill Contemporary Learning Series* titles visit www.mhhe.com/cls.

This convenient guide matches the units in **Annual Editions: Mass Media 10/11** with the corresponding chapters in three of our best-selling McGraw-Hill Mass Communication textbooks by Dominick, Rodman, and Baran.

Annual Editions: Mass Media 10/11	Dynamics of Mass Communication: Media in Transition, 11/e by Dominick	Mass Media in a Changing World, 3/e by Rodman	Introduction to Mass Communication: Media Literacy and Culture, 6/e Updated Edition by Baran
Unit 1: Living with Media	**Chapter 1:** Communication: Mass and Other Forms **Chapter 2:** Perspectives on Mass Communication **Chapter 3:** Historical and Cultural Context **Chapter 4:** Newspapers **Chapter 6:** Books **Chapter 9:** Motion Pictures **Chapter 10:** Broadcast Television **Chapter 19:** Social Effects of Mass Communication	**Chapter 1:** Introduction: Media in a Changing World **Chapter 2:** Media Impact: Understanding Research and Effects **Chapter 3:** Books: The Durable Medium **Chapter 4:** Newspapers: Where Journalism Begins **Chapter 6:** Movies: Magic from the Dream Factory	**Chapter 1:** Mass Communication, Culture, and Media Literacy **Chapter 3:** Books **Chapter 4:** Newspapers **Chapter 5:** Magazines **Chapter 6:** Film **Chapter 7:** Radio, Recording, and Popular Music **Chapter 8:** Television, Cable, and Mobile Video **Chapter 13:** Theories and Effects of Mass Communication
Unit 2: Telling Stories	**Chapter 4:** Newspapers **Chapter 10:** Broadcast Television **Chapter 13:** News Gathering and Reporting **Chapter 19:** Social Effects of Mass Communication	**Chapter 10:** The Internet: Convergence in a Networked World **Chapter 11:** Electronic Journalism: News in an Age of Entertainment	**Chapter 4:** Newspapers **Chapter 8:** Television, Cable, and Mobile Video **Chapter 15:** Global Media
Unit 3: Players and Guides	**Chapter 16:** Formal Controls: Laws, Rules, Regulations **Chapter 17:** Ethics and Other Informal Controls **Chapter 19:** Social Effects of Mass Communication	**Chapter 7:** Recordings and the Music Industry: Copyright Battles, Format Wars **Chapter 14:** Media Law: Understanding Freedom of Expression **Chapter 15:** Media Ethics: Understanding Media Morality	**Chapter 7:** Radio, Recording, and Popular Music **Chapter 14:** Media Freedom, Regulation, and Ethics
Unit 4: A Word From Our Sponsor	**Chapter 15:** Advertising	**Chapter 4:** Newspapers: Where Journalism Begins **Chapter 10:** The Internet: Convergence in a Networked World **Chapter 13:** Advertising: The Media Support Industry	**Chapter 4:** Newspapers **Chapter 5:** Magazines **Chapter 7:** Radio, Recording, and Popular Music **Chapter 8:** Television, Cable, and Mobile Video **Chapter 12:** Advertising

Topic Guide

This topic guide suggests how the selections in this book relate to the subjects covered in your course. You may want to use the topics listed on these pages to search the Web more easily.

On the following pages a number of websites have been gathered specifically for this book. They are arranged to reflect the units of this Annual Editions reader. You can link to these sites by going to *http://www.mhhe.com/cls*.

All the articles that relate to each topic are listed below the bold-faced term.

Internet References

The following Internet sites have been selected to support the articles found in this reader. These sites were available at the time of publication. However, because websites often change their structure and content, the information listed may no longer be available. We invite you to visit *http://www.mhhe.com/cls* for easy access to these sites.

Annual Editions: Mass Media 10/11

General Sources

Associated Press Managing Editors
http://www.apme.com/

Allows you to view all the front pages of newspapers across the nation.

The Center for Communication
http://www.cencom.org

The Center for Communication is an independent nonpartisan media forum that introduces issues, ethics, people and media business. The site provides archived seminars like the panel discussion on Marshall McLuhan entitled "Oracle of the Electronic Age." Students can tap into these seminars via video-streaming. This site also provides links to numerous other sites.

Current.org
http://www.current.org/

This is a newspaper about public broadcasting in the U.S. It is editorially independent and is an affiliate of the Educational Broadcasting Corporation.

Digital Forensics and Tampering
http://www.cs.dartmouth.edu/farid/research/tampering.html

Dartmouth scientist Hany Farid posts examples of photo editing, and illustrations of his work developing mathematical and computational algorithms to detect tampering in digital media. Links to articles including *http://www.cs.dartmouth .edu/farid/publications/deception07.html* "Digital Doctoring: can we trust photographs?" and *http://www.cs.dartmouth.edu/farid/ publications/significance06.pdf* "Digital Doctoring: How to tell the real from the fake" (pdf files), well-illustrated with examples, historical and current.

Iowa Scholar's Desktop Resources
http://www.uiowa.edu/~commstud/resources/scholarsdesktop/

An encyclopedic resource related to a host of mass communication issues, this site is maintained by the University of Iowa's Department of Communication Studies. It provides excellent links covering advertising, cultural studies, digital media, film, gender issues, and media studies.

Media Awareness Network
http://www.media-awareness.ca/

Media Awareness Network provides resources and support for parents and teachers interested in media and information literacy for kids. Concise, vest-pocket summaries if issues including media stereotyping, media violence, online hate, information privacy. Includes educational games (e.g. *Jo Cool or Jo Fool: Interactive Module and Quiz on Critical Thinking for the Internet*). From Canada.

Netcomtalk/Boston University
http://web.bu.edu/COM/communication.html

The College of Communication at Boston University presents this multimedia publication site for daily perusal of a wide variety of news items and topics in media and communications. Click on "COMNews Today" for the latest happenings in mass media.

NewsPlace
http://www.niu.edu/newsplace/

This site of Professor Avi Bass from Northern Illinois University will lead you to a wealth of resources of interest in the study of mass media, such as international perspectives on censorship. Links to government, corporate, and other organizations are provided.

The Web Journal of Mass Communication
http://www.scripps.ohiou.edu/wjmcr/

This site can also be easily accessed from *http://www.wjmcr.org*. The Web Journal of Mass Communication out of Ohio University focuses on articles that relate to how the web shapes mass communication.

Writers Guild of America
http://www.wga.org

The Writer's Guild of America is the union for media entertainment writers. The nonmember areas of this site offer useful information for aspiring writers. There is also an excellent links section.

UNIT 1: Living with Media

American Center for Children and Media
http://www.centerforchildrenandmedia.org

Continually amasses up-to-date research, news and writings about children and media, from which it digests, analyzes and disseminates information on trends and themes.

Children Now
http://www.childrennow.org

Children Now's site provides access to a variety of views on the impact of media on children. Public opinion surveys of young people, independent research on television and print media, industry conference proceedings, and more are available. An Internet resource list is included.

Freedom Forum
http://www.freedomforum.org

The Freedom Forum is a nonpartisan, international foundation dedicated to free press, free speech, and free spirit for all people. Its mission is to help the public and the news media understand one another better. The press watch area of this site is intriguing.

Geocities
http://www.geocities.com/Wellesley/1031/#media

This site presents a negative perspective on how the media portray women. By clicking on its many links, you can find such varied resources as an archive on misogynistic quotes and a discussion of newspeak and doublethink.

UNIT 2: Telling Stories

Cable News Network
http://www.cnn.com

CNN's interactive site is considered to be an excellent online news site.

Internet References

Fox News

http://www.foxnews.com

The Fox News site touts itself as being "fair and balanced"

Fairness and Accuracy in Reporting

http://www.fair.org

FAIR, a U.S. media watch group, offers well-documented criticism of media bias and censorship. It advocates structural reform to break up the dominant media conglomerates.

Organization of News Ombudsmen (ONO)

http://www.newsombudsmen.org

This ONO page provides links to journalism websites. ONO works to aid in the wider establishment of the position of news ombudsmen on newspapers and elsewhere in the media and to provide a forum for the interchange of experiences, information, and ideas among news ombudsmen.

Television News Archive

http://tvnews.vanderbilt.edu

By browsing through this Vanderbilt University site, you can review national U.S. television news broadcasts from 1968 onward. It will give you insight into how the broadcast news industry has changed over the years and what trends define the industry today.

UNIT 3: Players and Guides

The Electronic Journalist

http://spj.org

This site for The Electronic Journalist, an online service of the Society of Professional Journalists (SPJ), will lead you to a number of articles having to do with journalistic ethics, accuracy, and other topics.

Federal Communications Commission (FCC)

http://www.fcc.gov

The FCC is an independent U.S. government agency whose mission "is to encourage competition in all communications markets and to protect the public interest." Access to information about such topics as laws regulating the media is possible.

Index on Censorship

http://www.indexonline.org

This British site provides information and many international links to show "how free speech affects the political issues of the moment."

Internet Law Library

http://www.phillylawyer.com

Featuring abundant resources in communications law, this site includes the most recent developments on this subject.

Michigan Press Photographers Association (MPPA)

http://www.mppa.org

Ethical issues in photo journalism are featured at this site sponsored by the MPPA.

Poynter Online: Research Center

http://www.poynter.org

The Poynter Institute for Media Studies provides extensive links to information and resources on media ethics, media writing and editing, visual journalism, and much more. Many bibliographies and websites are included.

World Intellectual Property Organization (WIPO)

http://www.wipo.org

Click on the links at WIPO's home page to find general information on WIPO and intellectual property, publications and documents, international classifications, and more.

UNIT 4: A Word from Our Sponsor

Advertising Age

http://adage.com

Gain access to articles and features about media advertising, such as a history of television advertising, at this site.

Citizens Internet Empowerment Coalition (CIEC)

http://www.ciec.org

CIEC is a broad group of Internet users, library groups, publishers, online service providers, and civil liberties groups working to preserve the First Amendment and ensure the future of free expression. Find discussions of the Communications Decency Act and Internet-related topics here.

Educause

http://www.educause.edu

Open this site for an e-mailed summary of info-tech news from various major publications and for many other resources meant to facilitate the introduction, use, access to, and management of information resources in teaching, learning, scholarship, and research.

Media Literacy Clearing House

http://www.frankwbaker.com/default1.htm

Frank Baker's Media Literacy Clearing House provides access to a wealth of resources designed for teaching media literacy and of interest to anyone seeking to improve their own media literacy. Click "Math in the Media" for links to data on 30 second ad costs, calculating ratings and shares, and Nielsen markets.

UNIT 1

Living with Media

Unit Selections

1. **Off Course,** Michael Massing
2. **Tele[re]vision,** Jenny Price
3. **Research on the Effects of Media Violence,** Media Awareness Network
4. **True Crime: The Roots of an American Obsession,** Walter Mosley
5. **Wikipedia in the Newsroom,** Donna Shaw
6. **Journalist Bites Reality!** Steve Salerno
7. **The Future of Reading,** Steven Levy
8. **Are Newspapers Doomed?,** Joseph Epstein
9. **The Great Wall of Facebook,** Fred Vogelstein

Key Points to Consider

- What purpose do media serve in your life? What are your priorities in selecting entertainment media? In what ways are you satisfied and dissatisfied with the media information you consume?

- Where do social media fit into your life? There are only 24 hours in a day. What activities does time with Facebook et al. replace: Time with entertainment media? Time with informational media? In-person time with friends and family? Time sleeping?

- Why is it so difficult for research to definitively resolve media effects questions?

- Do you think the Internet will make print media, such as books and newspapers, obsolete? Would you miss them if it did?

- Select a comparison sample of old and new media—for example, television sitcoms from about the time you were born (*Nick at Night* is a good source) and current television sitcoms, or women's magazines from the time your mother came of age and current women's magazines, or romantic movies from the time your grandparents were teenagers and current romantic movies. What changes do you see?

- Does media content primarily reflect social reality or does it significantly shape social reality? Should it do otherwise? Why or why not?

Student Website
www.mhhe.com/cls

Internet References

American Center for Children and Media
http://www.centerforchildrenandmedia.org
Children Now
http://www.childrennow.org
Freedom Forum
http://www.freedomforum.org
Geocities
http://www.geocities.com/Wellesley/1031/#media

The media have been blamed for just about everything, from a decrease in attention span to an increase in street crime, to undoing our capacity to think. In *Amusing Ourselves to Death* (Penguin, 1986), social critic Neil Postman suggested that the cocktail party, the quiz show, and popular trivia games are reflections of society's trying to find a use for the abundance of superficial information given to us by the media. Peggy Noonan, a former network writer and White House speechwriter, has observed that experiences are not "real" unless they are ratified by media (which is why, she says, half the people in a stadium watch the game on monitors rather than the field). Marie Winn's memorable description of a child transfixed by television—slack-jawed, tongue resting on the front teeth, eyes glazed and vacant (*The Plug-In Drug,* Penguin, 1985, 2002)—has become an oft-quoted symbol of the passivity encouraged by television viewing. We, as a nation, have a distinct love-hate relationship with mass media.

Questions of whether, and to what extent, media influence our behaviors, values, expectations, and ways of thinking are difficult to answer. While one bibliographer has compiled a list of some 4,000 citations of English-language articles focusing just on children and television, the conclusions drawn in these articles vary. Isolating media as a causal agent in examining human behavior is a difficult task.

Media messages serve a variety of purposes: They inform, they influence public opinion, they sell, and they entertain—sometimes below the level of consumers' conscious awareness. Children watch *Sesame Street* to be entertained, but they also learn to count, to share, to accept physical differences among individuals, and (perhaps) to desire a Sesame Street lunch box. Adults watch crime dramas to be entertained, but they also learn that they have the right to remain silent when arrested, how (accurately or inaccurately) the criminal justice system works, and that the world is an unsafe place.

Nicholas Johnson, a former chairman of the Federal Communications Commission, has noted, "Every moment of television programming—commercials, entertainment, news—teaches us something." How such incidental learning occurs is most often explained by two theories. Social learning (or modeling) theory suggests that the behavior of media consumers, particularly children, is affected by their imitating role models presented via media. The degree to which modeling occurs depends upon the presence of *inhibitors,* lessons learned in real life that discourage imitation, and *disinhibitors,* experiences in real life that reinforce imitation.

Cultivation theory holds that media shape behavior by influencing attitudes. Media provide a "window to the world," exposing consumers to images of reality that may or may not jibe with personal experience. *Mainstreaming* effects occur when media introduce images of things with which the consumer has no personal experience. *Resonance* effects occur when media images echo personal experience. For example, recent research has found that knowing someone who is openly gay or lesbian is the single best predictor of tolerance of same-sex marriage, but seeing likable gay characters on television shows such as *Will & Grace* also has significant effects on attitude. In one study,

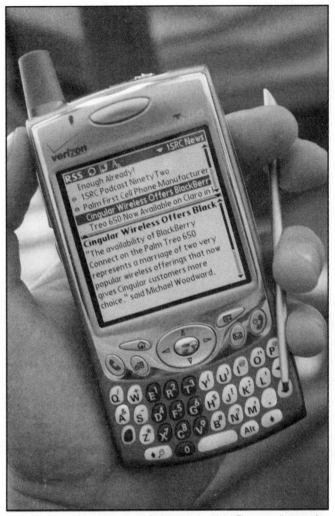

© The McGraw-Hill Companies, Inc./John Flournoy, photographer

anti-gay perceptions in students with little personal experience of interacting with gay men decreased by 12% after viewing ten episodes of HBO's *Six Feet Under*. This is a mainstreaming effect. Heavy media consumers are more likely to be affected than light consumers, since they spend more time absorbing information from media. People who have had real-world experiences similar to those in the media they consume may find that the media reinforce their beliefs (resonance). However, consumers who have had personal experiences that differ from the images portrayed in media are not as likely to believe "media reality" over what they have observed in real life.

The readings in this unit examine media use, media content, and media effects. All of them acknowledge the increasingly complex interactions among media producers, technology, forms, formats, and consumers. They share concerns over media influence on daily living and on society. Some take a *feedforward* perspective, holding media accountable for shaping changes in public attitude and behavior. Others argue a *feedback* viewpoint, in which media simply reflect what consumers choose to make popular.

"Off Course" provides an overview of the public concerns about popular culture and themes of entertainment media, as well as media's coverage of itself. "Tele[re]vision" explore prosocial effects of media and kids. The latter offers insight into *Sesame Street* lessons worldwide as well as in the United States. "Research on the Effects of Media Violence" summarizes some of the key questions that have grounded research on media effects, with findings explained using both social learning and cultivation theories.

"True Crime" addresses Americans' fascination with crime from a cultivation perspective: "Our relationship with guilt is as old as the DNA that defines our species. But the nature of culpability changes with technology and technique. These changes affect the way we see the world and the way we seek to understand our predicament.

True-crime stories, murder mysteries, up-to-the-minute online news reports, and (as always) rumor and innuendo grab our attention faster than any call for justice, human rights, or ceasefires."

"Wikipedia in the Newsroom" is about creation and ownership of information posted to the website that pops to the first page of most web searches—for better or for worse. "I like much of the new technology," states a Pulitzer Prize-winning reporter. "But to me rules, borders, guidelines, and transparency matter a lot." The argument presented in "Journalist Bites Reality!" is captured in the article's subtitle: "How broadcast journalism is flawed in such a fundamental way that its utility for informing viewers is almost nil."

The unit concludes with articles on electronic books ("The Future of Reading") and Facebook ("The Great Wall of Facebook") and the interface of consumer and business perspectives in their evolution.

Off Course

How the hip and ambitious coverage of pop culture at our most influential newspaper manages to miss half the story.

Michael Massing

Not too many years ago, *The New York Times* was so thoroughly high-minded in its approach to culture, so consumed with opera and museums and classical music, that it let critical trends in popular culture pass by unremarked. With the entertainment business expanding into a huge global combine reaching into every corner of the American psyche, however, the *Times* has recognized that, as a world-class newspaper—and one in need of younger readers—it must approach the subject with the same intensity and sense of purpose it brings to politics and economics, and for the last decade it has been moving in that direction. More recently, the paper has been reorganizing its coverage of culture—adding staff, mapping out new beats, and better coordinating coverage among the relevant sections, Arts & Leisure, The Arts, and Business Day. Now, with a culture staff of nearly one hundred reporters, critics, and editors, the *Times* can ferret out news about pop culture like few other publications.

Yet in boosting its coverage of this subject, the paper at times seems to have careened toward the opposite extreme, eagerly chronicling every up-and-down tick in the great fame-and-ambition sweepstakes. Its reports on TV, movies, pop music, video games, publishing, and advertising brim with news about boardroom struggles, mogul rivalries, high-stakes dealmaking, ratings shares, marketing strategies, publicity blitzes, technological innovations, branding, and franchising. The paper is drawn to the hot and the hip, to glamour and buzz, to the Weinsteins and Eisners, the Spielbergs and Bronfmans. With its heavy reliance on sources inside the media business, the paper's coverage at times seems indistinguishable from that of *Billboard, Variety, Advertising Age*, and other publications aimed at industry insiders.

In the process, the *Times* has neglected a critical aspect of pop culture—its effects on society. With the entertainment world grown so pervasive, with its products so thoroughly infiltrating the nation's households, its influence on kids, families, and communities has intensified as well. Yet the *Times*, like most mainstream news media, pays all that only sporadic attention. When Janet Jackson exposes her nipple during a halftime show, or desperate housewife Nicollette Sheridan drops her towel during an

NFL promo, the paper will jump on the story. When TV stations refuse to air *Saving Private Ryan* for fear of being sanctioned, or the secretary of education blasts PBS for distributing a show about an animated rabbit who visits a friend with lesbian parents, the *Times* is faithfully there.

But public concerns about popular culture run much deeper than such incidents, and point to stories that are not being written. In a poll of 1,001 parents conducted last year by the Kaiser Family Foundation, only 17 percent expressed high levels of concern about the Janet Jackson incident. But 63 percent said they were "very concerned" that children are being exposed to too much inappropriate content in entertainment media, and another 26 percent said they were "somewhat concerned." As these figures show, it's not just conservatives who feel this way. "The vast majority of parents," said the foundation, "believe that sexual and violent content on TV contributes to children's behavior."

As to what to do about it, Americans are much more conflicted. A survey of 1,505 adults conducted earlier this year by the Pew Research Center for the People and the Press found that 48 percent believe that government control of entertainment poses a greater danger than harmful programming, compared to 41 percent who felt the reverse. Yet when asked about specific control measures, they were far more supportive. For instance, 75 percent said they favored stricter enforcement of government rules about TV content when children are likely to be watching; 69 percent said they supported steeper fines for violations of indecency guidelines.

To some, all this might seem like yesterday's news. It has been nearly twenty years since Tipper Gore launched a campaign urging recording companies to place warning labels on records containing explicit language. And it has been six years since the shootings at Columbine generated a rash of articles on the effects of violent programming on kids. Yet far from ebbing, the issue has intensified as pop culture grows ever more invasive, polymorphous, and perverse. On an episode of Fox's short-lived *Keen Eddie*, three men trafficking in horse semen hire a prostitute to arouse their stud. In the plastic surgery drama *Nip/Tuck*, a character has sex with a life-sized doll of a porn star and has a threesome with a hooker and a guy named Christian. On MTV's *I Want a Famous Face*, young women undergo nose jobs, breast implants, and other forms of surgery to look like their favorite celebrities. On shows like *Survivor* and *The Bachelor*, lying, deceiving, and sheer meanness are not only tolerated but celebrated. (In the Pew study, 38 percent of those surveyed expressed serious concern over reality shows in which people "are made fun of or tricked.") On *The Sopranos*, one character beats his girlfriend (a stripper) to death and is later killed by Tony Soprano, who chops off his head and stuffs it in a bowling-ball bag. The Internet, meanwhile, gives youngsters access to all sorts of lewd and grotesque material at the stroke of a key.

The journalistic questions such fare provokes seem endless, and they extend far beyond the usual ones about sex and violence into the realms of sociology, politics, and religion. Consider, for instance, the surge of religious fervor across the country. Is it linked in any way to the growing reach, and grossness, of popular culture? To what extent does the spread of evangelical Christianity represent a reaction to the language on *South Park* and the lifestyles on *Sex and the City*? With so many TV shows built around the imperfections of women's bodies and the urgent need to correct them, what effect has this had on the health (both physical and psychological) of young women? Even more urgent are the questions raised by last November's postelection exit polls showing that "moral values" were a top concern for many voters. Many journalists automatically assumed that this finding referred to such traditional issues as abortion, gay rights, and school prayer, but might it not also have reflected mounting discomfort with ads showing preteens in low-rider jeans and kids miming the garb and gestures of gangsta rap? In March, Hillary Clinton, citing studies on the impact of violent images on children, denounced violent video games, including one that encourages players "to have sex with prostitutes and then murder them." How is such a stand likely to play with voters and with the entertainment executives who have traditionally backed her?

Is the surge in religious fervor across the country linked to the growing penetration, and grossness, of popular culture?

Answering these kinds of questions requires an approach no different from that involved in investigating other social issues like welfare reform and school vouchers—sending reporters into the field. It requires talking to parents and teachers, youth counselors and Little League coaches, young children and teenagers. It requires speaking with psychologists and sociologists and drawing on studies and statistics that can help provide context for the anecdotes gathered from the field. Finally, it requires fashioning all this into a lively and insightful report.

With such a large culture staff and newshole, the *Times* would seem in an ideal position to address the impact of pop culture. And over the years it has—in book reviews, op-eds, the magazine, and the style section, as well as in the culture pages. Yet actual reported pieces on the subject appear only rarely, making the paper's culture coverage seem strangely out of balance.

Now would seem a good time to address this imbalance, for the *Times* has just named a new culture editor, Sam Sifton. From 1990 to 1998, Sifton worked at *New York Press*, then left to become a founding editor of *Talk* magazine. Arriving at the *Time* in 2002, he became the deputy dining editor. For the last year, he has participated in a "bakeoff" with Jim Schachter, formerly an editor in the business section, for the top culture job. As the winner, the thirty-eight-year-old Sifton will oversee what executive editor Bill Keller recently called, in a memo, "quite simply the finest staff of culture journalists working anywhere, and working at the top of their game." Sifton is no doubt being pelted with ideas and suggestions, but, here, unsolicited, are some of my own.

Monday, May 23, was a typical day in the life of culture at the *Times*. The Arts section offered a rumination on three new museum exhibitions on the Jewish presence in early New York, plus reviews of dance, theater, classical music, world music, and the "tribal & textile arts show" at the Seventh Regiment Armory—an indication of the paper's deep commitment to covering the arts. Top billing, though, went to a long feature titled SKATEBOARDING'S UPSTART DAYS, by Sharon Waxman, one of the paper's Hollywood correspondents. It recounted the tale of Catherine Hardwicke, an up-and-coming director in Venice, California, who managed to convince Sony Pictures Entertainment to let her direct a movie about the early history of skateboarding. In SO LONG, GARAGE. LAPTOPS ROCK, David Carr described how musicians "are using powerful laptop tools to produce music that in an earlier age might have wailed out of a garage." Inside, another Waxman article noted that *Star Wars: Episode III* had become the "year's first movie blockbuster," breaking box-office records for a four-day opening.

This being a Monday, much of the day's media action was in Business Day. (For ten years now, the Monday business section has featured stories on the entertainment and media industries.) ON FALL TV, THE NETWORKS ARE PLANNING SOMETHING BORROWED, ran the headline across the section's front page. It was the latest in a series of *Times* pieces on the new fall TV lineups. The article cited the usual array of media buyers and strategists, one of whom declared that it was "shocking" that NBC "was leaving intact its sagging lineup on Thursday, the biggest night of the week for advertising." A column along the left-hand side of the front page, also by David Carr, described how two "very wealthy young men" were seeking to break Hollywood's habit of being "hooked on the big opening weekend" by releasing movies in DVD and on cable on the same day as their theatrical release. Inside were articles about the disappearance of the comedian Dave Chappelle; a new wrinkle in the feud between the rap stars Ja Rule and 50 Cent; Nintendo's efforts to bolster its market share in the video game console business; and Google's recent introduction of a service that lets users build a customized home page.

It was quite a yeasty mix for a single day, leavened with dashes of celebrity and gossip. The harvest on other days looks little different. Here's a brief sampler, culled from April and May:

- DVD producers "climbing up the Hollywood food chain"
- the revival of *Radar* as a magazine for the hip
- the move from New York to Los Angeles of the publishing industry "trend-setter" Judith Regan
- Hollywood's welcoming of a "new crop of moguls"
- PARIS INC., on Paris Hilton's burgeoning business empire
- *Gawker*, the "flagship chronicle of Manhattan's news and gossip" (offering blogs that are "sexy, irreverent, a tad elitist, and unabashedly coastal.")
- a deal by the founders of Miramax (i.e., the Weinsteins) to distribute video programs
- how CBS is planning to fill the void left in its lineup by *Everybody Loves Raymond*
- how ABC, celebrating a ratings comeback, "won't rest on its laurels"
- how ABC's schedule "emits that 'Housewives' vibe"
- how Fox and UPN are aiming for young viewers, and how Fox, in its fall lineup, is sticking with the "tried and true" (no surprise, given that Fox finished the season "as the top-rated network among those aged 18 to 49, the category most desired by advertisers")

That last reference, to 18- to 49-year-old viewers, is a fixture of TV stories in the *Times*. According to a Nexis search, the phrase appeared more than 200 times in the two-year period ending in April 2005. A variant, "18 to 34," appeared more than a hundred times, often accompanied by the words "most desirable," "coveted," and "sought after" by advertisers. Back in October 2002, the *Times Magazine* ran an article, headlined THE MYTH OF '18 TO 34,' by Jonathan Dee, that disputed the idea that this age group is of special value to advertisers; members of the aging baby-boom generation, he argued, have much more disposable income and so make up a more lucrative market. It remains true that many advertisers continue to pay a premium for younger viewers. But the frequency with which the *Times* mentions this demographic, and the reflexive, almost unthinking way it's cited, captures the extent to which the paper's culture coverage has been penetrated by the jargon and thinking of Madison Avenue and Hollywood.

In that same April–May period, meanwhile, I found little reporting on the social or political effects of culture. The closest entry seemed a March 30 article by Julie Salamon (HAS BIG BIRD SOLD OUT?) on a new deal to distribute PBS children's shows on a 24-hour commercial cable network, and the debate over whether or not that was good for children. Amid the outpouring of reports on ratings sweeps and marketing campaigns, though, this piece was easy to overlook.

How might pop culture be covered differently? One place to begin looking for an answer is Orlando, Florida, which is in the heart of the Bible Belt and has a burgeoning population of evangelical Christians. Mark I. Pinsky has covered religion for the *Orlando Sentinel* for ten years, and he says he has been struck by how many evangelicals "feel besieged by a toxic popular culture. It's public enemy number one. They see it as hypersexual and ultraviolent, and out of their control. These people are stuck in middle-class or lower-middle-class tract houses, and they can't get away from it."

Interestingly, Pinsky, the author of a forthcoming first-person book titled *A Jew Among the Evangelicals*, says he often finds himself in agreement with the evangelical critique of pop culture. He has a seventeen-year-old son and a fourteen-year-old daughter, and they are not allowed to watch TV on school nights. "I don't believe kids hear or see something and then go out and do it," he observes. "I don't think that if they see a murder on TV, they're going to go out and kill somebody." But the literature "does suggest a desensitizing and normalizing of behavior that takes place," he says, adding, "A friend gave me a DVD of *Deadwood*. I have no problem with my son watching that. But I won't let him watch a dumb-ass sitcom. We're not prudish people at all, but I won't let the stupidity on such shows seep into their minds. It's attitudinal. Twelve-year-olds who watch TV begin talking like thirty-year-olds to their parents. You can see it immediately."

Pinsky referred me to a recent article by a fellow *Sentinel* reporter, Linda Shrieves, about "sitcom kids"—children who mimic the behavior they see on TV. "Though most TV watchdog groups fret about violence and sex on television," Shrieves wrote, "some parents say they're increasingly concerned about TV's attitude problem. From cartoons to sitcoms, the stars are now sassy children who deliver flip one-liners, put down authority figures and revel in a laugh track. And their attitudes are contagious. Formerly polite kids are smart-aleck, eye-rolling and harrumphing, just like the kids on television." Douglas Gentile of the National Institute on Media and the Family was quoted as saying that "psychologists love to slice it up many different ways, but it boils down to this: Kids copy what they see on TV."

Gentile's institute, based in Minneapolis, is one of several nonpartisan groups in the United States that seeks to guide parents on pop culture. The groups are far less political than, say, the Parents Television Council, which is headed by the right-wing activist L. Brent Bozell and which generates many of the indecency complaints that flood the FCC. On its website, the National Institute on Media posts reviews of movies and video games, assessing their suitability for kids. Some are truly eye-opening. Of the video game "Grand Theft Auto: San Andreas," it writes, "Raunchy, violent and portraying just about every deviant act that a criminal could think of in full, living 3D graphics. . . . There are no redeeming qualities in this game for children. From glorifying drive-by-shootings to delivering prostitutes to their johns, this game teaches just about everything you wouldn't even want your kids to see." In the game, players are rewarded for stealing guns and squad cars from police officers and brutally murdering them. On the website, readers are urged to sign a petition to tell the makers of "Grand Theft Auto," Take Two Interactive Software, to "do the only decent thing: publicly apologize and STOP KILLING COPS AS ENTERTAINMENT!"

Last year, "Grand Theft Auto: San Andreas" was the top-selling video game in the United States, with 5.1 million units sold. Its popularity and violence raise obvious questions about its possible effects on kids. On the occasions when the *Times* runs articles about such questions, it's usually in its specialized Circuits section (recently reduced to a weekly page), which guarantees that many *Times* readers will not read them. In *The Washington Post*, by contrast, the subject has twice this year made page one. In March, for instance, the *Post* ran a front-page article about the popular game "Postal" (named after shootings by postal workers). While violence has always been vital to the game's success, Ariana Eunjung Cha wrote, things have reached the point where even the game's creative team worries about excessive gore. Steve Wik, the team's creative director, is quoted as saying that "too many games have become dependent on violence for violence's sake, and that has made violence boring." A colleague feels that "some games are too dark for even his taste." The article goes on to note that the surging popularity of video games has "prompted a backlash," with a number of states introducing bills to ban the sale of violent games to minors.

The market for pop culture no doubt includes many of the same people who express backlash outrage. This contradiction seems worth exploring.

The *Post* piece suggests another approach to writing about pop culture—probing the attitudes of entertainment executives about the products they create. A pioneer of the genre is Ken Auletta's "What Won't They Do?" Published in *The New Yorker* back in 1993, it recounts his exchanges with various Hollywood figures about movies and TV shows that push the edge on violence and sex. His subjects range from Oliver Stone, who suggests that some criticism of violent programming "borders on censorship," to Debra Winger, who, as the mother of a young boy, lashes out at movies with gratuitous violence and kinky sex and who won't even let her son see *Home Alone* because the parents "are idiots" and because the son, played by Macaulay Culkin, takes too much joy in committing acts of violence.

Most revealing is Auletta's conversation with Rupert Murdoch, the chairman of 20th Century Fox. Murdoch tells Auletta of his contempt for the liberal group-think of Hollywood and its reflexive suspicion of ideas like "family values." Auletta then asks him whether *A Current Affair*, a nightly stew of sex, scandal, and rumor produced by Murdoch's Fox network, has had a coarsening effect on American life. "Coarsening?" Murdoch says, seemingly caught off-guard. "I don't know. If you were to say there had been occasions when *A Current Affair* has treated some subjects sleazily in the past, I'd have to say yes." He adds, "If you want me to get up and defend every film, every program, I don't do it."

Since then, of course, Murdoch has started up the Fox News Channel. There, hosts like Bill O'Reilly and John Gibson inveigh against "Hollywood" and the "liberal media elite" for inflicting lurid movies and vulgar sitcoms on the upstanding folks of middle America. Needless to say, they almost never mention the part that Murdoch's own companies play in this. Nor do they acknowledge that much of the proliferating junk they so strenuously condemn is served up by entertainment corporations seeking to maximize their profits according to the principles of the unfettered market—the same market that these conservatives so noisily champion. This contradiction within conservatism is rarely examined by the *Times* or other newspapers.

One writer who has probed this issue is Thomas Frank. In his book, *What's the Matter with Kansas?*, he writes, "The truth is that the culture that surrounds us—and that persistently triggers new explosions of backlash outrage—is largely the product of business rationality."

It is made by writers and actors, who answer to editors and directors and producers, who answer to senior vice presidents and chief executive officers, who answer to Wall Street bankers, who demand profits above all else. From the megamergers of the media giants to the commercial time-outs during the football game to the plots of the Hollywood movies and to the cyberfantasies of *Wired* and *Fast Company* and *Fortune*, we live in a free-market world. . . . It is because of the market that our TV is such a sharp-tongued insulter of "family values" and such a zealous promoter of every species of social deviance.

Frank does not dwell much on who makes up that market. It no doubt includes many of the same people who express backlash outrage. This contradiction, too, would seem worth exploring. Those who produce toxic products often argue that they're simply giving the market what it wants. Even if one accepts that defense, it's still possible that such fare could have undesirable effects or feed a sense of insecurity and dismay. Last November, the *Times* ran a lively and informative piece on how the ratings of shows like *Desperate Housewives* are as high in conservative red states as in liberal blue ones. The piece quoted experts noting that those who most strenuously denounce salacious programs on TV are often those most drawn to them. Unfortunately, the article did not quote any viewers, nor did it seek to go inside any real communities to see what ordinary Americans might have to say about these shows. (By the way, *Desperate Housewives* was the eleventh-most-watched show among two-to-eleven-year-olds last year.)

Despite that oversight, Frank's account is refreshing, because, unlike many journalists, he takes seriously the anger and frustration that many ordinary Americans feel about the culture around them. His central thesis is that corporate elites have effectively taken the backlash outrage of ordinary people and directed it at liberals, thus helping those elites win electoral office, which they then use to adopt economic policies that further enrich corporations at the expense of these same ordinary people. Whether or not one agrees with this analysis, Frank convincingly shows that it's impossible to grasp the current political dynamic in

America without understanding pop culture and how ordinary Americans view it.

The same is true for the rest of the world. American movies, TV shows, and pop music have conquered foreign lands with far more ease than have American armies. (In *From Beirut to Jerusalem*, Thomas Friedman describes how two journalists traveling by taxicab in Beirut were stopped by a bunch of fierce-looking militiamen. When the militiamen learned that one of the journalists was from the *Dallas Times Herald*, they pointed their guns at him as if to shoot, then demanded to know, "Who shot J.R.?" Breaking into howls of laughter, they let the car pass.) But all those satellite dishes pulling down the signals of Howard Stern and *The Real World* have no doubt generated much reaction and animosity. And what about all those sadistic action pics churned out by Hollywood and avidly marketed abroad? To what degree have they fed the bloodlust of jihadis and suicide bombers? You rarely read about this in our top papers.

In early June, as I was completing this article, the *Times* finally ran a piece that took a serious look at the issue of culture and its impact. Written by Bruce Weber, it described a bitter dispute at a high school in the town of Muhlenberg, Pennsylvania, over *The Buffalo Tree*, a novel set in a juvenile detention center that includes a scene in a communal shower in which an adolescent boy becomes sexually aroused. After a sixteen-year-old student complained at a school board meeting about having to read this, the board voted to ban the book, and by the next morning all classroom copies had been collected and stored in a vault in the principal's office. As Weber noted, Muhlenberg, while conservative politically and with a growing evangelical population, "is not militantly right wing," and "even the more vociferous opponents of the book did not insist it come off the school library shelves." The school board's vote set off a period of "unusual activism," with students circulating petitions, teachers preparing defenses of the book, and letters on both sides appearing in the local paper. The schools' superintendent tried to broker a compromise, but as one teacher observed, "*The Buffalo Tree* isn't coming back anytime soon." Overall, the piece provided a sensitive and insightful look at a knotty cultural issue.

No doubt a thorough search of *Times* coverage in recent years would turn up other stories like this. But they remain rare. Now that the paper has a new culture editor, might we see more of them? Sam Sifton declined to be interviewed for this article, but I did speak with the man who, by all accounts, remains the real power in culture at the *Times*: Frank Rich. Like his mentor Arthur Gelb, who for decades dictated the paper's tastes in the arts, Rich is the *Times*'s culture czar, though he exercises his power with far more discretion. In Rich's weekly columns, he routs the indecency police, roasts right-wing politicians, and flays religious hypocrites, creating the ideological climate in which the culture staff operates. After more than two years on the front page of the Arts & Leisure section, his column in April returned to the op-ed page. Rich himself was assigned a new office on the tenth floor of the *Times*, where the opinion pages are housed, but he will also retain his old office on the fourth floor, where culture roosts, and from which he has played an instrumental part in the remaking of the culture department.

That process began under Howell Raines. On becoming executive editor of the *Times*, Raines had ambitious plans for building its circulation. The goal was to corral more readers, and two of the largest potential pools were affluent readers nationwide and the young. The key to getting both, Raines believed, was improving the *Times*'s "back of the book" sections. In his long, self-aggrandizing retrospective in the *Atlantic* in May 2004, Raines wrote that to get readers between the ages of twenty and forty, "you have to penetrate the worlds of style and popular culture." For national readers, he mentioned those same two subjects plus entertainment and travel as critical. Improving the coverage of these areas, he wrote, would help "to lure national readers who wanted to use the *Times* to experience the New Yorkness of New York—which is to say a point of view that could not be found in their local papers."

Do most *Times* readers really need to know which network delivers the most 18- to 49-year-olds to advertisers?

Among the decisions Raines faced after taking over the paper was naming a new editor for Arts & Leisure. For suggestions, he turned to Frank Rich. Rich, in turn, mentioned Jodi Kantor as someone to watch for the department. The New York editor of *Slate*, Kantor was only twenty-seven, but she had the hip, edgy sensibility that was seen as the route to young readers, and she was hired in March 2003. Before Raines could proceed, Jayson Blair intervened, but Bill Keller, his successor, decided to pursue the process. To prepare a culture plan, Keller appointed a committee that included Rich, Kantor, Adam Moss, Steve Erlanger, and Michael Kimmelman, among others. The blueprint they produced called for restructuring beats, improving coordination between the various sections responsible for culture, and increasing the emphasis on reporting.

"We wanted to beef up our reporting of culture, especially at a time when culture coverage is in decline almost everywhere in journalism," Rich told me. "We've had a huge expansion in our coverage." As the reporting on culture has been strengthened, so has the reporting on its business side. As Rich noted, it's become hard to "separate the coverage of show business from the coverage of the show. There's been a complete changeover in every cultural field. When I began as a theater critic, Broadway shows were produced by rich people like David Merrick and Alexander Cohen. Now Broadway is dominated by Clear Channel and Disney. Look at independent movies—today they're produced by companies like New Line, which is owned by Time Warner, the biggest media company in the world. As big money and large corporations take over the business, that becomes part of the story."

I asked Rich about the idea of doing more reporting from the field about the social impact of culture. He sounded dubious. Such reporting, he said, "has to be done very carefully." He cited the Columbine shootings and the initial reports that the perpetrators were influenced by *The Matrix*. "That turned out not to be true." He went on: "I'm skeptical of determinist correspondences. Michael Medved, the conservative critic, has observed that the generation raised on *Father Knows Best* produced the sixties." Rich cited the case of his own two sons: "All they did in high school was listen to hip hop and watch video games. They saw Quentin Tarantino at a young age. I rarely censored what they did. Now one at the age of twenty-five has just had a book published by a division of *The New York Review of Books*. Another is studying fiction at Harvard and wants to be a novelist." I did not have the presence of mind to suggest that the kids of a renowned cultural critic like Rich might have one or two more cultural advantages over most kids in the country.

But pursuing the point, I asked, Wouldn't the *Times*'s coverage benefit from sending reporters into local communities to talk with parents, teachers, and counselors? "It's all anecdotal," Rich said. "No one seems able to agree on what it all means."

I wondered, though, if reporting on culture and its effects would be any more anecdotal than, say, reporting on class in America, a subject on which the *Times* just published a very extended series, most of it consisting of anecdotes about individuals, backed up by occasional citations from studies and experts. Given those nearly one hundred people on the *Times* culture staff, would it hurt to spare one or two to visit Florida or Kansas or Colorado and report back on the debates over pop culture taking place there? Is it really necessary to run all those stories about the new fall TV lineups? Do most *Times* readers really need to know which network wins the ratings war or delivers the most 18- to 49-year-olds to advertisers? Do they really need to be apprised of the every move of Paris Hilton and Harvey Weinstein? The *Times* does a good job of giving its readers around the country a taste of New York. Isn't it time it gave its New York readers more of a taste of what's going on in the rest of the country?

If it did, the *Times* could help spark a debate about pop culture and its consequences. And that in itself would be healthy. Looming over every discussion of this subject is the threat of censorship. That threat is serious. But contrary to Oliver Stone's fear, the mere discussion of whether some forms of pop culture hurt society does not constitute censorship. Given its vast influence, the *Times*, by covering pop culture more fully, could help get a national discussion going. That, in turn, might give entertainment executives new incentives—apart from FCC fines or congressional intervention—to consider the social effects of what they produce.

MICHAEL MASSING, a contributing editor to *CJR,* is the author of *Now They Tell Us: The American Press and Iraq*.

Tele[re]vision

Researchers are taking a new look at TV. Instead of just filling time or acting as a passive babysitter, can the medium be a good teacher?

JENNY PRICE

Society gives parents plenty of reasons to feel guilty about the time their children spend in front of the television. Nicknames for the medium—boob tube or idiot box, for example—do little to help alleviate their worries.

For years, researchers have shown the negative effects of TV violence and, more recently, they have found links between childhood obesity and too much viewing. President Obama implored parents to "turn off the TV" during a campaign ad pitching his education policy. Still, the average child in the United States spends nearly four hours watching television each day, even though pediatricians recommend no more than two hours of educational programming for kids two years and older.

TV viewing is a given in the average household, but in many cases, parents have no idea what programs their children are watching or whether they understand them at all.

"What we seldom get—and need—is solid, research-based advice about when to turn the TV on," noted Lisa Guernsey, an author and journalist who covers media effects on children, in a column she wrote for the *Washington Post*.

Researchers, including UW-Madison faculty and an alumnus who is behind some groundbreaking work in the field, are working to fill that void, showing that some TV can actually be good for kids.

Their efforts have improved educational programming for children, pinpointing what engages their developing brains and how they learn as they watch. Now the researchers are exploring whether children are really getting the lessons from programs that adults think they are, and how exposure to television might affect children as young as babies and toddlers.

Spoonful of Sugar

Well-crafted shows for children can teach them the alphabet, math, and basic science concepts, as well as manners and social skills. But what really makes for good television when it comes to younger viewers? That's a key question Marie-Louise Mares MA'90, PhD'94, a UW-Madison associate professor of communication arts, is trying to answer.

Much of the educational programming aimed at children falls into the category of "prosocial"—meaning that it's intended to teach lessons, such as healthy eating habits, self-esteem, or how to treat others. The classic example of a prosocial program is *Mister Rogers' Neighborhood.* Mares has shown that a prosocial program's positive influence can be just as strong as a violent program's negative influence.

But good messages can get lost.

"Children's interpretations of what a show is about are very different from what an adult thinks," Mares says. "Some kids take away the completely wrong message."

Mares began studying children's comprehension of prosocial messages after watching the movie *Mary Poppins* with a four-year-old fan. Although the child predicted each scene before it appeared on screen, she had difficulty doing what Mares calls "making sense of the story." The girl did not know why the character Bert, played by Dick Van Dyke, was on the roof dancing or that the "spoonful of sugar" Julie Andrews sings about was a metaphor. As they continued to watch the movie together, Mares learned that what is obvious to an adult doesn't necessarily sink in with children.

She demonstrated that confusion in a study involving a TV episode of *Clifford the Big Red Dog,* in which the cartoon character and friends meet a three-legged dog named K.C. The intent of the program was to teach children to be accepting of those with disabilities. But throughout much of the episode, Clifford and his friends behave badly toward the dog. At one point, one of the dogs expresses fear of catching three-legged dog disease. Sure enough, in follow-up interviews, one-third of the children thought the dogs could catch the disease, and many of them interpreted the lesson of the episode along the lines of this child's comment: "You should be careful . . . not to get sick, not to get germs."

"Showing the fear can actually be more conflicting and more frightening to kids," Mares says.

Her findings are important because much of kids' programming attempts to teach lessons by showing characters behaving badly in some way and then having them learn better behavior. That's confusing for children, Mares says, and could even lead them to focus on the bad behavior.

Her findings are important because much of kids' programming attempts to teach lessons by showing characters behaving badly in some way and then having them learn better behavior. That's confusing for children and could even lead them to focus on the bad behavior.

In the end, 80 percent of the kids in the study said the lesson of the *Clifford* episode was to be nice to dogs with three legs. Although that's a nice sentiment, Mares says, "You don't encounter many [three-legged dogs]."

The producers of prosocial programs also should consider the methods they use to portray the behaviors they're trying to teach kids, Mares says, as well as ensure that the content is relevant and realistic to young viewers. That might be one of the reasons why stories involving dogs or other animal characters don't seem to get the message across to children. One group of youngsters in Mares' study watched a *Clifford* episode that had been edited to remove the dogs showing fear of K.C.—yet the children still interpreted the story as being about dogs, not about inclusiveness and tolerance.

Mares is in new territory; virtually no research has been conducted to identify programming that would effectively foster inclusiveness in children. She has experimented, with mixed results, by embedding some kind of prompt within children's programs that could help young viewers comprehend the intended message, especially since most parents aren't watching along with their kids. Attempts include having the main character start off the show or interrupt mid-lesson to say, "Hey kids, in this story we're going to learn that we shouldn't be afraid of people who are different."

She's still looking for answers on how that practice—which she calls scaffolding—could work effectively. But balance is essential, Mares says, noting that she could create the "ideal" show, but then kids wouldn't want to watch.

Making over *Sesame Street*

The end of the 1960s saw the debut of two landmark educational programs for young people: *Sesame Street* and *Mister Rogers' Neighborhood.* Not long after, Daniel Anderson '66 began trying to discover what exactly was going on with children while they watched TV.

Anderson, a professor at the University of Massachusetts-Amherst who has advised the producers of children's shows including *Sesame Street* and *Captain Kangaroo,* dispelled one of the central myths on the subject—that when the TV is turned on, children's brains turn off. In fact, parents are more likely than their children to become couch potatoes while watching television, says Anderson, who holds a UW bachelor's degree in psychology.

He observed children watching television and witnessed them turning away from the screen several times during a broadcast to play with toys, fight with siblings, or talk to their parents. After they were done watching, he tested their understanding of what they had just seen. Anderson's findings were the exact opposite of what most people thought.

"It was very clear that children were mentally active, that they were constantly posing questions for themselves, [asking], 'What's going to happen next, why are they doing that . . . is this real?' " he says. "And it was also clear that when television invited participation, that kids would become very active—pointing at the screen or talking to the characters on the TV."

This finding ushered in a new era of children's programming, with the cable channel Nickelodeon enlisting Anderson's help to develop a new generation of shows in the late 1990s, most notably *Blue's Clues* and *Dora the Explorer,* that were centered on the concept that children would dance, sing, and follow along with programs they enjoyed rather than sit and stare vacantly at the screen.

Blue's Clues features a mix of animated characters—including a cute blue puppy—and backgrounds, with a live host who invites children who are watching to look for and decipher clues to solve a puzzle, such as, "What does Blue want for her birthday?" Along the way, the show focuses on information such as colors or shapes or numbers.

Anderson pushed producers to make the show visually simple, with very little editing or transitions that require viewers to process jumps in time or location—something young children have a hard time doing, his research showed.

While most researchers "focus on the negative contributions of media," experts such as Anderson and Mares have been "at the forefront of recognizing that television that is designed to be educational really can be beneficial for children," says Amy Jordan, who oversees research on children's media policy for The Annenberg Public Policy Center.

In his best-selling book *The Tipping Point,* which examines how ideas and trends spread, author Malcolm Gladwell labeled *Blue's Clues* as one of the "stickiest"—meaning the most irresistible and involving—television shows ever aired, and noted that its creators "borrowed those parts of *Sesame Street* that did work."

In turn, the success of *Blue's Clues* prompted the producers of *Sesame Street* to seek Anderson's help in giving the long-running staple a makeover. With the new millennium approaching, the show needed to catch up with the way kids watch TV. Rather than the repetitive narrative format children delighted in following as they watched *Blue's Clues, Sesame Street* featured a series of about forty short segments, ranging in length from ten seconds to four minutes.

Even venerable *Sesame Street,* airing since the late 1960s, has evolved, thanks to research about children's TV. The show's original concept assumed short attention spans, cramming as many as forty short segments into each hour.

What Is Educational Television?

POP QUIZ

**Is the TV show *Hannah Montana* educational?
If your answer is no, guess again.**

The ubiquitous Disney Channel sitcom featuring pop star Miley Cyrus airs during ABC's Saturday morning block of shows aimed at children. And, believe it or not, it helps the network's affiliates fulfill their obligation under federal law to air educational and informational (E/I) programming for kids.

Congress first passed legislation in 1990—the Children's Television Act—requiring broadcast stations to increase E/I programming, but what followed were some laughable claims of compliance. For example, *The Jetsons* was labeled educational because it taught children about the future, and stations were sometimes airing educational shows at times when children weren't likely to be awake and watching. So in 1997, lawmakers revisited the act, putting in place what's known as the "three-hour rule," stipulating that the networks air at least three hours of E/I programming for kids per week. Although the rule isn't enforced unless viewers complain, it is used as a guideline when the Federal Communications Commission reviews a station's license for renewal.

So have things gotten better? The FCC has acted on complaints, such as when it fined Univision affiliates $24 million for claiming that serial melodramas known as telenovelas were educational. But even under the three-hour rule, broadcasters maintain shows featuring professional athletes, such as *NBA Inside Stuff* or *NFL Under the Helmet,* count toward the requirement.

Amy Jordan, who oversees research on children's media policy for The Annenberg Public Policy Center and has studied implementation of the three-hour rule, says most commercial network programs are prosocial in nature, aimed at teaching children lessons. *Hannah Montana* falls into that category.

"We actually don't know the take-away value of those kinds of programming," Jordan acknowledges. "And that's an important question, because it speaks to whether or not the broadcasters are living up to the spirit of the Children's Television Act."

A study released last fall by advocacy organization Children Now found that only one in eight shows labeled E/I meets the standard of "highly educational." The majority of the programs studied—a little more than 60 percent—were deemed "moderately educational." The picture looked better at PBS, where the programming for kids was rated significantly higher than E/I shows on commercial stations.

Another issue is that the E/I label is confusing for many parents, with some mistaking programs such as *The Oprah Winfrey Show* and *Who Wants to Be a Millionaire?* as educational.

"In theory, I think parents believe they have a sense of what their kids are exposed to, but in fact, their knowledge is pretty limited," Jordan says. "So to get parents to direct their children to positive programming . . . it's an uphill battle for broadcasters."

Part of the misunderstanding, she says, results from broadcasters doing little to promote which shows carry the E/I label, thereby keeping parents and their children in the dark about which shows are intended to be educational.

"They have this concern about the spinach syndrome—if children think [a program is] good for them, they won't watch it," she says.

—J.P.

"The original conception was that you needed a lot of novelty and change to hold a preschooler's attention. And so they quite explicitly would put things together in unpredictable orders," Anderson says. "A story that was happening on the street with Big Bird and the human characters might be followed by a film about buffalos, which in turn might be followed by a Muppet piece about the letter *H.*"

Sesame Street offered children no connection or context among the concepts and segments, and, not surprisingly, it lost viewers when shows like *Blue's Clues* began airing. At Anderson's suggestion, producers made the show more storylike and predictable, reducing the number of characters and sets, and connecting more concepts. Now the typical episode features around ten segments per hour.

"You're dealing with children who don't need complexity," Anderson says. "In a sense, a lot of what they were doing was almost for the adults and not so much for their audience."

Research Gap

The notion of children and television as a research prospect first confronted Anderson when he was a young assistant professor. He had just given an undergraduate lecture on child development, in which he said younger children tend to have more trouble sustaining attention than older children, when one of his students asked, "Well, if those things are true, how come my four-year-old brother can just sit and stare [at *Sesame Street*]?"

"I kind of glibly answered him," Anderson recalls, "that 'Oh, it's because television is just being a distractor. It just looks like your brother's sustaining attention, but the picture is constantly changing and so on.' I just made that up—I had no idea."

Feeling guilty, Anderson sent a graduate student to the library with orders to find out everything he could about children's attention to television.

"He kept coming back and saying he couldn't find anything, and that's what got me started," Anderson says.

> **"Television that has a clear curriculum in mind—that studiously avoids problematic content like violence—has been shown in dozens of studies to really enhance the way children think, the kinds of things that they know, and even how they get along with one another."**
>
> —Amy Jordan

Beginning in the 1980s, Anderson and his colleagues followed 570 children from preschool until high school graduation to see what effect watching *Sesame Street* had on their school performance, behavior, and attitudes. They found that children who had watched when they were young earned better grades in high school, read more books, placed more value on achievement, and showed less aggression. Anderson's study included controls for many other factors, including family size, exposure to media in adolescence, and parents' socioeconomic status.

"We think that the effects are really traceable and cumulative all the way, at least, through high school. So television, I think, can be a powerful educator," Anderson says.

Jordan says those findings hold up in other research. "Television that has a clear curriculum in mind—that studiously avoids problematic content like violence—has been shown in dozens of studies to really enhance the way children think, the kinds of things that they know, and even how they get along with one another," she says.

An Uncontrolled Experiment

So where does that leave guilt-ridden parents looking for answers about television? It seems it comes down to what and how much kids are watching, and at what age.

Anderson, who has been working in the field for decades, thinks that despite educational programming, children are growing up within a vast, uncontrolled experiment. And he draws a sharp distinction about TV's potential value for children over age two.

His recent research focuses on how very young children are affected by simply playing or spending time in a room where adult programming, such as news programs or talk shows, is on the television. Anderson's latest study observed what happened when fifty children ages one to three played in a room for an hour. Half of the time, there was no TV in the room; for the last thirty minutes, the game show *Jeopardy!*—not exactly a toddler favorite—was showing.

The conventional wisdom, based on previous research, was that very young children don't pay attention to programs that they can't understand. But Anderson's study found clear signs that when the television was on, children had trouble concentrating, shortened and decreased the intensity of their play, and cut in half the time they focused on a particular toy.

When the TV was on, the children played about ninety seconds less overall. The concern is whether those effects could add up and harm children's playtime in the long term, impairing their ability to develop sustained attention and other key cognitive skills.

The Annenberg center's Jordan says more studies looking at the effects of TV on younger children are essential, in part because surveys have found that as many as two-thirds of children six years and under live in homes where the TV is on at least half the time, regardless of whether anyone is watching.

"Babies today are spending hours in front of screens . . . and we don't really understand how it's affecting their development," she says. "We can no longer assume children are first exposed to TV when they're two years old because it's happening at a much younger age."

JENNY PRICE '96 is a writer for *On Wisconsin.*

Research on the Effects of Media Violence

Whether or not exposure to media violence causes increased levels of aggression and violence in young people is the perennial question of media effects research. Some experts, like University of Michigan professor L. Rowell Huesmann, argue that fifty years of evidence show "that exposure to media violence causes children to behave more aggressively and affects them as adults years later." Others, like Jonathan Freedman of the University of Toronto, maintain that "the scientific evidence simply does not show that watching violence either produces violence in people, or desensitizes them to it."

Many Studies, Many Conclusions

Andrea Martinez at the University of Ottawa conducted a comprehensive review of the scientific literature for the Canadian Radio-television and Telecommunications Commission (CRTC) in 1994. She concluded that the lack of consensus about media effects reflects three "grey areas" or constraints contained in the research itself.

First, media violence is notoriously hard to define and measure. Some experts who track violence in television programming, such as George Gerbner of Temple University, define violence as the act (or threat) of injuring or killing someone, independent of the method used or the surrounding context. Accordingly, Gerber includes cartoon violence in his data-set. But others, such as University of Laval professors Guy Paquette and Jacques de Guise, specifically exclude cartoon violence from their research because of its comical and unrealistic presentation.

Second, researchers disagree over the type of relationship the data supports. Some argue that exposure to media violence causes aggression. Others say that the two are associated, but that there is no causal connection. (That both, for instance, may be caused by some third factor.) And others say the data supports the conclusion that there is no relationship between the two at all.

Third, even those who agree that there is a connection between media violence and aggression disagree about how the one effects the other. Some say that the mechanism is a psychological one, rooted in the ways we learn. For example, Huesmann argues that children develop "cognitive scripts" that guide their own behaviour by imitating the actions of media heroes. As they watch violent shows, children learn to internalize scripts that use violence as an appropriate method of problem-solving.

Other researchers argue that it is the physiological effects of media violence that cause aggressive behaviour. Exposure to violent imagery is linked to increased heart rate, faster respiration and higher blood pressure. Some think that this simulated "fight-or-flight" response predisposes people to act aggressively in the real world. Still others focus on the ways in which media violence primes or cues pre-existing aggressive thoughts and feelings. They argue that an individual's desire to strike out is justified by media images in which both the hero and the villain use violence to seek revenge, often without consequences.

In her final report to the CRTC, Martinez concluded that most studies support "a positive, though weak, relation between exposure to television violence and aggressive behaviour." Although that relationship cannot be "confirmed systematically," she agrees with Dutch researcher Tom Van der Voot who argues that it would be illogical to conclude that "a phenomenon does not exist simply because it is found at times not to occur, or only to occur under certain circumstances."

What the Researchers Are Saying

The lack of consensus about the relationship between media violence and real-world aggression has not impeded ongoing research. Here's a sampling of conclusions drawn to date, from the various research strands:

> Research strand: Children who consume high levels of media violence are more likely to be aggressive in the real world.

In 1956, researchers took to the laboratory to compare the behaviour of 24 children watching TV. Half watched a violent episode of the cartoon *Woody Woodpecker,* and the other 12 watched the non-violent cartoon *The Little Red Hen.* During play afterwards, the researchers observed that the children who watched the violent cartoon were much more likely to hit other children and break toys.

Six years later, in 1963, professors A. Badura, D. Ross and S.A. Ross studied the effect of exposure to real-world violence, television violence, and cartoon violence. They divided 100 pre-school children into four groups. The first group watched a real person shout insults at an inflatable doll while hitting it with a mallet. The second group watched the incident on television. The third watched a cartoon version of the same scene, and the fourth watched nothing.

When all the children were later exposed to a frustrating situation, the first three groups responded with more aggression than the control group. The children who watched the incident on television were just as aggressive as those who had watched the real person use the mallet; and both were more aggressive than those who had only watched the cartoon.

Over the years, laboratory experiments such as these have consistently shown that exposure to violence is associated with increased heartbeat, blood pressure and respiration rate, and a greater willingness to administer electric shocks to inflict pain or punishment on others. However, this line of enquiry has been criticized because of its focus on short term results and the artificial nature of the viewing environment.

Other scientists have sought to establish a connection between media violence and aggression outside the laboratory. For example, a number of surveys indicate that children and young people who report a preference for violent entertainment also score higher on aggression indexes than those who watch less violent shows. L. Rowell Huesmann reviewed studies conducted in Australia, Finland, Poland, Israel, Netherlands and the United States. He reports, "the child most likely to be aggressive would be the one who (a) watches violent television programs most of the time, (b) believes that these shows portray life just as it is, [and] (c) identifies strongly with the aggressive characters in the shows."

A study conducted by the Kaiser Family Foundation in 2003 found that nearly half (47 percent) of parents with children between the ages of 4 and 6 report that their children have imitated aggressive behaviours from TV. However, it is interesting to note that children are more likely to mimic positive behaviours—87 percent of kids do so.

Recent research is exploring the effect of new media on children's behaviour. Craig Anderson and Brad Bushman of Iowa State University reviewed dozens of studies of video gamers. In 2001, they reported that children and young people who play violent video games, even for short periods, are more likely to behave aggressively in the real world; and that both aggressive and non-aggressive children are negatively affected by playing.

In 2003, Craig Anderson and Iowa State University colleague Nicholas Carnagey and Janie Eubanks of the Texas Department of Human Services reported that violent music lyrics increased aggressive thoughts and hostile feelings among 500 college students. They concluded, "There are now good theoretical and empirical reasons to expect effects of music lyrics on aggressive behavior to be similar to the well-studied effects of exposure to TV and movie violence and the more recent research efforts on violent video games."

Research Strand: Children who watch high levels of media violence are at increased risk of aggressive behaviour as adults.

In 1960, University of Michigan Professor Leonard Eron studied 856 grade three students living in a semi-rural community in Columbia County, New York, and found that the children who watched violent television at home behaved more aggressively in school. Eron wanted to track the effect of this exposure over the years, so he revisited Columbia County in 1971, when the children who participated in the 1960 study were 19 years of age. He found that boys who watched violent TV when they were eight were more likely to get in trouble with the law as teenagers.

When Eron and Huesmann returned to Columbia County in 1982, the subjects were 30 years old. They reported that those participants who had watched more violent TV as eight-year-olds were more likely, as adults, to be convicted of serious crimes, to use violence to discipline their children, and to treat their spouses aggressively.

Professor Monroe Lefkowitz published similar findings in 1971. Lefkowitz interviewed a group of eight-year-olds and found that the boys who watched more violent TV were more likely to act aggressively in the real world. When he interviewed the same boys ten years later, he found that the more violence a boy watched at eight, the more aggressively he would act at age eighteen.

Columbia University professor Jeffrey Johnson has found that the effect is not limited to violent shows. Johnson tracked 707 families in upstate New York for 17 years, starting in 1975. In 2002, Johnson reported that children who watched one to three hours of television each day when they were 14 to 16 years old were 60 percent more likely to be involved in assaults and fights as adults than those who watched less TV.

Kansas State University professor John Murray concludes, "The most plausible interpretation of this pattern of correlations is that early preference for violent television programming and other media is one factor in the production of aggressive and antisocial behavior when the young boy becomes a young man."

However, this line of research has attracted a great deal of controversy. Pulitzer Prize-winning author Richard Rhodes has attacked Eron's work, arguing that his conclusions are based on an insignificant amount of data. Rhodes claims that Eron had information about the amount of TV viewed in 1960 for only 3 of the 24 men who committed violent crimes as adults years later. Rhodes concludes that Eron's work is "poorly conceived, scientifically inadequate, biased and sloppy if not actually fraudulent research."

Guy Cumberbatch, head of the Communications Research Group, a U.K. social policy think tank, has equally harsh words for Johnson's study. Cumberbatch claims Johnson's group of 88 under-one-hour TV watchers is "so small, it's aberrant." And, as journalist Ben Shouse points out, other critics say that Johnson's study "can't rule out the possibility that television is just a marker for some unmeasured environmental or psychological influence on both aggression and TV habits."

Research Strand: The introduction of television into a community leads to an increase in violent behaviour.

Researchers have also pursued the link between media violence and real life aggression by examining communities before and after the introduction of television. In the mid 1970s, University of British Columbia professor Tannis McBeth Williams studied a remote village in British Columbia both before and after television was introduced. She found that two years after TV arrived, violent incidents had increased by 160 percent.

Researchers Gary Granzberg and Jack Steinbring studied three Cree communities in northern Manitoba during the 1970s and early 1980s. They found that four years after television was introduced into one of the communities, the incidence of fist fights and black eyes among the children had increased significantly. Interestingly, several days after an episode of *Happy Days* aired, in which one character joined a gang called the Red Demons, children in the community created rival gangs, called the Red Demons and the Green Demons, and the conflict between the two seriously disrupted the local school.

University of Washington Professor Brandon Centerwall noted that the sharp increase in the murder rate in North America in 1955 occurred eight years after television sets began to enter North American homes. To test his hypothesis that the two were related, he examined the murder rate in South Africa where, prior to 1975, television was banned by the government. He found that twelve years after the ban was lifted, murder rates skyrocketed.

University of Toronto Professor Jonathan Freedman has criticized this line of research. He points out that Japanese television has some of the most violent imagery in the world, and yet Japan has a much lower murder rate than other countries, including Canada and the United States, which have comparatively less violence on TV.

Research Strand: Media violence stimulates fear in some children.

A number of studies have reported that watching media violence frightens young children, and that the effects of this may be long lasting.

In 1998, Professors Singer, Slovak, Frierson and York surveyed 2,000 Ohio students in grades three through eight. They report that the incidences of psychological trauma (including anxiety, depression and post-traumatic stress) increased in proportion to the number of hours of television watched each day.

A 1999 survey of 500 Rhode Island parents led by Brown University professor Judith Owens revealed that the presence of a television in a child's bedroom makes it more likely that the child will suffer from sleep disturbances. Nine percent of all the parents surveyed reported that their children have nightmares because of a television show at least once a week.

Tom Van der Voort studied 314 children aged nine through twelve in 1986. He found that although children can easily distinguish cartoons, westerns and spy thrillers from reality, they often confuse realistic programmes with the real world. When they are unable to integrate the violence in these shows because they can't follow the plot, they are much more likely to become anxious. This is particularly problematic because the children reported that they prefer realistic programmes, which they equate with fun and excitement. And, as Jacques de Guise reported in 2002, the younger the child, the less likely he or she will be able to identify violent content as violence.

In 1999, Professors Joanne Cantor and K. Harrison studied 138 university students, and found that memories of frightening media images continued to disturb a significant number of participants years later. Over 90 percent reported they continued to experience fright effects from images they viewed as children, ranging from sleep disturbances to steadfast avoidance of certain situations.

Research Strand: Media violence desensitizes people to real violence.

A number of studies in the 1970's showed that people who are repeatedly exposed to media violence tend to be less disturbed when they witness real world violence, and have less sympathy for its victims. For example, Professors V.B. Cline, R.G. Croft, and S. Courrier studied young boys over a two-year period. In 1973, they reported that boys who watch more than 25 hours of television per week are significantly less likely to be aroused by real world violence than those boys who watch 4 hours or less per week.

When researchers Fred Molitor and Ken Hirsch revisited this line of investigation in 1994, their work confirmed that children are more likely to tolerate aggressive behaviour in the real world if they first watch TV shows or films that contain violent content.

Research Strand: People who watch a lot of media violence tend to believe that the world is more dangerous than it is in reality.

George Gerbner has conducted the longest running study of television violence. His seminal research suggests that heavy TV viewers tend to perceive the world in ways that are consistent with the images on TV. As viewers' perceptions of the world come to conform with the depictions they see on TV, they become more passive, more anxious, and more fearful. Gerbner calls this the "Mean World Syndrome."

Gerbner's research found that those who watch greater amounts of television are more likely to:

- overestimate their risk of being victimized by crime
- believe their neighbourhoods are unsafe
- believe "fear of crime is a very serious personal problem"
- assume the crime rate is increasing, even when it is not

André Gosselin, Jacques de Guise and Guy Paquette decided to test Gerbner's theory in the Canadian context in 1997. They surveyed 360 university students, and found that heavy television viewers are more likely to believe the world is a more dangerous place. However, they also found heavy viewers are not more likely to actually feel more fearful.

Research Strand: Family attitudes to violent content are more important than the images themselves.

A number of studies suggest that media is only one of a number of variables that put children at risk of aggressive behaviour.

For example, a Norwegian study that included 20 at-risk teen-aged boys found that the lack of parental rules regulating what the boys watched was a more significant predictor of aggressive behaviour than the amount of media violence they watched. It also indicated that exposure to real world violence, together with exposure to media violence, created an "overload" of violent events. Boys who experienced this overload were more likely to use violent media images to create and consolidate their identities as members of an anti-social and marginalized group.

On the other hand, researchers report that parental attitudes towards media violence can mitigate the impact it has on children. Huesmann and Bacharach conclude, "Family attitudes and social class are stronger determinants of attitudes toward aggression than is the amount of exposure to TV, which is nevertheless a significant but weaker predictor."

True Crime

The Roots of an American Obsession

WALTER MOSLEY

Everybody is guilty of something. This is a truism of the West. It goes all the way back to Cain and original sin and has been a central topic of discourse among members of society from the construction of the laws of ancient Rome, through the Inquisition, into the Jim Crow system of the South (and North), stopping to wallow in the culture of the Soviet Union, and going right to the rotted heart of the race laws of Nazi Germany.

In 2,000 years of Western civilization we have been guilty of heresy, perversion, theft, and murder; of fighting and refusing to fight; of loving, lusting after, and sometimes just looking. We have been guilty of speaking out and keeping silent, of walking, marching, and running away. We have been found culpable for following orders and for refusing to follow them, for adultery, child endangerment, sexual harassment, and elder abuse. We have also been guilty of our religion, national origin, skin color, sexual preference, gender, and, now and then, of the blood in our veins.

Guilt is the mainstay of who we are and how we are organized, and is, seemingly, our undeniable destiny, along with Death and Taxes.

Our relationship with guilt is as old as the DNA that defines our species. But the nature of culpability changes with technology and technique. These changes affect the way we see the world and the way we seek to understand our predicament. True-crime stories, murder mysteries, up-to-the-minute online news reports, and (as always) rumor and innuendo grab our attention faster than any call for justice, human rights, or ceasefires.

These stories grab our attention faster than any call for justice, human rights, or ceasefires.

This is because most of us see ourselves as powerless cogs in a greater machine; as potential victims of a society so large and insensitive that we, innocent bystanders in the crowd, might be caught at any time in the crossfire between the forces of so-called good and evil.

Because of this vulnerability we have questions that need to be answered to ensure our safety. One such question is, what would happen if . . .? What if you saw a man shoot somebody? Should you tell the police? Would they protect you from murky vengeance? You saw a true-crime TV show once that profiled a man who identified a murderer and was himself murdered for giving evidence. Would you be guilty of being stupid for doing what you were taught was right?

Another question is, is it safe? Is it safe for you to walk the streets, drink the water, fly on commercial airliners, speak to an attractive stranger, to believe the words of political, religious, corporate, and social leaders?

In smaller societies we worked side by side with leaders, wealthy property owners, and local ministers. Face-to-face meetings and friendly gossip gave us at least the illusion of understanding where we stood and what was right. But today the working urban dweller gets all this information from TV and computer screens . . . and so often, we know, the media misinform.

The feeling of being lied to brings about a hunger for truth. We want to know if the man on death row was really guilty. Were there actually WMDs in the hills of Iraq? Are people being tortured, and am I morally responsible for my government's actions?

In order to answer these questions we first turn, with a mistrustful eye, to objective opinion sources. Editorials in newspapers and magazines, talk shows and news programs, public radio, blogs, and (because there's just too much for one person to read, listen to, and view) friends who have gleaned information from other impartial venues.

But even as we take in the information shoveled out at a stupendous rate from dozens of different sources, we begin to worry. Who owns the news? How do bloggers pay their rent? Why, in spite of what I'm being told, is the economy, and the world in general, getting worse?

This dissatisfaction brings us to fictional accounts. Crime shows, mysteries, and films speak to the bystander in a dangerous world. These forms of entertainment corroborate our feelings of distrust and allow us to think about how we might fit into a world that wouldn't even be aware of us getting crushed under its collective weight.

Fiction, better than reality, gives us heroes who can't let us down, who cannot be arrested, convicted, or vilified. Maybe these stories won't be able to resolve our dilemmas in the real world, but they can offer escape through a fantasy where even a common everyday Joe (or Jane) can be saved.

This salvation has always been our goal. Forgiveness for our sinful desires and secret trysts, for our failures and broken commandments, for our weakness beside the machine that covers the world with its cold, gray shadow.

This is why we have TV psychologists and mother substitutes, confessionals and paparazzi. On the one hand we're looking for deliverance, and on the other we seek to show how even the rich and famous are flawed.

We need forgiveness and someone to blame. So the story of crime fills our TVs, theaters, cinemas, computer files, and bookshelves. We are fascinated with stories of crime, real or imagined, because we need them to cleanse the modern world from our souls.

MOSLEY is the author, most recently, of *The Long Fall.*

Wikipedia in the Newsroom

While the line "according to Wikipedia" pops up occasionally in news stories, it's relatively rare to see the user-created online encyclopedia cited as a source. But some journalists find it very valuable as a road map to troves of valuable information.

DONNA SHAW

When the Las Vegas Review-Journal published a story in September about construction cranes, it noted that they were invented by ancient Greeks and powered by men and donkeys.

Michigan's Flint Journal recently traced the origins of fantasy football to 1962, and to three people connected to the Oakland Raiders.

And when the Arizona Republic profiled a controversial local congressman in August, it concluded that his background was "unclear."

What all three had in common was one of the sources they cited: Wikipedia, the popular, reader-written and -edited online encyclopedia. Dismissed by traditional journalism as a gimmicky source of faux information almost since it debuted in 2001, Wikipedia may be gaining some cautious converts as it works its way into the mainstream, albeit more as a road map to information than as a source to cite. While "according to Wikipedia" attributions do crop up, they are relatively rare.

To be sure, many Wikipedia citations probably sneak into print simply because editors don't catch them. Other times, the reference is tongue-in-cheek: The Wall Street Journal, for example, cited Wikipedia as a source for an item on "turducken" (a bizarre concoction in which a chicken is stuffed into a duck that is stuffed into a turkey) in a subscriber e-mail update just before Thanksgiving. In the e-mail, the Journal reporter wrote that some of his information was "courtesy of Wikipedia's highly informative turducken entry. As my hero Dave Barry says, 'I'm not making this up. Although, I'll admit that somebody on Wikipedia might have.'"

And when Time Inc. Editor-in-Chief John Huey was asked how his staffers made sure their stories were correct, he jokingly responded, "Wikipedia."

It's unclear if many newsrooms have formal policies banning Wikipedia attribution in their stories, but many have informal ones. At the Philadelphia Inquirer, which cited Wikipedia in an article about the death of television personality Tom Snyder last July, Managing Editor Mike Leary recently sent an e-mail to staff members reminding them they are never to use Wikipedia "to verify facts or to augment information in a story." A news database search indicates that "according to Wikipedia" mentions are few and far between in U.S. papers, and are found most frequently in opinion columns, letters to the editor and feature stories. They also turn up occasionally in graphics and information boxes.

Such caution is understandable, as for all its enticements, Wikipedia is maddeningly uneven. It can be impressive in one entry (the one on the Naval Battle of Guadalcanal includes 138 endnotes, 18 references and seven external links) and sloppy in another (it misspells the name of AJR's editor). Its topics range from the weighty (the Darfur conflict) to the inconsequential (a list of all episodes of the TV series "Canada's Worst Handyman"). Its talk pages can include sophisticated discussions of whether fluorescent light bulbs will cause significant mercury pollution or silly minutiae like the real birth date of Paris Hilton's Chihuahua. Some of its commentary is remarkable but some contributors are comically dense, like the person who demanded proof that 18th-century satirist Jonathan Swift wasn't serious when he wrote that landlords should eat the children of their impoverished Irish tenants.

Hubble Smith, the Review-Journal business reporter who wrote the crane story, says he was simply looking for background on construction cranes for a feature on the Las Vegas building boom when the Wikipedia entry popped up during a search. It was among the most interesting information he found, so he used it. But after his story went to the desk, a copy editor flagged it.

"He said, 'Do you realize that Wikipedia is just made up of people who contribute all of this?'" Smith recalls. "I had never used it before." The reference was checked and allowed to remain in the story.

Indeed, the primary knock against Wikipedia is that its authors and editors are also its users—an unpaid, partially anonymous army, some of whom insert jokes, exaggeration and even outright lies in their material. About one-fifth of the editing is done by anonymous users, but a tight-knit community of 600 to 1,000 volunteers does the bulk of the work, according to Wikipedia cofounder Jimmy Wales. Members of this group can delete material or, in extreme cases, even lock particularly outrageous entries while they are massaged.

The extent of the potential for misinformation became clearer in August, when a new tool called WikiScanner (wikiscanner .virgil.gr/) began providing an ingenious database to identify propagandists and hoaxers. It gave Wikipedia critics plenty of new ammunition, as it revealed that among those surreptitiously rewriting entries were employees of major corporations, politicians and the CIA trying to make their bosses look better. And then there was the John Seigenthaler Sr. episode, in which someone edited the prominent retired journalist's Wikipedia biography to insinuate that he briefly had been a suspect in the assassinations of John and Robert F. Kennedy. In an op-ed piece for USA Today in 2005, Seigenthaler, who once worked for Bobby Kennedy and was one of his pallbearers, railed against Wikipedia, calling it "a flawed and irresponsible research tool." (A Nashville man later admitting inserting the material as a joke aimed at a coworker, and apologized.)

No one is more aware of such pitfalls than the leadership of Wikipedia, whose online disclaimer reminds users that "anyone with an Internet connection" can alter the content and cautions, "please be advised that nothing found here has necessarily been reviewed by people with the expertise required to provide you with complete, accurate or reliable information." An even more blunt assessment appears in the encyclopedia's "Ten things you may not know about Wikipedia" posting: "We do not expect you to trust us. It is in the nature of an ever-changing work like Wikipedia that, while some articles are of the highest quality of scholarship, others are admittedly complete rubbish." It also reminds users not to use Wikipedia as a primary source or for making "critical decisions."

Wales says it doesn't surprise him to hear that some journalists are cautiously trying it out. "I think that people are sort of slowly learning how to use Wikipedia, and learning its strengths and its weaknesses," he says. "Of course, any reasonable person has to be up front that there are weaknesses. . . . On the other hand, there are lots of sources that have weaknesses." Wales thinks the encyclopedia's best journalistic use is for background research rather than as a source to be quoted.

Wales, a board member and chairman emeritus of the nonprofit Wikimedia Foundation Inc., which owns Wikipedia, says the company constantly strives to improve its product. "Right now we're tightly focused on making sure that, for example, the biographies are well sourced," he says. The foundation is also developing new tools "to block people who are misbehaving," including one for new German-language Wikipedia users that will vet their contributions. If it works, Wales says, it can be rolled out for Wikipedia encyclopedias in other languages.

He also defends the right of Wikipedia—and perhaps even reporters—to have a little fun. "I subscribe to Google alerts and I saw that turducken [item in the Wall Street Journal e-mail] and I thought, well, what other source would you use? Britannica doesn't cover this nonsense," he says.

There are still plenty of journalists who aren't convinced of Wikipedia's worth, among them the denizens of testycopyeditors .org, where contributors to the online conversation have names like "crabby editor" and "wordnerdy." Asked his opinion of Wikipedia, Phillip Blanchard, the Washington Post copy editor who started testycopyeditors, responds, "I'm not sure what I could add, beyond 'don't use it' and 'it's junk.'"

While the Post has no written policy against it, "I can't imagine a circumstance under which a fact would be attributed to Wikipedia," says Blanchard, who works on the financial desk. "'According to Wikipedia' has appeared only a couple of times in the Washington Post, once in a humor column and once in a movie review."

Gilbert Gaul, a Pulitzer Prize-winning reporter at the Post, describes himself as a "dinosaur in the changing world" when it comes to rules about sourcing stories. Wikipedia, he says, doesn't meet his personal test—for one thing, "there is no way for me to verify the information without fact-checking, in which case it isn't really saving me any time." He prefers to do his own research, so he can "see and touch everything," rather than rely on the mostly anonymous content of Wikipedia.

"I like much of the new technology. . . . But to me rules, borders, guidelines and transparency matter a lot," Gaul said in an e-mail interview. "I need and want to be able to trust the people I am reading or chatting with. If I can't, what is the point?"

Other journalists, though, are at least somewhat won over by what can be an impressive feature: those sometimes lengthy Wikipedia citations that lead to other, more authoritative sources. David Cay Johnston, a Pulitzer-winning reporter for the New York Times, says

he recently looked up "thermodynamics" to see where it led him, and found that Wikipedia's entry listed numerous references from reliable sources.

"I have a solid understanding of the concept, but once we get into fine points, I have nothing beyond my skepticism as a reporter to judge the accuracy, validity and reliability of what is there," he says. "However, this entry appears to be useful as a source guide. It has names of researchers whose books were published by eminent organizations, and you can take that as a quick way to find sources. So as a tip sheet, as a road map to reliable sources, Wikipedia seems valuable."

Jim Thomsen, a copy editor at the Kitsap Sun in Bremerton, Washington, has no problem with attributing information to the online encyclopedia in certain cases. "If I see something in Wikipedia I might want to cite for background and context for a story, I trace back the cites to their original sources," Thomsen said in an e-mail interview. "If I feel the origins are solid, I'll use the info.

For a student who just uses a search engine and they use the first thing that pops up . . . this undermines the kind of thing we're trying to teach them.

"I know there's been a lot of hullabaloo about people with agendas seeding Wikipedia with slanted or even false information, but as I see it, that sort of stuff can be easily sniffed out—by looking at the cites, and tracking them back. No cites? Fuhgeddaboudit. The bottom line is that Wikipedia can be a great tool as a central Clearinghouse for contextual information. But not a single syllable there should be taken at face value."

The Los Angeles Times is one of many newspapers that have allowed an occasional "according to Wikipedia" in their pages in the last several months. One was in a commentary piece about Barack Obama; another appeared in a staff-written story about a professional "man in the street" who managed to be interviewed repeatedly. The reference in the latter story drew rapid fire on testycopyeditors.org, with comments including "Shame on the Los Angeles Times" and "No, no, a thousand times no."

Melissa McCoy, the Times' deputy managing editor in charge of copy desks, says the paper occasionally allows Wikipedia attribution. "We're certainly not going to use Wikipedia as a standalone news source, but we're not going to exclude it if it takes us somewhere," she says. "If a reporter spots something in there and it makes them do an extra phone call, it's silly" not to use it.

There's no unanimity about Wikipedia among academic experts, who have engaged in vigorous debates about the online encyclopedia. While many professors refuse to allow students to cite it, it has attracted some prominent defenders, including historians and scientists who have analyzed its content.

"If a journalist were to find something surprising on Wikipedia and the journalistic instincts suggested it was correct, the journalist might add that as an unsubstantiated Wiki-fact and invite Comment," says Cathy Davidson, a professor at Duke University and cofounder of HASTAC (Humanities, Arts, Science, and Technology Advanced Collaboratory, www.hastac.org), a network of researchers developing new ways to collect and share information via technology. "Perhaps an online version of the printed piece, for example, might include a blog inviting people to comment on the Wiki-fact. It may be that there would be Wikifacts online that were not in the printed piece. In other words, why not use the new technologies available to expand knowledge in all kinds of ways?"

Journalists also should consider, Davidson says, whether some of the sources they deem reliable have their own inadequacies. For example, when she recently researched the origins of calculus, she found that standard Western histories generally credited England's Isaac Newton and Germany's Gottfried Wilhelm Leibniz. But Wikipedia went much further, tracing the discovery of basic calculus functions back to the Egyptians in 1800 BC, and then to China, India and Mesopotamia—all hundreds of years before the Europeans.

So while journalists should be cautious no matter what resources they use, "What Wikipedia does reveal to those in the Euro-American world is knowledge which most of our sources, even the most scholarly, have, in the past, neglected because it did not fit in our intellectual genealogies, in our history of ideas," Davidson says.

In December 2005, the science journal Nature published a survey of several experts about the content of comparable Wikipedia and online Encyclopedia Britannica entries. In a conclusion hotly disputed by Britannica, Nature said that Wikipedia "comes close to Britannica in terms of the accuracy of its science entries," in that the average Wikipedia article contained four errors to Britannica's three. Britannica's 20-page response said that "almost everything about the journal's investigation . . . was wrong and misleading . . . the study was so poorly carried out and its findings so error-laden that it was completely without merit." The company further asserted that Nature had misrepresented its own data—its numbers, after all, showed that Wikipedia had a third more inaccuracies than Britannica—and asked for "a full and public retraction of the article." Nature stood by its story.

"The Nature piece profoundly undermined the authority upon which Britannica depends," says Gregory Crane, editor in chief of the Perseus Digital Library at Tufts University. He is a recent convert to the pro-Wikipedia camp, calling it "the most important intellectual phenomenon of the early 21st century."

He recognizes its faults, especially when Wikipedians write about controversial topics. So "people have to do some critical thinking," Crane says, by evaluating their sources, "whether it's Wikipedia or the New York Times."

In an article he wrote in 2005, Crane acknowledged that Wikipedia "is an extreme case whose success so far has shocked skeptical scholars." But he noted as well that other, more mainstream reference works had similar foundations—for example, the Oxford English Dictionary was written over a period of 70 years by thousands of people, including "an inmate at an asylum for the criminally insane."

A 2006 analysis by another scholar and Wikipedia fan, George Mason University historian Roy Rosenzweig, found some inaccuracies, omissions, uneven writing and even plagiarism in selected entries. But his comparison of several Wikipedia biographies against comparable entries in two other encyclopedias found that Wikipedia "roughly matches" Microsoft's Encarta in accuracy while still falling short of the Oxford University Press' American National Biography Online. "This general conclusion is supported by studies comparing Wikipedia to other major encyclopedias," wrote Rosenzweig, who was director of the university's Center for History and New Media until his death last year.

Still, many if not most in the academic community think that Wikipedia, if used at all, should be no more than a secondary source, and they frequently tell their students as much. For Cornell University professor Ross Brann, that position was reinforced in early 2007, after the outing of a salaried Wikipedia employee and editor who called himself "Essjay" and claimed to be a tenured professor with doctorates in theology and canon law. Turns out he had seriously padded his résumé: The New Yorker discovered after interviewing Essjay that he was actually a 24-year-old community college dropout. To Brann, a professor of Judeo-Islamic Studies and director of graduate studies for the Department of Near Eastern Studies, the incident confirmed that Wikipedia could not be trusted as a primary source.

"I just tell students, 'Do not use Wikipedia, do not cite it, do not go there for my classes.' We're trying to teach them how to use sources, how to evaluate different sources, and I think that in general, although obviously a wonderful resource, for a student who just uses a search engine and they use the first thing that pops up . . . this undermines the kind of thing we're trying to teach them," Brann says.

Brann notes that Wikipedia's popularity probably has a lot to do with the fact that its entries so frequently pop up first, because that's the nature of search engines. "Many of them just work by the multiplicity of uses, others by virtue of ad arrangements—somebody is deciding for you what you're going to look at," he says.

And what about college journalists, a group that has never known life without computers? A news database search suggests that they are just as reluctant to cite Wikipedia as their professional colleagues. In August, for example, the University of Iowa newspaper, the Daily Iowan, used the WikiScanner database to determine that thousands of Wikipedia entries had been made or modified by people using the campus computer network. Some involved obvious but harmless enough vandalism: "Hawkeyes Rule" was inserted into text about the college's football stadium; less generously, a former university president was called an "eater of monkey brains," according to the paper's story.

Jason Brummond, editor in chief of the Daily Iowan, says he considers Wikipedia a good initial source, "but you go from there to find what most people would consider a more reputable source." Reporters in his newsroom generally understand that, he adds.

Brummond thinks the age of the journalist doesn't necessarily have that much to do with accepting Wikipedia: "It's more a personal awareness of how Wikipedia works."

In September, the University of Kansas student newspaper ran an editorial calling upon Wikipedia to do a better job of restoring "adulterated pages," noting that "despite a thousand recitations by our professors that Wikipedia is not a genuine source, students trust the site to give them accurate information." Nevertheless, Erick Schmidt, editor of the University Daily Kansan, says he doesn't rely much on Wikipedia, in part because his reporters write mostly about college and community issues. Plus, "we're taught to be cautious of things and skeptical," he says.

Schmidt rejects the notion that college students uncritically accept Wikipedia because they are infatuated with all things Internet. "We don't want to move things to technology because we think it's cool or paper is lame," he says. "But honestly, we are pressed for time, and if technology speeds things up . . . that's why we're being drawn to it."

For his part, Wales maintains that the more people use Wikipedia, the more they'll come to understand and accept it. His conclusion, he says, "comes from people who have used the site for a long time and know, 'I have to be careful'. . . which is what good reporting is supposed to be about anyway."

But whatever the verdict on Wikipedia, one thing should not change, says the New York Times' Johnston: "No matter who your sources are, when you sign your name, you are responsible for every word, every thought, every concept."

Contributing writer **DONNA SHAW** (shaw@tcnj.edu) has written about front-page ads, hyperlocal websites and Pulitzer Prizes for *AJR*.

From *American Journalism Review,* February/March 2008, pp. 40–45. Copyright © 2008 by the Philip Merrill College of Journalism at the University of Maryland, College Park, MD 20742-7111. Reprinted with permission.

Journalist Bites Reality!

How broadcast journalism is flawed in such a fundamental way that its utility as a tool for informing viewers is almost nil.

STEVE SALERNO

It is the measure of the media's obsession with its "pedophiles run amok!" story line that so many of us are on a first-name basis with the victims: Polly, Amber, JonBenet, Danielle, Elizabeth, Samantha. And now there is Madeleine. Clearly these crimes were and are horrific, and nothing here is intended to diminish the parents' loss. But something else has been lost in the bargain as journalists tirelessly stoke fear of strangers, segueing from nightly-news segments about cyberstalkers and "the rapist in your neighborhood" to prime-time reality series like *Dateline*'s "To Catch a Predator." That "something else" is reality.

According to the U.S. Department of Justice, in a given year there are about 88,000 documented cases of sexual abuse against juveniles. In the roughly 17,500 cases involving children between ages 6 and 11, strangers are the perpetrators just 5% of the time—and just *3%* of the time when the victim is under age 6. (Further, more than a third of such molesters are themselves juveniles, who may not be true "predators" so much as confused or unruly teens.) Overall, the odds that one of America's 48 million children under age 12 will encounter an adult pedophile at the local park are startlingly remote. The Child Molestation Research & Prevention Institute: "Right now, 90 percent of our efforts go toward protecting our children from strangers, when what we need to do is to focus 90% of our efforts toward protecting children from the abusers who are not strangers." That's a diplomatic way of phrasing the uncomfortable but factually supported truth: that if your child is not molested in your own home—by you, your significant other, or someone else you invited in—chances are your child will never be molested anywhere. Media coverage has precisely inverted both the reality and the risk of child sexual assault. Along the way, it has also inverted the gender of the most tragic victims: Despite the unending parade of young female faces on TV, boys are more likely than girls to be killed in the course of such abuse.

We think we know Big Journalism's faults by its muchballyhooed lapses—its scandals, gaffes, and breakdowns—as well as by a recent spate of insider tell-alls. When Dan Rather goes public with a sensational exposé based on bogus documents; when the *Atlanta Journal-Constitution* wrongly labels

Richard Jewell the Olympic Park bomber; when *Dateline* resorts to rigging explosive charges to the gas tanks of "unsafe" trucks that, in *Dateline*'s prior tests, stubbornly refused to explode on their own; when the *New York Times*' Jayson Blair scoops other reporters working the same story by quoting sources who don't exist. . . . We see these incidents as atypical, the exceptions that prove the rule.

Sadly, we're mistaken. To argue that a decided sloppiness has crept into journalism or that the media have been "hijacked by [insert least favorite political agenda]" badly misses the real point; it suggests that all we need to do to fix things is filter out the gratuitous political spin or rig the ship to run a bit tighter. In truth, today's system of news delivery is an enterprise whose procedures, protocols, and underlying assumptions all but guarantee that it cannot succeed at its self-described mission. Broadcast journalism in particular is flawed in such a fundamental way that its utility as a tool for illuminating life, let alone interpreting it, is almost nil.

"You Give Us 22 Minutes, and We'll Give You . . . What, Exactly?"

We watch the news to "see what's going on in the world." But there's a hitch right off the bat. In its classic conception, newsworthiness is built on a foundation of anomaly: *man-bites-dog,* to use the hackneyed journalism school example. The significance of this cannot be overstated. It means that, by definition, journalism in its most basic form deals with what life *is not.*

Today's star journalist, however, goes to great lengths to distance himself from his trade's man-bites-dog heritage. To admit that what he's presenting is largely marginalia (or at best "background music") deflates the journalist's relevance in an environment where members of Major Media have come to regard themselves as latter day shamans and oracles. In a memorable 2002 piece, "The Weight of the Anchor," columnist Frank Rich put it this way, regarding the then-Big 3 of Brokaw, Jennings, and Rather: "Not quite movie stars, not quite officialdom, they are more famous than most movie stars and more powerful than most politicians."

Thus, journalism as currently practiced delivers two contradictory messages: that what it puts before you (a) is newsworthy (under the old man-bites-dog standard), but also (b) captures the *zeitgeist*. ("You give us 22 minutes, we'll give you the world," gloat all news radio stations across the country.) The news media cannot simultaneously deliver both. In practice, they fail at both. By painting life in terms of its oddities, journalism yields not a snapshot of your world, but something closer to a photographic negative.

Even when journalism isn't plainly capsizing reality, it's furnishing information that varies between immaterial and misleading. For all its *cinema-verité* panache, embedded reporting, as exemplified in Iraq and in *Nightline*'s recent series on "the forgotten war" in Afghanistan, shows only what's going on in the immediate vicinity of the embedded journalist. It's not all that useful for yielding an overarching sense of the progress of a war, and might easily be counterproductive: To interpret such field reporting as a valid microcosm is the equivalent of standing in a spot where it's raining and assuming it's raining everywhere.

Journalism's paradoxes and problems come to a head in the concept of *newsmagazination,* pioneered on *60 Minutes* and later the staple tactic of such popular clones as *Dateline, 48 Hours,* and *20/20.* One of the more intellectually dishonest phenomena of recent vintage, newsmagazination presents the viewer with a circumstantial stew whipped up from:

- a handful of compelling sound-bites culled from anecdotal sources,
- public-opinion polls (which tell us nothing except what people *think* is true),
- statistics that have no real evidentiary weight and/or scant relevance to the point they're being used to "prove,"
- logical flaws such as *post hoc ergo propter hoc* (after the fact) reasoning,
- faulty or, at best, unproven "expert" assumptions, or "conventional wisdom" that is never seriously examined,
- a proprietary knowledge of people's inner thoughts or motives (as when a White House correspondent discounts a president's actual statements in order to reveal to us that president's "true agenda"), etc.

Case in point: On Nov. 5, 2004, NBC's *Dateline* built a show around the dangers of gastric bypass surgery. The topic was a natural for *Dateline,* inasmuch as *The Today Show*'s own Al Roker, who did much of the reporting, had undergone the surgery and achieved a stunning weight loss. In setting the scene, anchor Stone Phillips noted that the expected mortality rate for gastric bypass is 1 in 200. (Translation: The *survival* rate is 199 in 200, or 99.5%.) Phillips then handed off to Roker; the affable weatherman spent a few cheery moments on his own success, then found his somber face in segueing to the tragic saga of Mike Butler, who died following surgery. The Butler story consumed the next 30 minutes of the hour long broadcast, punctuated by the obligatory wistful soliloquy from Butler's young widow. So, in covering a procedure that helps (or at least doesn't kill) roughly 99.5% of patients, *Dateline* elects to tell the story in terms of the 0.5% *with tragic outcomes.* Had NBC sought to equitably represent the upside and downside of gastric bypass, it would've devoted 1/200th of the show—a mere 18 seconds—to Butler. Further, wouldn't it have been journalistically responsible for *Dateline* to devote a good portion of the broadcast to the risks of morbid obesity itself, which far outweigh the risks of surgical bypass?

Do the Math . . . *Please*

One underlying factor here is that journalists either don't understand the difference between random data and genuine statistical proof, or they find that distinction inconvenient for their larger purpose: to make news dramatic and accessible. The media need a story line—a coherent narrative, ideally with an identifiable hero and villain. As Tom Brokaw once put it, perhaps revealing more than he intended, "It's all storytelling, you know. That's what journalism is about." The mainstream news business is so unaccustomed to dealing with issues at any level of complexity and nuance that they're wont to oversimplify their story to the point of caricature.

The best contemporary example is the Red State/Blue State dichotomy, invoked as an easy metaphor to express the philosophical schism that supposedly divides "the two Americas." Watching CNN's Bill Schneider hover over his maps on Election Night 2004, drawing stark lines between colors, one would've thought there were no Republicans in California, or that a Democrat arriving at the Texas border would be turned back at gunpoint. Well, guess what: The dichotomy doesn't exist—certainly not in the way journalists use the term. It's just a handy, sexy media fiction. Although California did wind up in the Kerry column in 2004, some 5.5 million Californians voted for George W. Bush. They represented about 45% of the state's total electorate and a much larger constituency in raw numbers than Bush enjoyed *in any state he won,* including Texas. Speaking of Texas: That unreconstituted Yankee, John Kerry, collected 2.8 million votes there. *Two point eight million.* Yet to hear the media tell it, California is deep, cool Blue, while Texas is a glaring, monolithic Red. Such fabrications aren't just silly. They become institutionalized in the culture, and they color—in this case literally—the way Americans view the nation in which they live.

The mythical Red State/Blue State paradigm is just one of the more telling indications of a general disability the media exhibit in working with data. A cluster of random events does not a "disturbing new trend!" make—but that doesn't stop journalists from finding patterns in happenstance. Take lightning. It kills with an eerie predictability: about 66 Americans every year. Now, lightning could kill those 66 people more or less evenly all spring and summer, or it could, in theory, kill the lot of them on one *really* scary Sunday in May. But the scary Sunday in May wouldn't necessarily mean we're going to have a year in which lightning kills 79,000 people. (No more than if it killed a half-dozen people named Johanssen on that Sunday would it mean that lightning is suddenly targeting Swedes.) Yet you can bet that if *any* half-dozen people are killed by lightning one Sunday, you'll soon see a special report along the lines of, *LIGHTNING: IS IT OUT TO GET US?* We've seen this propensity on display with shark attacks, meningitis, last year's rash of amusement-park fatalities, and any number of other "random event clusters" that occur for no reason anyone can explain.

Journalists overreact to events that fall well within the laws of probability. They treat the fact that something happened as if we never before had any reason to think it *could* happen—as if it were a brand-new risk with previously unforeseen causation. Did America become more vulnerable on 9/11? Or had it been vulnerable all along? Indeed, it could be argued that America today is far *less* vulnerable, precisely because of the added vigilance inspired by 9/11. Is that how the media play it? Similarly, a bridge collapse is no reason for journalists to assume in knee-jerk fashion that bridges overall are any less safe than they've been for decades. Certainly it's no reason to jump to the conclusion that the nation's infrastructure is crumbling, which is how several major news outlets framed the collapse of the Interstate 35W Bridge this past summer. As Freud might put it, sometimes a bridge collapse is just a bridge collapse. Alas, journalism needs its story line.

For a textbook example of the intellectual barrenness of so much of what's presented even as "headline" news, consider the Consumer Confidence Index and media coverage of same. For decades, such indices have been telling America how it feels about its economic prospects. The best known index has been compiled each month since 1967 by the Conference Board, a nonprofit organization dating to 1916. The Board's index is an arbitrary composite of indicators rooted in five equally arbitrary questions mailed to 5000 households. ("Do you see jobs as being easier or harder to get next year?") On Tuesday, October 30, 2007, the Board reported that its latest CCI had dipped to a two-year low. The media jumped on the story, as is ever the case when the CCI dips. (CCI upticks are seldom reported with the same fervor.) Like many of its counterparts nationally, no doubt, a Philadelphia network affiliate sent its consumer-affairs reporter trudging out to find consumers who lacked confidence. She succeeded.

Few reporters bother to mention that, customarily, there has been only a tenuous connection between CCI numbers and actual consumer spending or the overall health of the economy as objectively measured. In fact, just days after the release of the downbeat CCI, the Labor Department reported that the economy had generated 166,000 new jobs in October—twice the forecast. That statistic, which measures reality, got nowhere near the same play as the CCI, which measures perception.

Let's recap. We have a fanciful metric that's just a compilation of opinion, which is layered with further opinion from passersby, and then subjected to in-studio analysis (still more opinion). All of which is presented to viewers as . . . news.

The problem for society is that giving headline prominence to meaningless or marginal events exalts those events to the status of conventional wisdom. "Reporting confers legitimacy and relevance," writes Russell Frank, Professor of Journalism

Ethics at Penn State University. "When a newspaper puts a certain story on page one or a newscast puts it at or near the top of a 22-minute program, it is saying to its audience, in no uncertain terms, that 'this story is important.'" The self-fulfilling nature of all this should be clear: News organizations decide what's important, spin it to their liking, cover it *ad nauseam,* then describe it—without irony—as "the 800-pound gorilla" or "the issue that just won't go away." This is not unlike network commercials promoting sit-coms and dramas that "everyone is talking about" in the hopes of getting people to watch shows that apparently no one is talking about.

Tonight at 11 . . . the Apocalypse!

Far worse than hyping a story that represents just 0.5% reality, is covering "news" that's *zero* percent reality: There literally is no story. Even so, if the non-story satisfies other requirements, it will be reported anyway. This truism was not lost on the late David Brinkley, who, towards the end of his life, observed, "The one function that TV news performs very well is that when there is no news, we give it to you with the same emphasis as if there were."

On June 9, 2005, as part of its ongoing series of "Security Updates," CNN airs a special report titled "Keeping Milk Safe." Over shots of adorable first-graders sipping from their pint cartons, CNN tells viewers that the farm-to-shelf supply chain is vulnerable at every point, beginning with the cow; with great drama, the report emphasizes the terrifying consequences such tampering could have. Nowhere does the network, mention that in the history of the milk industry, *no incident of supply-chain tampering has ever been confirmed,* due to terrorism or anything else.

Similarly, after the Asian tsunamis struck over Christmas 2004, *Dateline* wasted no time casting about for an alarmist who could bring the tragedy closer to home: the familiar *Could It Happen Here?* motif. The show's producers found Stephen Ward, PhD, of the University of California at Santa Cruz. In January, *Dateline*'s East Coast viewers heard Ward foretell a geological anomaly in their very own ocean that could generate the equivalent of "all the bombs on earth" detonating at once. The event Ward prophesied would unleash on New York City a wave containing "15 or 20 times the energy" of the Asian tsunamis. As a helpful backdrop, *Dateline* treated its viewers to spectacular visuals from *The Day After Tomorrow,* showing Manhattan's heralded landmarks disappearing beneath an onrushing, foamy sea.

But for sheer overwrought absurdity, it's hard to beat what took place in mid-September 1999. For six full days, journalists behaved as if there was one story and one story only: Hurricane Floyd. The TV tempest commenced as the actual tempest still lolled hundreds of miles offshore, with no one certain how much of a threat Floyd posed, or whether it might fizzle before it hit land (as so often happens—Katrina has changed the way we think about hurricanes, but Katrina was a once-in-a-generation event). This was Saturday. By Tuesday the hurricane-in-absentia had engulfed the nightly news. While residents of areas in Floyd's projected path evacuated, the other side of the highway was clotted with news crews on their way *in.* By Wednesday all of the networks had their parka-clad correspondents standing on some coastal beach, each correspondent bent on looking wetter and more windblown than the next. Sprinkled among all this were the requisite interviews with men (and women) on the street—as well as in insurance companies, emergency-services offices, local restaurants, and the like. Bereft of an actual hurricane to show during this feverish build-up, *The Today Show* aired old footage of Hurricane Hugo's plunder of Charleston, in sledgehammer foreshadowing of the disaster to come.

Floyd caused a fair amount of damage when it finally hit on Thursday: 57 deaths and an estimated $6 billion in property loss. But here's where things get curious. By the time Floyd blew in, media interest clearly had ebbed. On television at least, coverage of the aftermath was dispatched in a day or so, with occasional backward glances occupying a few moments of air time in subsequent newscasts. Bottom line, the coverage of Floyd *before* it was a real story dwarfed the coverage given the storm once it *became* a story. Evidently the conjured image of tidal waves crashing on shore was more titillating to news producers than film of real life homeowners swabbing brownish muck out of their basements.

Today's newspeople have substantially improved on one of the timeless axioms of their craft: "If it bleeds, it leads." They prefer the mere prospect of bad news to most other kinds of news that did occur. The result is journalism as Stephen King might do it: the dogged selling of the cataclysm 'round the corner, complete with stage lighting and scenes fictionalized for dramatic purposes. Sure, the camera loves suspense. But . . . is suspense news? Is it really news that someone *thinks* a hurricane *might* kill thousands? It might kill no one, either, which is historically closer to the truth. Honest journalism would wait to see what the storm does, then report it.

Granted, Floyd blew in during a slow week. Following, though, is a sampling of the events that were largely ignored while the assembled media were waiting for Floyd:

- The House of Representatives took a hard stand on soft money, approving limits on campaign spending.
- The Equal Employment Opportunity Commission launched an investigation of corporate America's fondness for cash balance pension plans, an issue that affected millions of workers, and stood to affect millions more.
- The 17-member Joint Security Commission released a chilling report on America's handling of security-clearance applications. This, let us remember, was two years before the terror attacks of 9/11.
- The terrorist bombings in Russia and the gruesome, continuing holocaust in East Timor.

The advance billing given to Floyd bespeaks a gloomy trend in broadcast news' continuing slide toward theater. We witnessed this same phenomenon during the run-up to Desert Storm, Y2K, and the Clinton impeachment, among others.

The Crusades—Postmodern Style

Nowhere are these foibles more noticeable—or more of a threat to journalistic integrity—than when they coalesce into a cause: so-called "advocacy" or "social" journalism. To begin with, there are legitimate questions about whether journalism should even have causes. Does the journalist alone know what's objectively, abstractly good or evil? What deserves supporting or reforming? The moment journalists claim license to cover events sympathetically or cynically, we confront the problem of what to cover sympathetically or cynically, where to draw such lines and—above all—who gets to draw them. There are very few issues that unite the whole of mankind. Regardless, as Tom Rosenstiel of the Project for Excellence in Journalism told *USA Today,* "News outlets have found they can create more . . . identity by creating franchise brands around issues or around a point of view."

Even worse, the data on which journalists premise their crusades are drawn from the same marginalia discussed above. When Francisco Serrano was discovered to be living in the Minnesota high school he once attended, the media covered the 2005 story as if every American high school had a half-dozen homeless people living in it. The actual episode, though exceedingly rare if not one-of-a-kind, became a window to the nation's social failings.

In his thinking and methodology, today's journalist resembles the homicide cop who, having settled on a suspect, begins collecting evidence specifically against that suspect, dismissing information that counters his newfound theory of the crime. Too many journalists think in terms of buttressing a preconceived argument or fleshing out a sense of narrative gained very early in their research. This mindset is formalized in journalism's highest award: the Pulitzer Prize. Traditionally, stories deemed worthy of Pulitzer consideration have revealed the dark (and, often as not, statistically insignificant) underbelly of American life. In 2007 the Pulitzer for "public-service journalism" went to *The Wall Street Journal,* for its "creative and comprehensive probe into backdated stock options for business executives. . . ." The *Journal* reported on "possible" violations then under investigation at 120 companies. There are 2764 listed companies on the New York Stock Exchange; NASDAQ adds another 3200. Not to dismiss the sincerity and diligence of the *Journal*'s work, but what's the final takeaway here? That 120 companies (0.02) "possibly" cheated? Or that—so far as anyone knows—at least 5844 others didn't?

Food for thought: Every time I fly, I'm amazed that these huge, winged machines get off the ground, stay off the ground, and don't return to ground until they're supposed to. Think about the failure rate of commonplace products: Light bulbs burn out. Fan belts snap. refrigerators stop refrigerating. But planes don't crash. Actuarially speaking, they simply don't. The entire process of commercial flight and the systems that support it is remarkable. Do you fully understand it? I don't. I'm sure lots of people don't. Still, you won't win a Pulitzer for a piece that sheds light on the myriad "little miracles" that conspire to produce aviation's normalcy, stability and success. You'd be laughed out of today's newsrooms for even proposing such a piece (unless you were doing it as the kind of feel-good feature that editors like to give audiences as gifts for the holidays). Have a flight go down, however—*one* flight, *one* time—and have a reporter find some overworked ATC operator or other aberration that may have caused the disaster, and *voila!* You're in Pulitzer territory for writing about something that—statistically—never happens.

Just as journalists who run out of news may create it, journalists who run out of real causes may invent them. It's not hard to do. All you need is a fact or two, which you then "contextualize" with more so-called expert opinion. December 10, 2004 was a banner night for exposing those well-known dens of iniquity that masquerade as Amish settlements. Stories about rape and incest among the Amish appeared on both *Dateline* and *20/20*. The *Dateline* story even made reference to the principal character in the story that aired an hour later on *20/20*—which gives you some idea how common the abuse may be, if seasoned journalists must choreograph their exposés around the same incident. That brings us to Elizabeth Vargas and her question for *20/20*'s expert on Amish affairs: Just how widespread *is* this abuse? Amid stock footage of adorable children strolling down a dusky road in suspenders and bonnets, the expert tells America that it's "not a gross exception."

What kind of reporting is that? Does it indicate that 1% of Amish children are abused? Ten percent? Forty percent? Who knows?

This is what passes for investigative journalism nowadays.

Their World . . . and They're Welcome to It

The world we're "given" has an indisputable impact on how Americans see and live their lives. (How many other events are set in motion by the "truths" people infer from the news?) Here we enter the realm of iatrogenic reporting: provable harms that didn't exist until journalism itself got involved.

In science journalism in particular, the use of anecdotal information can create impressions that would be comical, were it not for the amount of public alarm they generate.

Pop quiz: How many Americans have died of Mad Cow Disease? Before you answer, let's look to Britain, where the scare began in earnest around 1995 after a few herd of cattle were found to be infected. First of all, in the cows themselves, what we call "Mad Cow" is technically *bovine spongiform encephalopathy,* or BSE. When BSE species-jumps to humans, it manifests itself as something called *variant Creutzfeldt Jacob Disease,* or *v*CJD. ("Non-variant" CJD occurs independently of cows and can even be inherited.) A link between BSE and *v*CJD was established in 1996. British reporters went scurrying to find epidemiologists who were alarmed by the discovery, some of whom obligingly put the death toll in the coming years above 500,000.

By late 2006, the end of Mad Cow's first documented decade, the U.K. had confirmed a total of 162 human deaths—nothing to be glib about. But that's a long way from 500,000. And here in the U.S.? The CDC describes two confirmed deaths, both involving people born and raised abroad. A third case involves a man from Saudi Arabia who remains alive at this writing.

Not what you might've expected, eh?

Nevertheless, when a New Jersey woman, Janet Skarbek, became convinced that an outbreak had killed off her neighbors, she found a warm welcome in newsrooms. Her dire pronouncements touched off a mini-hysteria. Even after the CDC eliminated *v*CJD as a factor, the media kept fanning the fires of public concern, typically by quoting Dr. Michael Greger, a part-time chef and full-time alarmist who labels Mad Cow "the plague of the 21st Century." When journalists want a fatalistic sound bite on the disease, they dial Greger's number.

However history may remember Mad Cow as an actual pathology, this much is sure: The media-inflamed scare has been fatal to jobs—most directly in the meat-packing industry, but in related enterprises as well. It has soured consumers on beef. It has caused volatile swings in livestock prices. It has mandated new protocols that add hundreds of thousands of dollars to the average cattle rancher's cost of doing business. It has caused us to cut ourselves off from key beef suppliers, fomenting minor crises in diplomacy and commerce. A 2005 survey reckoned the total cost of Mad Cow to U.S. agricultural interests at between $3.2 billion and $4.7 billion. This, for something that has killed far fewer Americans in 10 years than the 200 who die each month from *choking* on food or food substances.

To hear the media tell it, we're under perpetual siege from some Terrifying New Disease That Threatens to End Life as We Know It. It's too soon to render verdicts on the ultimate impact of avian flu, but that pathogen would have to wipe out many millions in order to justify the hype. Lyme Disease? The Cleveland Clinic has this to say: "Although rarely fatal and seldom a serious illness, Lyme Disease has been widely publicized, frequently overdramatized, and sometimes linked to unproven conditions." Is it coincidence that visits to national parks began tracking downward in 1999, amid media coverage that made it sound as if deer ticks and the rest of Mother Nature's foot-soldiers had declared war on humankind? Maybe. Maybe not.

In science reporting and everywhere else, there's no minimizing the psychic effects of regularly consuming a world-view rooted in peculiarity, much of which is pessimistic. In a 2003 Gallup poll, just 11% of respondents rated crime in their own neighborhoods as "very serious" or "extremely serious," yet 54% of those same respondents deemed crime in America as a whole "very serious" or "extremely serious." The catch-22 should be apparent: If crime were that pervasive, it would have to be occurring in a lot more than 11% of the respondents' "own neighborhoods." Such an enigmatic skew can only be explained in terms of the difference between what people personally experience—what they know firsthand—and the wider impressions they get from the news.

Figuratively speaking, we end up drowning in the tides of a hurricane that never makes shore.

I give you, herewith, a capsule summary your world, and in far less than 22 minutes:

- The current *employment* rate is 95%.
- Out of 300 million Americans, roughly 299.999954 million were not murdered today.
- Day after day, some 35,000 commercial flights traverse our skies without incident.
- The vast majority of college students who got drunk last weekend did not rape anyone, or kill themselves or

anyone else in a DUI or hazing incident. On Monday, they got up and went to class, bleary-eyed but otherwise okay.

It is not being a Pollyanna to state such facts, because they *are* facts. Next time you watch the news, keep in mind that what you're most often seeing is trivia framed as Truth. Or as British humorist/philosopher G.K. Chesteron whimsically put it some decades ago, "Journalism consists in saying 'Lord Jones is dead' to people who never knew Lord Jones was alive."

From *Skeptic* by Steve Salerno, Volume 14, Number 1, 2008, pp. 52–59. Copyright © 2008 by Skeptic Magazine. Reprinted by permission of Millenium Press.

The Future of Reading

Amazon's Jeff Bezos already built a better bookstore. Now he believes he can improve upon one of humankind's most divine creations: the book itself.

STEVEN LEVY

"Technology," computer pioneer Alan Kay once said, "is anything that was invented after you were born." So it's not surprising, when making mental lists of the most whiz-bangy technological creations in our lives, that we may overlook an object that is superbly designed, wickedly functional, infinitely useful and beloved more passionately than any gadget in a Best Buy: the book. It is a more reliable storage device than a hard disk drive, and it sports a killer user interface. (No instruction manual or "For Dummies" guide needed.) And, it is instant-on and requires no batteries. Many people think it is so perfect an invention that it can't be improved upon, and react with indignation at any implication to the contrary.

"The book," says Jeff Bezos, 43, the CEO of Internet commerce giant Amazon.com, "just turns out to be an incredible device." Then he uncorks one of his trademark laughs.

Books have been very good to Jeff Bezos. When he sought to make his mark in the nascent days of the Web, he chose to open an online store for books, a decision that led to billionaire status for him, dotcom glory for his company and countless hours wasted by authors checking their Amazon sales ratings. But as much as Bezos loves books professionally and personally—he's a big reader, and his wife is a novelist—he also understands that the surge of technology will engulf all media. "Books are the last bastion of analog," he says, in a conference room overlooking the Seattle skyline. We're in the former VA hospital that is the physical headquarters for the world's largest virtual store. "Music and video have been digital for a long time, and short-form reading has been digitized, beginning with the early Web. But long-form reading really hasn't." Yet. This week Bezos is releasing the Amazon Kindle, an electronic device that he hopes will leapfrog over previous attempts at e-readers and become the turning point in a transformation toward Book 2.0. That's shorthand for a revolution (already in progress) that will change the way readers read, writers write and publishers publish. The Kindle represents a milestone in a time of transition, when a challenged publishing industry is competing with television, Guitar Hero and time burned on the BlackBerry; literary critics are bemoaning a possible demise of print culture, and Norman Mailer's recent death underlined the dearth of novelists who cast giant shadows. On the other hand, there are vibrant pockets of book lovers on the Internet who are waiting for a chance to refurbish the dusty halls of literacy.

As well placed as Amazon was to jump into this scrum and maybe move things forward, it was not something the company took lightly. After all, this is the *book* we're talking about. "If you're going to do something like this, you have to be as good as the book in a lot of respects," says Bezos. "But we also have to look for things that ordinary books can't do." Bounding to a whiteboard in the conference room, he ticks off a number of attributes that a book-reading device—yet another computer-powered gadget in an ever more crowded backpack full of them—must have. First, it must project an aura of *bookishness;* it should be less of a whizzy gizmo than an austere vessel of culture. Therefore the Kindle (named to evoke the crackling ignition of knowledge) has the dimensions of a paperback, with a tapering of its width that emulates the bulge toward a book's binding. It weighs but 10.3 ounces, and unlike a laptop computer it does not run hot or make intrusive beeps. A reading device must be sharp and durable, Bezos says, and with the use of E Ink, a breakthrough technology of several years ago that mimes the clarity of a printed book, the Kindle's six-inch screen posts readable pages. The battery has to last for a while, he adds, since there's nothing sadder than a book you can't read because of electile dysfunction. (The Kindle gets as many as 30 hours of reading on a charge, and recharges in two hours.) And, to soothe the anxieties of print-culture stalwarts, in sleep mode the Kindle displays retro images of ancient texts, early printing presses and beloved authors like Emily Dickinson and Jane Austen.

But then comes the features that your mom's copy of "Gone With the Wind" can't match. E-book devices like the Kindle allow you to change the font size: aging baby boomers will appreciate that every book can instantly be a large-type edition. The handheld device can also hold several shelves' worth of books: 200 of them onboard, hundreds more on a memory card and a limitless amount in virtual library stacks maintained by Amazon. Also, the Kindle allows you to search within the book for a phrase or name.

Some of those features have been available on previous e-book devices, notably the Sony Reader. The Kindle's real breakthrough springs from a feature that its predecessors never offered: wireless connectivity, via a system called Whispernet. (It's based on the EVDO broadband service offered by cellphone carriers, allowing it to work anywhere, not just Wi-Fi hotspots.) As a result, says Bezos, "This isn't a device, it's a service."

Specifically, it's an extension of the familiar Amazon store (where, of course, Kindles will be sold). Amazon has designed the Kindle to operate totally independent of a computer: you can use it to go to the store, browse for books, check out your personalized recommendations, and read reader reviews and post new ones, tapping out the words on a thumb-friendly keyboard. Buying a book with a Kindle is a one-touch process. And once you buy, the Kindle does its neatest trick: it downloads the book and installs it in your library, ready to be devoured. "The vision is that you should be able to get any book—not just any book in print, but any book that's *ever* been in print—on this device in less than a minute," says Bezos.

Amazon has worked hard to get publishers to step up efforts to release digital versions of new books and backlists, and more than 88,000 will be on sale at the Kindle store on launch. (Though Bezos won't get terribly specific, Amazon itself is also involved in scanning books, many of which it captured as part of its groundbreaking Search Inside the Book program. But most are done by the publishers themselves, at a cost of about $200 for each book converted to digital. New titles routinely go through the process, but many backlist titles are still waiting. "It's a real chokepoint," says Penguin CEO David Shanks.) Amazon prices Kindle editions of New York Times best sellers and new releases in hardback at $9.99. The first chapter of almost any book is available as a free sample.

The Kindle is not just for books. Via the Amazon store, you can subscribe to newspapers (the Times, The Wall Street Journal, The Washington Post, Le Monde) and magazines (The Atlantic). When issues go to press, the virtual publications are automatically beamed into your Kindle. (It's much closer to a virtual newsboy tossing the publication on your doorstep than accessing the contents a piece at a time on the Web.) You can also subscribe to selected blogs, which cost either 99 cents or $1.99 a month per blog.

In addition, the Kindle can venture out on the Web itself—to look up things in Wikipedia, search via Google or follow links from blogs and other Web pages. You can jot down a gloss on the page of the book you're reading, or capture passages with an electronic version of a highlight pen. And if you or a friend sends a word document or PDF file to your private Kindle e-mail address, it appears in your Kindle library, just as a book does. Though Bezos is reluctant to make the comparison, Amazon believes it has created the iPod of reading.

The Kindle, shipping as you read this, costs $399. When Bezos announces that price at the launch this week, he will probably get the same raised-eyebrow reaction Steve Jobs got in October 2001, when he announced that Apple would charge that same price for its pocket-size digital music player. No way around it: it's pricey. But if all goes well for Amazon, several

years from now we'll see revamped Kindles, equipped with color screens and other features, selling for much less. And physical bookstores, like the shuttered Tower Records of today, will be lonelier places, as digital reading thrusts us into an exciting—and jarring—post-Gutenberg era.

Will the Kindle and its kin really take on a technology that's shone for centuries and is considered the bedrock of our civilization? The death of the book—or, more broadly, the death of print—has been bandied about for well over a decade now. Sven Birkerts, in "The Gutenberg Elegies" (1994), took a peek at the future and concluded, "What the writer writes, how he writes and gets edited, printed and sold, and then read—all the old assumptions are under siege." Such pronouncements were invariably answered with protestations from hard-liners who insisted that nothing could supplant those seemingly perfect objects that perch on our night tables and furnish our rooms. Computers may have taken over every other stage of the process—the tools of research, composition and production—but that final mile of the process, where the reader mind-melds with the author in an exquisite asynchronous tango, would always be sacrosanct, said the holdouts. In 1994, for instance, fiction writer Annie Proulx was quoted as saying, "Nobody is going to sit down and read a novel on a twitchy little screen. Ever."

Oh, Annie. In 2007, screens are ubiquitous (and less twitchy), and people have been reading *everything* on them—documents, newspaper stories, magazine articles, blogs—as well as, yes, novels. Not just on big screens, either. A company called Daily-Lit this year began sending out books—new ones licensed from publishers and classics from authors like Jane Austen—straight to your e-mail IN BOX, in 1000-work chunks. (I've been reading Boswell's "Life of Johnson" on my iPhone, a device that is expected to be a major outlet for e-books in the coming months.) And recently a columnist for the Chicago Tribune waxed rhapsodically about reading Jane Austen on his BlackBerry.

But taking on the tome directly is the challenge for handheld, dedicated reading devices, of which the Kindle is only the newest and most credible effort. An early contender was the 22-ounce Rocket eBook (its inventors went on to create the electric-powered Tesla roadster). There were also efforts to distribute e-books by way of CD-ROMs. But the big push for e-books in the early 2000s fizzled. "The hardware was not consumer-friendly and it was difficult to find, buy and read e-books," says Carolyn Reidy, the president of Simon & Schuster.

This decade's major breakthrough has been the introduction of E Ink, whose creators came out of the MIT Media Lab. Working sort of like an Etch A Sketch, it forms letters by rearranging chemicals under the surface of the screen, making a page that looks a lot like a printed one. The first major implementation of E Ink was the $299 Sony Reader, launched in 2006 and heavily promoted. Sony won't divulge sales figures, but business director Bob Nell says the Reader has exceeded the company's expectations, and earlier this fall Sony introduced a sleeker second-generation model, the 505. (The Reader has no wireless—you must download on your computer and then move it to the device—and doesn't enable searching within a book.)

Now comes the Kindle, which Amazon began building in 2004, and Bezos understands that for all of its attributes, if one aspect of the physical book is not adequately duplicated, the entire effort will be for naught. "The key feature of a book is that *it disappears*," he says.

While those who take fetishlike pleasure in physical books may resist the notion, that vanishing act is what makes electronic reading devices into viable competitors to the printed page: a subsuming connection to the author that is really the basis of our book passion. "I've actually asked myself, 'Why do I love these physical objects?' " says Bezos. " 'Why do I love the smell of glue and ink?' The answer is that I associate that smell with all those worlds I have been transported to. What we love is the words and ideas."

Long before there was cyberspace, books led us to a magical nether-zone. "Books are all the dreams we would most like to have, and like dreams they have the power to change consciousness," wrote Victor Nell in a 1988 tome called "Lost in a Book." Nell coined a name for that trancelike state that heavy readers enter when consuming books for pleasure—"ludic reading" (from the Latin *ludo,* meaning "I play"). Annie Proulx's claim was that an electronic device would never create that hypnotic state. But technologists are disproving that. Bill Hill, Microsoft's point person on e-reading, has delved deep into the mysteries of this lost zone, in an epic quest to best emulate the conditions on a computer. He attempted to frame a "General Theory of Readability," which would demystify the mysteries of ludic reading and why books could uniquely draw you into a rabbit hole of absorption.

"There's 550 years of technological development in the book, and it's all designed to work with the four to five inches from the front of the eye to the part of the brain that does the processing [of the symbols on the page]," says Hill, a boisterous man who wears a kilt to a seafood restaurant in Seattle where he stages an impromptu lecture on his theory. "*This* is a high-resolution scanning machine," he says, pointing to the front of his head. "It scans five targets a second, and moves between targets in only 20 milliseconds. And it does this repeatedly for hours and hours and hours." He outlines the centuries-long process of optimizing the book to accommodate this physiological marvel: the form factor, leading, fonts, justification . . . "We have to take the same care for the screen as we've taken for print."

Hill insists—not surprisingly, considering his employer—that the ideal reading technology is not necessarily a dedicated e-reading device, but the screens we currently use, optimized for that function. (He's read six volumes of Gibbon's "The Decline and Fall of the Roman Empire" on a Dell Pocket PC.) "The Internet Explorer is not a browser—it's a reader," he says. "People spend about 20 percent of the time browsing for information and 80 percent reading or consuming it. The transition has already happened. And we haven't noticed."

But even Hill acknowledges that reading on a televisionlike screen a desktop away is not the ideal experience. Over the centuries, the sweet spot has been identified: something you hold in your hand, something you can curl up with in bed. Devices like the Kindle, with its 167 dot-per-inch E Ink display, with type set in a serif font called Caecilia, can subsume consciousness in the same way a physical book does. It can take you down the rabbit hole.

Though the Kindle is at heart a reading machine made by a bookseller—and works most impressively when you are buying a book or reading it—it is also something more: a perpetually connected Internet device. A few twitches of the fingers and that zoned-in connection between your mind and an author's machinations can be interrupted—or enhanced—by an avalanche of data. Therein lies the disruptive nature of the Amazon Kindle. It's the first "always-on" book.

What kinds of things will happen when books are persistently connected, and more-evolved successors of the Kindle become commonplace? First of all, it could transform the discovery process for readers. "The problem with books isn't print or writing," says Chris Anderson, author of "The Long Tail." "It's that not enough people are reading." (A 2004 National Endowment for the Arts study reported that only 57 percent of adults read a book—any book—in a year. That was down from 61 percent a decade ago.) His hope is that connected books will either link to other books or allow communities of readers to suggest undiscovered gems.

The connectivity also affects the publishing business model, giving some hope to an industry that slogs along with single-digit revenue growth while videogame revenues are skyrocketing. "Stuff doesn't need to go out of print," says Bezos. "It could shorten publishing cycles." And it could alter pricing. Readers have long complained that new books cost too much; the $9.99 charge for new releases and best sellers is Amazon's answer. (You can also get classics for a song: I downloaded "Bleak House" for $1.99.) Bezos explains that it's only fair to charge less for e-books because you can't give them as gifts, and due to restrictive antipiracy software, you can't lend them out or resell them. (Libraries, though, have developed lending procedures for previous versions of e-books—like the tape in "Mission: Impossible," they evaporate after the loan period—and Bezos says that he's open to the idea of eventually doing that with the Kindle.)

Publishers are resisting the idea of charging less for e-books. "I'm not going along with it," says Penguin's David Shanks of Amazon's low price for best sellers. (He seemed startled when I told him that the Alan Greenspan book he publishes is for sale at that price, since he offered no special discount.) Amazon is clearly taking a loss on such books. But Bezos says that he can sustain this scheme indefinitely. "We have a lot of experience in low-margin and high-volume sale—you just have to make sure the mix [between discounted and higher-priced items] works." Nonetheless the major publishers (all of whom are on the Kindle bandwagon) should loosen up. If you're about to get on a plane, you may buy the new Eric Clapton biography on a whim for $10—certainly for $5!—but if it costs more than $20, you may wind up scanning the magazine racks. For argument's sake, let's say cutting the price in half will double a book's sales—given that the royalty check would be the same, wouldn't an author prefer twice the number of readers? When I posed the question to best-selling novelist James Patterson, who was given an early look at the Kindle, he said that if the royalty fee were the same, he'd take the readers. (He's also a believer that the Kindle will succeed: "The baby boomers have a love affair with paper," he says. "But the next-gen people, in their 20s and below, do everything on a screen.")

The model other media use to keep prices down, of course, is advertising. Though this doesn't seem to be in Kindle's plans, in some dotcom quarters people are brainstorming advertiser-supported books. "Today it doesn't make sense to put ads in books, because of the unpredictable timing and readership," says Bill McCoy, Adobe's general manager of e-publishing. "That changes with digital distribution."

Another possible change: with connected books, the tether between the author and the book is still active after purchase. Errata can be corrected instantly. Updates, no problem—in fact, instead of buying a book in one discrete transaction, you could *subscribe* to a book, with the expectation that an author will continually add to it. This would be more suitable for nonfiction than novels, but it's also possible that a novelist might decide to rewrite an ending, or change something in the middle of the story. We could return to the era of Dickens-style serializations. With an always-on book, it's conceivable that an author could not only rework the narrative for future buyers, but he or she could reach inside people's libraries and make the change. (Let's also hope Amazon security is strong, so that we don't find one day that someone has hacked "Harry Potter" or "Madame Bovary.")

Those are fairly tame developments, though, compared with the more profound changes that some are anticipating. In a connected book, the rabbit hole is no longer a one-way transmission from author to reader. For better or for worse, there's company coming.

Talk to people who have thought about the future of books and there's a phrase you hear again and again. *Readers will read in public. Writers will write in public.* Readers, of course, are already enjoying a more prominent role in the literary community, taking star turns in blogs, online forums and Amazon reviews. This will only increase in the era of connected reading devices. "Book clubs could meet inside of a book," says Bob Stein, a pioneer of digital media who now heads the Institute for the Future of the Book, a foundation-funded organization based in his Brooklyn, N.Y., town house. Eventually, the idea goes, the community becomes part of the process itself.

Stein sees larger implications for authors—some of them sobering for traditionalists. "Here's what I don't know," he says. "What happens to the idea of a writer going off to a quiet place, ingesting information and synthesizing that into 300 pages of content that's uniquely his?" His implication is that that intricate process may go the way of the leather bookmark, as the notion of author as authoritarian figure gives way to a Web 2.0 wisdom-of-the-crowds process. "The idea of authorship will change and become more of a process than a product," says Ben Vershbow, associate director of the institute.

This is already happening on the Web. Instead of retreating to a cork-lined room to do their work, authors like Chris Anderson, John Battelle ("The Search") and NYU professor Mitchell Stephens (a book about religious belief, in progress) have written their books with the benefit of feedback and contributions from a community centered on their blogs.

"The possibility of interaction will redefine authorship," says Peter Brantley, executive director of the Digital Library Federation, an association of libraries and institutions. Unlike some writing-in-public advocates, he doesn't spare the novelists. "Michael Chabon will have to rethink how he writes for this medium," he says. Brantley envisions wiki-style collaborations where the author, instead of being the sole authority, is a "superuser," the lead wolf of a creative pack. (Though it's hard to believe that lone storytellers won't always be toiling away in some Starbucks with the Wi-Fi turned off, emerging afterward with a narrative masterpiece.)

All this becomes even headier when you consider that as the e-book reader is coming of age, there are huge initiatives underway to digitize entire libraries. Amazon, of course, is part of that movement (its Search Inside the Book project broke ground by providing the first opportunity for people to get search results from a corpus of hundreds of thousands of tomes). But as an unabashed bookseller, its goals are different from those of other players, such as Google—whose mission is collecting and organizing all the world's information—and that of the Open Content Alliance, a consortium that wants the world's books digitized in a totally nonproprietary manner. (The driving force behind the alliance, Brewster Kahle, made his fortune by selling his company to Amazon, but is unhappy with the digital-rights management on the Kindle: his choice of an e-book reader would be the dirt-cheap XO device designed by the One Laptop Per Child Foundation.) There are tricky, and potentially showstopping, legal hurdles to all this: notably a major copyright suit filed by a consortium of publishers, along with the Authors Guild, charging that Google is infringing by copying the contents of books it scans for its database. Nonetheless, the trend is definitely to create a back end of a massively connected library to supply future e-book devices with more content than a city full of libraries. As journalist Kevin Kelly wrote in a controversial New York Times Magazine article, the goal is to make "the entire works of humankind, from the beginning of recorded history, in all languages, available to all people, all the time."

Google has already scanned a million books from its partner libraries like the University of Michigan and the New York Public Library, and they are available in its database. (Last week my wife searched for information about the first English edition of the journals of Pehr Kalm, a Swedish naturalist traveling in Colonial America. In less than two seconds, Google delivered the full text of the book, as published in 1771.)

Paul LeClerc, CEO of the New York Public Library, says that he's involved in something called the Electronic Enlightenment, a scholarly project (born at the University of Oxford) to compile all the writings of and information about virtually every major figure of the Enlightenment. It includes all the annotated writings, correspondence and commentary about 3,800 18th-century writers like Jefferson, Voltaire and Rousseau, completely cross-linked and searchable—as if a small room in a library were compressed to a single living document. "How could you do that before?" he asks.

Now imagine that for *all* books. "Reading becomes a community activity," writes Kelly. "Bookmarks can be shared with fellow readers. Marginalia can be broadcast . . . In a very curious way, the universal library becomes one very, very, large single text: the world's only book."

Google's people have thought about how this connectivity could actually affect how people read. Adam Smith, product director for Book Search, says the process is all about "getting rid of the idea that a book is a [closed] container." One of his colleagues, Dan Lansing, describes how it might work: "Say you are trying to learn more about the Middle East, and you start reading a book, which claims that something happened in a particular event in Lebanon in '81, where the author was using his view on what happened. But actually his view is not what [really] happened. There's newspaper clippings on the event, there are other people who have written about it who disagree with him, there are other perspectives. The fact that all of that is at your fingertips and you can connect it together completely changes the way you do scholarship, or deep investigation of a subject. You'll be able to get all the world's information, all the books that have been published, all the world's libraries."

Jim Gerber, Google's content-partnerships director, suggests that it might be an interesting idea, for example, for someone on the liberal side of the fence to annotate an Ann Coulter book, providing refuting links for every contention that the critic thought was an inaccurate representation. That commentary, perhaps bolstered and updated by anyone who wants to chime in, could be woven into the book itself, if you chose to include it. (This would probably make Ann Coulter very happy, because you'd need to buy her book in order to view the litany of objections.)

All these ideas are anathema to traditionalists. In May 2006, novelist John Updike, appalled at reading Kelly's article ("a pretty grisly scenario"), decided to speak for them. Addressing a convention of booksellers, he cited "the printed, bound and paid-for book" as an ideal, and worried that book readers and writers were "approaching the condition of holdouts, surly hermits who refuse to come out and play in the electric sunshine of the post-Gutenberg village." (Actually, studies show that heavy Internet users read many more books than do those not on the Net.) He declared that the "edges" of the traditional book should not be breached. In his view, the stiff boards that bound the pages were not just covers but ramparts, and like-minded people should "defend the fort."

That fort will stand, of course, for a very long time. The awesome technology of original books—and our love for them—will keep them vital for many years to come. But nothing is forever. Microsoft's Bill Hill has a riff where he runs through the energy-wasting, resource-draining process of how we make books now. We chop down trees, transport them to plants, mash them into pulp, move the pulp to another factory to press into sheets, ship the sheets to a plant to put dirty marks on them, then cut the sheets and bind them and ship the thing around the world. "Do you *really* believe that we'll be doing that in 50 years?" he asks.

The answer is probably not, and that's why the Kindle matters. "This is the most important thing we've ever done," says Jeff Bezos. "It's so ambitious to take something as highly evolved as the book and improve on it. And maybe even change the way people read." As long as the batteries are charged.

Are Newspapers Doomed?

JOSEPH EPSTEIN

"Clearly," said Adam to Eve as they departed the Garden of Eden, "we're living in an age of transition." A joke, of course—but also not quite a joke, because when has the history of the world been anything other than one damned transition after another? Yet sometimes, in certain realms, transitions seem to stand out with utter distinctiveness, and this seems to be the case with the fortune of printed newspapers at the present moment. As a medium and as an institution, the newspaper is going through an age of transition *in excelsis*, and nobody can confidently say how it will end or what will come next.

To begin with familiar facts, statistics on readership have been pointing downward, significantly downward, for some time now. Four-fifths of Americans once read newspapers; today, apparently fewer than half do. Among adults, in the decade 1990–2000, daily readership fell from 52.6 percent to 37.5 percent. Among the young, things are much worse: in one study, only 19 percent of those between the ages of eighteen and thirty-four reported consulting a daily paper, and only 9 percent trusted the information purveyed there; a mere 8 percent found newspapers helpful, while 4 percent thought them entertaining.

From 1999 to 2004, according to the Newspaper Association of America, general circulation dropped by another 1.3 million. Reflecting both that fact and the ferocious competition for classified ads from free online bulletin boards like craigslist.org, advertising revenue has been stagnant at best, while printing and productions costs have gone remorselessly upward. As a result, the New York Times Company has cut some 700 jobs from its various papers. The *Baltimore Sun*, owned by the *Chicago Tribune*, is closing down its five international bureaus. Second papers in many cities have locked their doors.

This bleeding phenomenon is not restricted to the United States, and no bets should be placed on the likely success of steps taken by papers to stanch the flow. *The Wall Street Journal*, in an effort to save money on production costs, is trimming the width of its pages, from 15 to 12 inches. In England, the once venerable *Guardian*, in a mad scramble to retain its older readers and find younger ones, has radically redesigned itself by becoming smaller. London's *Independent* has gone tabloid, and so has the once revered *Times*, its publisher preferring the euphemism "compact."

For those of us who grew up with newspapers in our daily regimen, sometimes with not one but two newspapers in our homes, it is all a bit difficult to take in. As early as 1831, Alexis de Tocqueville noted that even frontier families in upper Michigan had a weekly paper delivered. A.J. Liebling, the *New Yorker's* writer on the press, used to say that he judged any new city he visited by the taste of its water and the quality of its newspapers.

The paper to which you subscribed, or that your father brought home from work, told a good deal about your family: its social class, its level of education, its politics. Among the five major dailies in the Chicago of my early boyhood, my father preferred the *Daily News*, an afternoon paper reputed to have excellent foreign correspondents. Democratic in its general political affiliation, though not aggressively so, the *Daily News* was considered the intelligent Chicagoan's paper.

My father certainly took it seriously. I remember asking him in 1952, as a boy of fifteen, about whom he intended to vote for in the presidential election between Dwight Eisenhower and Adlai Stevenson. "I'm not sure," he said. "I think I'll wait to see which way Lippmann is going."

The degree of respect then accorded the syndicated columnist Walter Lippmann is hard to imagine in our own time. In good part, his cachet derived from his readers' belief not only in his intelligence but in his impartiality. Lippmann, it was thought, cared about what was best for the country; he wasn't already lined up; you couldn't be certain which way he would go.

Of the two candidates in 1952, Stevenson, the intellectually cultivated Democrat, was without a doubt the man Lippmann would have preferred to have lunch with. But in the end he went for Eisenhower—his reason being, as I recall, that the country needed a strong leader with a large majority behind him, a man who, among other things, could face down the obstreperous Red-baiting of Senator Joseph McCarthy. My father, a lifelong Democrat, followed Lippmann and crossed over to vote for Eisenhower.

My father took his paper seriously in another way, too. He read it after dinner and ingested it, like that dinner, slowly, treating it as a kind of second dessert: something at once nutritive and entertaining. He was in no great hurry to finish.

Today, his son reads no Chicago newspaper whatsoever. A serial killer could be living in my apartment building, and I would be unaware of it until informed by my neighbors. As for the power of the press to shape and even change my mind, I am in the condition of George Santayana, who wrote to his sister in 1915 that he was too old to "be influenced by newspaper argument. When I read them I form perhaps a new opinion of the newspaper but seldom a new opinion on the subject discussed."

I do subscribe to the *New York Times*, which I read without a scintilla of glee. I feel I need it, chiefly to discover who in my cultural world has died, or been honored (probably unjustly), or has turned out some new piece of work that I ought to be aware of. I rarely give the daily *Times* more than a half-hour, if that. I begin with the obituaries. Next, I check the op-ed page, mostly to see if anyone has hit upon a novel way of denigrating President Bush; the answer is invariably no, though they seem never to tire of trying. I glimpse the letters to the editor in hopes of finding someone after my own heart. I almost never read the editorials, following the advice of the journalist Jack Germond who once compared the writing of a newspaper editorial to wetting oneself in a dark-blue serge suit: "It gives you a nice warm feeling, but nobody notices."

The arts section, which in the *Times* is increasingly less about the arts and more about television, rock 'n' roll, and celebrity, does not detain me long. Sports is another matter, for I do have the sports disease in a chronic and soon to be terminal stage; I run my eyes over these pages, turning in spring, summer, and fall to see who is pitching in that day's Cubs and White Sox games. And I always check the business section, where some of the better writing in the *Times* appears and where the reporting, because so much is at stake, tends to be more trustworthy.

Finally—quickly, very quickly—I run through the so-called hard news, taking in most of it at the headline level. I seem able to sleep perfectly soundly these days without knowing the names of the current presidents or prime ministers of Peru, India, Japan, and Poland. For the rest, the point of view that permeates the news coverage in the *Times* is by now so yawningly predictable that I spare myself the effort of absorbing the facts that seem to serve as so much tedious filler.

Am I typical in my casual disregard? I suspect so. Everyone agrees that print newspapers are in trouble today, and almost everyone agrees on the reasons. Foremost among them is the vast improvement in the technology of delivering information, which has combined in lethal ways with a serious change in the national temperament.

The technological change has to do with the increase in the number of television cable channels and the astonishing amount of news floating around in cyberspace. As Richard A. Posner has written, "The public's consumption of news and opinion used to be like sucking on a straw; now it's like being sprayed by a fire hose."

The temperamental change has to do with the national attention span. The critic Walter Benjamin said, as long ago as the 1930's, that the chief emotion generated by reading the newspapers is impatience. His remark is all the more pertinent today, when the very definition of what constitutes important information is up for grabs. More and more, in a shift that cuts across age, social class, and even educational lines, important information means information that matters to *me*, now.

And this is where the two changes intersect. Not only are we acquiring our information from new places but we are taking it pretty much on our own terms. The magazine *Wired* recently defined the word "egocasting" as "the consumption of on-demand music, movies, television, and other media that cater to individual and not mass-market tastes." The news, too, is now getting to be on-demand.

Instead of beginning their day with coffee and the newspaper, there to read what editors have selected for their enlightenment, people, and young people in particular, wait for a free moment to go online. No longer need they wade through thickets of stories and features of no interest to them, and least of all need they do so on the websites of newspapers, where the owners are hoping to regain the readers lost to print. Instead, they go to more specialized purveyors of information, including instant-messaging providers, targeted news sites, blogs, and online "zines."

Much cogitation has been devoted to the question of young people's lack of interest in traditional news. According to one theory, which is by now an entrenched cliché, the young, having grown up with television and computers as their constant companions, are "visual-minded," and hence averse to print. Another theory holds that young people do not feel themselves implicated in the larger world; for them, news of that world isn't where the action is. A more flattering corollary of this is that grown-up journalism strikes the young as hopelessly out of date. All that solemn good-guy/bad-guy reporting, the taking seriously of *opéra-bouffe* characters like Jesse Jackson or Al Gore or Tom DeLay, the false complexity of "in-depth" television reporting à la *60 Minutes*—this, for them, is so much hot air. They prefer to watch Jon Stewart's *The Daily Show* on the Comedy Central cable channel, where traditional news is mocked and pilloried as obvious nonsense.

Whatever the validity of this theorizing, it is also beside the point. For as the grim statistics confirm, the young are hardly alone in turning away from newspapers. Nor are they alone responsible for the dizzying growth of the so-called blogosphere, said to be increasing by 70,000 sites a day (according to the search portal technorati.com). In the first half of this year alone, the number of new blogs grew from 7.8 to 14.2 million. And if the numbers are dizzying, the sheer amount of information floating around is enough to give a person a serious case of Newsheimers.

Astonishing results are reported when news is passed from one blog to another: scores if not hundreds of thousands of hits, and, on sites that post readers' reactions, responses that can often be more impressive in research and reasoning than anything likely to turn up in print. Newspaper journalists themselves often get their stories from blogs, and bloggers have been extremely useful in verifying or refuting the erroneous reportage of mainstream journalists. The only place to get a reasonably straight account of news about Israel and the Palestinians, according to Stephanie Gutmann, author of *The Other War: Israelis, Palestinians, and the Struggle for Media Supremacy*, is in the blogosphere.

The trouble with blogs and Internet news sites, it has been said, is that they merely reinforce the reader's already established interests and views, thereby contributing to our much-lamented national polarization of opinion. A newspaper, by contrast, at least compels one to acknowledge the existence of other subjects and issues, and reading it can alert one to affecting or important matters that one would never encounter if left to one's own devices, and in particular to that primary device of our day, the computer. Whether or not that is so, the argument has already been won, and not by the papers.

Another argument appears to have been won, too, and again to the detriment of the papers. This is the argument over politics, which the newspapers brought upon themselves and which, in my view, they richly deserved to lose.

One could put together an impressive little anthology of utterances by famous Americans on the transcendent importance of the press as a guardian watchdog of the state. Perhaps the most emphatic was that of Thomas Jefferson, who held that freedom of the press, right up there with freedom of religion and freedom of the person under the rights of habeas corpus and trial by jury, was among "the principles [that] form the bright constellation which has gone before us, and guided our steps through an age of revolution and reformation." Even today, not many people would disagree with this in theory; but like the character in a Tom Stoppard play, many would add: "I'm with you on the free press. It's the damned newspapers I can't stand."

The self-proclaimed goal of newsmen used to be to report, in a clear and factual way, on the important events of the day, on subjects of greater or lesser parochialism. It is no longer so. Here is Dan Rather, quoting with approval someone he does not name who defines news as "what somebody doesn't want you to know. All the rest is advertising."

"What somebody doesn't want you to know"—it would be hard to come up with a more concise definition of the target of the "investigative journalism" that has been the pride of the nation's newspapers for the past three decades. Bob Woodward, Carl Bernstein, Seymour Hersh, and many others have built their reputations on telling us things that Presidents and Senators and generals and CEO's have not wanted us to know.

Besides making for a strictly adversarial relationship between government and the press, there is no denying that investigative journalism, whatever (very mixed) accomplishments it can claim to its credit, has put in place among us a tone and temper of agitation and paranoia. Every day, we are asked to regard the people we elect to office as, essentially, our enemies—thieves, thugs, and megalomaniacs whose vicious secret deeds it is the chief function of the press to uncover and whose persons to bring down in a glare of publicity.

All this might have been to the good if what the journalists discovered were invariably true—and if the nature and the implications of that truth were left for others to puzzle out. Frequently, neither has been the case.

Much of contemporary journalism functions through leaks—information passed to journalists by unidentified individuals telling those things that someone supposedly doesn't want us to know. Since these sources cannot be checked or cross-examined, readers are in no position to assess the leakers' motives for leaking, let alone the agenda of the journalists who rely on them. To state the obvious: a journalist fervently against the U.S. presence in Iraq is unlikely to pursue leaks providing evidence that the war has been going reasonably well.

Administrations have of course used leaks for their own purposes, and leaks have also become a time-tested method for playing out intramural government disputes. Thus, it is widely and no doubt correctly believed that forces at the CIA and in the State Department have leaked information to the *New York Times* and the *Washington Post* to weaken positions taken by the White House they serve, thereby availing themselves of a mechanism of sabotage from within. But this, too, is not part of the truth we are likely to learn from investigative journalists, who not only purvey slanted information as if it were simply true but then take it upon themselves to try, judge, and condemn those they have designated as political enemies. So glaring has this problem become that the *Times*, beginning in June, felt compelled to introduce a new policy, designed, in the words of its ombudsman, to make "the use of anonymous sources the 'exception' rather than 'routine.'"

No wonder, then, that the prestige of mainstream journalism, which reached perhaps an all-time high in the early 1970's at the time of Watergate, has now badly slipped. According to most studies of the question, journalists tend more and more to be regarded by Americans as unaccountable kibitzers whose self-appointed job is to spread dissension, increase pressure on everyone, make trouble—and preach the gospel of present-day liberalism. Aiding this deserved fall in reputation has been a series of well-publicized scandals like the rise and fall of the reporter Jayson Blair at the *New York Times*.

The politicization of contemporary journalists surely has a lot to do with the fact that almost all of them today are university-trained. In *Newspaper Days*, H.L. Mencken recounts that in 1898, at the age of eighteen, he had a choice of going to college, there to be taught by German professors and on weekends to sit in a raccoon coat watching football games, or of getting a job on a newspaper, which would allow him to zip off to fires, whorehouse raids, executions, and other such festivities. As Mencken observes, it was no contest.

Most contemporary journalists, by contrast, attend schools of journalism or study the humanities and social sciences. Here the reigning politics are liberal, and along with their degrees, and their sense of enlightened virtue, they emerge with locked-in political views. According to Jim A. Kuypers in *Press Bias and Politics*, 76 percent of journalists who admit to having a politics describe themselves as liberal. The consequences are predictable: even as they employ their politics to tilt their stories, such journalists sincerely believe they are (a) merely telling the truth and (b) doing good in the world.

Pre-university-educated journalists did not, I suspect, feel that the papers they worked for existed as vehicles through which to advance their own political ideas. Some among them might have hated corruption, or the standard lies told by politicians; from time to time they might even have felt a stab of idealism or sentimentality. But they subsisted chiefly on cynicism, heavy boozing, and an admiration for craft. They did not treat the news—and editors of that day would not have permitted them to treat the news—as a trampoline of which to bounce their own tendentious politics.

To the degree that papers like the *New York Times*, the *Washington Post*, and the *Los Angeles Times* have contributed to the political polarization of the country, they much deserve their fate of being taken less and less seriously by fewer and fewer people. One can say this even while acknowledging that the cure, in the form of on-demand news, can sometimes seem as bad as the disease, tending often only to confirm users, whether liberal or conservative or anything else, in the opinions they already hold. But at least the curious or the bored can, at a click, turn elsewhere on the Internet for variety or relief—which is more than can be said for newspaper readers.

Nor, in a dumbed-down world, do our papers of record offer an oasis of taste. There were always a large number of newspapers in America whose sole standard was scandal and entertainment. (The crossword puzzle first appeared in Joseph Pulitzer's *New York World*.) But there were also some that were dedicated to bringing their readers up to a high or at least a middling mark. Among these were the *New York Times*, the *St. Louis Post-Dispatch*, the *Washington Post*, the *Milwaukee Journal*, the *Wall Street Journal*, the now long defunct *New York Herald-Tribune*, and the *Chicago Daily News*.

These newspapers did not mind telling readers what they felt they ought to know, even at the risk of boring the pajamas off them. The *Times*, for instance, used to run the full text of important political speeches, which could sometimes fill two full pages of photograph-less type. But now that the college-educated are writing for the college-educated, neither party seems to care. And with circulation numbers dwindling and the strategy in place of whoring after the uninterested young, anything goes.

What used to be considered the serious press in America has become increasingly frivolous. The scandal-and-entertainment aspect more and more replaces what once used to be called "hard news." In this, the serious papers would seem to be imitating the one undisputed print success of recent decades, *USA Today*, whose guiding principle has been to make things brief, fast-paced, and entertaining. Or, more hopelessly still, they are imitating television talk shows or the Internet itself, often mindlessly copying some of their dopier and more destructive innovations.

The editor of the *London Independent* has talked of creating, in place of a newspaper, a "viewspaper," one that can be viewed like a television or a computer. The *Los Angeles Times* has made efforts to turn itself interactive, including by allowing website readers to change the paper's editorials to reflect their own views (only to give up on this initiative when readers posted pornography on the page). In his technology column for the *New York Times*, David Carr speaks of newspapers needing "a podcast moment," by which I take him to mean that the printed press must come up with a self-selecting format for presenting on-demand news akin to the way the iPod presents a listener's favorite programming exactly as and when he wants it.

In our multitasking nation, we already read during television commercials, talk on the cell-phone while driving, listen to music while working on the computer, and much else besides. Some in the press seem in their panic to think that the worst problem they face is that you cannot do other things while reading a newspaper except smoke, which in most places is outlawed anyway. Their problems go much deeper.

In a speech given this past April to the American Society of Newspaper Editors, the international publisher Rupert Murdoch catalogued the drastic diminution of readership for the traditional press and then went on to rally the troops by telling them that they must do better. Not different, but better: going deeper in their coverage, listening more intently to the desires of their readers, assimilating and where possible imitating the digital culture so popular among the young. A man immensely successful and usually well anchored in reality, Murdoch here sounded distressingly like a man without a plan.

Not that I have one of my own. Best to study history, it is said, because the present is too complicated and no one knows anything about the future. The time of transition we are currently going through, with the interest in traditional newspapers beginning to fade and news on the computer still a vast confusion, can be likened to a great city banishing horses from its streets before anyone has yet perfected the automobile.

Nevertheless, if I had to prophesy, my guess would be that newspapers will hobble along, getting ever more desperate and ever more vulgar. More of them will attempt the complicated mental acrobatic of further dumbing down while straining to keep up, relentlessly exerting themselves to sustain the mighty cataract of inessential information that threatens to drown us all. Those of us who grew up with newspapers will continue to read them, with ever less trust and interest, while younger readers, soon enough grown into middle age, will ignore them.

My own preference would be for a few serious newspapers to take the high road: to smarten up instead of dumbing down, to honor the principles of integrity and impartiality in their coverage, and to become institutions that even those who disagreed with them would have to respect for the reasoned cogency of their editorial positions. I imagine such papers directed by editors who could choose for me—as neither the Internet nor I on my own can do—the serious issues, questions, and problems of the day and, with the aid of intelligence born of concern, give each the emphasis it deserves.

In all likelihood a newspaper taking this route would go under; but at least it would do so in a cloud of glory, guns blazing. And at least its loss would be a genuine subtraction. About our newspapers as they now stand, little more can be said in their favor than that they do not require batteries to operate, you can swat flies with them, and they can still be used to wrap fish.

JOSEPH EPSTEIN contributed "Forgetting Edmund Wilson" to last month's *Commentary*. His new book, *Friendship, An Exposé,* will be published by Houghton Mifflin in July.

The Great Wall of Facebook

FRED VOGELSTEIN

L arry Page should have been in a good mood. It was the fall of 2007, and Google's cofounder was in the middle of a five-day tour of his company's European operations in Zurich, London, Oxford, and Dublin. The trip had been fun, a chance to get a ground-floor look at Google's ever-expanding empire. But this week had been particularly exciting, for reasons that had nothing to do with Europe; Google was planning a major investment in Facebook, the hottest new company in Silicon Valley.

Originally Google had considered acquiring Facebook—a prospect that held no interest for Facebook's executives—but an investment was another enticing option, aligning the Internet's two most important companies. Facebook was more than a fast-growing social network. It was, potentially, an enormous source of personal data. Internet users behaved differently on Facebook than anywhere else online: They used their real names, connected with their real friends, linked to their real email addresses, and shared their real thoughts, tastes, and news. Google, on the other hand, knew relatively little about most of its users other than their search histories and some browsing activity.

But now, as Page took his seat on the Google jet for the two-hour flight from Zurich to London, something appeared to be wrong. He looked annoyed, one of his fellow passengers recalls. It turned out that he had just received word that the deal was off. Microsoft, Google's sworn enemy, would be making the investment instead—$240 million for a 1.6 percent stake in the company, meaning that Redmond valued Facebook at an astonishing $15 billion.

As the 767 took off, Page tersely but calmly shared the news with the others on the plane and answered their questions for about 15 minutes. "Larry was clearly, clearly unhappy about it," the passenger says.

Page soon got over it, but Facebook's rejection was still a blow to Google; it had never lost a deal this big and this publicly. But according to Facebookers involved in the transaction, Mountain View never had much of a chance—all things being equal, Microsoft was always the favored partner. Google's bid was used primarily as a stalking horse, a tool to amp up the bidding. Facebook executives weren't leaping at the chance to join with Google; they preferred to conquer it. "We never liked those guys," says one former Facebook engineer. "We all had that audacity, 'Anything Google does, we can do better.' No one talked about MySpace or the other social networks. We just talked about Google."

Today, the Google-Facebook rivalry isn't just going strong, it has evolved into a full-blown battle over the future of the Internet—its structure, design, and utility. For the last decade or so, the Web has been defined by Google's algorithms—rigorous and efficient equations that parse practically every byte of online activity to build a dispassionate atlas of the online world. Facebook CEO Mark Zuckerberg envisions a more personalized, humanized Web, where our network of friends, colleagues, peers, and family is our primary source of information, just as it is offline. In Zuckerberg's vision, users will query this "social graph" to find a doctor, the best camera, or someone to hire—rather than tapping the cold mathematics of a Google search. It is a complete rethinking of how we navigate the online world, one that places Facebook right at the center. In other words, right where Google is now.

All this brave talk might seem easy to dismiss as the swagger of an arrogant upstart. After all, being Google is a little like being heavyweight champion of the world—everyone wants a shot at your title. But over the past year, Facebook has gone from glass-jawed flyweight to legitimate contender. It has become one of the most popular online destinations. More than 200 million people—about one-fifth of all Internet users—have Facebook accounts. They spend an average of 20 minutes on the site every day. Facebook has stolen several well-known Google employees, from COO Sheryl Sandburg to chef Josef Desimone; at least 9 percent of its staff used to work for the search giant. And since last December, Facebook has launched a series of ambitious initiatives, designed to make the social graph an even more integral part of a user's online experience. Even some Googlers concede that Facebook represents a growing threat. "Eventually, we are going to collide," one executive says.

It is remarkable that the most powerful company on the Web would feel threatened by one that has yet to turn a profit. (Last year, one insider estimates, Facebook burned through $75 million plus the $275 million in revenue it brought in; Google made $4.2 billion on an astounding $15.8 billion in net revenue.) And even Facebook executives concede that Google has secured an insurmountable lead in search advertising—those little text ads that pop up next to search results—which

Facebook's 4-Step Plan for Online Domination

Mark Zuckerberg has never thought of his company as a mere social network. He and his team are in the middle of a multiyear campaign to change how the Web is organized—with Facebook at the center. Here's how they hope to pull it off.

1. Build Critical Mass

In the eight months ending in April, Facebook has doubled in size to 200 million members, who contribute 4 billion pieces of info, 850 million photos, and 8 million videos every month. The result: a second Internet, one that includes users' most personal data and resides entirely on Facebook's servers.

2. Redefine Search

Facebook thinks its members will turn to their friends—rather than Google's algorithms—to navigate the Web. It already drives an eyebrow-raising amount of traffic to outside sites, and that will only increase once Facebook Search allows users to easily explore one another's feeds.

3. Colonize the Web

Thanks to a pair of new initiatives—dubbed Facebook Connect and Open Stream—users don't have to log in to Facebook to communicate with their friends. Now they can access their network from any of 10,000 partner sites or apps, contributing even more valuable data to Facebook's servers every time they do it.

4. Sell Targeted Ads, Everywhere

Facebook hopes to one day sell advertising across all of its partner sites and apps, not just on its own site. The company will be able to draw on the immense volume of personal data it owns to create extremely targeted messages. The challenge: not freaking out its users in the process.

To understand Facebook's challenge to Google, consider my friend and neighbor Wayne, a PhD in computer science from UC Berkeley and a veteran of many big-time programming jobs. I know a lot about him because we are friends. I know even more because we are Facebook friends. On his online profile, I not only find the standard personal-blog-type information—his birthday, address, résumé, and pictures of his wife, son, and step-kids. I also discover that he likes to make beer, that he had dinner at one of my favorite restaurants last week, and that he likes to watch cartoons. Indeed, he has posted something about his life almost every day for the past two months—wondering whether his son's Little League game will get rained out, asking his friends what the impeller in his central heating unit does.

But if I type Wayne's name into Google, I learn very little. I am directed to an old personal website, with links that have almost all expired, and a collection of computer-science papers he has written over the years. That's about it.

Hardly any of Wayne's Facebook information turns up on a Google search, because all of it, along with similar details about the other 200 million Facebook users, exists on the social network's roughly 40,000 servers. Together, this data comprises a mammoth amount of activity, almost a second Internet. By Facebook's estimates, every month users share 4 billion pieces of information—news stories, status updates, birthday wishes, and so on. They also upload 850 million photos and 8 million videos. But anyone wanting to access that stuff must go through Facebook; the social network treats it all as proprietary data, largely shielding it from Google's crawlers. Except for the mostly cursory information that users choose to make public, what happens on Facebook's servers stays on Facebook's servers. That represents a massive and fast-growing blind spot for Google, whose long-stated goal is to "organize the world's information."

Facebook isn't just kneecapping Google's search engine; it is also competing with it. Facebook encourages its 200 million members to use Microsoft's search engine, which it installed on its homepage late last year as part of the deal struck between the two companies. At press time, it was also planning to launch Facebook Search, allowing users to scour one another's feeds. Want to see what some anonymous schmuck thought about the *Battlestar Galactica* finale? Check out Google. Want to see what your friends had to say? Try Facebook Search. And it will not only be for searching within Facebook. Because Facebook friends post links to outside sites, you will be able to use it as a gateway to the Web—making it a direct threat to Google. Why settle for articles about the Chrysler bankruptcy that the Google News algorithm recommends when you can read what your friends suggest? Already, Facebook is starting to horn in on Google's role as the predominant driver of Web traffic. According to Hitwise, Facebook in recent months has sent more traffic than Google to Evite, video site Tagged.com, and gossip mills Perez Hilton.com and Dlisted. That trend should only grow with the advent of Facebook Search.

These are just the latest moves in an ambitious campaign to make the social graph an integral, ubiquitous element of life online. In December, Facebook launched Connect, a network

accounts for about 90 percent of Google's net revenue. But they say they are going after an even bigger market: the expensive branding campaigns that so far have barely ventured online. Once, Google hoped an alliance with Facebook would help attract those huge ad budgets. Now, instead of working together to reach the promised land of online brand advertising, Facebook and Google are racing to see who can get there first.

Like typical trash-talking youngsters, Facebook sources argue that their competition is old and out of touch. "Google is not representative of the future of technology in any way," one Facebook veteran says. "Facebook is an advanced communications network enabling myriad communication forms. It almost doesn't make sense to compare them."

of more than 10,000 independent sites that lets users access their Facebook relationships without logging in to Facebook.com. Go to Digg, for instance, and see which stories friends recommended. Head to Citysearch and see which restaurants they have reviewed. Visit TechCrunch, Gawker, or the Huffington Post and read comments they have left. On Inauguration Day, millions of users logged in to CNN.com with their Facebook ID and discussed the proceedings with their friends in real time.

In April, Facebook announced its Open Stream API, allowing developers to create mashups using Facebook's constantly updated stream of user activity. Previously, users who wanted to read their friends' News Feeds had to go to the Facebook site. Now developers can export that information to any site—or to freestanding applications, much as Twitter desktop clients do for Tweets.

Connect and Open Stream don't just allow users to access their Facebook networks from anywhere online. They also help realize Facebook's longtime vision of giving users a unique, Web-wide online profile. By linking Web activity to Facebook accounts, they begin to replace the largely anonymous "no one knows you're a dog" version of online identity with one in which every action is tied to who users really are.

To hear Facebook executives tell it, this will make online interactions more meaningful and more personal. Imagine, for example, if online comments were written by people using their real names rather than by anonymous trolls. "Up until now all the advancements in technology have said information and data are the most important thing," says Dave Morin, Facebook's senior platform manager. "The most important thing to us is that there is a person sitting behind that keyboard. We think the Internet is about people."

But you don't build a competitor to Google with people alone. You need data. And Connect and Open Stream are intended to make Facebook a much more powerful force for collecting user information. Any time someone logs in to a site that uses Connect or Open Stream, they give Facebook the right to keep track of any activity that happens there—potentially contributing tons more personal data to Facebook's servers. Facebook Connect and Open Stream are also designed to make each user's friend network, which belongs to Facebook, even more valuable and crucial to the Web experience. Together, they aim to put Facebook users' social networks at the center of all they do online.

Facebook aims to put its users' social networks at the center of all they do online.

Mark Zuckerberg is notoriously cocky, even by the standards of Silicon Valley. Two years ago, he walked away from a reported nearly $1 billion offer from Yahoo for his company. He could have sold to Google or Microsoft for a lot more. His business cards once famously read: I'M CEO . . . BITCH. And he has described Facebook as a once-in-a-century communications revolution, implying that he is right up there with Gutenberg and Marconi.

Still, you'd think he might play it a little cool when discussing Google, not wanting to antagonize the most powerful company on the Internet. But Zuckerberg doesn't pull any punches, describing Google as "a top-down way" of organizing the Web that results in an impersonal experience that stifles online activity. "You have a bunch of machines and algorithms going out and crawling the Web and bringing information back," he says. "That only gets stuff that is publicly available to everyone. And it doesn't give people the control that they need to be really comfortable." Instead, he says, Internet users will share more data when they are allowed to decide which information they make public and which they keep private. "No one wants to live in a surveillance society," Zuckerberg adds, "which, if you take that to its extreme, could be where Google is going."

It's ironic to hear Zuckerberg paint Google as Big Brother. After all, many observers worry that Facebook itself has grown too controlling. Unlike Google, Facebook makes it difficult for users to export their contacts, mail, photos, and videos—a practice Web 2.0 evangelists say is a sign that the company values its proprietary data more than its users' experience. In November 2007, Facebook launched Beacon, a ham-fisted attempt to inject advertising into News Feeds. Users felt violated; after a month of protest, Zuckerberg publicly apologized and effectively shut Beacon down. Then, in February 2009, Facebook quietly changed its terms of service, appearing to give itself perpetual ownership of anything posted on the site, even after members closed their accounts. Users complained so vociferously—millions joined Facebook groups and signed online petitions protesting the change—that the company was forced to backtrack. The event left many people fearful of the amount of personal information they were ceding to a private, profit-hungry enterprise. "DO YOU OWN FACEBOOK?" a *New York* magazine cover story asked warily in April. "OR DOES FACEBOOK OWN YOU?" (Facebook executives say that the company was merely updating the terms of service to match those of other sites and that there was no nefarious intent. They reinstated a version of the amendment after subjecting it to a vote of Facebook members.)

The drumbeat of controversy surrounding Facebook illustrates the catch-22 the social network faces: It has a massive storehouse of user data, but every time it tries to capitalize on that information, its members freak out. This isn't an academic problem; the company's future depends on its ability to master the art of behavioral targeting—selling customized advertising based on user profiles. In theory, this should be an irresistible opportunity for marketers; Facebook's performance advertising program allows them to design and distribute an ad to as narrow an audience as they would like. (It has also developed a program to create ads that are designed to be spread virally.) But as the Beacon debacle showed, there is a fine line between "targeted and useful" and "creepy and stalkerish"—and so far, not enough advertisers have been willing to walk that line.

In a way, Facebook's dilemma extends from its success. Users see the site as sanctified space, a place to engage in intimate conversations with friends—not to be laser-beamed by weirdly personal advertising. But with initiatives like Connect and Open Stream, Facebook can sell ads beyond its own site. Just as Google's AdSense program sells ads on any participating website, Connect and Open Stream will eventually push Facebook-brokered advertising to any member site or app. But unlike with AdSense, Facebook's ads could be exquisitely tailored to their targets. "No one out there has the data that we have," says COO Sandberg.

That's where the big-budget brand advertisers come in. Google has courted them for four years, to no avail. That's because, while search ads are great at delivering advertising to users who are seeking specific products, they are less effective at creating demand for stuff users don't yet know they want. Google has tried everything to lure brand advertisers—from buying and selling radio ads to purchasing YouTube. And it is easy to see why it keeps trying. Today, global online brand advertising accounts for just $50 billion a year. Offline brand advertising, meanwhile, accounts for an estimated $500 billion.

Google's desire to crack the brand-advertising conundrum is so intense, some company executives have even considered swallowing their pride and pursuing another deal with Facebook. But whether or not it ultimately friends the social network, Google has clearly been influenced by it. On December 4, the same day that Facebook Connect launched, Google unveiled its own version, Friend Connect, which allows websites to link to accounts on any of the major social networks—including MySpace, LinkedIn, Ning, Hi5, and Bebo. In March, four months after Facebook reportedly offered $500 million in a failed bid for Twitter, reports surfaced that Google was holding similar talks. (A Google insider confirms the discussions.) It is easy to see the appeal: Twitter is growing even faster than Facebook—doubling its membership in March—and would give Google access to the kind of personal information that fills Facebook News Feeds. And Google recently announced Wave, a Web communications platform that encourages Facebook-like sharing and conversations. The company even seems to have conceded Zuckerberg's point about its impersonal search results. In April, Google announced a plan to allow individuals to create detailed profiles that would show up whenever anyone searches for their name. If they opt for this service—a big if—users gain greater control over how they are portrayed online, which will give them the incentive to share with Google the kind of personal information they had previously shared only with Facebook.

Google has even shown a willingness to join Facebook in gingerly tapping the third rail of Internet marketing—behavioral targeting. The search giant has long assured its users that it would never use their personal information to deliver targeted advertising, relying instead on aggregate data or search activity that preserves anonymity. ("There is a line with users that you don't want to cross," Google CEO Eric Schmidt said in the wake of the Beacon controversy.) But in March, Google started its own behavioral targeting campaign—tracking users' browsing to deliver more-customized ads. Users have the option to either edit their profiles or opt out entirely.

In September 2007, Gideon Yu was hired as Facebook's CFO. Before that, the 38-year-old had been CFO at YouTube, where he negotiated its acquisition by Google. He'd also put in four years as Yahoo's treasurer and was one of its top dealmakers. Facebook announced the hire with much fanfare. "I consider it kind of a coup that we were able to recruit him here," Zuckerberg told the *Wall Street Journal*. "He's just excellent."

Nineteen months later, Yu was gone. It was a short tenure—not unprecedented for a private-company CFO. But Zuckerberg turned Yu's departure into a kerfuffle by publicly trashing him, saying that the job had simply outgrown him and that Facebook now needed a CFO with "substantial public company experience." To many, the performance was a stark reminder that the Facebook CEO, while undeniably ambitious and brilliant, was still just 24 years old. (He's 25 now.)

Zuckerberg's youth has given Googlers some confidence. After all, even under the most sage and steady leadership, Facebook would be confronted with a difficult challenge: turning a massive user base into a sustainable business. (Just ask Friendster, MySpace, YouTube, and Twitter.) Through Google's own experience with YouTube, they have seen how expensive it can be to keep up with exploding user growth. They inked a disastrous $900 million partnership with MySpace in 2006, a failure that taught them how hard it is to make money from social networking. And privately, they don't think Facebook's staff has the brainpower to succeed where they have failed. "If they found a way to monetize all of a sudden, sure, that would be a problem," says one highly placed Google executive. "But they're not going to."

Facebook's naysayers have a point. But before they get too complacent, they might remember another upstart that figured out a new way to organize the Internet. For five years, it worked on building its user base and perfecting its product, resisting pleas from venture capitalists to figure out how to make money. It was only after it had made itself an essential part of everyone's online life that its business path became clear—and it quickly grew to become one of the world's most powerful and wealthy companies. The name of that company, of course, was Google.

Contributing editor **Fred Vogelstein** (*fred_vogelstein@wired.com*) wrote about Google in issue 17.02.

UNIT 2
Telling Stories

Unit Selections

Key Points to Consider

- What is your take on media coverage of war and politics? What are your primary sources of information on these topics?

- Analyze coverage of a news story in print media (newspapers and/or news magazines) and online. Note examples of editorial viewpoints and/or subjectivity in the selection and presentation of information. If you were the editor, what would you do differently? Why?

- Watch newscasts on two different networks on the same evening (in many markets, you can find one network's early evening news airing on the half hour and another on the hour, or you can record one while watching another). List the stories covered, in the order in which they are reported and the time devoted to each. Did you notice any patterns in the reporting? Were there any differences in the way stories on the same topic were presented? Did you note any instances in which editorial or entertainment values were reflected in the story selection or coverage? What conclusions do you draw from your findings?

- What do you think accounts for the American public's increasing disinterest in hard news topics? Is it the media's fault? Should making news more interesting/appealing be a media priority? Why or why not?

Student Website
www.mhhe.com/cls

Internet References

Cable News Network
  http://www.cnn.com
Fox News
  http://www.foxnews.com
Fairness and Accuracy in Reporting
  http://www.fair.org
Organization of News Ombudsmen (ONO)
  http://www.newsombudsmen.org
Television News Archive
  http://tvnews.vanderbilt.edu

The reporting of news and information was not, in the beginning, considered an important function within broadcast media organizations. Television news was originally limited to 15-minute commercial-free broadcasts, presented as a public service. Over the years, however, the news business became big business. News operations grew intensely competitive, locked in head-to-head popularity races in which the loss of one ratings point translated into a loss of millions of dollars in advertising revenue. The government spent time debating how many newspapers and television stations a single company could own. There were articles written speculating on how online news and information would change business-as-usual, and traditional news media took steps to become online players. In the past several years, however, layoffs and buyouts have rocked the most noble of news organizations. As put in "The News Mausoleum," "If one new medium, television, had wounded the institution of the daily newspaper with happy results for those who survived, a second new medium, the Internet, has slowly been slowly garroting the survivors."

News, by definition, is timely: It is "news," not "olds." Decisions regarding what stories to play and how to play them are made under tight deadlines. Media expert Wilbur Schramm has noted that "hardly anything about communication is so impressive as the enormous number of choices and discards and interpretations that have to be made between [an] actual news event and the symbols that later appear in the mind of a reporter, an editor, a reader, a listener, or a viewer. Therefore, even if everyone does his job perfectly, it is hard enough to get the report of an event straight and clear and true." Schramm's comments point to the tremendous impact of selectivity in crafting news messages. The process is called *gatekeeping*.

Gatekeeping is necessary. News operations cannot logistically cover or report every event that happens in the world from one edition or broadcast or posting to the next. The concerns associated with the reality of gatekeeping relate to whether the gatekeepers abuse the privilege of deciding what information or viewpoints mass audiences receive. Simply being selected for media coverage lends an issue, an event, or an individual a certain degree of celebrity—the "masser" the medium, the greater the effect.

Traditional news media are under enormous pressure to remain competitive in a changing media environment. Daily U.S. newspaper circulation peaked at 62.3 million in 1990. Since then, market share in large markets has dropped as much as 10 percent per year. Some 50,000 news industry employees lost their jobs between 2001 and 2006. Between 1970 and 2006, the percentage of U.S. homes with televisions turned on at news time and tuned to the nightly news (in Nielsen terms, the combined news "share") declined from 75% to 35%. The average age of viewers of prime-time television is 42, about the median age of the population as a whole; the median age of network evening news viewers is 60. The percentage of people who report that they never watch a nightly news broadcast has more than doubled.

In his novel *The Evening News,* Arthur Hailey observed: "People watch the news to find out the answers to three questions,

© Photodisc/PunchStock

Is the world safe? Are my home and family safe? and, Did anything happen today that was interesting?" Given cursory answers to those questions, viewers are satisfied that they are "keeping up," although the total amount of news delivered in a half-hour newscast would, if set in type, hardly fill the front page of a daily newspaper. Many adults report that they are too busy to follow the news, or are suspicious of the media, or find the news too depressing. In one recent study, 27% of television viewers described themselves as "stressed" while watching the evening news (51% reported feeling "stressed" watching Martha Stewart). Availability and consumption of *information,* however, is on the rise. Knowledge of sports and celebrities has increased, while knowledge of local and national politics has decreased.

The articles in this section explore the changing landscape of contemporary news and information coverage and consumption. The first three selections center on significant changes in the news business that both reflect and shape messages in the media pipeline. "The News Mausoleum" and "Don't Blame the Journalism" review turning points in the collapse of newspapers, which depend on diminishing advertising revenue to run their businesses. "Overload!" offers an intriguing application of insights from cognitive psychology to analyzing media consumers' response to information overload.

The next set of articles explores gatekeeping. "Whatever Happened to Iraq?" suggests reasons for the declining coverage of the Iraq War. "What the Mainstream Media Can Learn from Jon Stewart" proposes "lessons for newspapers and networks struggling to hold on to fleeting readers, viewers, and advertisers in a tumultuous era of transition for old media." Jon Stewart aficionados fare well.

"Climate Change: Now What?" and "Double Whammy" examine questions of bias or spin in the reporting on global warming. "Climate Change" takes the position that media have appropriately moved beyond debating the presence of global warming to advocating for political, economic, and consumer actions to mitigate its progress. "Double Whammy" presents a case study of news coverage of race and racism by the national media.

"Charticle Fever" discusses attempts to package print information in formats attractive to 18- to 35-year-olds accustomed to getting news online. "Beyond News" recommends news organizations "flip" from reporting to analyzing information, rather than trying to compete with the Web. "Maybe It *Is* Time to Panic" proposes changes in content and business models aimed at making acceptable profits in a "right-brain, digital world."

Communicating news and information is a critical function of mass media, and the degree to which media perform and are perceived to perform their gatekeeping and watchdog functions are of critical importance. In his book *Tuned Out: Why Americans Under 40 Don't Follow the News,* David T.Z. Mindich writes, "Robert Putnam's 2000 book, *Bowling Alone,* charted the decay of what the author called "social capital," the important resource of public and quasi-public dialogue. For example, Putnam discovered that more people bowl than ever before, but fewer bowl in leagues; hence, the title of his book. But bowling is just the start. The last half century has seen a decline in membership in unions, Elks clubs, and PTAs; fewer people give dinner parties, speak in public, go to church, and attend the theater. . . . Putnam convincingly demonstrated a correlation between the lack of social capital and news consumption. The same people who join groups and write their representatives also read newspapers. The same people who have trust in the system, and their ability to change it, use the news for ammunition. The same people who distrust each other, drop out of society, and become isolated, find news irrelevant to their lives." It is arguable that a decline in careful and credible coverage of important events and issues among media has contributed to decline in social capital. However, in a market-driven media climate, it is difficult for news media to sustain an economically viable hard news orientation when a declining number of consumers express interest in that product.

The News Mausoleum

JOHN PODHORETZ

The Newseum, a dazzling edifice of glass, marble, and steel that recently opened in Washington after seven years of planning and construction at a cost of $475 million, sits directly across Pennsylvania Avenue from the National Gallery of Art and cater-corner from the National Archives. Though the location was not chosen for this reason, it suggests that the subject matter of the Newseum (a blend of "news" and "museum") is as crucial to America and the West as the masterpieces hanging in the National Gallery and the foundational documents of the United States preserved within the Archives.

Its president, Peter Prichard, told me as he showed me around the almost-finished Newseum a few months ago that the purpose of the institution is the celebration of free speech. A 50-ton, 74-ft.-high slab of yellow Tennessee marble hangs from the front of the building; on it are etched the 45 words of the First Amendment. There could indeed be no nobler cause, but the Newseum addresses it primarily by inference. The slogan adorning its press kit gives the real game away: "Newseum. Where the News Comes to Life."

This half-billion-dollar enterprise is not really a tribute to an important idea or a celebration of a basic human freedom. It is, rather, the news industry's tribute to itself. And it is a tribute on a scale that would have gladdened the heart of Ramses II. The original Newseum, which opened in 1997, was a modest facility housed in the USA Today building across the Potomac from Washington in Rosslyn, Virginia. The current iteration, conceived by the Freedom Forum, a non-profit organization with a $700-million endowment courtesy of a huge block of Gannett Company stock, has been graced with eye-opening donations from almost every major-media corporation in America.[1]

The ebullient Prichard, who edited *USA Today* from 1988 to 1994, has reason to be proud. The Newseum is an overwhelming space. It was designed by James Polshek, who also mapped out the extraordinary Rose Center for Earth and Space on the site of the old Hayden Planetarium in New York. The two institutions are similar in scope and analogous in presentation. Like the Rose Center, the Newseum is a gigantic diorama, with a clear exterior wall of glass exposing the inside to full view. While the Rose Center pivots on a giant sphere, the Newseum is dominated by the world's largest LCD display, 90 feet square, with photographs and headlines and video in constant motion.

Visitors to the Rose Center ride an elevator to the top, where their tour of the universe begins with the Big Bang, after which they walk downward in a spiral around the mammoth globe, approaching ground level as the universe ages. Prichard took me by elevator to the top floor of the Newseum and then walked me down five levels through 28 different galleries and fifteen theaters. An endless row of display cases features newspapers from every era in American history, which can be examined in the climate-controlled drawers in which they are being perfectly preserved. Another endless row of screens allows visitors to pull up almost every front page of every newspaper in the world at any time.

"World's most Interactive Museum," says the Newseum's literature, trumpeting 130 "interactive stations featuring more than two dozen interactive programs." For once, the rules of contemporary museum design—which favor showing the visitor a good time rather than insisting on his aesthetic or spiritual elevation—are entirely congruent with institutional purpose. There is, for example, something faintly ridiculous in the notion that pressing buttons in a natural-history museum will teach visitors something about the rain forest that they could not get from reading a wall display. But news is an interactive medium by definition—the original interactive medium. The newspaper, the wellspring of the industry, was created to cover the actions of some and relay the report to others, who are then encouraged to respond to what they have read.

What is more, while neither the rain forest nor great art is a consumer product, news is a business. A museum dedicated to promoting an industry *should* pull out all the stops to make its visitors think they are having the time of their lives. Do vast numbers of people today find news arid, boring, or dull? Well, they won't after they visit this Space Mountain of a museum. And perhaps, just perhaps, upon leaving, they will awaken on the morrow with an unfamiliar yearning—an itch to hold an actual newspaper in their hands or to tune in later in the day to the evening news on television.

The Newseum is chock-a-block with television studios, both actual (ABC's *This Week with George Stephanopoulos* is now broadcast from it) and pretend (facilities allow visitors to anchor their own "newscasts"). Nonetheless, its true subject is the glorious history of the newspaper and its vital role in American life since the early 1700's. But herein lies a stark and bitter irony.

For the simple fact is that, slogan or no slogan, the news is *not* coming to life, at least as far as newspapers are concerned.

For newspapers, these are the end times, or something very much like them. Every week provides a new marker on the road to apocalypse: hundreds of layoffs in Los Angeles, circulation scandals in Dallas and Long Island, buyout packages in New York and Washington. Newspaper-circulation numbers are released twice a year, and for the past decade those numbers have charted an uninterrupted downward curve, accelerating at speeds now approaching an avalanche.

Designed as a monument to the daily, the Newseum may in fact be its mausoleum, with the marble First Amendment slab serving as its tombstone.

Newspapers have been dying for a half-century, of course. For each big city in the United States there is a name—the *Chicago Daily News,* the *Washington Star,* the *Baltimore News American,* the *Dallas Times Herald,* the *Houston Post,* the *Nashville Banner,* the *St. Louis Globe Democrat*—that serves as a Proustian madeleine, instantly conjuring up the memory of a beloved comic strip or an elegiac sports columnist or a hard-bitten crime reporter. And this is to say nothing of the vanished papers of New York, each of which summons a little universe: the *World Telegram,* the *Herald Tribune,* the *Mirror,* the *Graphic,* and the original *Sun* (whose name has been revived by the only big-city broadsheet to have been launched in the United States in the past twenty years).

Evening papers, timed to report on news events occurring after the late-night printing of morning papers, not to mention the afternoon baseball scores and closing stock prices, were killed off by the advent of the dinner-hour TV anchorman. At the same time, the mass migration of Americans from the city to the suburbs buried all but a handful of papers that depended for their circulation not on home delivery but on people tossing a coin to a newsie.

These simultaneous shakeouts were basically completed twenty years ago or more. What is happening to newspapers now is something very different. In the wake of the industry's consolidation, the survivors prospered mightily. But they are now being drained of their value, and at a quickened rate.

Newsday, the high-end Long Island tabloid that was once one of the most profitable enterprises in all of American industry, is on the block at a rumored price of $350 million. Five years ago, it would have sold for at least $1 billion. The seller is the Tribune Co., which in 2007 was bought outright by the Chicago billionaire Sam Zell. Tribune made $240 million in profit in 2006; in the fourth quarter of 2007, it lost $78 million. Zell sought to explain his decision to sell *Newsday* by saying he had "started with the assumption that print would be down 2 or 3 percent this year, not 18 percent."

The most ominous aspect of the industry's collapse is that monopoly newspapers—whose competitors folded long ago and left them in sole possession of an entire local market—are the worst afflicted. Such institutions, being the only game in town, should have been immune from decline. And yet falling they are. Over the past few years, for example, the *Dallas*

Morning News had to "restate" its paid circulation twice when it was discovered that the figures had been fraudulently inflated.[2] There have been layoffs and buyouts by the hundreds, and the news-gathering staff has been cut by a third.

When a monopoly begins to lose market share by as much as ten percent per year, withering and fading on its own and not on account of specific competitive pressure, it is a sure sign that the structural integrity of an entire industry has been compromised. Implosion is sure to follow—and is indeed taking place in every city in every region of the country. For anyone who depends on newspapering for his livelihood, there is simply no mistaking the death rattle.

The newspaper is a classic product of the Industrial Revolution. Its manufacture, which has barely changed in 150 years, requires a huge physical plant dominated by complex machines that cost hundreds of millions of dollars to purchase and maintain. Crews of manual laborers must load and unload many tons of paper, take care of the machinery as the newspaper is inked and colored and cut and folded, and oversee the interweaving of its sections. After all that, a brigade of truckers shows up to take the papers on an hours-long delivery tour. This must happen seven days a week, under any conceivable weather condition, every day of the year, forever.

And that is merely the blue-collar side of the business. The white-collar side employs hundreds of workers as well: writers and editors and photographers and graphic designers to fill the pages with copy and images, advertising salesmen to fill them with ads, a circulation department to make sure the paper gets to paying customers, and dozens of executives supervising it all.

This labor-intensive process is precisely the model that has been upended in industry after industry, driven to painful change by technological innovation and competitive threats. When the first such major threat hit the newspaper industry, it came in the form of television news, another labor-intensive and expensive medium. But in helping to shutter newspapers, TV proved to be a boon for the ones that weathered the storm.

However dangerous the challenge from television, the number of stations was, fortunately for the print business, fixed by federal fiat. Meanwhile, there was usually one money-making newspaper in the same local market—the only venue for print advertising by supermarkets and department stores and other businesses needing to let their customers know about weekly sales and bargains. For two decades, those newspapers cornered their markets, generated an enormous amount of cash, produced unheard-of profit margins of 20 to 30 percent, and were as valuable as their TV rivals, if not more so.

This period came to an end with the end of the 20th century. If one new medium, television, had wounded the institution of the daily newspaper with happy results for those who survived, a second new medium, the Internet, has been slowly garroting the survivors.

The substantive reason almost goes without saying. The Internet has turned the daily newspaper into an atavism. By providing readers with news and features every second of the day, cleanly and quickly, it has basically destroyed the rationale behind a once-a-day compendium printed on paper.

I began in the news business 25 years ago, and one of the first things I learned was that the profession was on the cusp of a profound and epochal change. The culprit was the rise of the personal computer. At conferences of newspaper editors in the 1980's and 90's, the drumbeat was constant: what we are we will not be in ten, fifteen, or twenty years.

At one conference, a futurist sketched a scenario in which we would all be carrying screens that would roll up in our briefcases like a tabloid—an early and only slightly fanciful imagining of what has actually taken place with handheld devices like the BlackBerry and the iPhone. Another visionary suggested that in some Brave New World, newspaper companies would install a special printer in every subscriber's home, into which the electronic content of the newspaper would be delivered over phone lines. The cost of manufacturing and maintaining these home devices would be far less than the mammoth expense of printing and delivering an actual daily newspaper. And here was the best part—the subscriber would be paying for the paper he was printing on. Something not too dissimilar from this vision has come to pass as well. Tens of millions of people now get their news from a special "box" in their homes that is the radically faster, vastly more powerful, and better-designed personal computer. Whether they print what they read or not is up to them.

So clearly did news organizations see the threat posed by the computer that they mobilized to address it, to get ahead of it, and to manage it. In the 1980's, they spent hundreds of millions and perhaps billions of dollars in the effort. To take one example, the Washington Post Co., a well-run and far-thinking industry leader, sank nearly $50 million into an electronic news service called Datatext. But the system was hard to understand, and made demands on the memory of the personal computer and the bandwidth of telephone lines that neither could meet at the time. The experiment was folded after three years, but it or something like it was repeated again and again by other major news companies, with similarly dire results.

These efforts were motivated by more than the desire to master a new technology for its own sake. It was universally understood that the mass audience for news was shrinking—the same audience on which the business relied in order to sell subscriptions and advertising. Readership had already declined by 50 percent since the advent of television. Young adults who had never developed the habit of reading a paper as children were showing no inclination to pick it up later in life.

The personal computer was going to be the way to reach these and other new people, if only someone could figure out how. Ironically, the breakthrough in this regard—the development in 1993 of the graphic interface called Mosaic, which gave birth to the creature known as the "website"—turned out to be far cheaper than any of the visionaries could have imagined.

Still, they were more forward-thinking than their counterparts in most other industries when faced with similar challenges. Not only did the news business know what was coming, it even knew where it was going to be hurt most severely. Katharine Graham, who ran the *Washington Post,* once told me that the primary reason she was worried about the future of her paper lay with the threat posed by the computer to, of all things, classified advertising.

That conversation took place in 1987—seven years before a man in San Francisco started a local bulletin board to let his friends know about cultural events in town. His name was Craig Newmark, and he, more than any other person, is the Shiva of the newspaper business, the destroyer of worlds.

Newmark began publishing his "list" as a website in 1995, only two years after the invention of the web browser and in the only region in the United States where people had grown truly comfortable using the new medium then known as the World Wide Web.

In short order, his friends told other friends, and Craigslist .org became popular. His readers began posting both job listings and items for sale. These were arranged in a simple and comprehensible manner, were easily searched, and were free. The site soon expanded to other cities. Craigslist became the first place any urban dweller under the age of thirty would go to find a used couch, a part-time job, or a roommate. In short order, realtors, too, began listing apartments and houses for rent. There arose an entire web-based industry following the Craigslist model: help-wanted sites like Monster.com, journalismjobs.com, and media-bistro.com.

Classifieds have always been the most profitable element in any newspaper. They divide a broadsheet page into as many as 200 ads, each one sold separately and at full price (unlike larger display advertising, which is often sold at a discount). The rule of thumb is that the more spaces can be sold on any given page, the more money can be made per ad. Thus, two half-page ads can be sold for more than a full page, four quarter-page pages can be sold for more than two half-pages, and so on.

The rise of the Craigslist model has devastated classified advertising in newspapers, once the only place in a city to sell a used car or list a job opening. True, today's newspapers have duplicated all their classified ads on their websites, and they have attempted to best Craigslist and its emulators by offering different features, new ways to search, and so forth. But the result is harder to use, and in any case why should you spend $100 putting something up for sale in the paper when you can post it on Craigslist for free? Why list a job for $200 when you can list it for $10?

There is no answer to these questions. The only solution is for newspapers to lower their prices to Craigslist levels, but at that point someone else will come along and restore the entirely free model, and the end result will be the same. Last year, classified advertising dropped nationally by more than 16 percent; overall, it is down 34 percent since 2000. Over the next ten years, the cash cow of any newspaper will dry up entirely.

Feverishly anticipating the demise of their 19th-century industrial product, newspapers are once again renewing their efforts to take advantage, somehow, of the growth of the Internet. But they are uniquely ill-positioned to do so. When it comes to reporting the news, their greatest competitive asset is the size of their news-gathering and news-writing staffs. But they can afford those staffs only because of advertising revenue. And, on the web, they will generate only a fraction of the advertising revenue they have been able to generate in print as an effective monopoly. Moreover, and unlike the case with every other rival they have faced in the past, the technical cost of competing with them is astonishingly low.

All they will have left is a very powerful brand—the term we now use for what used to be called a name. That brand will be worth a very great deal, but it will not be worth enough on its own to produce the kind of comprehensive news portrait that has been the defining purpose of urban and regional newspapers for a century and a half. That is why, to many observers, it seems a certainty that these brands will eventually be bought out by Internet monoliths, like Google and Yahoo, which are hungry for "content."

The prospect is a very stark one for people who work in, write, and edit newspapers. For these people do not think of themselves as "content providers." They think much more highly of themselves than that. They believe they play a vital role, perhaps the most vital role, in the defense of the freedoms of every citizen. After all, who else is there to keep a vigilant watch over the official custodians of society? Who else is there to protect the people from the depredations of business and government? Is not freedom of speech—the very freedom that enables journalists to ply their trade—the first of our freedoms, *primus inter pares,* and who will guard it if not they?

Historically speaking, this attitude is of relatively recent vintage. It may, in fact, be an artifact of the rise of the same highly profitable monopoly newspapers and shared-monopoly television networks that were so profitable and consequently grew so powerful that they gave the members of their news force reason to believe they were not just working stiffs—the general attitude of newspapermen throughout most of the preceding era—but akin to a democratic nobility.

The immodesty of this idea led many newspaper professionals of the late 20th century into a category error. They came to confuse the significance of the subjects they were covering with the act of covering them. Proximity to the news made *them* a species of news. They wrote about government; therefore, they were equivalent to the government in importance. They reported a war, and their act of reporting a war came to loom as large as the war itself. Today, the death of a journalist in a war zone is assigned vastly more weight than the death of a soldier.

This error is very much in evidence in the Newseum. Its grandest displays are giant artifacts. On the third floor, there is an East German guard tower attached to a slab of the Berlin Wall; on the first floor, there is a huge twisted piece of metal that was the World Trade Center's broadcast antenna. These are remarkable to behold and to contemplate, and they encourage one to reflect deeply on totalitarianism, Islamofascism, and terrorism. But what is important about them, what is thought-provoking about them, has absolutely nothing to do with journalism or with journalists; it has to do with actuality. If anything, the unearned grandiosity at work in the news business is one of the key elements behind the deep and abiding disdain that the American people have come to harbor for it.

After much study, the Newseum's researchers have determined that Katharine Graham's husband, Philip, the editor of the *Washington Post,* was the first person to utter the phrase, "News is the rough first draft of history." The phrase appears on the wall of the News History Gallery on the fifth level. It was a pithy and clever way to describe the role of the industry, and it has been cited ever since by professionals who believe it places journalism in the highest possible context.

But read the sentence again: "news is the rough first draft of history." There is a very becoming modesty at work here. For as every writer knows in his marrow, and every editor knows to his annoyance and grief, the central quality of a rough first draft is that it is full of mistakes.

Nor is this very rough first draft expected to improve on a second reading. It is supposed to be superseded by something else. Something better.

Notes

1. Collectively, the New York Times Co., News Corporation, Hearst Corporation, ABC, NBC, Time Warner, and Cox Enterprises have given $45 million; another $52 million has come from foundations and individual philanthropists.

2. *Newsday,* sued by hundreds of its advertisers for overcharging on the basis of falsified circulation claims, settled out of court.

JOHN PODHORETZ is the editorial director of *Commentary* and the author of *Bush Country* and *Can She Be Stopped?* He blogs regularly about politics on *contentions* at www.commentarymagazine.com.

Overload!

Journalism's Battle for Relevance in an Age of Too Much Information

BREE NORDENSON

In 2007, as part of the third round of strategic planning for its digital transformation, The Associated Press decided to do something a little different. It hired a research company called Context to conduct an in-depth study of young-adult news consumption around the world. Jim Kennedy, the AP's director of strategic planning, initially agreed to the project because he thought it would make for a "fun and entertaining" presentation at the annual meeting. It turned out to be more than that; the AP believed that the results held fundamental implications for the role of the news media in the digital age. Chief among the findings was that many young consumers craved more in-depth news but were unable or unwilling to get it. "The abundance of news and ubiquity of choice do not necessarily translate into a better news environment for consumers," concluded the researchers in their final report. "Participants in this study showed signs of news fatigue; that is, they appeared debilitated by information overload and unsatisfying news experiences. . . . Ultimately news fatigue brought many of the participants to a learned helplessness response. The more overwhelmed or unsatisfied they were, the less effort they were willing to put in."

The idea that news consumers, even young ones, are overloaded should hardly come as a surprise. The information age is defined by output: we produce far more information than we can possibly manage, let alone absorb. Before the digital era, information was limited by our means to contain it. Publishing was restricted by paper and delivery costs; broadcasting was circumscribed by available frequencies and airtime. The Internet, on the other hand, has unlimited capacity at near-zero cost. There are more than 70 million blogs and 150 million websites today—a number that is expanding at a rate of approximately ten thousand an *hour.* Two hundred and ten billion e-mails are sent each day. Say goodbye to the gigabyte and hello to the exabyte, five of which are worth 37,000 Libraries of Congress. In 2006 alone, the world produced 161 exabytes of digital data, the equivalent of three million times the information contained in all the books ever written. By 2010, it is estimated that this number will increase to 988. Pick your metaphor: we're drowning, buried, snowed under.

The information age's effect on news production and consumption has been profound. For all its benefits—increased transparency, accessibility, and democratization—the Internet has upended the business model of advertising-supported journalism.

This, in turn, has led news outlets to a ferocious focus on profitability. Over the past decade, they have cut staff, closed bureaus, and shrunk the newshole. Yet despite these reductions, the average citizen is unlikely to complain of a lack of news. Anyone with access to the Internet has thousands of free news sources at his fingertips. In a matter of seconds, we can browse *The New York Times* and *The Guardian, Newsweek* and *The Economist,* CNN and the BBC.

News is part of the atmosphere now, as pervasive—and in some ways as invasive—as advertising. It finds us in airport lounges and taxicabs, on our smart phones and PDAs, through e-mail providers and Internet search engines. Much of the time, it arrives unpackaged: headlines, updates, and articles are snatched from their original sources—often as soon as they're published—and excerpted or aggregated on blogs, portals, social-networking sites, RSS readers, and customizable homepages like My MSN, My Yahoo, myAOL, and iGoogle. These days, news comes at us in a flood of unrelated snippets. As Clay Shirky, author of *Here Comes Everybody: The Power of Organizing without Organizations,* explains, "The economic logic of the age is unbundling." But information without context is meaningless. It is incapable of informing and can make consumers feel lost. As the AP noted in its research report, "The irony in news fatigue is that these consumers felt helpless to change their news consumption at a time when they have more control and choice than ever before. When the news wore them down, participants in the study showed a tendency to passively receive versus actively seek news."

There has always been a large swath of the population that is not interested in news, of course, just as there has always been a portion that actively seeks it out. What's interesting about the current environment is that despite an enormous increase in available news and information, the American public is no better informed now than it has been during less information-rich times. "The basic pattern from the forties to today is that the amount of information that people have and their knowledge about politics is no worse or no better than it's been over that sixty-year period," explains Michael X. Delli Carpini, dean of the Annenberg School for Communication at the University of Pennsylvania. For example, a 2007 survey conducted by the Pew Research Center for the People & the Press found that 69 percent of Americans could correctly name the vice president, only a slight decrease from the 74 percent who could in 1989.

This phenomenon can be partially explained by our tendency to become passive in the face of too much information. It can also be attributed to the fact that the sheer number of specialized publications, the preponderance of television channels, the wide array of entertainment options, and the personalization and customization encouraged by digital technologies have made it far easier to avoid public-affairs content. "As choice goes up, people who are motivated to be politically informed take advantage of these choices, but people who are not move away from politics," explains Delli Carpini. "In the 1960s, if you wanted to watch television you were going to watch news. And today you can avoid news. So choice can be a mixed blessing."

Markus Prior writes in his book, *Post-Broadcast Democracy: How Media Choice Increases Inequality in Political Involvement and Polarizes Elections,* "Political information in the current media environment comes mostly to those who want it." In other words, in our supersaturated media environment, serendipitous exposure to political-affairs content is far less common than it used to be. Passive news consumers are less informed and less likely to become informed than ever before.

The tragedy of the news media in the information age is that in their struggle to find a financial foothold, they have neglected to look hard enough at the larger implications of the new information landscape—and more generally, of modern life. How do people process information? How has media saturation affected news consumption? What must the news media do in order to fulfill their critical role of informing the public, as well as survive? If they were to address these questions head on, many news outlets would discover that their actions thus far—to increase the volume and frequency of production, sometimes frantically and mindlessly—have only made things more difficult for the consumer.

> **To win the war for our attention, news organizations must make themselves indispensable by producing journalism that helps make sense of the flood of information that inundates us all.**

While it is naïve to assume that news organizations will reduce their output—advertising dollars are involved, after all—they would be wise to be more mindful of the content they produce. The greatest hope for a healthy news media rests as much on their ability to filter and interpret information as it does on their ability to gather and disseminate it. If they make snippets and sound bites the priority, they will fail. Attention—our most precious resource—is in increasingly short supply. To win the war for our attention, news organizations must make themselves indispensable by producing journalism that helps make sense of the flood of information that inundates us all.

The Limits of Human Attention

Ours is a culture of multitasking, of cramming as many activities as possible into as short a period of time as possible. We drive and talk on our cell phones, check e-mail during meetings and presentations, eat dinner while watching TV. In part, says Maggie

Jackson, author of *Distracted: The Erosion of Attention and the Coming Dark Age,* such multitasking "is part of a wider value system that venerates speed, frenetic activity, hyper-mobility, etcetera, as the paths to success. That's why we're willing to drive like drunks or work in frenzied ways, although it literally might kill us."

Many young people multitask to the extreme, particularly when it comes to media consumption. I've witnessed my twenty-two-year-old brother watch television while talking on the phone, IMing with several friends, composing an e-mail, and updating his Facebook page. A widely cited 2006 study by the Henry J. Kaiser Family Foundation found that 81 percent of young people engage in some form of media multitasking during a given week. But as cognitive psychologists have long known, human attention is quite limited. Despite our best efforts, when we try to do more than one thing at once, we are less efficient and more prone to error. This is because multitasking is actually a process of dividing attention, of toggling back and forth between tasks.

Acquiring new information requires particularly focused attention, which includes the ability to ignore distractions. In order to absorb the information contained in a CNN newscast, for example, we must not only direct our attention to the person talking, but also filter out the running headlines, news updates, and financial ticker on the lower part of the screen. Torkel Klingberg, a professor of cognitive neuroscience at Karolinska Institute in Sweden and author of *The Overflowing Brain,* puts it simply: "If we do not focus our attention on something, we will not remember it." In other words, attention is a critical component of learning.

Michael Posner, a researcher who has dedicated his career to studying attention and a professor emeritus of psychology at the University of Oregon, explains attention as a system of three networks—alerting, orienting, and executive. Alerting refers to the state of wakefulness necessary to attend to information, while orienting is the process by which we respond to stimuli, such as movement, sound, or noise. Executive attention is the highest-order network, the one that we have conscious control over. If we are trying to study for a test or read a novel, we use it to direct and maintain our focus, as well as to suppress our reaction to competing stimuli like the din of a nearby conversation or television.

The information-saturated environment that we live in is, unsurprisingly, extremely demanding of our attention. Modern life—both at work and at home—has become so information-rich that Edward Hallowell, a Boston-area psychiatrist, believes many of us suffer from what he calls an attention-deficit trait, a culturally induced form of attention-deficit disorder. As he pointed out in a 2005 interview with CNET News, "We've been able to overload manual labor. But never before have we so routinely been able to overload brain labor." According to Hallowell and other psychiatrists, all these competing inputs prevent us from assimilating information. "What your brain is best equipped to do is to think, to analyze, to dissect, and create," he explains. "And if you're simply responding to bits of stimulation, you won't ever go deep." Journalist John Lorinc noted as much in an elegant article on distraction in the April 2007 issue of *The Walrus:*

> It often seems as though the sheer glut of data itself has supplanted the kind of focused, reflective attention that might make this information useful in the first place. The dysfunction of our information environment is an outgrowth of its extraordinary fecundity. Digital communications technology

has demonstrated a striking capacity to subdivide our attention into smaller and smaller increments; increasingly, it seems as if the day's work has become a matter of interrupting the interruptions.

In a recent report, *Information Overload: We Have Met the Enemy and He Is Us,* the research firm Basex concluded that interruptions take up nearly 30 percent of a knowledge worker's day and end up costing American businesses $650 billion annually. Other studies show that interruptions cause significant impairments in performance on IQ tests.

In many ways, the modern age—and the Internet, in particular—is a veritable minefield of distractions. This poses a central challenge to news organizations whose mandate is to inform the public. Research by Pablo Boczkowski, who teaches communication studies at Northwestern University, has revealed that when we consume news online we do so for significantly less time than in print and that we do it while we're working. Further complicating matters is the disruptive nature of online advertising. Intrusive Web advertisements—washingtonpost.com recently featured one in which a Boeing helicopter flies right across the text of a news story—exploit our orienting network, which evolved to respond quickly to novel stimuli. Could we train ourselves to suppress our tendency to be distracted by such advertising? "You can get somewhat better, but it's hard to resist because it'll produce orienting," Posner explains. "The way you resist it is you bring your attention back as quickly as you can." Yet even if we were somehow able to eliminate ads, the sheer number of articles, headlines, and video and audio feeds on news websites makes focused attention difficult. Having to decide where to direct our attention and then maintain it makes reading and retaining news online a formidable task.

The Attention Economy

One of the most useful frameworks for understanding journalism's challenges and behavior in the information age is the notion of the attention economy. Economics is the study of the allocation of resources and the basic principles of supply and demand, after all, and about a decade ago a handful of economists and scholars came up with the concept of the attention economy as a way of wrestling with the problem of having too much information—an oversupply, if you will—and not enough time or people to absorb it all.

The dynamics of the attention economy have created a complicated and hypercompetitive arena for news production and consumption. News media must not only compete with one another, as well as with an ever-increasing assortment of information and entertainment options, but also with the very thing that supports their endeavors—advertising. In fact, the advertising industry has been struggling with the dynamics of the attention economy for a couple of decades now. As the advertising landscape becomes more saturated, advertisers must work harder to get their messages to the consumer. But as Mark Crispin Miller, professor of media ecology at New York University, notes in the *Frontline* documentary *The Persuaders:*

Every effort to break through the clutter is just more clutter. Ultimately, if you don't have clean, plain borders and backdrops for your ads, if you don't have that blank space, that commons, that virgin territory, you have a very hard time

making yourself heard. The most obvious metaphor is a room full of people, all screaming to be heard. What this really means, finally, is that advertising is asphyxiating itself.

The news media also run the risk of self-asphyxiation in an information landscape crowded with headlines, updates, and news feeds. In order to garner audience attention and maintain financial viability, media outlets are increasingly concerned with the "stickiness" of their content. According to Douglas Rushkoff, host of *The Persuaders* and author of the forthcoming book *Life Incorporated,* the question for these organizations has become, "How do we stick the eyeballs onto our content and ultimately deliver the eyeballs to our sponsors?" As he dryly points out, "That's a very different mandate than how do we make information—real information—available to people. The information economy, then, is a competitive space. So as more people who are information providers think of themselves as competing for eyeballs rather than competing for a good story, then journalism's backwards." The rise of sound bites, headlines, snippets, infotainment, and celebrity gossip are all outgrowths of this attempt to grab audience attention—and advertising money. Visit a cable-news website most any day for an example along the lines of POLICE: WOMAN IN COW SUIT CHASED KIDS (CNN); or MAN BEATS TEEN GIRL WAITING IN MCDONALD'S LINE (Fox News). As Northwestern's Boczkowski points out, "Unlike when most of the media were organized in monopolistic or oligopolistic markets, now they are far more competitive; the cost of ignoring customer preferences is much higher."

Meanwhile, the massive increase in information production and the negligible cost of distributing and storing information online have caused it to lose value. Eli Noam, director of the Columbia Institute for Tele-Information, explains that this price deflation is only partly offset by an increase in demand in the digital age, since the time we have to consume information is finite. "On the whole—on the per-minute, per-line, per-word basis—information has continuously declined in price," says Noam. "The deflation makes it very difficult for many companies to stay in business for a long time."

Thus, we come to the heart of journalism's challenge in an attention economy: in order to preserve their vital public-service function—not to mention survive—news organizations need to reevaluate their role in the information landscape and reinvent themselves to better serve their consumers. They need to raise the value of the information they present, rather than diminish it. As it stands now, they often do the opposite.

More-Faster-Better

"Living and working in the midst of information resources like the Internet and the World Wide Web can resemble watching a firefighter attempt to extinguish a fire with napalm," write Paul Duguid and John Seely Brown, information scientists, in *The Social Life of Information.* "If your Web page is hard to understand, link to another. If a 'help' system gets overburdened, add a 'help on using help.' If your answer isn't here, then click on through another 1,000 pages. Problems with information? Add more."

Like many businesses in the information age, news outlets have been steadily increasing the volume and speed of their output. As the proliferation of information sources on the Web continues at a breakneck pace, news media compete for attention by adding content and features—blogs, live chat sessions with journalists, video and audio streams, and slideshows. Much of this is of excellent quality. But taken together, these features present a quandary: Do we persevere or retreat in the face of too much information? And as the AP study showed, even young news consumers get fatigued.

In psychology, passivity resulting from a lack of control is referred to as "learned helplessness." Though logic would suggest that an increase in available news would give consumers more control, this is not actually the case. As Barry Schwartz, the Dorwin Cartwright Professor of Social Theory and Social Action at Swarthmore College, argues in his book *The Paradox of Choice: Why More is Less,* too many choices can be burdensome. "Instead of feeling in control, we feel unable to cope," he writes. "Freedom of choice eventually becomes a tyranny of choice."

Too many choices can be burdensome: 'Instead of feeling in control, we feel unable to cope. Freedom of choice becomes a tyranny of choice.'

A recent study by Northwestern University's Media Management Center supports this phenomenon. It found that despite their interest in the 2008 election, young adults avoid political news online "because they feel too much information is coming at them all at once and too many different things are competing for their attention." The study participants said they wanted news organizations to display *less* content in order to highlight the essential information. "Young people want the site design to signal to them what's really important . . . instead of being confronted by a bewildering array of choices," write the researchers in their final report, *From "Too Much" to "Just Right": Engaging Millennials in Election News on the Web.*

The instinct that more is better is deeply ingrained in the modern psyche. David Levy, a professor at The Information School of the University of Washington, uses the phrase "more-better-faster" to describe the acceleration of society that began with the Industrial Revolution. According to Levy, we tend to define productivity in terms of speed and volume rather than quality of thought and ideas. "We are all now expected to complete more tasks in a smaller amount of time," writes Levy in a 2007 journal article. "And while the new technologies do make it remarkably efficient and easy to search for information and to collect masses of potentially relevant sources on a huge variety of topics, they can't, in and of themselves, clear the space and time needed to absorb and to reflect on what has been collected." In the case of news production, Swarthmore's Schwartz agrees. "The rhythm of the news cycle has changed so dramatically that what's really been excluded," he says, "is the time that it takes to think."

Implications for Democracy

Our access to digital information, as well as our ability to instantly publish, share, and improve upon it at negligible cost, hold extraordinary promise for realizing the democratic ideals of journalism. Yet as we've seen, many news consumers are unable or unwilling to navigate what Michael Delli Carpini refers to as the "chaotic and gateless information environment that we live in today."

When people had fewer information and entertainment options, journalistic outlets were able to produce public-affairs content without having to worry excessively about audience share. As the Internet and the 24/7 news cycle splinter readership and attention

spans, this is no longer the case. "Real journalism is a kind of physician-patient relationship where you don't pander to readers," says Bob Garfield, a columnist for *Advertising Age* and co-host of NPR's *On the Media*. "You give them some of what they want and some of what you as the doctor-journalist think they ought to have." Unfortunately, many news outlets feel they can no longer afford to strike the right balance.

As information proliferates, meanwhile, people inevitably become more specialized both in their careers and their interests. This nichification—the basis for *Wired* editor Chris Anderson's breakthrough concept of the Long Tail—means that shared public knowledge is receding, as is the likelihood that we come in contact with beliefs that contradict our own. Personalized home pages, newsfeeds, and e-mail alerts, as well as special-interest publications lead us to create what sociologist Todd Gitlin disparagingly referred to as "my news, my world." Serendipitous news—accidentally encountered information—is far less frequent in a world of TiVo and online customization tools.

Viewed in this light, the role of the journalist is more important than ever. "As society becomes splintered," writes journalist and author David Shenk in *Data Smog,* "it is journalists who provide the vital social glue to keep us at least partly intact as a common unit." Journalists work to deliver the big picture at a time when the overload of information makes it hard to piece it together ourselves. "The journalist's job isn't to pay attention simply to one particular field," explains Paul Duguid. "The job is to say, 'Well, what are all the different fields that bear on this particular story?' They give us the breadth that none of us can have because we're all specialists in our own particular area." In other words, the best journalism does not merely report and deliver information, it places it in its full and proper context.

Journalism's New Role

The primacy placed on speed and volume in the information age has led to an uneven news landscape. "There is an over-allocation of resources on breaking and developing news production and constant updates," observes Boczkowski. "I think many news organizations are overdoing it." While headlines and updates are undoubtedly important, their accumulation is problematic. "Increasingly, as the abundance of information overwhelms us all, we need not simply more information, but people to assimilate, understand, and make sense of it," write Duguid and Seely Brown.

The question, then, is how?

As David Shenk presciently noted more than a decade ago, "In a world with vastly more information than we can process, journalists are the most important processors we have." The researchers who conducted the study for the AP concluded that the news fatigue they observed among young adults resulted from "an overload of basic staples in the news diet—the facts and updates that tend to dominate the digital news environment." In other words, the news they were encountering was underprocessed.

"In a world with vastly more information than we can process, journalists are the most important processors we have."

—David Shenk

In order to address the problem, the AP has made a number of changes in the way it approaches news production. For starters, it instituted a procedure it calls 1-2-3 filing, which attempts to reduce news clutter and repetition (the days of endless write-throughs are over) while also acknowledging the unpackaged and real-time nature of news in the digital world. With 1-2-3 filing, reporters produce news content in three discrete parts, which they file separately: a headline, a short present-tense story, and, when appropriate, a longer in-depth account. By breaking down the news in this way, the AP hopes to eliminate the redundancy and confusion caused by filing a full-length article for every new story development. In 1-2-3 filing, each component replaces the previous component: the headline is replaced by the present-tense story, which is then replaced by the in-depth account.

The AP has also launched a series of initiatives aimed at providing consumers with deeper, more analytical content. It has created a Top Stories Desk at its New York headquarters to identify and "consider the big-picture significance" of the most important stories of the day. It has also begun developing interactive Web graphics to help explain complicated and ongoing stories like Hurricane Katrina and the Minnesota bridge collapse. And for 2008, the AP launched "Measure of a Nation," a multimedia series dedicated to examining the election "through the prism of American culture, rather than simply the candidates and the horse race." "Measure of a Nation" packages take a historical approach to covering such notions as myth, elitism, and celebrity in American presidential politics. In one article published in late August, for example, journalist Ted Anthony explains the powerful political influence of the Kennedy family over the past fifty years, drawing parallels between the campaigns of JFK and RFK and that of Barack Obama. As the AP writes in its report, these changes in approach represent "a concerted effort to think about the news from an end-user's perspective, re-emphasizing a dimension to news gathering and editing that can get lost in the relentless rush of the daily news cycle."

Much like educational institutions, the best news organizations help people convert information into the knowledge they need to understand the world. As Richard Lanham explains in *The Economics of Attention,* "Universities have never been simply data-mining and storage operations. They have always taken as their central activity the conversion of data into useful knowledge and into wisdom. They do this by creating attention structures that we call curricula, courses of study." Institutions of journalism do it by crafting thoughtful and illuminating stories. "Journalists who limit their role to news flashes are absolving themselves of any overarching obligation to the audience," writes Shenk in *The End of Patience.* "Mere telling focuses on the mechanics of transmitting information of the moment, while education assumes a responsibility for making sure that knowledge sticks." The most valuable journalism is the kind that *explains.* "The first and foremost role that a journalist plays is to provide the information in a context that we wouldn't be able to get as amateurs," says Delli Carpini. "And I think that's where journalism should be focusing."

As it turns out, explanatory journalism may have a promising future in the market for news. On May 9, in partnership with NPR News, *This American Life* dedicated its hour-long program to explaining the housing crisis. "The Giant Pool of Money" quickly became the most popular episode in the show's thirteen-year history. CJR praised the piece (in "Boiler Room," the essay by Dean Starkman in our September/October issue) as "the most comprehensive and insightful look at the system that produced the credit crisis." And on his blog, *PressThink,* Jay Rosen, a journalism professor at New York University, wrote that the program was "probably the best work of explanatory journalism I have ever heard." Rosen went on to note that by helping people understand an issue, explanatory journalism actually creates a market for news. It gives people a reason to tune in. "There are some stories—and the mortgage crisis is a great example—where until I grasp the *whole,* I am unable to make sense of *any* part," he writes. "Not only am I not a customer for news reports prior to that moment, but the very frequency of the updates alienates me from the providers of those updates because the news stream is adding daily to my feeling of being ill-informed, overwhelmed, out of the loop."

> **"There are some stories—and the mortgage crisis is a great example—where until I grasp the *whole,* I am unable to make sense of *any* part."**
>
> —Jay Rosen

Rather than simply contributing to the noise of the unending torrent of headlines, sound bites, and snippets, NPR and *This American Life* took the time to step back, report the issue in depth, and then explain it in a way that illuminated one of the biggest and most complicated stories of the year. As a result of the program's success, NPR News formed a multimedia team in late August to explain the global economy through a blog and podcast, both of which are called "Planet Money." And on October 3, *This American Life* and NPR aired a valuable follow-up episode, "Another Frightening Show About the Economy," which examined the deepening credit crisis, including how it might have been prevented and Washington's attempts at a bailout.

Along with supplying depth and context, another function of the modern news organization is to act as an information filter. No news outlet better embodies this aim than *The Week,* a magazine dedicated to determining the top news stories of the week and then synthesizing them. As the traditional newsweeklies are struggling to remain relevant and financially viable, *The Week* has experienced steady circulation growth over the past several years. "The purpose of *The Week* is not to tell people the news but to make sense of the news for people," explains editor William Falk. "Ironically, in this intensive information age, it's in some ways harder than ever to know what's important and what's not. And so I often say to people, 'With *The Week,* you're hiring this group of really smart, well-versed people that read for you fifty hours a week and then sit down and basically give you a report on what they learned that week.' "

Rather than merely excerpting and reprinting content, this slim magazine takes facts, text, and opinions from a variety of sources—approximately a hundred per issue—to create its own articles, columns, reviews, and obituaries. As Falk explains, there's a certain "alchemy" that occurs when you synthesize multiple accounts of a news story. And *The Week*'s success suggests that consumers are willing to pay for this. "We're a service magazine as much as we are a journalism magazine," says Falk. "People work ten, eleven hours a day. They're very busy. There are tremendous demands on their time. There are other things competing for your leisure time—you can go online, you can watch television or a DVD. So what we do is deliver to you, in a one-hour package or less, is a smart distillation of what happened last week that you need to pay attention to."

One ally in journalism's struggle to deal with information overload, meanwhile, may be the digital machinery that brought it about in the first place. While digital archiving and data tagging cannot replace human interpretation and editorial judgment, they have an important role to play in helping us navigate the informational sea. As any news consumer knows, searching for or following a story can be frustrating on the Internet, where information is both pervasive and transient. In its study, the AP observed that young consumers struggled to find relevant in-depth news. So the wire service stepped up an effort begun in 2005 to tag all its articles, images, and videos according to a classification system of major news topics and important people, places, and things. These tags allow consumers, as well as news organizations and aggregators, to more effectively find and link to AP content. A number of other organizations, including *The New York Times* (check out the Times Topics tab on nytimes.com), *The Washington Post,* and CNN have similar projects under way, promising an opportunity to rapidly—and often automatically—provide consumers with a high level of detail, context, and graphical means of explanation.

The website for BBC News may be the best example of how journalistic organizations can deliver context in the digital environment. A news story about the Russia-Georgia crisis, for example, is displayed alongside a list of links to a map of the region, a country profile, an explanation of the crisis, a summary of Russian foreign policy, and related news articles and video footage. All online BBC News stories are presented in this manner, giving consumers multiple ways to learn about and understand an issue. While no American site is this comprehensive, a handful of major news outlets, from CNN to NPR to the *National Journal,* have used this approach in creating special election 2008 Web pages. By linking stories to one another and to background information and analysis, news organizations help news consumers find their way through a flood of information that without such mediation could be overwhelming and nearly meaningless.

Why Journalism Won't Disappear

While it's true that the Web allows the average individual to create and disseminate information without the help of a publishing house or a news organization, this does not mean journalism institutions are no longer relevant. "Oddly enough, information is one of the things that in the end needs brands almost more than anything else," explains Paul Duguid. "It needs a recommendation, a seal of approval, something that says this is reliable or true or whatever. And so journalists, but also the institutions of journalism as one aspect of this, become very important."

Moreover, the flood of news created by the production bias of the Internet could, in the end, point to a new role for journalistic institutions. "We're expecting people who are not librarians, who

are not knowledge engineers to do the work of knowledge engineers and librarians," says Jonathan Spira, CEO and chief analyst for the business research firm Basex and an expert in information overload. In other words, most of us lack the skills—not to mention the time, attention, and motivation—to make sense of an unrelenting torrent of information. This is where journalists and news organizations come in. The fact that there is more information than there are people or time to consume it—the classic economy-of-attention problem—represents a financial opportunity for news organizations. "I think that the consumers, being subjects to this flood, need help, and they know it," says Eli Noam. "And so therefore they want to have publications that will be selecting along the lines of quality and credibility in order to make their lives easier. For that, people will be willing to pay." A challenge could become an opportunity.

In fact, journalism that makes sense of the news may even increase news consumption. As Jay Rosen points out on his blog, explanatory journalism creates a "scaffold of understanding in the users that future reports can attach to, thus driving demand for the updates that today are more easily delivered." In a similar fashion—by providing links to background information and analysis alongside every news story—the BBC gives consumers frameworks for understanding that generate an appetite for more information.

The future of news depends on the willingness of journalistic organizations to adjust to the new ecology and new economy of information in the digital age. "I think in some ways, we need a better metaphor," says Delli Carpini. "The gatekeeping metaphor worked pretty well in the twentieth century, but maybe what news organizations should be now is not gatekeepers so much as guides. You don't want gatekeepers that can say you can get this and you can't get that. You want people who can guide you through all this stuff."

> "Maybe what news organizations should be now is not gatekeepers so much as guides. You want people who can guide you through all this stuff."
>
> —Delli Carpini

Ironically, if out of desperation for advertising dollars, news organizations continue to chase eyeballs with snippets and sound bites, they will ultimately lose the war for consumer attention. Readers and viewers will go elsewhere, and so will advertisers. But if news organizations decide to rethink their role and give consumers the context and coherence they want and need in an age of overload, they may just achieve the financial stability they've been scrambling for, even as they recapture their public-service mission before it slips away.

BREE NORDENSON is a freelance writer.

From *Columbia Journalism Review,* November/December 2008, pp. 30–42. Copyright © 2008 by Columbia Journalism Review. Reprinted by permission.

Don't Blame the Journalism

The Economic and Technological Forces behind the Collapse of Newspapers

Paul Farhi

When the obituaries are written for America's newspapers, count on journalists to indict themselves in their own demise. You've heard it before, from a thousand bloggers and roundtable know-it-alls: We were too slow to adapt, too complacent, too yoked to our tried-and-true editorial traditions and formulas. We could have saved ourselves, goes the refrain, if only we had been more creative and aggressive and less risk averse.

To which I can only reply: Oh, please.

As newspapers shuffle toward the twilight, I'm increasingly convinced that the news has been the least of the newspaper industry's problems. Newspapers are in trouble for reasons that have almost nothing to do with newspaper journalism, and everything to do with the newspaper business. Even a paper stocked with the world's finest editorial minds wouldn't have a fighting chance against the economic and technological forces arrayed against the business. The critics have it exactly backward: Journalists and journalism are the victims, not the cause, of the industry's shaken state.

We've lost readers, to be sure. But that's been happening for decades, and not necessarily because of editorial quality. Disagree? Then try answering this: Did editorial quality kill afternoon newspapers?

Contemporary newspapers have their own problems, but the usual analysis about what ails us misses the point. Let's take a quick tour:

Fact No. 1

Despite everything you've heard, newspapers, even these days, remain remarkably popular. Some readers have left us (and many, it should be said, were dropped by cost-conscious publishers who no longer wanted to deliver papers to far-flung subscribers). But what's largely overlooked in the gloom is how many people newspapers reach each day. Almost 50 million buy one daily, and nearly 117 million read one, according to the Newspaper Association of America's research. Throw in 66 million unique visitors to newspaper websites each month, and the conclusion is inescapable: Lots of people want what newspaper journalists produce.

Fact No. 2

Newspaper readers—so often derided as old and unattractive to advertisers—are actually better educated and more affluent than TV news viewers. The average newspaper, for example, reaches about seven in 10 households with incomes of more than $60,000 annually, compared with about four in 10 for CNN and Fox News, according to Mediamark Research.

Fact No. 3

Every traditional news medium has lost market share, and some have lost more than newspapers. According to the Project for Excellence in Journalism, ratings for late local newscasts on network-affiliated stations across the country were 6.7 percent lower during the November 2007 sweeps than the previous year—a faster decline than newspaper circulation (down 2.6 percent daily, 3.5 percent on Sunday) during roughly the same period. This isn't a one-time aberration, either. Local TV stations in Washington, D.C., for example, have seen the ratings for their 6 p.m. newscasts plunge 37 percent from 1997 to 2007. Over the same period, the Washington Post's Sunday circulation has dropped 16 percent. Yet the local TV news business remains relatively strong, with far fewer layoffs and cutbacks and less end-of-an-era weariness than in most print newsrooms.

So if the problem with newspapers really isn't too few customers, or too many undesirable ones, why are they so threatened these days?

The problem has little to do with the reporting, packaging and selling of information. It's much bigger than that. The gravest threats include the flight of classified advertisers, the deterioration of retail advertising and the indebtedness of newspaper owners. Wrap all these factors together and you've set in motion the kind of slash-and-burn tactics that will hasten, not forestall, the end.

For decades, newspapers enjoyed what economists call a "scarcity" advantage. In most cities, there was only one outfit that could profitably collect, print and distribute the day's news, and it could raise prices even as it delivered fewer readers each year. Indeed, monopoly daily newspapers enjoyed enormous profit margins—sometimes as much as 25 percent or more—until very recently. But the scarcity advantage has faded; the Internet has essentially handed a free printing press and a distribution network to anyone with a computer.

The real revelation of the Internet is not what it has done to newspaper readership—it has in fact expanded it—but how it has sapped newspapers' economic lifeblood.

The real revelation of the Internet is not what it has done to newspaper readership—it has in fact expanded it—but how it has sapped newspapers' economic lifeblood. The most serious erosion has occurred in classified advertising, which once made up more than 40 percent of a newspaper's revenues and more than half its profits. Classified advertisers didn't desert newspapers because they disliked our political coverage or our sports sections, but because they had alternatives. Craigslist and eBay and dozens of other low-cost and no-cost classified sites began gobbling newspapers' market share a few years ago. What they didn't wipe out, the tanking economy did. During the first half of 2008, print classified advertising nosedived more than 25 percent, as withering job, real-estate and auto listings erased $1.8 billion in revenue from newspaper companies' books. Newspapers have been uniquely hurt—television never had classifieds to lose.

Similarly, the disappearance of local chain stores over the past two decades has fallen like a series of hammer blows on newspapers. In my city, the names of the dearly departed included such homegrown advertisers as Hechinger hardware stores, Trak Auto Parts, Crown Books, Dart Drug, Peoples Drug, Raleigh's clothing stores and the department stores Woodward & Lothrop, Garfinckel's and Hecht's. TV lost some of these advertisers, too, but has gained the likes of Wal-Mart and other big-box outlets, which tend to buy airtime, not newspaper space.

Newspapers that were hoping to be rescued by their online ad businesses woke up to a sobering reality in mid-2007. By then, it was becoming clear that online advertising wasn't growing fast enough to make up for the rapid disappearance of print ads (see "Online Salvation?" December 2007/January 2008). In fact, at the moment, online ads aren't growing at all. Sales at newspaper websites fell 2.4 percent in the second quarter of 2008. This may be as ominous a development as the meltdown of print. Online newspaper revenues had grown smartly in every quarter since the Newspaper Association of America began tracking them in 2003. No longer.

There's still much that many newspapers can do to improve their websites: adding Twitter feeds, social networking applications, Google map mashups (maps over-laid with data), on-demand mobile information and, of course, more video. All good. But let's not kid ourselves. The online business model is still uncertain, at best. An online visitor isn't as valuable to advertisers as a print customer. Online readers tend to dart in and out, spending far less time on a newspaper site than a subscriber spends with a paper. And a portion of the traffic (how much depends on the paper) comes from outside the paper's circulation area, making these visitors irrelevant to local advertisers. I'm not really surprised that newspapers haven't figured out how to make the Web pay for all the things that print traditionally has. There may not even be a business model for it. But again: Can you really blame the newsroom for that?

Newspapers that were hoping to be rescued by their online ad businesses woke up to a sobering reality in mid-2007.

The last wound is self-inflicted. Newspaper companies and other investors completed highly leveraged takeover deals just as the newspaper business rolled off the table. It's no coincidence that the most troubled newspapers are the ones owned by companies that took on enormous IOUs just as the newspaper apocalypse began. Some of these companies—Tribune, McClatchy, Journal Register, MediaNews Group, Avista Capital Partners, GateHouse Media—are now cutting like mad to stay ahead of the debt boulder bearing down on them. Meanwhile, Copley, Advance, Cox, Landmark and Blethen have all put some of their newspaper holdings up for sale. This all but guarantees more debt for the papers' new owners—assuming, of course, that the sellers can find buyers in the first place.

So add it up. Could smarter reporting, editing and photojournalism have made a difference? Can a spiffy new website or paper redesign win the hearts of readers? Surely, they can't hurt. But if we, and our critics, were realistic, we'd admit that much is beyond our control, and that insisting otherwise is vain. As British media scholar and author Adrian Monck put it in an essay about the industry's troubles earlier this year: "The crops did not fail because we offended the gods."

As is, I fear we're deep into the self-fulfilling prophecy stage now. In many ways, newspapers are dying . . . because they're dying. As their cash flow shrivels, owners aren't willing, or able, to invest in their papers to arrest the rate of decline, if not reverse it. Each cut in editorial staffing and newshole makes the newspaper less useful and attractive, which makes the next round of cuts inevitable, and so on. Some newspapers entered their death spiral months ago.

I suspect someday our former readers will be peering forlornly toward their empty doorsteps and driveways and wondering where the paper they once loved has gone. I will share their sadness, but not their shock. I've got some news for you, dear readers: Our disappearance wasn't your fault. And as a journalist, I can safely say, it wasn't ours, either.

PAUL FARHI (farhip@washpost.com), a Washington Post reporter, writes frequently about the media for the Post and AJR.

Climate Change: Now What?

**Scientists agree it's real, but there's no consensus on solutions.
Readers need a guide to the options.**

Cristine Russell

Media coverage of climate change is at a crossroads, as it moves beyond the science of global warming into the broader arena of what governments, entrepreneurs, and ordinary citizens are doing about it. Consider these recent examples: a decade from now, Abu Dhabi hopes to have the first city in the world with zero carbon emissions. In a windswept stretch of desert, developers plan to build Masdar City, a livable environment for fifty thousand people that relies entirely on solar power and other renewable energy. Science correspondent Joe Palca reported from Masdar's construction site as part of National Public Radio's yearlong project "Climate Connections."

The *Christian Science Monitor*'s Peter N. Spotts went to the Biesbosch, a small inland delta near the Netherlands' city of Dordrecht, to research "How to Fight a Rising Sea." In an effort that could be instructive for others, the Dutch are developing ways to protect their small country's vulnerable coast against rising sea levels that could result from climate change.

Wang Suya lives in Japan but sends a YouTube greeting to fellow visitors at Dot Earth, the innovative blog started by Andrew C. Revkin, the *New York Times* environment reporter. Having traveled the globe to cover global warming, Revkin now posts and exchanges ideas on Dot Earth about climate and sustainability issues, particularly the energy, food, and water demands on a planet that may house nine billion people by mid-century.

These reporters are in the advance guard of an army of journalists around the world who are covering what *Time* magazine has dubbed the "War on Global Warming." Journalists will play a key role in shaping the information that opinion leaders and the public use to judge the urgency of climate change, what needs to be done about it, when and at what costs. It is a vast, multifaceted story whose complexity does not fit well with journalism's tendency to shy away from issues with high levels of uncertainty and a time-frame of decades, rather than days or months.

In 2009, climate-change coverage will grow in significance on a number of domestic and international fronts:

In science, the impact of global warming will be followed closely at the two poles as well as Pacific island hot spots, like the low-lying islands of Papua New Guinea, that are in the greatest danger.

In politics, after eight years of relative inaction by the Bush administration, the new U.S. president and Congress will be under pressure to pass legislation to curb emissions of greenhouse gases.

Internationally, the United Nations has scheduled key conferences—in Poznan, Poland, in December 2008 and in Copenhagen in December 2009—to hammer out a new international treaty that is practically and politically feasible. Shortages and high prices are bringing the role of biofuels in the global food crisis under added scrutiny.

Meanwhile, the efforts of countries, businesses, communities, and even individuals to reduce their "carbon footprints" will increasingly be examined.

Climate change will require thoughtful leadership and coordination at news organizations. Editors will need to integrate the specialty environment, energy, and science reporters with other beats that have a piece of the story—everything from local and national politics to foreign affairs, business, technology, health, urban affairs, agriculture, transportation, law, architecture, religion, consumer news, gardening, travel, and sports. "News organizations are increasingly asking what other beats are going to be affected by climate," says veteran environment reporter Bud Ward, who edits a respected online journalism site, The Yale Forum on Climate Change & The Media. He notes that even *Sports Illustrated* has tackled climate change and its potential impact on everything from cancelled games to baseball bats. But, Ward worries, "it will be extremely difficult to explain the policy side of the debate" in the months ahead. Unless editors push hard for it, "there's generally not the time or space for that kind of explanatory coverage."

To that end, Ward has organized media workshops on global warming for top editors as well as reporters. A daylong meeting last fall at Stanford University attracted heavy hitters like Washington Post executive editor Leonard Downie Jr. and top editors from *The New York Times,* the *Los Angeles Times,* and metropolitan papers from Detroit to Des Moines. Eighteen news executives spent the morning with leading scientists, who emphasized the strong agreement among international experts that the earth is warming and that man-made greenhouse gas emissions are largely to blame. The UN Intergovernmental Panel on Climate Change (IPCC) last year issued a widely publicized report (in four parts) that provided the most comprehensive scientific agreement to date on the causes and potentially devastating impact of global warming. Yet, recalls Stephen H. Schneider, a Stanford climatologist, "several editors were surprised there was so much consensus."

In the afternoon session, the consensus dissipated when it came to a discussion of the potential economic impact of climate actions. One expert saw climate change as a profitable business opportunity; another warned that solutions would be difficult and costly: "There are no silver bullets . . . only silver birdshot." Ward says that one editor later commented: "It looks like economists are going to need their own IPCC."

Daniel P. Schrag, a climate geologist who directs the Harvard University Center for the Environment, says, "We're in a transition in which the climate science is no longer the primary issue. More and more it's about how we stop it, not whether it is happening."

And Matthew C. Nisbet, an American University communications professor, says, "We have had more science coverage on climate change than at any time in history. The next challenge is to find ways to cover the story across news beats and in ways that engage new readers."

Here are some thoughts as to how coverage might be sharpened in the year ahead in the broad areas of science, politics, and business.

Science and Technology

The ongoing science story. After several years of stumbling, mainstream science and environmental coverage has generally adopted the scientific consensus that increases in heat-trapping emissions from burning fossil fuels and tropical deforestation are changing the planet's climate, causing adverse effects even more rapidly than had once been predicted.

The process of science often involves studies that contradict one another along the way. . . . Journalists should avoid 'yo-yo' coverage with each new study and try to put the latest findings in context.

But the devil is in the details. New findings on why, where, how fast, and with what impact climate change might occur will take time to assess, and there is a danger that the subtleties of the science, and its uncertainty, might be missed by reporters unfamiliar with the territory. The process of science often involves studies that contradict one another along the way; scientists look for consistency among several reports before concluding that something is true. Journalists should avoid "yo-yo" coverage with each new study and try to put the latest findings in context.

Scientists are debating, for example, how global warming may affect hurricanes, with an "ongoing tempest among meteorologists and climatologists spouting off at one another on whether hurricane activity in the Atlantic is up due to a warming ocean," noted Charles Petit in the MIT Knight Science Journalism Tracker. He cited a recent computer simulation of late twenty-first-century hurricane patterns by National Oceanic and Atmospheric Administration scientists that predicted *fewer* tropical storms and hurricanes in the Atlantic. Experienced journalists reported the findings cautiously, noting that some studies have suggested *more* and *more powerful* hurricanes due to global warming. Jim Loney, a Reuters reporter, concluded his story with a scientist's caveat: "We don't regard this as the last word on this topic."

You can't see climate change out the window. "Weather is what you get; climate is what you expect," says Stanford's Schneider. "Weather is the day-to-day fluctuations; climate is the long-term averages, the patterns and probability of extremes." The basic difference is time: weather equals short-term, climate the long haul. Ward uses a clothes analogy—weather helps us decide what to wear each day; climate influences the wardrobe we buy.

"The earth is getting hotter," says John P. Holdren, a Harvard scientist and international climate-policy leader who has addressed the UN—and been on the *Late Show with David Letterman*. He cites climate patterns showing that twenty-three out of twenty-four of the hottest years on record have occurred since 1980. The thirteen hottest all have occurred since 1990, with 2005 the hottest ever recorded. But "the heating is not uniform geographically," cautioned Holdren, who uses the term "global climate disruption" because some regions may experience more extreme—and less predictable—environmental changes than others.

This message was echoed in a landmark Agriculture Department report, released in late May and signed by three Cabinet secretaries, that Juliet Eilperin, the national environment and politics reporter for *The Washington Post,* called the "most detailed look in nearly eight years at how climate change is reshaping the American landscape." It concluded that the West is already vulnerable to forest fires, reduced snow pack, and drought.

It is a good rule of thumb to avoid attributing any specific weather event directly to climate change. A single summer heat wave may or may not be part of a long-term climate trend. A cold winter in New England does not mean that global warming is not happening.

Environmental forces may also interact in ways that can be hard to explain. German researchers, writing recently in *Nature,* used a new climate model to suggest that natural variation in ocean circulation might "temporarily offset" temperature increases from human-caused global warming in Europe and North America over the next decade. Some misleading media reports turned the preliminary forecast into a definitive statement that, as a British *Telegraph* reporter put it, "global warming will stop until at least 2015."

Watch out for techno-optimism. Proponents of new energy technologies often hype the potential benefits—without knowing the effectiveness, cost, time frame (always longer than expected), risks, or potential impact on the larger energy picture. It's a reporter's duty to explain the potential downside as well as conflicts of interests.

Renewable energy sources, such as solar, wind, and geothermal, have garnered enthusiastic publicity. But it will take time for them to make a dent in the overall U.S. energy marketplace because of higher costs, lower scale, and public opposition to sitings of wind farms and solar grids. Nuclear power is popular in France but still largely radioactive in the American public's mind. Another area for further media follow-up is the touted technology for carbon capture and storage at coal-burning power plants, which has stalled in the U.S. because of political squabbling and unexpected cost overruns.

In a related vein, beware the law of unintended consequences. The biofuel ethanol was ballyhooed as a big win for U.S. energy security, farmers, and the environment, but a funny thing happened on the way to the fuel tank. A February 2008 study in *Science* magazine concluded that producing ethanol from corn may exceed or match the greenhouse gas emissions from fossil fuels.

More recently, of course, ethanol has been blamed for contributing to the world food crisis, since farm acreage previously used for food is now devoted to lucrative fuel-producing corn. Suddenly many elected officials want to cut back on congressional mandates to produce far more ethanol. Once again, the public is left wondering what happened. An excellent April 30 front-page piece from Charles City, Iowa, by *Washington Post* energy reporter Steven Mufson, explored the links between "food and fuel prices." But where were the skeptical scientists, politicians, and journalists earlier, when ethanol was first being promoted in Congress?

Choose your experts carefully. Experts are always a minefield, so the *Times*'s Revkin has a simple rule: when writing about climate science, seek comments from respected scientific experts who have published in major journals in the field, not the experts offered by various policy think tanks and interest groups with axes to grind.

The era of "equal time" for skeptics who argue that global warming is just a result of natural variation and not human intervention seems to be largely over—except on talk radio, cable, and local television. Last year, a meteorologist at CBS's Chicago station did a special report entitled "The Truth about Global Warming." It featured local scientists discussing the hazards of global warming in one segment, well-known national skeptics in another, and ended with a cop-out: "What is the truth about global warming? . . . It depends on who you talk to." Not helpful, and not good reporting.

As the climate issue moves further into public policy, journalists will need to sort out the political and economic interests of experts with a dizzying array of opinions about costs and benefits.

As the climate issue moves further into public policy, journalists will face new challenges in sorting out the political and economic interests of experts with a dizzying array of opinions

about the costs and benefits of combating global warming. The he-said, she-said reporting just won't do. The public needs a guide to the policy, not just the politics.

Politics and Policy

After the horse race. A Gallup election poll in early February about what issues would influence Americans' votes put the economy, Iraq, education, health care, and gas prices in the top five considered "extremely or very important." Environment and global warming weighed in at number thirteen.

Politicians pay attention to public opinion, of course. In the 2008 presidential race, Obama and McCain both favor mandatory caps to reduce greenhouse gas emissions—though McCain's plan is not as strict on this—and both candidates push nuclear power, though McCain pushes it more aggressively and with fewer caveats.

In Congress, a groundbreaking cap-and-trade "climate security" bill to reduce key greenhouse gas emissions by about 70 percent by 2050 came to the Senate floor for the first time in June. GOP critics argued that it would raise energy costs further, and the bill was blocked. The debate foreshadowed the difficulties such measures may face in the next Congress.

Think China. Estimates suggest China has passed the U.S. for the dubious distinction as the world's leader in total greenhouse gas emissions. Its rising emissions are fueled by coal-burning power plants—on average, about one new one fires up each week—to meet the energy demands of a growing middle class. But the Pew Center on Global Climate Change said that, on a per-capita basis, U.S. carbon emissions are still about five times greater than those of China, whose enormous 1.3 billion population dwarfs America's three-hundred million.

Neither the U.S. nor China has agreed to international restrictions on greenhouse gas emissions. While the conventional wisdom is that China will wait for the U.S. to act first, a recent opinion piece in the *San Francisco Chronicle* predicted that "China just might surprise the U.S. on climate change" because of growing domestic concerns about pollution, droughts, flooding, and other environmental hazards. The University of California authors predicted that China could also take the lead in the development of clean-energy technology—a good area for journalists to track, in addition to coal and cars.

Business and Commerce

Costs and benefits. Evaluating economic forecasts is even tougher than evaluating the science and precipitates fierce debate. A seven-hundred-page report for the British government in 2006 by economist Nicholas Stern said the costs of enacting global measures to reduce greenhouse gas emissions could amount to about 1 percent of world economic output annually. But not doing so, he said, might ultimately lead to a massive global "market failure," ranging from five to more than twenty times that amount. It drew international coverage for its methods and both praise and criticism from fellow economists. Yale economist William D. Nordhaus's new book concludes that the

Stern approach is too "ambitious" in requiring "extreme immediate action" and is therefore not cost-effective. He favors global carbon taxes that ramp up more gradually.

Many players are weighing in on the how-to-fix-it political issue. A May Reuters story, that ran before the Senate floor debate on cap-and-trade legislation, cited environmental groups as saying "the cost of doing nothing would be far higher" than taking action, while *Washington Post* columnist George Will called the bill a "radical government grab for control of the American economy." A *New York Times* editorial noted that despite Bush administration contentions that "mandatory cuts in carbon dioxide would bankrupt the country," every "serious study" has found that a market-based program "could yield positive economic gains" and that the "costs of inaction will dwarf the costs of acting now."

Times science writer Cornelia Dean wrote last year about the Interface Corporation, a Georgia carpet tile manufacturer that went on a full-court sustainability press by cutting waste, recycling, lowering energy use, and reducing greenhouse gas emissions—and saved money in doing so. "We have made the point in everybody's mind that the cost of reducing carbon emissions will be painful," Dean noted. But "it can also work to your advantage."

Track "green" promises. In the absence of federal action, more than 850 mayors have signed the U.S. Conference of Mayors Climate Protection Agreement to reduce local carbon emissions by using goals set by signatories to the international Kyoto Protocol. States like California and regional efforts in New England have also led in climate-change initiatives. Some corporations, too, have set ambitious goals for reducing their carbon footprints. Reporters need to hold private and public enterprises accountable by analyzing and comparing how well all of these bodies are doing in carrying out their bold promises.

In the meantime, there's a great risk of green fatigue in the media. The number of articles in U.S. newspapers mentioning "going green" in the first quarter of 2008 was about twelve times greater than the comparable period in 2005, according to LexisNexis. Worse, it is also the darling of the advertising business, and the mixing of news and commercial messages is starting to give the phrase a sour green-apple taste.

Still, the trend does give reporters an opportunity to expose examples of "green-washing" that promise eco-friendliness but don't deliver.

A s climate change encompasses virtually all aspects of contemporary life, reporters need to tell the story on their watch. A number of websites provide helpful information (see the list posted with this story on CJR.org). In the meantime, here is a starter set of possible stories for reporters to consider and readers to request:

In the realm of science, what is the stability of ice sheets in Greenland and West Antarctica, and how will this affect rising sea-level estimates? What plants and animals are at most risk of extinction, and what can be done about that?

What about adaptation to climate change, both here and abroad? Regardless of new control efforts, greenhouse gas emissions already in the pipeline will continue to have warming-related impacts for decades to come. How will Americans cope with changing conditions?

In land use and transportation, what efforts are under way to push auto makers to improve gas mileage? What can drivers do today? Hint: it's not just what you drive, it's how often and how far (eco-driving anyone?). How does air travel compare? How can city planners encourage compact living to reduce a community's carbon footprint? What else can consumers do?

In technology, what are the R&D prospects for biofuel alternatives like cellulosic ethanol, made from grass, wood chips, and other inedible plants? What about futuristic ideas like genetically engineered carbon-eating trees?

In policy, what lessons does the European Union's experience have for the U.S. about possible carbon cap-and-trade schemes? How are the world's countries doing at meeting their Kyoto Protocol targets, which expire in 2012, and how do they compare to the U.S.?

In economics, what can be done to make tough emission caps in the U.S. more cost-efficient? How can developing countries balance economic growth and better living conditions against rising greenhouse gases?

Internationally, what is being done to slow deforestation in the tropics, from Indonesia to the Amazon, which is estimated to cause almost one-fifth of human-induced global carbon emissions? What about population growth and the increasing number of environmental refugees forced to flee because of flooding, drought, or other problems? How will global health be affected by climate change?

How will climate negotiations affect the geopolitics of energy, and what does "energy security" really mean?

There are countless such questions for reporters to tackle on a story that is only going to get bigger and more complicated in the decades (yes, decades) ahead.

And there is some urgency. Despite increased coverage of climate change, it is still not at the top of the media or public priority list. "If you don't have climate change as a headline in the press," says Nisbet, who writes the blog Framing Science, "it's unlikely to be a top-tier issue in the public or among policy makers." A 2007 ranking by the Project for Excellence in Journalism found that among all media, environmental coverage ranked nineteenth, at 1.7 percent of the newshole—just behind sports and celebrity coverage.

There is some urgency. A Gallup report last year found that just one in four Americans believes there will be extreme effects from global warming in fifty years without immediate, drastic action.

A Gallup report last November found that only about four in ten Americans believes that immediate, drastic action is needed to deal with global warming, and just one in four says there will be "extreme" effects of global warming in fifty years if efforts are not increased. Is this a failure of the experts and politicians to communicate the situation or a failure of journalists to dig and report?

Yet journalists should not be cheerleaders. As climate change moves further into the policy and political arena, the traditional wall between analytical reporting and advocacy is in danger. The issue is coming to the fore at a time of major change in mainstream journalism and the growth of opinionated websites and blogs that have helped to blur the old lines.

Nisbet, for one, sees a dramatic shift in media rhetoric on climate change. In the spring of 2006, fear was at the heart of Al Gore's documentary film, *An Inconvenient Truth,* which jump-started media coverage of global warming after years on the back burner. Suddenly, climate change—that term is gaining ground over global warming, by the way—was on front pages and magazine covers, including *Time*'s iconic image of a lone polar bear and the warning, "Be Worried. Be Very Worried."

Today, says Nisbet, "the underlying appeal is a moral message: 'We're all in this together.' It's a moral call to arms." Gore's new $300-million "We" media campaign seeks to cross the partisan divide with the optimistic motto: "We Can Solve It." The cover of *Time*'s Spring 2008 environment issue, bordered in green instead of *Time*'s customary red, took the famous World War II photo of Marines raising a U.S. flag on Iwo Jima and substituted a tree to illustrate its bold headline: "How to Win the War on Global Warming."

Did *Time* cross the line into environmental cheerleading? It would seem so, perhaps reflecting the magazine's more general shift into opinion and away from pure news. Managing editor Richard Stengel called the cover story "our call to arms to make this challenge—perhaps the most important one facing the planet—a true national priority."

Others are feeling their way more carefully. "Sure, I care about the environment," says Steve Curwood, host of "Living on Earth," a weekly environmental show on more than three hundred public radio stations. "But it's not our job to decide what should be done. It's our job to inform the citizenry. Right now we have an alarmed citizenry, but still not a very well-informed one," he said at a recent journalism forum.

"We don't set policy, we tell stories," says David Ledford, executive editor of *The News Journal* in Wilmington, Delaware, and president of The Associated Press Managing Editors. "But it's important to not just throw out that the earth is on fire without giving a sense of what they can do."

"It's very simple. The job of a professional journalist is to give the audience information that is a good thing for them to know," says seasoned ABC News correspondent Bill Blakemore, who has led the network's new multiplatform approach to global warming. Yet he finds that the momentous nature of the climate-change story carries even more of a responsibility and psychological burden than the dozen wars he has covered. "The unprecedented nature of this story," says Blakemore, "is quite grave."

CRISTINE RUSSELL is a freelance science journalist, president of the Council for the Advancement of Science Writing and a senior fellow at Harvard's Belfer Center for Science and International Affairs. She is a former Shorenstein Center fellow and *Washington Post* reporter, and writes regularly for *The Observatory,* the science desk on CJR.org.

Whatever Happened to Iraq?

How the Media Lost Interest in a Long-Running War with No End in Sight

SHERRY RICCHIARDI

Armando Acuna, public editor of the Sacramento Bee, turned a Sunday column into a public flogging for both his editors and the nation's news media. They had allowed the third-longest war in American history to slip off the radar screen, and he had the numbers to prove it.

The public also got a scolding for its meager interest in a controversial conflict that is costing taxpayers about $12.5 billion a month, or nearly $5,000 a second, according to some calculations. In his March 30 commentary, Acuna noted: "There's enough shame . . . for everyone to share."

He had watched stories about Iraq move from 1A to the inside pages of his newspaper, if they ran at all. He understood the editors' frustration over how to handle the mind-numbing cycles of violence and complex issues surrounding Operation Iraqi Freedom. "People feel powerless about this war," he said in an interview in April.

Acuna knew the Sacramento Bee was not alone.

For long stretches over the past 12 months, Iraq virtually disappeared from the front pages of the nation's newspapers and from the nightly network newscasts. The American press and the American people had lost interest in the war.

The decline in coverage of Iraq has been staggering. During the first 10 weeks of 2007, Iraq accounted for 23 percent of the newshole for network TV news. In 2008, it plummeted to 3 percent during that period. On cable networks it fell from 24 percent to 1 percent, according to a study by the Project for Excellence in Journalism.

The numbers also were dismal for the country's dailies. By Acuna's count, during the first three months of this year, front-page stories about Iraq in the Bee were down 70 percent from the same time last year. Articles about Iraq once topped the list for reader feedback. By mid-2007, "Their interest just dropped off; it was noticeable to me," says the public editor.

A daily tracking of 65 newspapers by the Associated Press confirms a dip in page-one play throughout the country. In September 2007, the AP found 457 Iraq-related stories (154 by the AP) on front pages, many related to a progress report delivered to Congress by Gen. David Petraeus, the top U.S. commander in Iraq. Over the succeeding months, that number fell to as low as 49. A spike in March 2008 was largely due to a rash of stories keyed to the conflict's fifth anniversary, according to AP Senior Managing Editor Mike Silverman.

During the early stages of shock and awe, Americans were glued to the news as Saddam Hussein's statue was toppled in Baghdad and sweat-soaked Marines bivouacked in his luxurious palaces. It was a huge story when President Bush landed on the aircraft carrier USS Abraham Lincoln on May 1, 2003, and declared major combat operations were over.

By March 2008, a striking reversal had taken place. Only 28 percent of Americans knew that 4,000 military personnel had been killed in the conflict, according to a survey by the Pew Research Center for the People & the Press. Eight months earlier, 54 percent could cite the correct casualty rate.

TV news was a vivid indicator of the declining interest. The three broadcast networks' nightly newscasts devoted more than 4,100 minutes to Iraq in 2003 and 3,000 in 2004. That leveled off to 2,000 annually. By late 2007, it was half that, according to Andrew Tyndall, who monitors the nightly news (tyndall report.com).

In broadcast, there's a sense that the appetite for Iraq coverage has grown thin.

"In broadcast, there's a sense that the appetite for Iraq coverage has grown thin. The big issue is how many people stick with it. It is not less of a story," said Jeffrey Fager, executive producer of "60 Minutes," during the Reva and David Logan Symposium on Investigative Reporting in late April at the Graduate School of Journalism at the University of California, Berkeley. The number of Iraq-related stories aired on "60 Minutes" has been consistent over the past two years. The total from April 2007 through March 2008 was 15, one fewer than during the same period the year before.

Despite the pile of evidence of waning coverage, news managers interviewed for this story consistently maintained there was no conscious decision to back off. "I wasn't hearing that in our newsroom," says Margaret Sullivan, editor of the Buffalo News. Yet numbers show that attention to the war plummeted at the Buffalo paper as it did at other news outlets.

Why the dramatic drop-off? Gatekeepers offer a variety of reasons, from the enormous danger for journalists on the ground in

Iraq (see "Obstructed View," April/May 2007) to plunging newsroom budgets and shrinking news space. Competing megastories on the home front like the presidential primaries and the sagging economy figure into the equation. So does the exorbitant cost of keeping correspondents in Baghdad.

No one questioned the importance of a grueling war gone sour or the looming consequences for the United States and the Middle East. Instead, newsroom managers talked about the realities of life in a rapidly changing media market, including smaller newsholes and, for many, a laser-beam focus on local issues and events.

Los Angeles Times' foreign editor Marjorie Miller attributes the decline to three factors:

The economic downturn and the contentious presidential primaries have sucked oxygen from Iraq. "We have a woman, an African American and a senior running for president," Miller says. "That is a very big story."

With no solutions in sight, with no light at the end of the tunnel, war fatigue has become a factor. Over the years, a bleak sameness has settled into accounts of suicide bombings and brutal sectarian violence. Insurgents fighting counterinsurgents are hard to translate to an American audience.

The sheer cost of keeping correspondents on the ground in Baghdad is trimming the roster of journalists. The expense is "unlike anything we've ever faced. We have shouldered the financial burden so far, but we are really squeezed," Miller says. Earlier, the L.A. Times had as many as five Western correspondents in the field. The bureau is down to two or three plus Iraqi staff.

Other media decision-makers echo Miller's analysis.

When Lara Logan, the high-profile chief senior foreign correspondent for CBS News, is rotated out of Iraq, she might not be replaced, says her boss, Senior Vice President Paul Friedman. The network is sending in fewer Westerners from European and American bureaus and depending more on local staff, a common practice for media outlets with personnel in Iraq. "We won't pull out, but we are making adjustments," Friedman says.

Friedman defends the cutbacks: "One of the definitions of news is change, and there are long periods now in Iraq when very little changes. Therefore, it's difficult for the Iraq story to fight its way on the air against other news where change is involved," such as the political campaign, he says.

John Stack, Fox News Channel's vice president for newsgathering, has no qualms about allotting more airtime to the presidential campaign than to Iraq. "This is a very big story playing out on the screen every night . . . . The time devoted to news is finite," Stack says. "It's a matter of shifting to another story of national interest."

Despite diminished emphasis on the war, Fox has no plans to cut back its Baghdad operation. "We still have a full complement of people there, operating in a very difficult environment. That hasn't gone down at all," he says. Fox has two full reporting teams in Iraq as well as a bureau chief and some local staff, for a total of 25 to 30 people, according to Stack.

In late 2007, the networks—CBS, NBC, ABC, CNN and Fox—entertained the notion of pooling resources in Iraq to cut expenses. After much discussion, the idea was tabled. "It turned out not to be possible," Friedman says. "To some extent, our needs are very different." Cable TV is all about constant repetition; even during lulls it features correspondents standing in front of cameras making reports. "The networks don't do that and don't need the same kind of facilities," Friedman says.

McClatchy Newspapers maintains a presence in Baghdad—a bureau chief, a rotating staffer generally from one of the chain's papers and six local staffers—but the decline in violence since the U.S. troop buildup last year has resulted in fewer daily stories, says Foreign Editor Roy Gutman. "We produce according to the news. During the [Iraqi] government's offensive in Basra [in March], we produced lengthy stories every day." To add another dimension to the coverage, McClatchy tapped into its Iraqi staff for compelling first-person accounts posted on its Washington bureau's website (mcclatchydc.com—see "A Blog of Heartbreak," April/May 2007).

New York Times Foreign Editor Susan Chira says she is content to run fewer stories than in the past. "But we want them to have impact. And, of course, when there are big running stories, we will stay on them every day."

Midsize dailies around the country face a different set of challenges. Many operate under mandates from their bosses to push local stories over national or international news in hope of boosting readership and advertising. In those publications, it often takes a strong community tie to propel Iraq onto page one.

Case in point: During the first week of February, the one story about Iraq that made 1A in the Buffalo News was headlined, "Close to home while far off at war." It told how the latest gadgetry helps local service members stay in touch with loved ones. During the same week a year ago, four Iraq-related stories made 1A. None appeared to have a local angle.

"There is strong local interest because we have a lot of service members over there and we have had quite a few deaths of local soldiers," Editor Sullivan says. "In my mind, there is no bigger nonlocal story. It's the expense, the lives, the policy issues, and what it means to the country's future. There is a general feeling that the media have tired of Iraq, but I have not."

At Alabama's Birmingham News, it takes a significant development to get an Iraq-related story prominent play without a local link, says Executive Editor Hunter George. During the first week in February, the Birmingham paper ran only one story related to the war. The topic: "Brownies send goodies, cards to troops in. Iraq."

Editors did not sit in a news budget meeting and make a conscious decision to cut back on Iraq coverage, George says. He believes the repetitiveness of the storyline has something to do with the decline. "I see and hear it all the time. It seems like a bad dream, and the public's not interested in revisiting it unless there is a major development. If I'm outside the newsroom and Iraq comes up, I hear groans. People say, 'More bad news,' Stories about the economy are moving up the news scale."

It was big news for Pennsylvania's Reading Eagle when a wounded soldier came home from Iraq and was met by some 50 bikers at the airport. The "Patriot Guard," as they are called, provided an escort. Townspeople slapped together a carnival to help raise money for a wheelchair ramp. "For us, it comes down to the grassroots level," says Eagle reporter Dan Kelly.

Earlier that day, Kelly's editor had handed him an assignment about a Marine from nearby Exeter Township who rushed home from the war zone to visit his ailing grandfather. By the time he got there, he was facing a funeral instead. "We look for special circumstances like this," Kelly says. "We pick our battles."

The Indianapolis Star ramped up coverage in January when the 76th Infantry Brigade Combat Team from the Indiana National Guard was redeployed to Iraq. The newspaper created a special Web page to help readers stay in touch with the more than 3,000 soldiers from around the state, including graphics showing their hometowns and how the combat gear they wear works in the war zone.

"I don't want to mislead you and say our coverage has been consistent over the past 12 months. It has rolled and dipped. We have had calls from people who believe we underplay events like bombings where several people are killed," says Pam Fine, the *Star*'s managing editor until early April. Front-page coverage of Iraq was the same in the first three months of 2007 and 2008. A total of 23 stories ran in each period. Fine left the paper to become the Knight Chair in News, Leadership and Community at the University of Kansas.

The reader representative for the San Francisco Chronicle doesn't think placement of stories about Iraq makes much difference. He reasons that five years in, most readers have formed clear opinions about the war. They're not likely to change their minds one way or another if a story runs on page one or page three, says Dick Rogers. "The public has become accustomed to the steady drumbeat of violence out of Iraq. A report of 20 or 30 killed doesn't bring fresh insight for a lot of people."

Americans might care if they could witness more of the human toll. That's the approach the Washington Post's Dana Milbank took in an April 24 piece titled, "What the Family Would Let You See, the Pentagon Obstructs."

When Lt. Col. Billy Hall was buried in Arlington National Cemetery in April, his family gave the media permission to cover the ceremony—he is among the highest-ranking officers to be killed in Iraq. But, according to Milbank, the military did everything it could to keep the journalists away, isolating them some 50 yards away behind a yellow rope.

The "de facto ban on media at Arlington funerals fits neatly" with White House efforts "to sanitize the war in Iraq," and that, in turn, has helped keep the bloodshed out of the public's mind, Milbank wrote in his Washington Sketch feature. There have been similar complaints over the years about the administration's policy that bans on-base photography of coffins returning from Iraq and Afghanistan. (See Drop Cap, June/July 2004.)

D espite the litany of reasons, some journalists still take a "shame on you" attitude toward those who have relegated the Iraq war to second-class status.

Sig Christenson, military writer for the San Antonio Express-News, has made five trips to the war zone and says he would go back in a heartbeat. "This is not a story we can afford to ignore," he says. "There are vast implications for every American, right down to how much gasoline costs when we go to the pump."

Christenson, a cofounder of the organization MRE—Military Reporters and Editors—believes the media have an obligation to provide context and nuance and make clear the complexities of the war so Americans better understand its seriousness. "That's our job," he says.

Along the same lines, Greg Mitchell, editor of Editor & Publisher, faults newsroom leaders for shortchanging "the biggest political and moral issue of our time."

"You can forgive the American public for being shocked at the recent violence in Basra [in March]. From the lack of press coverage that's out there, they probably thought the war was over," says Mitchell, who wrote about media performance in the book "So Wrong for So Long: How the Press, the Pundits—and the President—Failed on Iraq."

Both journalists point to cause and effect: The public tends to take cues from the media about what is important. If Iraq is pushed to a back burner, the signal is clear—the war no longer is a top priority. It follows that news consumers lose interest and turn their attention elsewhere. The Pew study found exactly that: As news coverage of the war diminished, so too did the public interest in Iraq.

Ellen Hume, research director at the MIT Center for Future Civic Media and a former journalist, believes the decline in Iraq news could be linked to a larger issue—profits. "The problem doesn't seem to be valuing coverage of the war; it's more about the business model of journalism today and what that market requires," Hume says.

"There is no sense that [the media] are going to be able to meet the numbers that their corporate owners require by offering news about a downer subject like Iraq. It's a terrible dilemma for news organizations."

Still, there has been some stunningly good reporting on Iraq over the past year.

Two of the Washington Post's six Pulitzer Prizes were war-related. Anne Hull and Dana Priest won the public service award for revealing the neglect of wounded soldiers at Walter Reed Army Medical Center (see Drop Cap, April/May 2007). Steve Fainaru won in the international reporting category for an examination of private security contractors in Iraq.

McClatchy's Baghdad bureau chief, Leila Fadel, collected the George R. Polk Award for outstanding foreign reporting. Judges offered high praise for her vivid depictions of the agonizing plight of families in ethnically torn neighborhoods.

CBS took two Peabody Awards, one for Scott Pelley's report on the killings of civilians in the Iraqi city of Haditha (see "A Matter of Time," August/September 2006) on "60 Minutes," another for Kimberly Dozier's report about two female veterans who lost limbs in Iraq on "CBS News Sunday Morning." Dozier herself was wounded in Iraq in May 2006.

ABC News correspondent Bob Woodruff, who was injured in Iraq in January 2006, received a Peabody Award for "Wounds of War," a series of reports about injured veterans.

There have been a series of groundbreaking investigations over the past year. In one of the most recent, the New York Times' David Barstow documented how the Pentagon cultivated military analysts to generate favorable news for the Bush administration's wartime performance. Many of the talking heads, including former generals, were being coached on what to tell viewers on television.

The Times continues to have a dominant presence on the ground in Iraq, sinking millions into maintaining its Baghdad complex, home and office to six or seven Western correspondents and a large Iraqi staff. Foreign Editor Chira says it has been more challenging to recruit people to go to Baghdad, but "we remain completely committed to maintaining a robust presence in Iraq."

Those are notable exceptions; no doubt there are more. But overall, Iraq remains the biggest nonstory of the day unless major news is breaking.

Mark Jurkowitz, associate director of the Project for Excellence in Journalism, points to May 24, 2007, as a major turning point in the coverage of U.S. policy toward Iraq. That's the day Congress voted to continue to fund the war without troop withdrawal timetables, giving the White House a major victory in a clash with the Democratic leadership over who would control the purse strings and thus the future of the war. Democrats felt they had a mandate from Americans to bring the troops home. President Bush stuck to a hard line and came out the victor. "The political fight was over," Jurkowitz says. "Iraq no longer was a hot story. The media began looking elsewhere."

Statistics from a report by Jurkowitz released in March 2008 support his theory. From January through May 2007, Iraq accounted for 20 percent of all news measured by PEJ's News Coverage Index. That period included the announcement of the troop "surge."

"But from the time of the May funding vote through the war's fifth anniversary on March 19, 2008, coverage plunged by about 50 percent. In that period, the media paid more than twice as much attention to the presidential campaigns than the war," according to PEJ.

"You could see the coverage of the political debate [over Iraq] shrink noticeably. The drop was dramatic," says Jurkowitz, who believes the press has an obligation to cover stories about Iraq even when the political landscape changes. "It is hard to say that the media has spurred any meaningful debate in America on this."

Is there anything to the concept of war fatigue or a psychological numbing that comes with rote reports of violence? Susan Tifft, professor of journalism and public policy at Duke University, believes there is.

She reasons that humans do adapt when the abnormal gradually becomes normal, such as a bloody and seemingly endless conflict far from America's shores. Tifft explains that despite tensions of the Cold War, America's default position for many years had been peace. Now the default position—the environment in which Americans live—is war. "And somehow we have gotten used to it. That's why it seems like wallpaper or Muzak. It's oddly normal and just part of the atmosphere," she says.

Does an acceptance of the status quo indicate helplessness or rational resignation on the part of the public and the press? Is it a survival mechanism?

Harvard University Professor Howard Gardner, a psychologist and social scientist, has explored what it is about the way humans operate that might allow this to happen.

Gardner explains that when a news story becomes repetitive, people "habituate"—the technical term for what happens when they no longer take in information. "You can be sure that if American deaths were going up, or if there was a draft, then there would not be acceptance of the status quo," Gardner wrote in an April 17 e-mail.

"But American deaths are pretty small, and the children of the political, business and chattering classes are not dying, and so the war no longer is on the radar screen most of the time. The bad economy has replaced it, and no one has yet succeeded in tying the trillion-dollar war to the decline in the economy."

New York Times columnist Nicholas D. Kristof is one who has tried. In a March 23 op-ed column, he quoted Nobel Prize-winning economist Joseph Stiglitz as saying the "present economic mess" is very much related to the Iraq war, which also "is partially responsible for soaring oil prices." Stiglitz calculated the eventual total cost to be about $3 trillion.

Kristof tossed out plenty of fodder for stories: "A congressional study by the Joint Economic Committee found that the sums spent on the Iraq war each day could enroll an additional 58,000 children in Head Start or give Pell Grants to 153,000 students to attend college . . . . [A] day's Iraq spending would finance another 11,000 border patrol agents or 9,000 police officers."

In Denver, Jason Salzman has been thinking along the same lines. The media critic for the Rocky Mountain News suggested in a February 16 column that news organizations "treat the economic costs of the war as they've treated U.S. casualties." After the death of the 3,000th American soldier, for instance, his newspaper printed the names of all the dead on the front page. To mark economic milestones, Salzman would like to see page one filled with graphics representing dollars Colorado communities have lost to the war.

"It's hard for me to realize why more reporters don't do these stories about the impact of the cost of the war back home," he said in an interview.

Another aspect of the war that could use more scrutiny is the Iraqi oil industry: Where is the money going? Who is benefiting? Why isn't oil money paying for a fair share of reconstruction costs?

Similarly, much more attention could be paid to the ramifications of stretching America's military to the limit.

And what about the impact of the war on the lives of ordinary Iraqis (see "Out of Reach," April/May 2006)? In April, Los Angeles Times correspondent Alexandra Zavis filed a story about a ballet school in Baghdad that had become an oasis for children of all ethnic and religious backgrounds.

"Now, more than ever," Zavis wrote in an e-mail interview, it "is the responsibility of journalists to put a name and a face on the mind-numbing statistics, to take readers in to the lives of ordinary Iraqis, and to find ways to convey what this unimaginable bloodshed means to the people who live it."

Jurkowitz's March 2008 report cited the "inverse relationship between war coverage and the coverage of the 2008 presidential campaign—an early-starting, wide-open affair that has fascinated the press since it began in earnest in January 2007. As attention to Iraq steadily declined, coverage of the campaign continued to grow in 2007 and 2008, consuming more of the press' attention and resources.

"Moreover, the expectation that Iraq would dominate the campaign conversation proved to be wrong," the report said. It was the economy instead. Jurkowitz cites what he calls an eye-catching statistic: In the first three months of 2008, coverage of the campaign outstripped war coverage by a ratio of nearly 11 to 1, or 43 percent of newshole compared with 4 percent.

But all that soon could change. "The [Iraq] story, we believe, remains as important as ever, and the debate about the future conduct of the war and the level of American troop presence in Iraq during the presidential campaign makes it crucial for the American public to be well informed," says the New York Times' Chira.

Jurkowitz agrees. That's why he's predicting a renaissance in Iraq coverage in the coming months. Battle lines already have been drawn: Sen. John McCain, the presumed Republican candidate, has vowed to stay the course in Iraq until victory is achieved. The Democrats favor withdrawing U.S. forces, perhaps beginning as early as six months after taking the oath of office.

"When we get in the general election mode, Iraq will be a big issue. The candidates will set the agenda for the discussion and the media will pick it up. This could reinvigorate the debate," Jurkowitz says. "The war will be back in the headlines."

Senior contributing writer **SHERRY RICCHIARDI** (sricchia@iupui.edu), who writes frequently about international coverage for *AJR,* assessed reporting on Iran in the magazine's February/March issue. Editorial assistant Roxana Hadadi (rhadadi@ajr.umd.edu) contributed research to this report.

From *American Journalism Review,* June/July 2008, pp. 20–27. Copyright © 2008 by the Philip Merrill College of Journalism at the University of Maryland, College Park, MD 20742-7111. Reprinted with permission.

Myth-Making in New Orleans

The impressive media coverage of Hurricane Katrina was marred by the widespread reporting—sometimes attributed to public officials—of murders and rapes that apparently never took place. What can news outlets learn from this episode to prevent similar problems in the future?

BRIAN THEVENOT

A s I walked briskly through the dimly lit area inside the food service entrance of New Orleans' Ernest N. Morial Convention Center, the thought of pulling back the sheets covering the four stinking, decomposing corpses in front of me seemed wrong, even perverse. Before I'd even thought to ask, one of the two soldiers who escorted me, Arkansas National Guardsman Mikel Brooks, nixed the prospect of looking inside the freezer he and another soldier said contained "30 or 40" bodies.

"I ain't got the stomach for it, even after what I saw in Iraq," he said.

I didn't push it. Now I wish I had, as gruesome as that may seem. The soldiers might have branded me a morbid fiend and run me the hell out of there, but my story in the September 6 edition of the Times-Picayune would have been right, or at least included a line saying I'd been denied the opportunity to lay eyes on the freezer.

Instead, I quoted Brooks and another soldier, by name, about the freezer's allegedly grim inventory, including the statement that it contained a "7-year-old with her throat cut."

Neither the mass of bodies nor the allegedly expired child would ever be found. As I later reported, an internal review by Arkansas Guard Lt. Col. John Edwards found that Brooks and others who repeated the freezer story had heard it in the food line at Harrah's Casino, a law enforcement and military staging area a block away. Edwards told me no soldier had actually seen bodies in a freezer.

I retell this story not to deflect blame— factual errors under my byline are mine alone—but as an example of how one of hundreds of myths got reported in the early days of Hurricane Katrina's aftermath.

I retell this story not to deflect blame—factual errors under my byline are mine alone—but as an example of how one of hundreds of myths got reported in the early days of Hurricane Katrina's aftermath. I corrected the freezer report—along with a slew of other rumors and myths transmitted by the media—in a September 26 Times-Picayune story coauthored by my colleague Gordon Russell. In that piece, we sought to separate fact from fiction on the narrow issue of reported violence at the Louisiana Superdome and the Convention Center.

We hadn't anticipated the massive shockwave of self-correction that story would send through the international media. The examination of myths of violence—and their confirmation by New Orleans Mayor C. Ray Nagin and then-Police Superintendent Eddie Compass—became *the* story for days on end, a moment of mass-scale media introspection that ultimately resulted in a healthy revision of history's first draft.

The Los Angeles Times, the New York Times and the Washington Post followed up with similar, well-researched efforts debunking myths and coming to essentially the same conclusion we had: While anarchy indeed reigned in the city, and subhuman conditions in the Dome and the Convention Center shocked the nation's conscience, many if not most of the alarmist reports of violence were false, or at least could not be verified. Dozens of other newspapers and television outlets joined in, offering news and opinion pieces, many doggedly questioning what they and others had earlier reported.

Our myth-debunking story put me in the eye of the debate's swirling storm. National television outlets praised our work, quoted it frequently and sought me out for interviews as their latest instant expert. A few bloggers had the opposite reaction, hanging me in virtual effigy as a symbol of the failings of the dreaded "MSM"—the mainstream media, that evil monolith—and concocting conspiracy theories to explain the media's errant early reports. Questions of race and class pervaded the debate in all media: Did the reporting of violence stem from journalists' willingness to believe the worst about poor African Americans?

What role did the refugees themselves, along with local black public officials—both of whom served as sources for many of the false stories—play in creating the myths?

The New York Times tempered its assessment of false reports, writing "some, though not all, of the most alarming stories that coursed through the city appear to be little more than figments of frightened imaginations." But the Times' piece differed in scope from ours, assessing reports of crime citywide instead of only at the Dome and the Convention Center. The Times also reported on property crimes such as widespread looting—definitely not a myth, I can confirm as an eyewitness—as part of the paper's exhaustive review. We concentrated exclusively on violent crime.

Jim Dwyer, one of the lead reporters on the Times' story, says he came to Louisiana for two weeks specifically to ascertain the truth of early wild reports of crime. As we did at the Picayune, Dwyer says he had taken an interest when the tenor of some reports, many unattributed, relayed nightmarish scenes that seemed to defy common sense.

"I just thought that some of the reports were so garish, so untraceable and always seemed to stop short of having actual witnesses to the atrocities . . . like a galloping mythical nightmare had taken control," Dwyer told me.

The paper also dispatched stringers to shelters in Houston and Austin, Dwyer says, where they found no shortage of secondhand or thirdhand accounts of rape and murder—but none that seemed credible enough to discount Dwyer's original thesis. "Nobody could say they saw rapes and murders. It was always three or four steps removed, like 'my sister's uncle's cousin'" had seen the violence, he says.

Dwyer also reviewed his own paper's reporting, but found that, while the Times had reported unconfirmed accounts of treachery, as did many others, its reporters had generally couched them with the caveat that they couldn't be confirmed. "I read all of it. We certainly reported stuff that Compass said, that Nagin said, but with pretty clear markers that it couldn't be verified," he says. "Also, the reports hadn't taken over our coverage in as powerful a way [as they did in some other media]. The atrocities didn't become the story. The paper kept its eye on the perilous conditions the people were in."

By the time the Times-Picayune's story ran—followed quickly by the L.A. Times' and the New York Times' pieces—nearly a month after the storm, there was no shortage of reports to second-guess. Many were attributed to refugees, cops and soldiers and even top public officials. Others appeared with weak attribution or none at all. Consider one example, this unattributed September 1 exchange on Fox News Channel between host John Gibson and correspondent David Lee Miller, live from New Orleans:

Gibson: "These are pictures of the cops arriving on the scene, armed and ready to take on the armed thugs. . . . Thugs shooting at rescue crews . . ."

Miller: "Hi, John, as you so rightly point out, there are so many murders taking place. There are rapes, other violent crimes taking place in New Orleans."

Kicking it up a notch and taking it worldwide, the normally staid Financial Times of London offered this September 5 description of the Convention Center, attributed to unnamed refugees: "Girls and boys were raped in the dark and had their throats cut and bodies were stuffed in the kitchens while looters and madmen exchanged fire with weapons they had looted."

The story went on to quote some flood victims by name: "Geraldine Lavy said her son protected four Australian tourists from rapists in the convention centre. 'Can you imagine? Four white women on their own?'" A man named Larry Martin told the Times that looters and gunmen "were shooting at buses, the rapes, the murders, the sodomy." The piece also reported, with no attribution, the apocryphal tale that "several hundred corpses are reported to have been gathered by locals in one school alone" in St. Bernard Parish, the badly flooded community just east of the city.

That one struck me as familiar: The Picayune's small team of reporters in New Orleans—most of the staff had been forced to evacuate to Baton Rouge after our headquarters nearly flooded—heard a similar report of up to 300 bodies piled at Marion Abramson High School in Eastern New Orleans. We dispatched two reporters to the school in a delivery truck, which got stuck while driving through high water. The reporters then canoed to the school, went inside—and found no bodies, and had nothing to write for their trouble.

Immediately after our story broke, we found ourselves making the rather jarring transition from reporter to source. The cable networks—CNN, MSNBC and Fox—needed to act immediately. It had taken me and Russell a full week to research our piece. So they sought members of our rag-tag "New Orleans bureau" for interviews.

The day the story ran, I went on CNN's "NewsNight with Aaron Brown." Our on-the-ground editor, David Meeks, had appeared on the cable channel along with reporter Michael Perlstein earlier that evening with Paula Zahn. The next morning, I went on MSNBC while being trailed by a French television reporter, and appeared again that afternoon on CNN Headline News.

We came away with differing assessments of how the television media had handled the revision. Meeks and Perlstein felt Zahn, in the live interview, had tried to pile the entirety of the blame at the foot of the New Orleans mayor and police chief, fully exonerating the media and street-level sources.

Zahn started the interview by asking Perlstein: "So, Michael, how is it that the mayor got all of this wrong?"

Perlstein didn't bite, explaining that the mayor—along with much of the media—had gotten somewhat understandably engulfed in the hysteria that spread like wildfire through a city with a devastated communications apparatus. "I think that the mayor was caught up in the same thing that a lot of people were caught up, reporters, officials and everyone else here included, and that there was a communications blackout," Perlstein said. "He was getting reports from pretty credible sources. But, by then, it had been passed along four or five different times, the story exaggerated each time along the way."

Zahn didn't appear interested in spreading the blame.

Zahn: "So, Michael in the end, what do you think is the most egregious exaggeration the mayor made?" she asked.

Perlstein responded that Nagin would have been wise to wait for a more official review of the violence at the Dome and the Convention Center.

Apparently still unsatisfied, Zahn served up another mayor-bashing opportunity to Meeks.

"Clearly, there was a great sensitivity to race in covering this story. But you had an African American mayor. You had the head of the police department being an African American. And, clearly, they had to be sensitive that what they were saying was going to have some tremendous impact. You're not suggesting, David, that they intentionally exaggerated this story?"

Neither Meeks nor anyone reasonable had suggested anything of the kind.

"I really don't think they did," Meeks told her. "I think they got caught up in hysteria."

After Meeks and Perlstein prepped me on the line of questioning, I went on CNN later that night with Aaron Brown. Standing under a tent in front of the Baton Rouge emergency management center, I stood nervously fidgeting with my earpiece, listening to Brown's introduction.

"We often remind you, when reporting breaking news stories, that the first reports are often wrong," Brown started. "With Katrina, it turns out that some of those reports, and not just the early ones, were really wrong. Some were fueled by people who were tired and hungry and clearly desperate. But some were fueled by the people in charge."

Knowing I had little time to make a point, I made sure to shift some focus away from the criticism of Nagin and Compass and turn the attention forward, toward correcting the record rather than finger-pointing.

"I have some sympathy for their initial reporting of supposed atrocities at the Dome and the Convention Center," I said of the city leaders. "Their communication apparatus had completely broken down . . . I also think that the media, in some sense, has to take responsibility for this and to come back to check, to verify some of these stories, basically just to finish the job, as I think we tried to do today."

Brown took the point and moved the conversation toward explaining how confusion created misinformation. "It sounds like there was almost a giant game of post office being played," he said. "One person believes to have seen one thing, tells someone else, and as it goes down the line, it keeps getting bigger and bigger. Before you know it, you have hundreds of deaths."

One guy saw six bodies. Then another guy saw six bodies. And another guy saw the same six and all of a sudden, it become 18.

I concurred. "There was a quote in the story today, I think a smart one, from deputy chief Warren Riley," I told Brown.

"He says, 'One guy saw six bodies. Then another guy saw six bodies. And another guy saw the same six and all of a sudden, it becomes 18.'"

The broadcasters had a point about public officials fueling the rumor mill, a point we had made, but not dwelled on, in our original story. In the most extreme case, Nagin told Oprah Winfrey that people in the Dome had sunk to an "almost animalistic state" after "five days watching dead bodies, watching hooligans killing people, raping people."

Then-Police Chief Eddie Compass—pushed into retirement by Nagin immediately after our story broke—spoke of "babies" being raped.

Still, Brown got past the public-official bashing and grasped the point of our story that many others missed: It hadn't been an "investigation," as some termed it, but rather an explanatory piece. We never intended to write "gotcha" journalism or declare ourselves the holier-than-thou hometown paper, preaching to the rest of the media and the public officials we all quoted. We just wanted to get the story right, and explain, to the extent possible, how it came to be wrong.

Dwyer expressed a similar goal. In his story, he didn't explicitly challenge any early reporting from the Times or any other outlet. Instead, he referred generally to widespread reports of violence and concentrated on the story itself: what really happened.

"My purpose wasn't to flay the New York Times or anybody else. This wasn't another Jayson Blair or Judith Miller situation, although it seems like sometimes these days your integrity is judged on how much you beat yourself like a pious Shiite," he says. "Whatever people reported from there in the early days, getting cold, hard facts was no easy task. They were doing the best they could, while trying to find electricity every 30 minutes just to be able to file, or in the Times-Picayune's case, struggling just to publish a paper on the Web."

Keith Woods, dean of faculty at the Poynter Institute, as well as a former Times-Picayune reporter, city editor and opinion writer and a New Orleans native, takes an even harder line on what he describes as a fashionable but destructive self-flagellation by media outlets—particularly television—that amounts to the media undercutting their already fragile credibility with the public. The press has had its legitimate reporter-writing-fiction scandals—Jayson Blair, Stephen Glass, Mike Barnicle—and in those instances, the media should indeed police themselves—brutally, Woods says. But early Katrina reporting, in which reporters often attributed tales and/or couched stories of violence with qualifiers, isn't even in the same ballpark, much less the same league, as making up stories out of thin air.

Some television outlets' willingness to put media-haters on air to bash the press only made the problem worse. "It was the typical self-abuse that follows media mistakes, and it became an equally unhelpful debate, an 'are not! are too!' debate over whether the media are biased or whatever," Woods says. "This sort of cannibalization is of great concern to me. If we just continue to stick our fingers in the wind, and then when we feel the hot breath of the public, we continue this self-abuse, then we'll just continue to hold up this unrealistic expectation that we're perfect . . . If we're walking around expecting that every time somebody goes off and does their job that it's done perfectly, then, first of all, we wouldn't have jobs in journalism, and second, public officials wouldn't need term limits."

Woods, who has been interviewed several times about Katrina reporting, found himself silently boiling with anger during one television panel discussion. He had agreed to go on PBS' "The NewsHour with Jim Lehrer" for a discussion of hurricane coverage, hoping for the fair, reasonable treatment for which Lehrer and PBS have been long respected. Instead, he found himself in the midst of a near food fight between NBC reporter Carl Quintanilla—in one corner, defending the media—and conservative radio talk show host Hugh Hewitt in the other corner, clubbing them.

"They'd go to the NBC reporter, who I thought made reasonable comments, to Hewitt, whose message was basically, 'Shoot the media,' then turn to me and say, 'Keith, what do you think?'" Woods says. "I was incensed."

Av Westin, a former vice president and executive producer for ABC News, says television reporters' and anchors' repeating of mythical violence, with sloppy attribution, marred otherwise remarkable journalism that aggressively reported the catastrophic damage of Katrina. He chalked it up to a lesson the television media should already have learned in the era of 24-hour news: Journalism requires thoughtful editing often absent in the competitive rush to air emotional breaking news.

"When I was at ABC, nothing got on the air without having the piece read in to us," he says. "Now, they're on the air 24-7 and they have to fill airtime, and that leads frequently to the reporting of rumor and speculation . . . Rather than saying, 'Let's wait five minutes,' they just go with it because it's in front of them. They keep learning that lesson and forgetting that lesson."

Then the mistakes feed off one another and multiply, Westin says. "There's something I call the 'out there syndrome'—it's okay for us to publish it because someone else already has, so it's 'out there,'" he says, rather than each media outlet confirming its own facts. "With 24-7 news, the deadline is always now, you go with whatever you've got, you stick it on the air."

Even as I became temporarily famous (for the standard 15 minutes) in the television news world, I was taken aback to find myself vilified by a few bloggers. In the blogosphere, I served as a target for a seemingly unquenchable disdain for the MSM.

Some branded me a hypocrite for writing about myth-making after I'd earlier reported one of the myths, the "30 or 40" bodies. But what's curious about much of the criticism is that reporters from the dreaded MSM often did a more thorough and sober job of correcting mainstream reports than did their sworn enemies in the blogosphere. Indeed, because most bloggers do little or no original reporting, they used my story about myths, along with those of the L.A. Times and New York Times, as the tools with which to beat us about the ears. They clubbed us with our own sticks.

Some blogs offered fair criticism, but others hyperventilated with unchecked rage that contributed little or nothing to the larger public good of finding out what had really happened. Some simply piled myth upon myth, developing media conspiracies out of what in the vast majority of cases were honest mistakes.

Lester Dent of ChronWatch, a San Francisco-based "media watchdog and conservative news site," went so far as to compare me to Jayson Blair. Dent asserted I "obviously" had never even been at the Convention Center and then demanded my head on a platter.

"Thevenot should be disciplined, up to and including being fired," Dent wrote.

I asked Dent about his allegation in an e-mail. He sent pages of further criticism in response, but somewhat reluctantly dropped the charge that I hadn't been at the scene, along with the Blair comparison.

"I will accept that you were on site making the report," he wrote in an e-mail response. "So no Jayson Blair moment."

As New Orleanians, playing a key role in correcting the international image of our own citizens gave us a deep satisfaction. Mostly poor, overwhelmingly African American, flood victims in the two shelters had been, in the most egregious cases, portrayed as beasts, raping and killing one another and even shooting at rescue workers trying to save them.

As journalists, reporting myths and later correcting them offers vital lessons on ramping up skepticism in initial reporting from chaotic environments—even if the sources are authoritative ones. We have three basic tools to use here, one during the reporting, the other during publishing, the third during any needed correction of initial reports.

The first is the persistent questioning of sources—about their sources: How do you know that? Did you see it? Who told you this? Are you 100 percent sure this happened? Who else can confirm it?

The second, wisely suggested in a column by former Washington Post Ombudsman Michael Getler, is careful and frequent qualification: "There is a journalistic device that is informative, accurate and protective, but that too often doesn't get used. It is a simple sentence that says: 'This account could not be independently verified.'"

The second time I wrote about the bodies in the freezer, as part of a narrative piece I penned for this magazine, I added just such a qualification (see "Apocalypse in New Orleans," October/November). At the time, a few days after I'd been to the Convention Center, I still had no higher-level confirmation of a body count—because no official count had been taken. So I added a sentence saying the presence and number of bodies at the center was "still unconfirmed amid a swirl of urban myths churned up by the storm."

The revision came as a result of a conversation with an editor in which I initially recommended cutting the mention of 40 bodies altogether unless I could confirm it independently before deadline. We compromised, adding the qualifier and strict attribution of the number to the guardsmen.

The third tool, which lately has been on display by many, though not all, media outlets, is an attitude that embraces the correcting of major news stories as news itself, not something to be buried in a corrections box.

"I think you treat it as a separate story, and it should have A1 prominence," says Hub Brown, an associate professor of broadcast journalism at the S.I. Newhouse School of Public Communications at Syracuse University. "Of course, print journalists are so much more meticulous at correcting their mistakes . . . Why not have a segment in the newscast that says, 'We've reported this through the past day, and it turned out to be wrong'?"

That sort of record correction would be a lot less painful—indeed, not painful at all—if journalists' initial dispatches contained detailed attribution, especially for high-temperature reports out of disaster zones. With stories like Katrina, in which rock-solid information in many cases proved so elusive, that should extend even to the point of publishing exactly how official sources came to know the information in question.

David Carr, a media columnist for the New York Times, was one of the first to question some of the early Katrina reporting in a September 19 column headlined: "More Horrible Than Truth: News Reports."

While Carr, in his column and in an interview, asserted that the media should shoulder their share of the blame, he was stunned at the degree to which public officials solidified the myths. "In New Orleans, that's what set this apart" from other examples of misinformation reported by the media, he says. "I was actually prepared a week before and had a column set to go, but then I realized the top police official and the top elected official were confirming these rumors. So how could I go after reporters on the ground receiving confirmation that this happened?"

Carr revised the column to address public officials' roles. Many have given Nagin and Compass a pass, saying they probably repeated exaggerations by mistake in a desperate attempt to get help for a truly desperate situation. Carr, however, suggests they were driven in part by political motives.

"Usually the first reaction of officials in crisis is to obfuscate and tamp down the rumors," he says. "Nagin and Compass stood there with a can of gasoline . . . In part what they were trying to do was explain that they had a mess on their hands—and that the feds had dropped the ball—by communicating an atmosphere of chaos that rendered their inability understandable."

In the worst of the storm reporting, tales of violence, rapes, murders and other mayhem were simply stated as fact with no attribution at all.

I am among those who committed this sin. In my previous AJR piece, although I attributed the account of bodies in the freezer and added that it could not be confirmed, I got loose with the attribution at another point in the story, describing the Convention Center as "a nightly scene of murders, rapes and regular stampedes."

What I later confirmed is that occasional gunfire, stampedes and terror did indeed plague the Convention Center. But only one death could be called a suspected homicide, a body with a gunshot wound, according to Kristen Meyer, spokeswoman for the state Department of Health and Hospitals. Meyer also confirmed that four bodies were retrieved from just inside the food service entrance, the same place I witnessed the four bodies lying under sheets. Widespread reports of rapes could not be confirmed.

Only one of those bodies has since been identified by name by her family, that of 79-year-old Clementine Eleby, who was not the gunshot victim, Meyer says.

While the media should learn lessons from Katrina, appropriate caution can't lead to paralysis. Backing off aggressive reporting of scenes where "official" information and sources, in some cases, literally don't exist isn't an option.

While the media should learn lessons from Katrina, appropriate caution can't lead to paralysis. Backing off aggressive reporting of scenes where "official" information and sources, in some cases, literally don't exist isn't an option. The many early Katrina stories marred by exaggerations or errors still stand out as a point of pride for the media. The quick reaction to the storm by reporters put accounts—most of them true and confirmed—of dire suffering in the faces of the public and authorities, prompting them to take action that saved lives.

As the debate about misreported Katrina violence rolled though blogs and more mainstream outlets, a conventional wisdom emerged: White middle-class reporters only believed and reported atrocities because they were predisposed to accept the worst about poor, black flood victims.

The race and class dynamics here are far more complicated. Many of the worst stories were attributed to poor, black flood victims themselves, along with African American public officials.

Brown, the Syracuse professor and an African American who teaches about diversity in the media, says that's no surprise. Black people are sometimes unconsciously biased against black people, too. "The fact that racism exists in the country doesn't mean everybody of one race feels one way, and everybody of another race feels the other," he says. "Sometimes victims of racism believe the worst about themselves. That's part of what makes it so harmful."

Poynter's Woods, an African American who has been writing and teaching about reporting on racial issues for years, doesn't buy the charge that the reports were driven largely by racial bias. It's not necessarily a gigantic leap in logic, he says, to believe that New Orleanians would murder one another in desperate times—they murder one another with regularity during normal times.

"I spent most of my life in the city of New Orleans, and when I left, it was the murder capital of the country," Woods says. "If you were to tell me a bunch of people murdered each other in the Dome and Convention Center, why wouldn't I believe it? . . . Race played a role, but it's an indecipherable role. It's useless trying to spend a lot of time trying to figure it out because you have to climb into the psyche of the people who were there."

You also have to deal in hypothetical comparisons. What would the media have reported if the Dome had been packed with white people?

The reality of being white in New Orleans and most of America, of course, substantially increases the likelihood of being middle class, and thus substantially decreases the likelihood of being anywhere near a shelter of any kind during a disaster of Katrina proportions.

I'll offer another hypothetical comparison that takes class out of the issue and leaves only race: If Katrina had hit a poor, white trailer-park town in, say, the Florida Panhandle, and white refugees and white public officials had offered the media tales of rape and murder, would any of us have doubted their "eyewitness" or "official" accounts?

There's no simple answer. White trailer-park towns don't typically include a Dome that might end up packed with about 30,000 people, with no power, no working toilets and scant medical care.

While the role of race can't be definitively measured, I have little doubt that, consciously or unconsciously, some white reporters and probably a smaller number of black ones found it more plausible that babies had been raped and children knifed in a black crowd than they would in a theoretical white one.

But I don't think race was the overriding factor.

I'm more inclined to go with an expanded version of Aaron Brown's gossip-line theory: that stories that may have started with some basis in fact got exaggerated and distorted as they were passed orally—often the only mode of communication—through extraordinarily frustrated and stressed multitudes of people, including refugees, cops, soldiers, public officials and, ultimately, the press.

The confusion was created by a titanic clash of communications systems. Stone-age storytelling got amplified by space-age technology.

A person might have seen a man passed out from dehydration in the Superdome, for instance, and assumed he was dead, then assumed there must be more dead. In the retelling, it becomes, "There's bodies in the Dome." Retold a few more times by stressed and frightened people—all the way up to the mayor—and it became, "There's so many bodies in the Dome you can't count them."

Then the media arrived, with satellite phones and modems, BlackBerrys, television trucks with the ability to broadcast worldwide and the technology to post on the Internet in an instant—and most of them not realizing that normal rules of sourcing no longer ensured accuracy.

The gossip line then circled the globe, as officials, hurricane victims, and rescue and security personnel began to confirm nightmarish scenarios, sincerely believing what they were saying and wanting desperately to get the word out—and get help on the way.

I can assure you that Mikel Brooks and his fellow guardsman sincerely believed what they told me. They talked to me out of disgust at the horrors, real and imagined. They did not "lie," which implies intent. They were consumed with a more important job at the time than nailing down every report they heard and believed: giving food and water to the living to keep them from joining the dead. It was my job to make sure what they said was true.

Ultimately, I followed up and did that job, as did many others. What Woods finds curious about the media-bashing on the Katrina story is that critics don't credit the media for doing the research to prove their early reports wrong.

"Don't forget, the journalists kept reporting—the reason you know that things were reported badly is because the journalists told you."

BRIAN THEVENOT, a reporter at New Orleans' *Times-Picayune*, can be reached at brianthevenot@hotmail.com.

What the Mainstream Media Can Learn from Jon Stewart

No, not to be funny and snarky, but to be bold and to do a better job of cutting through the fog.

RACHEL SMOLKIN

When Hub Brown's students first told him they loved "The Daily Show with Jon Stewart" and sometimes even relied on it for news, he was, as any responsible journalism professor would be, appalled.

Now he's a "Daily Show" convert.

"There are days when I watch 'The Daily Show,' and I kind of chuckle. There are days when I laugh out loud. There are days when I stand up and point to the TV and say, 'You're damn right!' " says Brown, chair of the communications department at Syracuse University's S.I. Newhouse School of Public Communications and an associate professor of broadcast journalism.

Brown, who had dismissed the faux news show as silly riffing, got hooked during the early days of the war in Iraq, when he felt most of the mainstream media were swallowing the administration's spin rather than challenging it. Not "The Daily Show," which had no qualms about second-guessing the nation's leaders. "The stock-in-trade of 'The Daily Show' is hypocrisy, exposing hypocrisy. And nobody else has the guts to do it," Brown says. "They really know how to crystallize an issue on all sides, see the silliness everywhere."

Whether lampooning President Bush's disastrous Iraq policies or mocking "real" reporters for their credulity, Stewart and his team often seem to steer closer to the truth than traditional journalists. The "Daily Show" satirizes spin, punctures pretense and belittles bombast. When a video clip reveals a politician's backpedaling, verbal contortions or mindless prattle, Stewart can state the obvious—ridiculing such blather as it deserves to be ridiculed—or remain silent but speak volumes merely by arching an eyebrow.

Stewart and his fake correspondents are freed from the media's preoccupation with balance, the fixation with fairness. They have no obligation to deliver the day's most important news, if that news is too depressing, too complicated or too boring. Their sole allegiance is to comedy.

Or, as "The Daily's Show's" website puts it: "One anchor, five correspondents, zero credibility. If you're tired of the stodginess of the evening newscasts, if you can't bear to sit through the spinmeisters and shills on the 24-hour cable news networks, don't miss The Daily Show with Jon Stewart, a nightly half-hour series unburdened by objectivity, journalistic integrity or even accuracy."

That's funny. And obvious. But does that simple, facetious statement capture a larger truth—one that may contain some lessons for newspapers and networks struggling to hold on to fleeing readers, viewers and advertisers in a tumultuous era of transition for old media?

Has our slavish devotion to journalism fundamentals—particularly our obsession with "objectivity"—so restricted news organizations that a comedian can tell the public what's going on more effectively than a reporter? Has Stewart, whose mission is to be funny, sliced through the daily obfuscation more effectively than his media counterparts, whose mission is to inform?

This is, perhaps, a strange premise for a journalism review to explore. AJR's mission is to encourage rigorous ethical and professional standards, particularly at a time when fake news of the non Jon Stewart variety has become all too prevalent. Stewart's faux news is parody, a sharp, humorous take on the actual events of the day, not to be confused with fake news of the Jayson Blair, Jack Kelley, National Guard memos or even WMD variety, based only loosely on actual events yet presented as real news.

As I posed my question about lessons of "The Daily Show" to various journalism ethicists and professionals, some carefully explained why mainstream news organizations should refrain from engaging in such whimsy.

Ed Fouhy, who worked for all three broadcast networks in his 22-year career as a producer and network executive before retiring in 2004, is a regular "Daily Show" watcher. "Sometimes conventional journalism makes it difficult for a journalist to say what he or she really thinks about an incident. Sometimes you can cut closer to the bone with another form, another creative form, like a novel or a satire on television," Fouhy says. "I think what we're seeing is just a daily dose of it. You think back to 'Saturday Night Live,' and they've satirized the news for a long time with their 'Weekend Update.' 'That Was the Week That Was' was an early television satire on the news."

But Fouhy cringes at the idea that real journalists should model themselves after such a show. When readers pick up a newspaper or viewers turn on a news broadcast, they're looking for serious information, and they should be able to find it. "When you begin to blur the line . . . to attract more viewers and younger viewers, I think that's a lousy idea," he says.

Adds Robert Thompson, director of the Bleier Center for Television and Popular Culture at Syracuse University, "Journalists have a really inconvenient thing they've got to go through: a process of trying to get [the story] right. . . . I don't think journalists should try to be more hip. Journalists have to learn the one lesson which is important, which is to try to get it right."

Fouhy and Thompson are correct, of course. But Thompson's colleague Hub Brown and some others interviewed for this piece believe the lesson of "The Daily Show" is not that reporters should try to be funny, but that they should try to be honest.

"Stop being so doggone scared of everything," Brown advises journalists. "I think there is much less courageousness than there needs to be. There are people out there who stick out because of their fearlessness. Somebody like Lara Logan at CBS," the network's chief foreign correspondent who has reported extensively from Iraq and Afghanistan, "is a great example who is fearless about saying the truth."

In the hours and days following Hurricane Katrina, state and federal officials dithered while New Orleanians suffered inside the filth and chaos of the Louisiana Superdome. Many journalists, notably CNN's Anderson Cooper, jettisoned their usual care in handling all sides equally. They were bewildered, appalled and furious, and it showed.

"We saw a lot of that during Hurricane Katrina, but it shouldn't take a Hurricane Katrina to get journalists to say the truth, to call it as they see it," Brown says. "The thing that makes 'The Daily Show' stick out is they sometimes seem to understand that better than the networks do." He adds: "I think it's valuable because when the emperor has no clothes, we get to say the emperor has no clothes. And we have to do that more often here. . . . The truth itself doesn't respect point of view. The truth is never balanced. . . . We have to not give in to an atmosphere that's become so partisan that we're afraid of what we say every single time we say something."

Venise Wagner, associate chair of the journalism department at San Francisco State University, argues with her students over whether "The Daily Show" is real journalism. They think it is; she tells them it isn't, explaining that journalism involves not just conveying information but also following a set of standards that includes verification, accuracy and balance.

But she says "The Daily Show" does manage to make information relevant in a way that traditional news organizations often do not, and freedom from "balance" shapes its success.

" 'The Daily Show' doesn't have to worry about balance. They don't have to worry about accuracy, even. They can just sort of get at the essence of something, so it gives them much more latitude to play around with the information, to make it more engaging," Wagner says. "Straight news sometimes places itself in a box where it doesn't allow itself—it doesn't give itself permission to question as much as it probably should question." Instead, the exercise becomes one of: "I'm just going to take the news down and give it to you straight."

But what exactly is straight news, and what is balance? Is balance a process of giving equal weight to both sides, or of giving more weight to the side with more evidence? Does accuracy mean spelling everybody's name right and quoting them correctly, or does it also mean slicing to the heart of an issue? "Nowhere is the comedy show balanced," says Wagner, "but it allows them more balance in showing what is really going on."

As journalists, by contrast, "We've presented a balanced picture to the public. But is it accurate? Is it authentic?" She cites coverage of the global warming debate, which, until recently, often was presented as an equal argument between scientists who said global warming was occurring and scientists who denied it. "That reality was not authentic. There were very few scientists who refuted the body of evidence" supporting global warming, Wagner says, yet the coverage did not always reflect that.

Martin Kaplan, associate dean of the University of Southern California's Annenberg School for Communication, dislikes journalists' modern perception of balance. "Straight news is not what it used to be," he says. "It has fallen into a bizarre notion that substitutes something called 'balance' for what used to be called 'accuracy' or 'truth' or 'objectivity.' That may be because of a general postmodern malaise in society at large in which the notion of a truth doesn't have the same reputation it used to, but, as a consequence, straight journalists both in print and in broadcast can be played like a piccolo by people who know how to exploit that weakness.

"Every issue can be portrayed as a controversy between two opposite sides, and the journalist is fearful of saying that one side has it right, and the other side does not. It leaves the reader or viewer in the position of having to weigh competing truth claims, often without enough information to decide that one side is manifestly right, and the other side is trying to muddy the water with propaganda."

Kaplan directs USC's Norman Lear Center, which studies how journalism and politics have become branches of entertainment, and he has worked in all three worlds: former editor and columnist for the now-defunct Washington Star; chief speechwriter for Vice President Walter Mondale; deputy presidential campaign manager for Mondale; Disney studio executive and motion picture and television producer.

He borrows Eric Alterman's phrase "working the ref" to illustrate his point about balance. Instead of "reading a story and finding out that black is black, you now read a story and it says, 'Some say black is black, and some say black is white'. . . . So whether it's climate change or evolution or the impact on war policy of various proposals, it's all being framed as 'on the one hand, on the other hand,' as though the two sides had equal claims on accuracy."

Therein lies "The Daily Show's" appeal, he says. "So-called fake news makes fun of that concept of balance. It's not afraid to have a bullshit meter and to call people spinners or liars when they deserve it. I think as a consequence some viewers find that helpful and refreshing and hilarious."

In addition to the user-generated satire on YouTube, Kaplan thinks the Web is bursting with commentators, including Alterman and Salon's Glenn Greenwald, who brilliantly penetrate the fog—sometimes angrily, sometimes amusingly, sometimes a bit of both.

Broadcasters have tackled this least successfully, he says, citing CBS' ill-fated "Free Speech" segment. Launched on and then discarded from "The CBS Evening News with Katie Couric," the segment gave personalities such as Rush Limbaugh uninterrupted airtime to trumpet their views. And "the challenge for the great national papers," Kaplan adds, "is to escape from this straightjacket in which they're unable to say that official A was telling the truth, and official B was not."

Part of "The Daily Show's" charm comes from its dexterity in letting public figures from Bush to House Speaker Nancy Pelosi (D-Calif.) speak for—and contradict—themselves, allowing the truth to emanate from a politician's entanglement over his or her own two feet. It's one way to hold government officials accountable for their words and deeds. Some might even call it fact-checking.

Brooks Jackson directs FactCheck.org, a project of the Annenberg Public Policy Center of the University of Pennsylvania, which monitors the accuracy of prominent politicians' statements in TV ads, debates, speeches, interviews and press releases. Jackson himself is a former reporter for the Associated Press, Wall Street Journal and CNN who pioneered "ad watch" coverage at the cable network during the '92 presidential race.

"I'm totally buying it," he told me after I stumbled through my fake-news-gets-at-the-truth-better premise. "I am in awe of the ability of Stewart and however many people he has working for him to cull through the vast wasteland of cable TV and pick out the political actors at their most absurd. They just have an unerring eye for that moment when people parody themselves. And I guess while the cable news hosts are obliged to take those moments of idiocy seriously, Jon Stewart can give us that Jack Benny stare—Does anybody remember Jack Benny?—give us that Jon Stewart stare and let the hilarity of the moment sink in, often without saying a word."

Does this qualify as fact-checking? Not exactly, Jackson replies, but "one thing he does do that is fact-checking: If somebody says, 'I never said that,' and next thing you know, there's a clip of the same guy three months ago saying exactly that, that's great fact-checking," and a great lesson for journalists. Jackson thinks NBC's Tim Russert is the master of that art in the mainstream media, confronting his subjects as he puts their quotes on-screen and reading them verbatim. "Stewart does it for laughs, and Russert does it for good journalistic reasons, and we all can learn from the two of them."

The form has its limits as a fact-checking technique. Jackson doesn't envision Stewart giving a State of the Union address rigorous ad-watch-type treatment, complete with statistical analysis of the president's proposed budget. Why would he? He'd put his audience to sleep. "Not every misleading statement can be debunked out of the person's own mouth," notes Jackson. "That's a particular kind of debunking that's very effective as comedy. . . . There's plenty that needs debunking that isn't funny."

Asked about Stewart's influence on mainstream reporters, Jackson says: "Jon's been holding up the mirror to them for quite a while without any particular effect. The forces that are making the news more trivial and less relevant are frankly much more powerful than a show like Jon Stewart's can change."

Much of the allure of Stewart's show lies in its brutal satire of the media. He and his correspondents mimic the stylized performance of network anchors and correspondents. He exposes their gullibility. He derides their contrivances.

On March 28, the broadcast media elite partied with their government sources at the annual Radio and Television Correspondents' Association dinner. The disquieting spectacle of White House adviser Karl Rove rapping in front of a howling audience of journalists quickly appeared on YouTube. Quipped Stewart, only too accurately, the next night: "The media gets a chance to, for one night, put aside its cozy relationship with the government for one that is, instead, nauseatingly sycophantic."

His 2004 textbook satire, "America (The Book): A Citizen's Guide to Democracy Inaction," devotes a section to media in the throes of transformation and punctures this transition far more concisely, and probably more memorably, than the millions of words AJR has devoted to the subject:

"Newspapers abound, and though they have endured decades of decline in readership and influence, they can still form impressive piles if no one takes them out to the trash. . . . Television continues to thrive. One fifteen-minute nightly newscast, barely visible through the smoky haze of its cigarette company benefactor, has evolved into a multi-channel, twenty-four hour a day infotastic clusterfuck of factish-like material. The 1990s brought the advent of a dynamic new medium for news, the Internet, a magnificent new technology combining the credibility of anonymous hearsay with the excitement of typing."

Phil Rosenthal, the Chicago Tribune's media columnist, thinks part of the reason "The Daily Show" and its spinoff, "The Colbert Report," resonate is that they parody not only news but also how journalists get news. "It's actually kind of a surefire way to appeal to people because if the news itself isn't entertaining, then the way it's covered, the breathless conventions of TV news, are always bankable," Rosenthal says. "You can always find something amusing there."

He adds that "so much of the news these days involves managing the news, so a show like Stewart's that takes the larger view of not just what's going on, but how it's being manipulated, is really effective. I think there's general skepticism about the process that this plays into. . . . The wink isn't so much we know what's really going on. The wink is also we know you know what we're doing here. It's down to the way the correspondents stand [in front of] the green screen, offering commentary and intoning even when their commentary may not be important."

Irony-deficient journalists have rewarded Stewart over the last five years by devoting more than 150 newspaper articles alone to his show and to studies about his show. Most have discussed the program's popularity. ("The Daily Show" attracted an average 1.5 million viewers nightly from January 1 through April 19, according to Nielsen Media Research. Couric's beleaguered CBS newscast, by contrast, netted an average 7.2 million viewers nightly during the same period.)

Many stories have pondered whether "The Daily Show" has substance and credibility; mourned young people's alleged propensity to rely on such lighthearted fare for news; brooded over what this reliance says about the state of the news media; and grieved that the show poisons young people's outlook on government, leaving them cynical and jaded. Stewart, who declined to be interviewed for this article, has patiently explained that his show is supposed to be funny.

That hasn't stopped the onslaught of serious discourse and research about "The Daily Show." A 2004 survey by the Pew Research Center for the People and the Press found that 21 percent of people age 18 to 29 cited comedy shows such as "The Daily Show" and "Saturday Night Live" as places where they regularly learned presidential campaign news, nearly equal to the 23 percent who regularly learned something from the nightly network news or from daily newspapers.

Even if they did learn from his show, a more recent study indicates Stewart's viewers are well-informed. An April 15 Pew survey gauging Americans' knowledge of national and international affairs found that 54 percent of regular viewers of "The Daily Show" and "Colbert Report" scored in the high-knowledge category, tying with regular readers of newspaper websites and edging regular watchers of "The NewsHour with Jim Lehrer." Overall, 35 percent of people surveyed scored in the high-knowledge category.

In October, Julia R. Fox, who teaches telecommunications at Indiana University, and two graduate students announced the results of the first scholarly attempt to compare Stewart's show with traditional TV news as a political information source. Their study, which will be published this summer by the Journal of Broadcasting & Electronic Media, examined substantive political coverage in 2004 of the first presidential debate and political conventions on "The Daily Show" and the broadcast television networks' nightly newscasts. Fox concluded Stewart's show is just as substantive as network news.

Fox says she wasn't surprised by the study results, but she was surprised by the general lack of surprise. "People have e-mailed me and said, 'I think you're absolutely wrong. I think 'The Daily Show' is more substantive.'"

Beyond the debate over whether Stewart's show is a quality source of information or whether wayward young fans have lost their minds, the media have treated him with admiration bordering on reverence. In early 2005, press reports handicapped his chances of landing on the "CBS Evening News," which, like Comedy Central, was then owned by Viacom. After Dan Rather had announced his abrupt retirement following revelations that alleged memos about President Bush's National Guard Service

had not been authenticated, CBS chief Leslie Moonves said he wanted to reinvent the evening news to make it more relevant, "something that younger people can relate to." Asked at a news conference whether he'd rule out a role for Stewart, Moonves took a pass, fueling more speculation.

In 2004, the Television Critics Association bestowed the outstanding achievement in news and information award not on ABC's "Nightline" or PBS' "Frontline," but on "The Daily Show." Stewart, who had won for outstanding achievement in comedy the previous year, seemed bemused by the honor. Instead of accepting in person, he sent a tape of himself sitting at "The Daily Show" anchor desk. "We're fake," he informed the TV critics. "See this desk? . . . It folds up at the end of the day, and I take it home in my purse."

But Melanie McFarland, the critic who presented Stewart's award, calls him a "truth teller" who speaks plainly about the news and offers a "spoonful of sugar that helps the medicine, the news, go down."

That sugar is not just delightful; it's provocative. "Any comedian can do sort of a 'Saturday Night Live' presentation and just do the punch line," says McFarland, who writes for the Seattle Post-Intelligencer. "He actually gives you some stuff to consider in addition to the punch line. He and his staff show an awareness of the issues and [are] able to take a longer view than a 24-hour news cycle can, which is funny because it's also a daily show." Other news programs and journalists, including "Frontline" and Bill Moyers, do this also, she says, but not as often. "So much of the news is not digestion but regurgitation. He's sort of looking at the raw material and making a commonsense assessment of what it means."

McFarland says Stewart's mockery of the media should galvanize journalists to perform better. "If there's a guy who's making great headway in giving people information by showing people what you're not doing in giving them information, let's try to do our jobs."

For serious news organizations, change is easier advised than enacted. Take Stewart's imitation of the stylized anchor persona, which—with precious little exaggeration—makes TV personalities look silly and stilted. Altering that persona is no easy task, as Katie Couric discovered when she tried to make the nightly news chattier.

"While Jon Stewart is a guy in a suit pretending to be a newscaster, and he acts like a guy in a suit pretending to be a newscaster, there's a certain formality and rigidity we've come to expect from our news, so much so that when Katie Couric opens the news with 'Hi,' or now I think it's 'Hello,' this is thought of as some kind of breakdown in the proper etiquette of newscasting," says the Chicago Tribune's Rosenthal. He thinks perhaps the time has come to abandon the old formality of newscasting but says such a process will be evolutionary.

In other broadcast formats, incorporating a more sardonic tone can work well. Rosenthal cites MSNBC's "Countdown with Keith Olbermann" as one news program that does a pretty good job incorporating the same sorts of elements that make "The Daily Show" successful. "Keith Olbermann gets a lot of attention for his editorializing, but the meat of that show is this hybrid blend of the news you need to know, the news that's entertaining, with a little bit of perspective [in] taking a step back from what the news is and what the newsmakers want it to be," he says. (See "Is Keith Olbermann the Future of Journalism?" February/March.)

Rosenthal thinks ABC's quirky overnight show, "World News Now," also has achieved a more detached, looser tone, and says it's no accident that the program has been "such a fertile breeding ground for unorthodox newspeople," including Anderson Cooper and Aaron Brown.

Public radio, known for its sober (and sometimes stodgy) programming, is experimenting with a more freewheeling search for truth as well. In January, Public Radio International launched "Fair Game from PRI with Faith Salie," a one-hour satirical news and entertainment show that airs on weeknights. The Sacramento Bee's Sam McManis likened the new show to "the quirky love child of 'The Daily Show With Jon Stewart' and 'All Things Considered.' It's smart enough to slake the traditional public-radio fans' thirst for intellectual programming but satiric enough to catch the attention of the prematurely cynical Gen X and Gen Y sets."

Salie is a comedian and a Rhodes Scholar with a bachelor's degree from Harvard and a master of philosophy from Oxford in modern English literature. "I'm not a journalist, and I don't have to pretend to be one," she says, describing herself as her listeners' proxy. When she interviews newsmakers—topics have included the Taliban, Hillary Clinton and the Dixie Chicks—"I don't feel like I have to mask my incredulousness. I can say, 'For real? Are you kidding me?' That leads to spontaneity."

Sometimes humor results from a certain framing of the news. Each Monday, the show revisits metaphors from the Sunday morning news shows. On "Fox News Sunday" on April 8, Juan Williams first compared Republican presidential hopeful John McCain to a "deflated balloon," then declared the Arizona senator was on the "wrong path" with his Iraq policy and concluded that he shouldn't be "tying his tail" to such an albatross. On NBC's "Meet the Press," Judy Woodruff in January described the administration's Iraq policy as akin to "putting a fist in a sink full of water, leaving it there for a few minutes and taking it out."

Salie says "The Daily Show" has demonstrated that young people are savvier than many elders believe, and the mainstream media should learn from that. Young people "are aware of the news and can recognize the preposterousness of some of it." But don't try too hard to be funny, she cautions. "I don't think real news shows should try the scripted, cutesy, pithy banter. It gives me the heebie-jeebies. It makes me feel sad for them, and it feels pathetic."

For an informal, satirical or even humorous take on the news to work in a mainstream newspaper, the format must be exactly right. Gene Weingarten, the Washington Post humor writer, thinks the media would do their jobs better if they had more fun, and he cringes whenever editors insist on labeling his pieces as satire. "Nothing could be worse for satire than labeling it satire," he laments.

But he concedes his editors may have a point. In August, Paul Farhi, a reporter for the Post's Style section (and an AJR contributor), reviewed the debut of colleague Tony Kornheiser on ESPN's "Monday Night Football." The critique was not flattering, and an apoplectic Kornheiser retaliated by publicly trashing Farhi as "a two-bit weasel slug," whom he would "gladly run over with a Mack truck."

The smackdown drew national attention, and Weingarten decided he wanted a piece of the action. So he skewered Kornheiser's second show with an outrageous, over-the-top rant on the front of Style about the "failed Kornheiser stewardship" taking "yet another bumbling misstep toward its inevitable humiliating collapse."

"It was patently unfair," Weingarten says of his tongue-in-cheek diatribe, which was not labeled as satire. "A child would have understood this piece. No one could have misunderstood this."

And yet they did. Weingarten got hundreds, possibly thousands, of complaints from sports lovers pummeling him for attacking Kornheiser unfairly. (Kornheiser himself called Weingarten, unsure how to interpret the piece.) "The mail I got was just absolutely hilarious," Weingarten says. "There is a problem of applying irony, humorous satire, in a newspaper when readers are not accustomed to seeing it there."

Did he learn from the experience? "No," he replies. "Because my reaction was, 'These people are idiots.'"

Perhaps the hardest lesson to take away from "The Daily Show" is the most important one. How can journalists in today's polarized political climate pierce the truth, Edward R. Murrow-style, without a) being ideological, or b) appearing ideological?

Olbermann's show, cited in several interviews as a serious news program that excels in revealing hypocrisy, is unabashedly liberal, and "The Daily Show" itself is frequently tagged with that label. In February, Fox News Channel debuted "The 1/2 Hour News Hour," billed as the conservative riposte to Stewart's liberal bent; after two pilot shows, the network has agreed to pick up 13 additional episodes.

"Unfortunately, people are heading for news that sort of reinforces their own beliefs," says Washington Post reporter Dana Milbank. "That may be Jon Stewart on the left, or that may be Rush Limbaugh on the right. . . . Limbaugh isn't funny, but he's starting with something that has a kernel of truth and distorting it to the point of fakery as well, so I think they are parallel."

Milbank is the author of Washington Sketch, an experiment at slashing through the hazy words and deeds of federal power players. Milbank pitched the idea, based on British newspapers' parliamentary sketches, and argued for a few years before getting the green light in early 2005. "There was a lot of sort of figuring out the place, and first it really floated in the news section," he says. "I think we fixed that problem [by] putting it consistently on page two, and it's labeled more clearly."

Occasionally, Washington Sketch has appeared on page one, as it did March 6 when Milbank tartly contrasted the style of two generals who testified before Congress on the deplorable conditions at Walter Reed Army Medical Center. Then and at other times, Milbank's acerbic take has proved more enlightening than the longer, more traditional accompanying news story.

The column lacks a consistent ideology. Milbank says his goal is a "pox on both their houses sort of thing," and adds, "I'm not trying to be 50-50, particularly. The goal is to pick on all of them. . . . It's observational as opposed to argumentative." Too often, he says, "We seem to make the mistake of thinking that if you're not being ideological, you therefore have to be boring, and all sort of 50-50 down the middle and follow the inverted pyramid."

Jeff Jarvis, the blogger behind BuzzMachine.com, says journalists should engage in more open, honest conversations with readers. "I think what Stewart et al do is remind us of what our mission and voice used to be and should be," says Jarvis, who also is a media consultant and head of the interactive journalism program at the City University of New York Graduate School of Journalism. He notes that Stewart is "very much a part of the conversation. He's joking about things we're talking about. And then the next day, we're talking about him talking about it."

Jarvis wants journalists to unleash their inner Stewart. "After enough drinks, reporters talk like Stewart: 'You won't BELIEVE what the mayor said today!' Why don't we talk to our readers that way?" he asks, and then acknowledges: "OK. There's a lot of arguments: 'The mayor won't talk to us again.' 'It's biased.' 'We don't want to turn everything into blogs."

Jarvis doesn't mean that every story should become a first-person diatribe, and obviously the mainstream media can't fall back on Stewart's I'm-just-joking excuse after they've infuriated a thin-skinned politician. But there are instances when a little unorthodoxy may be appropriate, and speaking frankly may enhance credibility.

Eric Deggans, the TV and media critic for the St. Petersburg Times, also wants to see a little more pluck. "'The Daily Show' is pushing us to be less traditional about how we deliver people information," Deggans says. "Are we going to turn around and turn into the Onion?" (The cult publication parodies news in print and online; its facetious Onion News Network debuted on March 27.) "Of course not. But if you've got a longtime state

capitol bureau chief, and they see something go down in the capitol, and they have a great, acerbic take on it, why not let them go at it in a column?"

Or, he suggests, experiment just a bit with the sacred space on page one. "Sometimes editors have really rigid ideas about what can go on the front page," he says. "If somebody has a really good column on [Don] Imus, why wouldn't you put it on the front page, as long as you label it clearly as opinion? There are some editors who would say your first next-day story about Don Imus has to be traditional. Why? Why does it have to be traditional? As long as the reader isn't fooled, why do you let yourself be handcuffed like that?"

Deggans is quick to add some caveats, including the importance of fairness. "You always have to be careful because there's a good reason why we had those rules," Deggans says. "But we have to challenge ourselves to subvert them more often. You have to be subversive in a way that maintains your credibility. When you have smart, capable people who want to write in a different way, let them try it."

The mainstream media can not, should not and never will be "The Daily Show." The major news of our time is grimly serious, and only real news organizations will provide the time, commitment and professionalism necessary to ferret out stories such as the Washington Post's exposé of neglected veterans at Walter Reed or the New York Times' disclosures of secret, warrantless wiretapping by the federal government.

But in the midst of a transition, our industry is flailing. Our credibility suffers mightily. The public thinks we're biased despite our reluctance to speak plainly. Our daily newspapers often seem stale. Perhaps "The Daily Show" can teach us little, but remind us of a lot: Don't underestimate your audience. Be relevant. And be bold.

Says Deggans: "In a lot of news organizations, it's the fourth quarter. It's fourth down, man. It's time to show a little pizzazz. It's time to reinvent what's going on, so people get engaged."

RACHEL SMOLKIN (rsmolkin@ajr.umd.edu) is *AJR*'s managing editor. *AJR* editorial assistant Emily Groves contributed research to this report.

Double Whammy

It took an awfully long time for the national media to catch up to the racial turmoil in Jena, Louisiana. When they did, the results were not exactly a clinic in precision journalism.

RAQUEL CHRISTIE

To think of excellent reporting on racial issues, Gene Roberts must reach back 40 years, back to the Orangeburg massacre, when South Carolina State Police shot more than 20 students protesting segregation outside a bowling alley. Three students died. Surviving students insisted the police were the aggressors, but police swore they were attacked by the students.

Public opinion and the press sided with the officers—it was seen as an unfortunate side effect of upholding the law. And so the story went, until Jack Nelson decided there must be more to it than that. The Los Angeles Times reporter went to the local hospital and got a hold of the medical records.

Virtually all the students had been shot in the back, and some had bullets in the bottom of their feet. They weren't attacking the police—they were running away.

Such dogged, skeptical reporting, so common in the civil rights era, is what's missing from racial reportage today, says Roberts, Pulitzer Prize-winning author of "The Race Beat" and former executive editor of the Philadelphia Inquirer. It is an absence that has come back to haunt us in the case of the Jena 6.

The turmoil in Jena, Louisiana, began in late August 2006, when a black student asked at an assembly if he could sit under what some refer to as the "white tree" at Jena High School. The next day, nooses were strung from that tree—black and gold nooses, school colors. The students responsible for the nooses were disciplined but not expelled.

The atmosphere at the school grew tense. In November, the school's main building was severely damaged by a fire. Then a white kid beat up a black kid at a party and a white kid pulled a shotgun on black kids at a convenience store. Black on white, white on black, black on white, white on black, but the presses were largely silent.

Then, on December 4, 2006, white Jena High School student Justin Barker was beaten up by black students and knocked unconscious; three days later, six black students were charged with attempted second-degree murder. That day, 35 area religious leaders from black and white churches gathered to promote peace, and less than a week later 600 Jena residents filled the Guy Campbell Memorial Football Stadium for a prayer service.

And for five more months, the presses were silent.

Until last spring, until a May 20 article appeared in the Chicago Tribune, not a single story, not one column or comment, was published in the national media about the racial incidents in Jena. In a search for Jena on LexisNexis, "Jena Malone" pops up plenty, as does a "Jena" band of Choctaw Indians, but the town is entirely absent until mid-2007.

The Washington Post's first story on the situation ran on August 4, 2007. The New York Times and the Los Angeles Times published their initial pieces on September 15, 2007—a day after defendant Mychal Bell's second-degree battery conviction was overturned because, the court said, he was improperly tried as an adult.

U.S. News & World Report weighed in on September 20. Newsweek first mentioned Jena on June 4, but only as a blip in its "Perspectives: Quotes in the News" section. (The magazine didn't publish a story on Jena until August 20.) Time magazine first mentioned Jena in a September 27 story on Barack Obama.

Television missed out, too. CNN first addressed Jena on "Paula Zahn Now" on June 25, 2007. CBS News waited until September 15 to do its first segment, a 567-word interview with some of the parents of the defendants and a school board member. ABC News waited until the same day, and reporter Ron Claiborne almost acknowledged the folly: "[M]ostly by word of mouth, by e-mail, and yes, by the Internet, the case of the Jena Six, six black high school students originally charged with attempted murder in the beating of a white teenager, has been bubbling, or more like boiling for months, provoking accusations of racism and unequal justice."

Yet the story was out there. From September 7, 2006, to October 12, 2007, the Associated Press distributed 74 stories about the Jena nooses, 52 on state wires, 38 on national wires, 22 on North American wires and five on southern regional wires. In the same time period, "Jena High School" appeared in AP stories 77 times. Three AP stories covered the high school arson. Mychal Bell first appeared in an AP story on May 3, 2007—more than

Jena Timeline

2006

Late August/early September—A black student asks at an assembly if he can sit under a tree known as a gathering spot for white students in the high school courtyard. Two or three nooses are then found hanging from the tree.

The principal recommends expulsion for three white students, but the LaSalle Parish School District instead imposes a series of suspensions and detentions. Several black parents and students attend a meeting at a local church to discuss the noose incident. The local daily newspaper reports on the meeting, and area television stations follow up. Law enforcement officers are posted at the school after reports of tensions.

September 7—The Associated Press runs its first Jena report.

November 30—The main building of Jena High School is badly damaged by a fire determined to be arson and is later demolished. In December 2007, the sheriff-elect says the fire was unrelated to the turmoil at the school; instead, it was set to destroy records of bad grades. Eight people, black and white, are charged with arson.

December 1–2—Several fights occur that police say are racial in nature.

December 4—On the first day back after the fire, black students beat up a white male student who is knocked unconscious and treated in the emergency room. Six are later charged with conspiracy to commit second-degree murder and attempted second-degree murder. Five are expelled from school. The attack victim also is later expelled for having a firearm in his truck on school grounds.

December 7—About 35 religious leaders from black and white area churches meet. Prayer services are held at Jena schools a few days later.

December 13—Approximately 600 Jena residents fill the football stadium for a unity and prayer service.

2007

March 8 and May 2—Rallies for the Jena 6 are held at the LaSalle Parish Courthouse in Jena and draw a few dozen people each, including representatives of the national ACLU and state NAACP.

May 20—The Chicago Tribune runs its first article on Jena.

June 25–28—Mychal Bell, 17, is the first of the Jena 6 to go to trial, in adult court because of the nature of the charges. He is convicted of reduced charges of aggravated second-degree battery and conspiracy to commit that crime. Eventually charges against the remaining five also will be reduced to battery. CNN first reports the story on June 25.

Mid-July—The tree in the school courtyard is cut down.

July 31—About 300 people from around the country rally for the Jena 6 at the courthouse.

August 4—The Washington Post publishes its first Jena story.

August 5—Rev. Al Sharpton visits Jena. Martin Luther King III joins him there on August 14.

Late August to mid-September—Bell retains new attorneys, working pro bono, who seek to move his case to juvenile court and to free Bell on bond. The judge denies bond, citing Bell's prior criminal record involving battery and criminal damage, and sends the conspiracy case to juvenile court. He upholds the battery conviction. Rev. Jesse Jackson visits Jena and calls for a major rally for September 20, the sentencing date for Bell's battery conviction. An appellate court overrules the judge, vacating the battery conviction and sending that case to juvenile court.

September 15—The New York Times, Los Angeles Times, ABC and CBS run their first reports on Jena.

September 20—An estimated 20,000 people from around the nation hold peaceful rallies and marches in Jena.

December—Bell pleads guilty to second-degree battery in juvenile court and agrees to testify in upcoming Jena 6 cases. He is sentenced to 18 months, to be reduced by time already served, in state juvenile custody. He is also serving a separate, partially concurrent 18-month sentence for three earlier crimes.

2008

A white-power group has sued the town of Jena to march against the Jena 6, the civil rights movement and Martin Luther King Jr. Day. The rally had been planned for January 21, when Jena residents hold a march to honor King.

The parents of the December 4 attack victim have filed a civil lawsuit seeking unspecified damages from the school board, the Jena 6 parents, the defendants who are legal adults and a seventh student who was not charged.

---

two weeks before the mainstream media bothered to mention the person who became the most recognized member of the Jena 6.

All this awful bait, but the national media didn't bite. The story, instead, was the property of black bloggers and radio hosts, two local papers and activists. Only after they had interpreted it, only after they had dissected it, only after they had decided the right and the wrong of it—and dedicated a movement, the Afrospear, to it—only after big names like Al Sharpton

and Jesse Jackson stepped into the fray last summer did the news media give it to us.

And when the media got it, they often took it as it was told to them. They let the citizens do much of the journalism, instead of piecing it together for themselves. They took Jena as a handout, not as an opportunity. They ignored the shades of gray, and kept what could have been the most complex, most challenging racial story, the one that would drive thousands to march and thousands to question the media and thousands to question the American justice system, black and white.

Why? What happened to the race beat?

"Race is still an issue in society, but it's difficult for newspapers to get handles on it," says Roberts, who now teaches journalism at the University of Maryland. "These usually aren't the kinds of events that lead to sort of inverted-pyramid, hard news kinds of stories. They're more ooze-and-seep racial stories. And it requires a lot of time and attention to do them with the nuance they deserve. And a lot of papers, in an era of cutbacks and short staffs, are shortchanging the race story."

Last summer, Jena became a major national story, inspiring a thousands-strong march, protests, calls for equal justice and a flooding of the national media.

But not before Alan Bean got to it.

Bean is not a journalist. He's the cofounder and executive director of Friends of Justice, a grassroots organization designed "to create media scandals around questionable prosecutions as they unfold," according to its website (friendsofjustice.wordpress.com/). In January 2007, Bean began receiving phone calls from a few parents in the small Louisiana town, complaining of racial injustice in the case of six young black men.

Bean researched. He read the local papers. He visited Jena and met the defendants and their parents. He developed a sense of mission. "It became clear that if business as usually practiced was going to play out . . . then these kids were going to be dragging felony convictions for the rest of their lives," Bean says. "That would probably mean they'd never go to college, never have a professional job, never have a chance at the American Dream. The Jena defendants had a lot of support, but [there was also] a lot of fear, and a lot of people felt they didn't want to speak up."

After more than a month, Bean spoke up for them. He wrote a six-page, "media-friendly" report titled "RESPONDING TO THE CRISIS IN JENA, LOUISIANA." Here is some of what it says.

- "The competence and independence of investigators is seriously in doubt."
- "The behavior of school officials and school board members reflects a breathtaking insensitivity to the mixture of anger, intimidation and horror inspired by the hate crime of late August."
- "The ethical lapses and flawed professional judgment of LaSalle Parish District Attorney Reed Walters call for strong remedial action."

Bean concedes he connected many events: the noose hangings, the December assault on Barker, the fight between black and white students. He also says he set out clear characters in his story. Walters, who charged the boys with attempted murder, and the school officials, who Bean says did not give the white students harsh enough punishments, are cast as the villains. The six defendants are described as "good kids."

"I made it very clear that I tried to present this as a human drama," Bean says.

In April 2007, he sent his report directly to those he thought would cover Jena the way he wanted it covered: Howard Witt of the Chicago Tribune, Tom Mangold of the BBC and Jordan Flaherty of Left Turn Magazine. Shortly after, Witt broke the story in the national media on May 20; Mangold broadcast "This World: 'Stealth racism' stalks deep South" four days later.

Flaherty's first Jena piece, on May 9 (leftturn.org/?q=node/649), begins with a quote from Alan Bean: "'The highest crime in the Old Testament,' he declared, 'is to withhold due process from poor people. To manipulate the criminal justice system to the advantage of the powerful, against the poor and the powerless.'" It continues with emotional quotes from the Jena defendants' parents: "When asked how her life has changed, [Bryant] Purvis' mother described the sadness of having her son taken away from her without warning. 'You wake up in the morning and your son is there. You lay down at night and he's there. Then all of a sudden he's gone. That's a lot to deal with.'"

"Racial demons rear heads," reads the headline over Witt's story, and the story begins: "The trouble in Jena started with the nooses. Then it rumbled along the town's jagged racial fault lines. Finally, it exploded into months of violence between blacks and whites."

"Now the 3,000 residents of this small lumber and oil town deep in the heart of central Louisiana are confronting Old South racial demons many thought had long ago been put to rest."

From "Stealth racism" by Tom Mangold: "The bad old days of the 'Mississippi Burning' 60s, civil liberties and race riots, lynchings, the KKK and police with billy clubs beating up blacks might have ended."

"But in the year that the first serious black candidate for the White House, Barack Obama, is helping unite the races in the north, the developments in the tiny town of Jena are disturbing." It goes on to recount many examples of a so-called "stealth" racism in Jena: a barber who won't cut black people's hair but insists he's not racist; the fact that Caseptla Bailey, mother of Jena defendant Robert Bailey, can't get a job as a bank teller. And it echoes Martin Luther King Jr. in calling Sunday mornings "perhaps one of the most segregated times in all of America," noting that a church in a white Jena neighborhood only has one black member.

Soon, the blogs were afire with cries for justice in Jena—and for media respect. "I make a final plea to the American media," wrote black blogger Shawn Williams on the day of Blogging for Justice, created by dozens of black bloggers who latched on to the Jena movement. "I'd ask that you raise your right hand and admit under oath that you just don't give a damn about black people. Your non-coverage of missing black women and children, your demonization of hip hop culture, your initial labeling of Katrina survivors as 'refugees' and your daily lynching of black athletes called sports talk radio is evidence of this fact. The Jena Six deserve justice." (dallassouthblog.com/2007/08/30/jena-six-deserve-justice/)

Wrote D. Yobachi Boswell on The Black Perspective: "The Afrosphere Jena 6 Coalition 'ask that the mainstream traditional media step forward and discharge their duty to provide coverage of this vitally important event to their viewers and readers and act as "the fourth institution" of governmental "checks and balance" that constitutional framers intended the press to be.'" (blackperspective.net/index.php/day-of-blogging-for-justice-jena-6/)

Says Wayne Bennett, who wrote about the lack of national media coverage on his blog The Field Negro: "I don't think it was a sexy story. Stuff like that happens all the time, especially in Southern towns. That's not something the mainstream media would chase. . . . They got on the story because Jesse Jackson and Al Sharpton got involved, then the big march, then it became sexier." (field-negro.blogspot.com/)

"I think it goes back to the difference of how the general media feels about an issue and how African Americans might feel," says Williams, author of Dallas South Blog. "It's because the media is made up of non-African Americans in general, and because of that they cover the stories from their personal point of view and that point of view is not shared by everyone. That's why I've really enjoyed what's happened lately with the blooming of bloggers. People can use their own spin to report what happens and how they feel about it."

After the bloggers were well into their crusade, in late summer, Jackson and Sharpton visited Jena. The Washington Post's first story came shortly after they announced their plans for demonstrations; others gradually trickled in. Coverage boomed the week of the September marches, held steady in some papers in October and decreased markedly in November.

Many bloggers credit themselves with bringing the events in Jena into the national spotlight.

Bennett wrote on September 20, the day of the marches: "For those of us black activists who use the web as a tool for change, we have been e-mailing each other, blogging about Jena, calling each other, and organizing on the web for months about this travesty of justice down in Bayou country. Now, finally, the rest of America has caught on. This is now national news, and the Jena 6 has springboarded into our national conscience. It also reinforces my belief that the Internet and the world wide web can also be used as a tremendous tool for activism and organizing for social change."

With so much percolating in the blogosphere, why did it take so long for the national media to jump on the Jena story?

"I certainly didn't become aware of it during much of that time," says Washington Post Executive Editor Leonard Downie Jr. "Apparently there was a growing communication about it on the Web and on radio, but it didn't reach our attention until later. Then when it did reach our attention . . . it took a while to nail it down." Says Darryl Fears, who covered Jena for the Post, "I found out about it the same way marchers did, through e-mail blasts. I didn't read any of the blogs, but there were these e-mails about a story of injustice in Jena. . . . Then my editor said, 'Hey, have you heard about this thing in Jena? Maybe we should go down there.'"

The Chicago Tribune's Witt says he "didn't know anything about [Jena] until April," when he got an e-mail from Alan Bean.

Keith Woods, dean of faculty at the Poynter Institute, says that the problem wasn't that journalists didn't know about Jena, but that they failed to see the deep implications of the case in terms of race relations and the black community, which has doubted the fairness of the criminal justice system for years. At last, a flesh-and-blood example, and nobody caught it.

"What's at work here, I believe, is a journalistic news judgment process that remains invisible even within news organizations, but certainly invisible to the public, that somebody is deciding the guilt or innocence of these young men or the level of their guilt or innocence or the level of justice they deserve before they tell the first story—and that dictates whether they send a reporter to answer the first questions or not," Woods says.

Catherine J. Mathis, senior vice president of corporate communications for the New York Times Co., said Times editors declined to be interviewed for this article. James O'Shea, who was ousted in January as editor of the Los Angeles Times, did not return phone calls.

At a panel titled "News Coverage of Hate Crimes" at the University of Maryland in November, participants agreed the media's slow response to the developments in Jena can be attributed to the death of the race beat—and the death of sensitivity to small stories with deeper meanings.

"I wish we still had race beats in this country now, because we miss the continuity of coverage we used to have," Gene Roberts said. "The people I wrote about [in 'The Race Beat'] would have been right in the middle of it."

"I think that we do need a race beat," said University of Maryland journalism professor and former Washington Post journalist Alice Bonner during the discussion. "We get caught up in episode and event coverage because we fail to take them up routinely. We need to cover race because it's a live, active, dynamic part of society. If we covered it routinely we wouldn't have to be so frenzied when something like this happens."

A race beat won't solve anything, Bonner said, if hiring patterns don't change. "The biggest problem with journalism," Bonner continued, "is journalism is still too white. . . . It's too white for a society that is increasingly brown. . . . It is too white for its own good."

But diversifying hiring won't help, the panelists said, if cultural sensitivity isn't instilled in reporters and news gatekeepers. "I don't want us to think racial hiring is the answer. Having two, five, 10 people of color is not even going to make a dent," Bonner said. "The way you stay there is you conform. And conformity is staying with the status quo."

At the Post, Fears is the only reporter specifically assigned to cover race, Executive Editor Downie says. But he says other beats, such as politics, regularly touch on racial issues, like immigration.

And the Post is trying to diversify. "Our staff is around 25 percent journalists of color, and we do have targets for our hiring, and diversity is a very important priority for us," he says. "But diversity is large territory. . . . You have gay readers, readers of different backgrounds. We're trying to match the diversity of the [Metro] area, which we're a long way away from, like most newsrooms, because this area is more diverse all the time."

Has any of this hindered the Post's Jena coverage?

"For our readership," Downie says, "our coverage [of Jena] has been relatively thorough."

On August 24, 2007, a LaSalle Parish judge made one of the heaviest decisions in the Jena 6 case: Mychal Bell would not be granted bail. The 17-year-old would stay behind bars until the end of his then-undetermined sentence—until, we know now, September 27, for more than nine months, longer than any other member of the Jena 6.

Only two local reporters showed up to witness the proceedings. One of them was Abbey Brown, 26, of Alexandria, Louisiana's Town Talk newspaper. And at the hearing, she learned more than Bell's fate: She learned he had a prior criminal record.

Her story the following day said that record included four previous violent crimes, including two Bell committed "while on probation for a Christmas Day battery in 2005, according to testimony." He was adjudicated—the juvenile equivalent of conviction—for three of the crimes, the story says. It goes on to explain why Judge J.P. Mauffray Jr. decided to hold Bell without bail; the reasons included Bell's criminal record.

But no major papers reported this fact, Brown says—not that day, not that week, not for months, not, in some cases, ever. "A reporter for the Jena Times and I were the only two people at that hearing," Brown says. "I know that we thought it was important to go to every single hearing that we heard about, but even after we reported it, it wasn't something the other media were picking up."

The two local papers that have covered the case vigorously from the beginning insist mainstream news organizations are misrepresenting pertinent facts and unjustly skewing a story about justice.

The Town Talk, a 32,000-circulation daily that routinely covers Jena as well as a number of other small towns, published its first story on the Jena 6 case on September 6, 2006, a short piece about the hanging of the nooses at Jena High School.

As of last November 15, the paper, based 37 miles from Jena, had published more than 140 additional stories on the episode, all easily accessible from its homepage (thetowntalk.com). A click on a sizable black, yellow and white box with JENA SIX takes you to the paper's Jena Web page, with links not just to all its coverage of the case but also to 21 photo albums, downloads of videos and court filings, a Jena map, a Jena timeline, a message board and a list of frequently asked questions about Jena and its coverage.

Paul Carty, the Town Talk's executive editor, has his own list of gripes, gripes that have positioned him as the enemy of those who insist coverage of the Jena saga has been just and groundbreaking:

- The national media routinely refer to the jury that prosecuted Mychal Bell as "all white" without explaining why it was so. Carty says that explanation is simple—as well as enlightening. A Town Talk story on June 27 said that, according to court officials, the court summoned 150 people for the jury pool, but only 50 showed up, and those 50 were white. According to the story, Bell's attorney, Blane Williams, said some of the 100 who didn't show up were black—which is important to consider in such a racially charged case, Carty says. "I think there's an obligation there that if you say there's an all-white jury, that should raise some concerns as a writer, because talking about an all-white jury in the Deep South in a case that has to do with race, that's fairly inflammatory writing, unless you provide context."

- The labeling of the tree a black student asked to sit under, and the nooses were subsequently strung from, as the "white tree" is "unfair and unsupported." "We've never referred to it as the 'white tree' because it's not an official name for the tree, and it's kind of like one side says white kids just sat under, others say black and white sat under it . . . so we've left it alone," Brown says. "I'm kind of a purist as far as sourcing things, and people have shown me pictures of white students sitting under the tree, of white and black students sitting under the tree. . . . We've kind of left it as [the] tree where nooses were hung."

- Jena has been unfairly portrayed by the media as a racist town. "One thing that just about knocked me out of my chair was when a TV reporter did a live shot in September, the day of the demonstration, and he asks a member of the community, 'How long has Jena been a racist town?' That's not to say that Jena doesn't have some racial problems, but Jena has the same kind of racial problems that every other community in this country has," Carty says. He declines to name the reporter or the news outlet.

- Feeding this portrayal is the fact that reporters are not talking to sources on all sides of the story. They either talk to the Jena 6, their parents or civil rights activists, Carty says. What about the residents of Jena? The judges? Justin Barker?

- Poor descriptions of Barker's condition. Brown reported on June 11 that Barker's initial medical bills totaled $5,467 and that students described the fight in statements with phrases like "stomped him badly," "stepped on his face," "knocked out cold on the ground," and "slammed his head on the concrete beam." "I've seen pictures that were taken of him and I've got to tell you this, this was no normal schoolyard brawl, this was a kid with blood coming out of his ears," Carty says. "Where it gets reported that he was treated at a local hospital and released, that's true, but I can tell you right now that he's sitting at home with internal injuries."

Carty is not the only one who believes Jena coverage has been inadequate. Similar charges have been brought by Craig Franklin, assistant editor of the Jena Times, a small weekly that has covered the town since 1905 and the Jena 6 case since the nooses appeared. In an October 24 column in the Christian Science Monitor titled "Media Myths About the Jena 6," Franklin, the paper's sole reporter on the case and a 20-year Jena resident, lists 12 of the fundamental things the national media got wrong about the Jena 6. Some echo Carty's critique.

Franklin says the plethora of errors has led Jena residents to stop speaking to national reporters. And if the media continue to get it wrong, such boycotts will become commonplace, he says.

"What I'm fearful of is the more that these types of cases are exposed in the public's view"—such as the Duke lacrosse case (see "Justice Delayed," August/September)—"and the national media does not do its job and report its facts and not just go with the person who cries the loudest or gives the best headline, I think we're going to lose our purpose. Right here in Jena, Louisiana, you can walk down the street and pick out any person and ask them, 'Do you trust the national media?' And they'll say, 'No.'"

An independent assessment of the critics' main arguments shows many of them to be largely true.

An analysis of all news stories and briefs about Jena in four major newspapers—the Washington Post, the New York Times, the Los Angeles Times and the Chicago Tribune—from the beginning of their coverage until November 15, found the following. Out of 57 stories:

- Only eight stories allude to Mychal Bell's prior criminal record, and only three—two October stories in the Chicago Tribune and one short, late-September story in the New York Times—mention the specifics. The Washington Post's first major story on Jena incorrectly says "Bell had no prior criminal record." On October 17, it mentions that Bell "was recently re-incarcerated on a probation violation" but gives no hint that his record included violent acts.

- Ten stories use the phrase "all white" to describe the jury that found Mychal Bell guilty of aggravated second-degree battery and conspiracy to commit aggravated second-degree battery. None explains why the jury was all white, though the Town Talk laid it out in June. Only the New York Times does not use the description.

- Multiple stories describe the tree the nooses were found on as a "white tree," either directly calling it a "white tree" or using a more rounded term: "tree that was a traditional gathering place for whites" or tree "on the side of the campus that, by long-standing tradition, had always been claimed by white students." No stories question if the description is correct, and none asks students about the tree. Only the L.A. Times does not describe the tree as "white."

- Descriptions of white student Justin Barker's medical condition vary from paper to paper and from story to story. The first Post story to discuss Barker's injuries says he had "two hours of treatment for a concussion and an eye that was swollen shut." The concussion is never mentioned again, and subsequent Post stories simply say he was knocked unconscious and released from the hospital. The first New York Times story to mention Barker's injuries says he was "treated at a local hospital and released." The next says he was knocked unconscious and kicked. The last just says he was "knocked unconscious." The L.A. Times' first story says Barker was "kicked in the head and knocked unconscious" and "taken to the hospital and treated for injuries to the ears, face and eye." The next

mention simply says he was "beaten and knocked briefly unconscious." The Chicago Tribune's first story mentioning Barker's condition says he "spent only a few hours at the hospital." The next story says he was knocked unconscious and did not require hospitalization.

- The Washington Post, the L.A. Times and the Chicago Tribune never, in months of coverage, mention Barker's medical bills. The New York Times mentions them in only two stories, the first on September 22, more than three months after the Town Talk reported them in June.

- The phrase "schoolyard brawl" or "schoolyard fight" is used multiple times to describe the December 4 beating. Many times, it is the only description.

- All four papers link the events in Jena multiple times, without ever explaining why they're linked. The Washington Post calls them a "chain of events." The New York Times says the nooses "set off a series of events."

- Thirty stories quote civil rights activists, organizations or advocates. Eight stories quote Jesse Jackson; twelve quote Al Sharpton; others quote the ACLU, the Southern Poverty Law Center and the NAACP. Six quote Alan Bean of Friends of Justice—five of them in the Chicago Tribune. Many times these are the only people quoted.

- District Attorney Reed Walters is quoted in only five stories. Many of the quotes are paraphrased. The New York Times is a notable exception here—it printed a column by Walters on September 26. Only six stories quote the parents of the Jena 6.

- A point not raised by other critics: The L.A. Times, the Washington Post, the New York Times and the Chicago Tribune repeatedly say the white students accused of hanging the nooses were "suspended for three days" or "were suspended from school" or "received brief suspensions." None addresses additional facts, like these, reported in an October 8 correction by the Atlanta-Journal Constitution: "The students [who hung the nooses] were disciplined with nine days of alternative school, two weeks of in-school suspension, Saturday detentions, attendance in discipline court, evaluation before returning to school and participation in a state intervention program for families."

Part of the problem with the coverage, says Kansas City Star columnist Jason Whitlock, is that the national media relied too heavily on Jena According to Alan Bean. In a piece titled "How One Man Fired Up Jena 6 Case," Whitlock wrote that the media blindly accepted Bean's story—to the detriment of the truth. Why? Because it was easy, he says.

"If you're part of the mainstream media, I think that you see the story as something that should win you a lot of acclaim," Whitlock says. "The media is so lost right now. In the '60s, we were very important . . . and we don't know how to be important anymore. So if we can hop on some explosive case and appear like we're championing the right cause and protecting the defenseless or whatever, we will."

"He called attention to Jena with his agenda as a point of entry," Carty, the Town Talk editor, says of Bean. "He was spoon-feeding to the media what the story was all about. His perspective on the story is a partisan perspective; he thinks an injustice has been done, and that's his starting point, and it's picked up in the mainstream."

Jena Times Assistant Editor Franklin wrote in a column: "First, because local officials did not speak publicly early on about the true events of the past year, the media simply formed their stories based on one side's statements—the Jena 6. Second, the media were downright lazy in their efforts to find the truth. Often, they simply reported what they'd read on blogs, which expressed only one side of the issue."

Bean knew the media would bite. They did in 1999, when he told them about incidents in his hometown of Tulia, Texas. He exposed a corrupt cop and helped overturn more than a dozen drug convictions against minorities. Tulia was quickly labeled a racist town.

"I knew that it was probably the kind of case the media could be talked into covering because it had so many spectacular features: The fire—something that was terribly significant that nobody was picking up—the nooses and the racial tension. I thought that if the story was framed properly and people could see the connective tissue they could see how one thing led to another," Bean says.

While he is critical of the coverage, Whitlock doesn't cast Bean as the villain. "I'm not saying it's Bean's fault—that's unfair to him. If there's any bad guys in the Jena 6 story it's the media. We blew this."

The Chicago Tribune's Witt defends his coverage of Jena and says Bean was a reliable source. The reporter says he found factual problems with one story promoted by Bean, "and there's certain aspects of it that he was certainly trying to push one way or another, but, for me, that's no different from what other sources do. And the job of journalists is to listen, to try to find the good story in there, but not to be led by the nose with a particular spin. But by and large . . . he was a credible source."

As for his own work on Jena, says Witt, "I don't see where I've been inaccurate in anything I've described."

He acknowledges that he did not mention Barker's medical bills but stands by his description of Barker's condition: "I don't know what his medical bills are; I've seen some claims from his family that he had medical bills. But he was knocked unconscious, and he was in hospital I believe for three or four hours. That's all true."

He says his description of the punishment for the students who hung the nooses as a "three-day suspension" is incomplete, but says it is the fault of the school superintendent, who did not explain the depth of the students' punishment. The superintendent "did not reveal any of the other details about this other type of discipline," Witt says. "I know that subsequently when people started focusing on the story he gave a press conference in which he did detail the other dimensions of that discipline . . . but if he had chosen to tell me about the rest of discipline, I would have reported that, too."

What about the all white jury? Readers don't need an explanation of why it was all white, Witt says. "I guess that's a salient

detail, but I'm not sure in the scheme of things it makes that much of a difference."

Shortly after his interview, Witt sent AJR an e-mail, with "a couple of additional points." Part of it: "It's also inaccurate to intimate that I was somehow partisan in my reporting of this story. I have accurately reported all sides of this ongoing saga. You should note, for example, that last month I wrote a highly critical story about questions surrounding the fundraising for the Jena 6 families and how those funds were being accounted for. . . . I can assure you that story won me no fans among the Jena 6 families and their supporters, who believe that by writing that story I damaged their cause, even as it elated many right-wing bloggers and commentators. [Bill] O'Reilly invited me onto his Fox News show to talk about it. As a journalist, my role is not to support any particular cause but to report all the significant developments in the story without fear or favor."

In late October, Witt's Tribune, along with several other major news organizations, sued to force the courts to give the media access to all legal proceedings involving Mychal Bell, "whose prosecution had been shrouded in secrecy on orders of the trial judge," he wrote. The media won.

Post reporter Fears defends his reportage on grounds similar to Witt's. Why didn't he clarify the punishment for the students who hung the nooses? Because the suspension is the only part that matters, he says. "We weren't going to get into any long litany of things these students had to undergo. We wanted to look at one, the three-day suspension being out of school, versus what the parents [of other students] wanted, which was their expulsion."

Why didn't he correct his statement that Bell had no prior criminal record? "There was no correction because . . . I made several attempts to verify it. One, I flew to Jena and looked at Bell's court jacket, and it wasn't in there. And the prosecutor [Reed Walters] was not talking to the press. He didn't talk to press before the march. . . . That rests squarely on his shoulders.

"It's interesting to me that these explanations were out after Jena came squarely in public eye, after these marches. They could have come very early on but they didn't. . . . Someone needs to ask, 'Why is that happening just now? Why didn't you explain that before?' "

New information is coming out now. There are conflicting reports. Why doesn't Fears report on it? Why hasn't he investigated what really happened with the Jena 6?

"For a national newspaper, you don't generally go back and try and follow all of that out," he says. "I do think the Jena story was a very interesting story, but to go back and investigate in Jena based on this flashpoint incident. . . . It just didn't rise to that type of story. It wasn't Hurricane Katrina. It wasn't so many things. It just wasn't the biggest story that a newspaper like the Washington Post or even the New York Times or the Boston Globe would do."

Carty admits the story was easier for the Town Talk because of its proximity to Jena and its familiarity with the town. But it was far from a breeze. At times, the small paper had a dozen reporters—a good part of its staff—working on the story, limiting its ability to cover other things.

And at times, people were very unsatisfied with its coverage. Lead Jena reporter Abbey Brown has received threatening phone calls and e-mails. But Brown stayed on the story—if anything, because the efforts of the national media left her disenchanted. "I guess it just kind of disappointed me a little. I'm a young journalist, and I've always been sort of an idealist," Brown says.

"I know our goal as journalists is to be fair, and I've seen some things that I kind of thought weren't so fair," she continues. "I don't think it was malicious, but there was just not enough effort. I had to talk to more than 30 people to get five people to go on record, but if that's what it takes then that's what it takes. At least that's how we feel."

Sometimes, the facts came quite easily.

"We just walked into the courthouse and said, 'Can we see the court documents?'" Brown says. "I've got countless calls from people saying, 'Who's a good person to talk to for this and that' and I've directed each of them to go into the courthouse and ask for the documents. . . . There's a wealth of information for both sides; if one side isn't talking it doesn't mean that's the end of it."

Gene Roberts recalls the sit-in movement of the 1960s and the Montgomery bus boycott. Like Jena, they were initially brushed off, and early reporting was hearsay, Roberts says. But they ended up being turning points of the civil rights movement.

"As journalists, you have to get up and use shoe leather and talk to people and do the story in all its roundness. Constantly people of authority, no matter what race they are, will give you the established line of what's going on, and you have to dig beneath that. . . . It's just not one side said this, one side said that. . . . You have to dig beneath and see what's right. The truth doesn't always lie between them."

At a "Covering Immigration and Race" discussion at the Poynter Institute, dean of faculty Keith Woods wanted to focus on Jena. So he spoke to the Town Talk's Carty and Williams from Dallas South Blog. What he found was a serious disconnect— two very different perceptions of the Jena story.

"The most profound realization coming out of those two conversations was how utterly differently two people could see the same story," Woods says. "To essentially paint it as the participants did, in the case of Paul [Carty], a story about overblown and incorrect media coverage, as much as it was about Jena, and to Shawn [Williams], it was a story about injustice."

Which is it about? The media should tell us, he says.

"First, I do think that the national media—and this is a phenomenon of the national media, not specific to Jena—tends to come in and sweep broadly in its reporting. And I would say it's subject to cast things inaccurately by not delving down deeply enough into individual details of the story," Woods says. "We wind up with bickering over whether there were three nooses in the tree or two, whether white people alone sat under the tree or whether there was a period when black and white people sat under the tree, and that's because national media doesn't climb down and check on those facts itself. It tends to rely on previous reporting. In this conversation, those inaccuracies have become the implicit argument against national coverage or a more just treatment of the young men in the story, and I think both of those are illogical conclusions.

"But here is the thing: If we are a nation of paranoid people, we need to know that. And so if it is pure paranoia that's driving the busloads of people that drive down to Jena, some of us need to report that, and if we believe it's paranoia, our belief needs to be taken to the journalistic test of reporting, and not simply dismissed, while we go off and cover O.J. And if it's not paranoia, who but journalists to help us understand it and see the injustice? Either argument deserves national attention before [the first story appeared] May 20."

RAQUEL CHRISTIE (raquelchristie@gmail.com) wrote about coverage of onetime professional football player Pat Tillman's death in Afghanistan in *AJR*'s October/November issue.

Charticle Fever

Bite-sized combinations of words, images, and graphics called "charticles" are in vogue at a number of American newspapers. And they are not necessarily the enemy of compelling narrative.

DANE STICKNEY

Josh Awtry is known as a story killer.

Because of his steadfast support for the short, graphic-driven alternate story form known as the "charticle," some traditionalist reporters and editors have labeled the Salt Lake Tribune assistant managing editor of online and presentation an enemy of the narrative.

A few months ago, a story-hugging editor cornered Awtry, accusing him of trying to turn the whole newspaper into one giant graphic.

"I'm not out to destroy narrative," Awtry replied. "Just bad narrative."

For decades, news organizations have been seeking ways to stem the steady decline of newspaper circulation and woo those elusive 18-to-35 year-olds who are likely to get their news free on the Internet. Well, here's an equation that editors and designers in newsrooms ranging from small dailies in Oregon to major metros in Florida are increasingly turning to: Chart + article = charticle. (Think Brad + Angelina = Brangelina, but not nearly as hot and quite a bit geekier.)

Charticles—as defined by Omaha World-Herald Deputy Presentation Editor Josh Crutchmer—are combinations of text, images and graphics that take the place of a full article. But in many newsrooms, the term refers to a bunch of blurbs floating around with no byline, no transitions and—gasp!—no nut graph.

Say you've been asked to write a story about what people were doing with their federal rebates aimed at stimulating the flagging economy. You go out and find one person who's going to spend it on a new hi-def TV, another who's going to stick it in the bank and another who's going to try to cut that $3,000 credit card debt in half. Sure, you could think up a snappy lead, mix in some quotes from economic experts and write a nice little 12-inch story. Or you could try another approach. You assign photographers to take nice portraits of the sources. You put their personal information in an easy-to-digest form—name, age, job, what they're doing with the money, maybe a quote or an expert's opinion on what these people have chosen to do. Boom. You're done. You've got three local faces staring back at you. The entire package—probably laid out in a grid format—is quick to read and easy to digest.

At papers including the Salt Lake Tribune, Omaha World-Herald (where I work), Florida Times Union, St. Petersburg Times and Orlando Sentinel, charticles are all the rage. The merger of graphics and text also occasionally pop up on the pages of dozens of other dailies, from the 9,000-circulation Daily Astorian in Oregon to larger papers like the 200,000-circulation San Jose Mercury News. The form allows more design freedom, helps offset heavy public-policy coverage and makes design contest judges smile.

But, as always, there's a catch. Charticles rely on authoritative, punchy writing, leaving room for opinion to seep in. And when news and opinion mix under a reporter's byline, well, you see where that could lead. Because the writing needs to be so succinct and the approach is design-intensive, a lot of people are involved in the evolution of a charticle. That can leave reporters writing to an editor's idea instead of letting their reporting lead the way.

Whatever its pluses and minuses, though, the charticle is causing editors, reporters and designers to examine how they tell stories.

It's unclear exactly how the charticle was born. If you find yourself bellied up to a bar with a bunch of hardcore page designers and want to start a ruckus, ask them who invented the charticle. You're apt to get a bunch of different—and fervently held—opinions.

Some say Van McKenzie, the late sports editor at the Orlando Sentinel and St. Petersburg Times, pioneered the marriage of graphics and text in the 1970s.

Others theorize that Edward Tufte, the Yale University design professor emeritus whom the New York Times described as the "da Vinci of data," is behind the charticle. But Tufte says he's not the guy. He says he didn't coin that "awful word 'charticle'" and certainly didn't come up with the idea. He has, however, written a lot about it. In his book "Beautiful Evidence," he contends the practice has been around forever and segregating words and images started with modern technology that can handle either pictures or words but not both.

Awtry agrees with Tufte on both counts. Illuminated manuscripts stretching as far back as 400 AD featured what would be labeled today as at-a-glance boxes. Mayan temples constructed 1,500 years ago featured calendars of events in grid form. But it's hard to present information that way on your basic personal computer.

"Have you ever tried to do an alt form in [Microsoft] Word? Not gonna happen," Awtry says. "Newspaper front-end systems allow you to start a story under a byline, write it and file it when you reach the end. Even the most progressive of systems won't let you do anything more than add a glance box."

So it was up to designers to take the text out of its traditional form and present it in a more accessible way. People like McKenzie, Tim Harrower of Portland's Oregonian and the graphics addicts at USA Today did just that.

But the word "charticle" has only been buzzing around newsrooms for less than a decade ago. One of the earliest designers to use the term was Monica Moses, a progressive visual journalism star who helped raise the profile of alternate story forms in the late 1990s and early 2000s at the Charlotte Observer, Minneapolis' Star Tribune and the Poynter Institute.

Moses remembers hearing the mashed-up term while judging a design contest in the early 2000s. The staff of Texas Monthly described their mergers of visuals and text as charticles. Many designers credit magazines—like Wired, with its use of edgy info blurbs, and Maxim, which wraps some features around pictures of near-naked women—as inspiration for newspaper charticles.

Moses liked the Texas Monthly term and used it as inspiration for the development of a more reader-friendly presentation. She pushed the charticle not only as a replacement for boring, info-heavy narratives, but also as companions to in-depth pieces. People are much more likely to read an 80-inch story if they're given a brief, easy-to-understand primer before diving in, Moses says.

Poynter's EyeTrack07 study backs her up. It found that alternative story forms like charticles did a better job of catching readers' attention than traditional narratives. The pairing of short text with visual elements also helped readers better remember facts, according to the study.

Anecdotal evidence of the charticle's impact varies from paper to paper. Patrick Webb, managing editor of the Daily Astorian in Oregon, has recently run four or five charticles in his newspaper. Topics included child care shortages, fishing and competition between area hospitals, some of which ran as the main story on the front page. "Every one has prompted unsolicited reader comments that say, 'I like the way you explained that,' " Webb says.

The San Jose Mercury News uses charticles sparingly, often in its business section for such topics as holiday shopping and events that require a lot of data but not much storytelling. The staff buzzes about them more than readers, Managing Editor David Satterfield says. "I'd say we've really had no reader response—either positive or negative," he says. "But folks here [in the newsroom] enjoy them."

The Times in Shreveport, Louisiana, recently set up a newsroom committee charged with getting more charticles and other alternative story forms into the paper, Executive Editor Alan English says. The staff is still determining when it's best to use the form and how to free up designers to create charticles. But top editors have asked each reporter to propose one charticle-like story each week. "We are exploring these new forms more seriously to be an easier and better read for baby boomers with busy lifestyles," English says.

The charticle is perfect for those busy readers, says Julie Wright, managing editor of the Anchorage Daily News. "Newspapers are at their best and most memorable when they tell stories with people, conflict, drama, action," she says. "But a lot of what we give readers doesn't have those elements; it's essentially imparting information. Alternative story forms are great for imparting information as opposed to telling a story: What hours is downtown parking free, how much rain have we had this summer, how much have grocery prices risen, what are the 10 best summer reads?"

The leaders at Minneapolis' Star Tribune, early believers in alternative forms, hired Moses in 2002. Eventually, the paper embraced her ideas to the point that it covered a major gubernatorial address in charticle form.

Things changed when McClatchy sold the Star Tribune to Avista Capital Partners in December 2006. Moses, who had moved to the business side of the paper, quit a few months later and now works as a consultant. The Star Tribune doesn't run as many high-profile charticles as it did under Moses, but the paper still regularly uses the form.

About a year later and nearly 1,200 miles away, another editor who worked with charticles resigned as well. But Choire Sicha quit his job in protest of the form that Moses embraced. Sicha publicly blasted the charticle in January after resigning as managing editor of the news-gossip website Gawker. Owner Nick Denton had recently expressed his desire to keep much of the site's content—often presented in charticles, top 10 lists and other alt forms—to between 100 and 200 words. That didn't sit well with Sicha, who told the New York Times, "I don't want to write a top 10 list in my life, ever. I don't want to construct a charticle."

Sicha indeed is not forming lists and charts now: He writes for Radar Online and freelances for the Los Angeles Times. "Obviously the charticle is useful in that it consolidates information," he says. "A charticle makes it pleasant to read without, you know, all those awful words in the way."

However, Sicha isn't convinced newspapers are reacting to their readers' desire for easier-to-read presentation. Instead, he thinks newspapers may have in fact changed the way people read by force-feeding them easy-to-digest information.

Publications have become "an experience of looking, not of reading. And so nearly every publication looks like US Weekly and Cosmo: numbers in huge type, pictures, polls. Databits. Postliterate!"

—Choire Sicha

"It seems to me that the short attention span of the reader has become a self-fulfilling thing. USA Today made the reader what he is," Sicha says. Publications have become "an experience of looking, not of reading. And so nearly every publication looks like US Weekly and Cosmo: numbers in huge type, pictures, polls. Databits. Postliterate!"

Sicha doesn't see that changing, because many designers and editors—misguidedly, in his view—don't think people want to read traditional newspapers. "They doubt themselves too much," he says. "Many have become cowards."

He sees editors and designers over-thinking and getting too cute. They are dreaming up what he calls "half-baked" charticle ideas, sending staffers out to report them and having designers make them look pretty. "Charticles are in that way anti-journalistic," Sicha says.

The potential problems don't end with editors and designers. Not only is there the risk of reporters injecting opinion, there's also the risk that they will kiss them off. Moses, Awtry and Crutchmer noticed that reporters often approached charticles with lower standards than they did traditional pieces. Because they are not stories and contain less text, some journalists seem to believe they don't require the same level of reporting and attention to detail that narratives do.

Actually, they may require more. In narratives, reporters can cover up holes with flowery writing or storytelling devices. Charticles don't allow that luxury. They're straightforward and simple. If you don't have the goods, it shows.

The best writers—the ones who often aren't asked to write alternate forms because they're too busy with "real" stories—are the ones who tend to do the best job with charticles, says Awtry, the Salt Lake designer. "Good writers get it," he says. "They know when a story needs to be told—to write with authority, sure, but also with emotion, impact and subtle weaving of narrative and chronology. They also know when to get out of the way. They don't have any desire to write subpar stories or feel the need to try and weave a weather story into a narrative. They'd rather be clean, kick it out the door and move on to something riveting."

Crutchmer, whose charticle ideas have helped the Omaha World-Herald win two Society of News Design Awards of Excellence, does see a battle of story forms emerging, a sort of survival of the most readable. And he foresees a victim: "I hope charticles kill the 12-inch story."

In Crutchmer's view, readers want one of two things. They want to get their need-to-know info quickly and in an understandable way. Charticles can handle that. But readers also want to be told stories in longer, captivating ways, in compelling traditional narratives. What they don't want are medium-length, inverted-pyramid reports. Crutchmer sees newspapers becoming more like magazines—a combination of short, graphic-heavy blurbs and well-written long-form stories.

So are Crutchmer, Awtry and their beloved charticles actually preserving the narrative? Perhaps they are promoting a way for the best writers to quickly get through the mundane news items and spend more time with the stories that need to be told with scene-setting leads, drama and character development.

Some journalists—like Choire Sicha and that editor who cornered Awtry—might have trouble buying that. Awtry doesn't much care.

"There's a place in our industry for a bigger toolbox," he says. "There's a place for the long, compelling story that evokes emotion, incites passion and fuels reaction. And there's also a place for self-selecting information—a place where I can glance, pick what I want and get out."

DANE STICKNEY (dstickn1@gmail.com) is a features writer at the Omaha World-Herald, where he writes 40-inch narratives about aged calligraphers and four-inch charticles on "American Idol" contestants.

From *American Journalism Review*, October/November 2008, pp. 36–39. Copyright © 2008 by the Philip Merrill College of Journalism at the University of Maryland, College Park, MD 20742-7111. Reprinted with permission.

Beyond News

Journalists worry about how the Web threatens the way they distribute their product. They are slower to see how it threatens the product itself.

MITCHELL STEPHENS

Call it the morning letdown. Your muffin may be fresh, but the newspaper beside it is decidedly stale.

Chavez bashes Bush on Un stage reads the headline, to pick one morning's example, on the lead story of *The Miami Herald.* That was a Thursday in September. But Yahoo, AOL, and just about every major news website in the country had been displaying that story—President Hugo Chavez of Venezuela had called President Bush "the devil"—since around noon on Wednesday. The news had been all over the radio, all over cable, too: Fox News had carried, with gleeful indignation, twenty-three minutes of the speech live. Indeed, when Katie Couric introduced the Chavez story on the *CBS Evening News,* at 6:30 Wednesday, her audience may have experienced an evening letdown. By then—half a day before Chavez's name would appear in newsprint in Miami—his entry on Wikipedia, the online encyclopedia, had been updated to include an account of the speech in the United Nations.

Editors and news directors today fret about the Internet, as their predecessors worried about radio and TV, and all now see the huge threat the Web represents to the way they distribute their product. They have been slower to see the threat it represents to the product itself. In a day when information pours out of digital spigots, stories that package painstakingly gathered facts on current events—what happened, who said what, when—have lost much of their value. News now not only arrives astoundingly fast from an astounding number of directions, it arrives free of charge. Selling what is elsewhere available free is difficult, even if it isn't nineteen hours stale. Just ask an encyclopedia salesman, if you can find one.

Mainstream journalists can, of course, try to keep retailing somewhat stale morning-print or evening-television roundups to people who manage to get through the day without any contact with Matt Drudge, Wolf Blitzer, or Robert Siegel. They can continue to attempt to establish themselves online as a kind of après AP—selling news that's a little slower but a little smarter than what Yahoo displays, which is essentially what *The Washington Post* and *The New York Times* were up to when, about four or five hours after Chavez had left the UN podium, they published, online, their own accounts of his speech.

But another, more ambitious option is available to journalists: they could try to sell something besides news.

The notion that journalists might be in a business other than the collection, ordering, and distribution of facts isn't new. In the days when the latest news was available to more or less anyone who visited the market or chatted in the street, weekly newspapers (at the time, the only newspapers) provided mostly analysis or opinion—something extra. The growth of cities, the arrival of dailies, and the invention of swift fact-transmitting and fact-distributing machines (the telegraph and the steam press) encouraged the development of companies devoted to the mass production and sale of news. Their day lasted more than a hundred years. But the sun is setting.

Information is once again widely available to more or less everyone, and journalists, once again, are having difficulty selling news—at least to people under the age of fifty-five. If news organizations, large and small, remain in the business of routine newsgathering—even if they remain in the business of routine newsgathering for dissemination online—the dismal prophesy currently being proclaimed by their circulation and demographic charts may very well be fulfilled.

"If we don't do the basic reporting, who will?" journalists counter. Here's John S. Carroll, former editor of the *Los Angeles Times,* presenting, to the American Society of Newspaper Editors, this notion of mainstream journalists as the indispensable Prime Movers: "Newspapers dig up the news. Others repackage it." But the widely held belief that the Web is a parasite that lives off the metro desks and foreign bureaus of beleaguered yet civic-minded newspapers and broadcast news organizations is a bit facile.

For much of their breaking news, Yahoo and AOL often tap the same source as Drudge and *WashingtonPost.com:* The Associated Press, with Reuters, AFP, and a few others also playing a role. (Most of the early online Chavez reports linked to an AP story.) Nothing said here is meant to imply that the wire services, and whatever cousins of theirs may materialize on the Web, should stop gathering and wholesaling news in bulk.

However, the Web increasingly has other places to turn for raw materials: more and more cameras are being aimed at news events, and transcripts, reports, and budgets are regularly being placed on the Web, either by organizations themselves or by citizens trying to hold those organizations to account. We are still very early in the evolution of the form, but surely industrious bloggers won't always need reporters to package such materials before they commence picking them apart. Mainstream journalists are making a mistake if they believe their ability to collect and organize facts will continue to make them indispensable.

There will continue to be room, of course, for some kinds of traditional, thoroughly sourced reporting: exclusives, certainly. Investigations, certainly. That's something extra. Yahoo isn't in a position to muckrake.

But the extra value our quality news organizations can and must regularly add is analysis: thoughtful, incisive attempts to divine the significance of events—insights, not just information. What is required—if journalism is to move beyond selling cheap, widely available, staler-than-your-muffin news—is, to choose a not very journalistic-sounding word, wisdom.

Here's more historical precedent: In the days when dailies monopolized breaking news, slower journals—weeklies like *The Nation, The New Republic, Time*—stepped back from breaking news and sold smart analysis. Now it is the dailies, and even the evening news shows, that are slow. Now it is time for them to take that step back.

Insights into the significance of news events certainly do appear on one page or another in our dailies, in one segment or another on our evening newscasts; but a reader or viewer has no reason to believe that they will be there on any particular story on any particular day. It's hit or miss. And outside of the small patch of the paper that has been roped off for opinion, the chances of coming upon something that might qualify as wisdom are not great. Most reporters have spent too long pursuing and writing "just the facts" to move easily into drawing conclusions based on facts. Their editors have spent too long resisting the encroachment of anything that is not carefully sourced, that might be perceived as less than objective, to easily welcome such analyses now.

So you sometimes get, under a "news analysis" slug or not, pieces that construct their insights out of the unobjectionably obvious—proclaiming that "some" have "voiced concerns," that "developments" may have "profound ramifications," but "on the other hand" "it is too soon to tell." And you find situations as odd as this: In a column in June 2006, David Brooks of *The New York Times* introduced his "War Council"—the "twenty or thirty people" who, because of the soundness of their "judgments" and "analysis," he turns to for wisdom about Iraq. One of those people works at Brooks's own paper: the "übercorrespondent"—currently Baghdad bureau chief—John F. Burns. Brooks included two quotes from Burns about Iraq in his column, including: "I'd have to say the odds are against success, but they are better now than they were three months ago, that's for sure." However, neither of those quotes was taken from the newspaper that employs Burns, where he

ventures beyond the facts only rarely and very cautiously. Instead they were comments Burns made on the PBS program *Charlie Rose*.

"We would be of little value in our television appearances," Burns acknowledges, "if we offered no more than a bare-bones recitation of events, without any attempt to place them in a wider context, and to analyze what they mean." But shouldn't the same standard of "value" apply to Burns's appearances in his newspaper? He denies that *Times* reporters "are muzzled in conveying the full range of our experience and impressions" under the proper rubrics in the paper. Nonetheless, the "impressions" from this *Times* correspondent that most interested a *Times* columnist had not originally appeared in the *Times* itself.

The Wall Street Journal got a taste of this the-best-stuff-doesn't-make-the-paper problem two years ago when an e-mail found its way onto the Web from one of its reporters in Iraq, Farnaz Fassihi. It proved not only more controversial but arguably more interesting than the stories Fassihi had been filing from that country. For in this e-mail, intended to be private, Fassihi wrote in the first person and she noted what things looked like to her: "For those of us on the ground," she said, "it's hard to imagine what if anything could salvage [Iraq] from its violent downward spiral."

Outside the strictures of mainstream journalism, Fassihi, in other words, did not have to attempt the magic trick American reporters have been attempting for a hundred years now: making themselves and their conclusions disappear.

The switch to a new product line is moving forward at a pretty good pace on the pages of at least two newspapers—one large and foreign, one small and local.

The *Independent* is a serious English national daily in a market with three other serious national dailies. So the *Independent*, looking for an edge, has begun devoting most of its front page, weeklylike, to a single story—a story covered with considerable perspective and depth, a story in which the paper is not shy about exhibiting a point of view. The *Independent* weighed in recently, for example, on the debate on global warming with this headline, and a picture of a large wave, dominating its front page: TSUNAMI HITS BRITAIN: 5 NOVEMBER 2060.

Simon Kelner, the paper's editor in chief, explains that his understanding of the situation of the daily newspaper "crystallized" during coverage in England of the American presidential election in 2004. The *Independent* reported and interpreted the results along with the other papers. "It was a really expensive, exhaustive exercise for us all," Kelner recalls. Yet the next morning newsstand circulation actually fell. For up-to-the-minute results people had turned instead to the radio, television, and the Internet. However, he explains, "The next day *The Independent* published twenty-one pages of analysis and interpretation of the election—and we put on fifteen percent in sales."

Kelner got the message. "The idea that a newspaper is going to be peoples' first port of call to find out what's going on in the world is simply no longer valid. So you have to add another layer: analysis, interpretation, point of view." Kelner now dubs his daily a "viewspaper."

Compare the *Independent*'s response to a visit by Secretary of State Condoleezza Rice to the Middle East with that of *The Washington Post*. The *Post* reported on a joint press conference she held with the Palestinian Authority's president, Mahmoud Abbas, on page A26 under this headline: RICE CITES CONCERN FOR PALESTINIANS, BUT LOW EXPECTATIONS MARK VISIT. The *Independent,* that same morning, emblazoned this headline on its front page: THE ROAD MAP TO NOWHERE: FOUR YEARS AFTER GEORGE BUSH UNVEILED HIS MIDDLE EAST PLAN, CONDOLEEZZA RICE ARRIVED TO FIND PEACE AS FAR AWAY AS EVER.

It is not that shocking, by European standards, that *The Independent* has been saying what it thinks; what is fresh and vital is the magazine-like boldness and focus (think *The Economist*) with which it is saying it. Beneath the ROAD MAP TO NOWHERE headline on its front page, the *Independent* displayed a map of Jerusalem. Around the map were arranged five short items—each divided into THE PROMISE (headlined in red) and WHAT HAPPENED—in which the paper compared what the Bush administration had claimed for its "road map for peace" with the little, nothing, or worse (the Lebanon war was mentioned), it has achieved. Inside the paper, an article combined the history of the Bush Middle East plan with a report on Secretary Rice's current, seemingly futile visit to the region. Such a mix of graphic, list, and article—of news event, wider focus, and point of view—is now typical for the *Independent*.

Producing such a paper certainly makes for an interesting newsroom. "Our competitors each select the best news story of the day," notes John Mullin, the *Independent*'s executive editor for news. "What we try to do is something much more holistic. We try to capture the entire feel of something. It makes life much more—some would say difficult, some would say rewarding." Mullin adds that the effort to present a big chunk of news with a coherent viewpoint can be particularly "challenging" for journalists who are "used to thinking in the time-honored fashion: who, what, when and where."

Nowhere in the world has that fashion been as honored, and for such a long time, as it has been in the United States. Mainstream journalists in America today live in fear of the charge of bias. To achieve more vigorous analysis, they may have to get over that fear. After all, opinions—from "these are the times that try men's souls" to FORD TO CITY: DROP DEAD—have, historically, managed to hold their own with facts as ways of understanding the world. And it's not as if there aren't things besides the effort to be balanced for which journalists might stand. Old-fashioned reason might, for example, do, too.

Journalists also might stand for honesty. Sure, the analytic journalist can prove wrong: Burns, on *Charlie Rose,* had one take on the situation in Iraq; in her e-mail Fassihi, writing at a different time, had another. But there is something to be said for being openly right or wrong rather than hiding an assessment behind the carefully choreographed quotes of various named and unnamed sources.

No one is suggesting that reporters pontificate, spout, hazard a guess, or "tell" when it is indeed "too soon to tell." No one is suggesting that they indulge in unsupported, shoot-from-the-hip tirades. "It's not like talk radio," explains one of the champions of analytic journalism, Mike Levine, executive editor of the *Times Herald-Record* in Middletown, New York. But it's not traditional American journalism either. Levine, a former columnist, had noticed that the analyses reporters unburdened themselves of in conversations in the newsroom were often much more interesting than what ended up in the paper. Some of that conversation is mere loose talk and speculation, of course. Yet "walk into any newsroom in America," Levine says, "turn the reporters upside down, and a hundred stories will come falling out. They know so much about the communities they cover, but they don't get it in the newspaper."

When he took over the *Times Herald-Record* in 1999, Levine was determined to change that. "We simply asked reporters to give the readers the benefit of their intelligent analysis," he explains. This means paying less attention to the mere fact that a hospital administrator resigned in nearby Sullivan County. It may even mean leaving the account of the resignation to the paper's website. It definitely means more attention, in the paper, to what that resignation might signify.

"We're not the infantry anymore," Levine explains. "We don't just go out to board meetings and take dictation. That's not really much of a contribution to the community. What are needed are journalists who can connect the dots." Levine, in other words, is not afraid of letting his reporters—after they've done the reporting, when they know as much about a subject as most of their sources—find meaning in the dots.

Accomplishing this at a newspaper that may not be at the top of the hiring ladder has required, in Levine's words, relying on "some experienced people devoted to community journalism"; it has required finding and hiring some young reporters who are "curious" enough not to "shut down inquiry" and surrender to what Levine calls "a stale, petrified 'objectivity.'" But Levine adds, "not every reporter on staff does this kind of reporting. We're evolving into it."

Here is an example of what happens when journalists do Levine's kind of reporting, from a multipart *Times Herald-Record* series by the reporters Tim Logan and John Doherty, on a renaissance in the city of Newburgh:

> The city is shaking off three decades of inertia. It's an exciting time. The real-estate market is hot. City politics are more harmonious. And there are plans galore. Plans for a community college on lower Broadway, plans for the long-empty stretch of land on Water Street, a master plan under way for the city as a whole.

> But there's no plan for the city's poor. . . . If this city is truly going to rebuild, if it will ever fill the void at its heart, if it can transform itself from a drain on the rest of Orange County into the thriving hub the county desperately needs, Newburgh can no longer ignore its poverty.

Note: That's not, "Some observers suggest Newburgh can no longer ignore its poverty." Nor is that an editorial or a column. The point is being made in news pages, at a small, local newspaper, by journalists—based on what they have learned on their beats (the *Times Herald-Record* employs a traditional, geography-based beat structure), and based on their own reasoned and informed appraisal of the situation.

Burned-out reporters can be forgiven for dreaming that the coming of this analyzing and appraising will lead to a life of leisurely speculation. But, alas, more industrious reporting, not less, will be required. You'd better know an awful lot about plans for rebuilding Newburgh before you contemplate criticizing those plans. Getting at the meaning of events will demand looking beyond press conferences, escaping the pack, tracking down more knowledgeable sources, spending more time with those who have been affected, even seeking out those whom Levine of the *Times Herald-Record* calls "the invisible people— people who are not at board meetings who may not even show up at the voting booth." When Levine took over, his paper began a "sourcing project," designed to force reporters to avoid "going to the same three or four sources [for] every story." More and more diverse sources, the theory goes, should improve story ideas and stories, and help reporters know more when they say what they know.

Strategies developed at the *Times Herald-Record* might be of use at larger papers, too. As a source of timely and important analysis, our journalistic heavyweights are simply not—on a day-to-day, story-to-story basis—reliable. We will know that they have grasped their role in this staler-than-your-muffin news world only when they realize that being fast with the analysis is as important today as being fast with the news has been for the last hundred years.

For that to happen, our major news organizations—we need to begin thinking of them as "news-analysis organizations"— will have to develop a stable of knowledgeable analysts whom they can assign each day to the major stories—as they currently assign reporters. Some of these "wisdom journalists" might be obtained through raids on think tanks and weeklies. Smaller papers, less able to filch an expert on urban issues from the Brookings Institution, might regularly borrow some analytic talent from the less jargon-infested corners of local universities.

But daily news-analysis organizations must also develop their own career path for analysts.

Working your way up through the metro desk, the Washington bureau, and a few overseas beats certainly has its value, but it does not necessarily qualify you for untangling the underlying causes of fundamentalist Islamic terrorism. Some extensive university training might. News-analysis organizations will have no more room for the sort of scholars who never leave the library or their laptops than they'll have room for the sort who stuff sixty words, two of them unfamiliar, into a sentence. "I have a degree in East-Asian studies," Susan Chira, foreign editor of *The New York Times,* states. "But when I went to Asia myself and lived there, I found out a lot of things my teachers didn't know." We will continue— in journalism, not academic journals—to need theory to be tested and illuminated by experience, including on-the-street, eyes-open, with-the-victims experience. But an ability to go and get is simply no longer sufficient. The best journalistic organizations are going to be selling the best thinking on current events—and that often is furthered by deep, directed study.

The old saying is that reporters are only as good as their sources. We will require many more journalists who, when occasion demands, are better than their sources, journalists who are impeccably *informed*. Let's call this one of the five I's—a guide to what journalists need to be, now that at least four of the old five W's are more widely and easily available. *Intelligent* would be another, along with *interesting* and a holdover from the previous ethos: *industrious*. But the crucial quality is probably *insightful*.

It is significant how many of the most respected names in the history of journalism—from Joseph Addison to Dorothy Thompson and Tom Wolfe, from Charles Dickens to Ernie Pyle and I.F. Stone—were, indeed, known for stories that were exhaustively reported, marvelously written, and often startlingly insightful. The disruptions caused by the new news technologies will prove a blessing if they allow journalists to stop romanticizing the mere gathering and organization of facts and once again aspire to those qualities.

MITCHELL STEPHENS, a professor of journalism at New York University, is the author of *A History of News.*

Maybe It *Is* Time to Panic

Why news organizations have to act much more boldly if they are to survive.

CARL SESSIONS STEPP

Two dozen journalists from a national magazine have gathered to discuss their future and how to prepare. They seem somewhat anxious and uneasy, but what most intrigues me is where they focus their main concern.

It isn't about whether journalism will survive, or even whether they will have jobs.

Their rawest worry seems to be this: With all the stresses and cutbacks, will they be able to continue doing the job right? "The hardest question," as one puts it, "is how to maintain accuracy with less time."

This apprehension squares with what I hear repeatedly in visiting newsrooms and talking with journalists. To be sure, they are showing worrisome levels of battle-scarred doubt. But at the same time, they remain some of the most idealistic souls you'll ever come across.

For all their jaded posturing, journalists want to preserve something that has worked for two centuries: news media that can both make acceptable profits and perform essential public services.

Can this still be done? Probably.

How? By moving far faster than conventional media are moving now, accelerating into a space-race urgency to revolutionize their content and business.

The rank-and-file is ready. After a generation of fitful transition toward some elusive new age, journalists seem primed to move from the hand-wringing stage to decisive action.

If only their leaders knew what to do.

At a recent Carnegie Corporation conference in New York City on the future of media, Jim Willse, editor of Newark's Star-Ledger, pointedly framed the problem.

"The business model of newspapers that we all grew up with has blown up," Willse said. Now the issue is: "What is it that we have that is truly of value? What can we do that people are willing to spend something to get, even if it's just time?"

> ## "What can we do that people are willing to spend something to get, even if it's just time?"
>
> —Jim Willse

The bad omens are easy to see.

Today's newspeople know they have forfeited the edge on breaking news and lost the buzz in the online marketplace. They have been outflanked and out-thought by portal sites, aggregators, social networkers, indexers, video hosts, auction and classified sites and many others. They see advertisers retreating, and readers fleeing and Web viewers waffling.

Lots of statistics demonstrate these points, but consider just this one:

Daily newspaper circulation has declined every year since 1987.

Yet journalists own some sizable advantages, both new and old. They cling to their franchise strength of localness in both news and advertising, benefit from the seemingly infinite appetite for information and conversation, maintain strong credibility and brand presence, and are models of dependable longevity in an age where trendier bookmarks and blogs come and go by the hour.

No wonder journalists, who aren't necessarily all that normal to begin with, react in unorthodox, often contradictory ways, endorsing change but clinging to old ways, cynical on the outside but altruistic at heart.

This duality, and the perseverance it breeds, may well save them in the end. The tough part is that, for now, they're acting a lot like a nervous puppy about to be loaded into the family van.

Are we going to the park to play, or to the vet to get those shots?

When I visited the Charlotte Observer last year to interview its under-30 staff members (see "Caught in the Contradiction," April/May 2007), a 24-year-old copy editor named Christine Lee, in true headline-writer style, cut directly to the heart.

"We are all just kind of stuck in that old model," she said, "and we haven't figured out how to get out of it yet."

Now, after a generation of inconclusive lurching, journalists want to figure it out. The initiative falls to managers.

The next step calls for newspeople to focus their formidable collective brainpower on a quantum leap forward in quality and service. It probably won't cost nearly as much as they fear; from Gutenberg to Google, world-changing ideas have come from unknown upstarts with more imagination than money. The results can be transforming.

At some elemental level, neither journalism nor market economics has changed.

Journalism remains today, as it always has been, a blend of reliable information, entertainment, discussion and connection.

All that is required to prosper, as always, is to supply the audience with some of the above ingredients more attractively than the competition.

What has changed profoundly is not the role of journalists—as trusted monitors, watchdogs and guides—but their position.

For centuries, journalists stood at the mouth of a vast assembly line of information. They controlled the flow, which moved in an efficient line from producers to receivers. This model let producers dominate content and format.

Information came when journalists let you have it. If you wanted a magazine, you had no choice but to stand by your mailbox until it arrived, on the producers' schedule, not yours.

Today journalists stand not at the head of the pipeline but in the middle of a boundless web of interconnected media, messages, senders and receivers. This is the new, right-brain, digital world. The journalist-in-the-middle is a ringmaster, a maker and a consumer, a grand impresario of a two-way information flow that has no beginning, end or fixed schedule.

Journalists no longer control content and format. Anyone with a computer can become a publisher. An independent blogger can scoop the pros. A kid with a cell phone can distribute the day's most compelling video.

Ultimately this interactivity may be the most influential change of all.

It makes everyone a potential producer as well as a consumer. It transcends schedules and time restrictions. It produces instant feedback and amplification. It democratizes decision-making. And it lets the audience disregard the professionals when it chooses.

Again, none of this changes the definition of news. News remains, as always, fresh information of public value.

What changes is how news is assembled and shared. Here too power has slipped from journalists. News becomes a collaborative and cumulative work in progress pieced together by multiple contributors, rather than a media-certified byproduct carved in press plates and fixed in time.

In a widely discussed essay in the Washington Post in January, the outspoken former Baltimore Sun reporter David Simon, executive producer of HBO's "The Wire," asked, "Isn't the news itself still valuable to anyone?"

I would answer that the news itself is more valuable than ever. Information is power. In an information age, good information is not just valuable but invaluable.

What changes is how that value is apportioned in the marketplace.

Until recently, producers monopolized the information flow and the resulting revenue. Now they have less control and more competition. Because technology has fostered near-infinite ways of finding and spreading information, there is actually far more revenue available than ever. But it is spread thinner, and the mainstream media have proved sadly slow in corralling their share.

Why didn't they capture the market in online classifieds, long before Craigslist? Why didn't they become the home base for local video, long before YouTube? Why didn't they recognize the power of social connections, long before Facebook?

Preoccupied with trying to save their old model, they barely glanced up as one potential pot of gold after another floated right past them.

Now, as blogger Alan Mutter, a former print editor turned new-media chief, wrote recently, it's time "to stop whining about the glories of yesteryear and start thinking of creative ways to make or save more money."

In short, the challenge is this: News organizations need to think more imaginatively, turn duress into motivation and make their content irresistible and their business operations unstoppable. And fast.

Hyde Post, the Atlanta Journal-Constitution's vice president for Internet operations, was discussing change within his organization last year when he said something that has stuck with me ever since.

"If we really wanted to get in good with people," Post said only half-jokingly, "we would be the people who come to your house and hook up your machines."

I for one wouldn't trust most journalists, myself included, to hook up anything mechanical, but I appreciate his larger point. Today's journalists need to corner the market on information customer service.

This will demand dramatic, even radical, improvements.

Think about these figures, all based on published reports by professional groups or analysts:

- Thirty years ago, 71 percent of adults read a daily newspaper. Ten years ago, it was 59 percent. Last year's figure: 48 percent.
- Last December, 63 million unique visitors came to newspaper websites. Google's figure: 133 million.
- Ad revenue for newspaper websites rose 21 percent to $773 million in the third quarter of last year over the previous year. Print ad losses during the same period: $1 billion, wiping out the gain from the Web.
- In the third quarter of last year, print advertising dropped 9 percent, including a decline of 17 percent among classifieds. A Goldman Sachs prediction for overall newspaper advertising this year: a drop of 8 percent.

While most news organizations remain profitable, they are rapidly losing ground in readership, revenue and Web popularity.

Now is not the time to panic, of course. . . .

Wait.

Now is exactly the time to panic.

Circulation down every year for two decades? Ad categories plummeting at double-digit levels? Competitors siphoning off brainpower and market share?

These dire symptoms fully support panic, or at least a boldness beyond anything seen so far.

In too many cases, news organizations respond not with bold advances but with retrenchment, and its inevitable damage to staffing, resources, newsholes and overall investment in such quality items as foreign coverage, enterprise and investigations. Even the physical size of the page has shrunk.

Their shift of resources to online journalism, while impressive in many ways, has been sluggish by cyber standards. Few traditional news organizations have built dominant websites. Cooperation and coordination between print and digital units remain grudging.

Now let me take a breath and acknowledge that exceptional work is being done on many media sites, that audacious experimentation can be found every day and that numerous news companies, foundations and organizations are underwriting exciting and promising initiatives.

But even conceding all that, how many mainstream journalists can look at either the tangibles (revenue and audience) or the intangibles (buzz and momentum) and truly feel good about the current situation? How many people, inside or outside the business, consider news organizations on the cutting edge?

While managers might argue that revenue problems require the print cutbacks and online caution, they should also ponder this question:

Do you really think that strategy is working?

My parents recently received a letter from the newspaper they have subscribed to since I was in the first grade 50 years ago. It informed them the paper was ending home delivery in their rural town.

It is no exaggeration to describe them as heartbroken.

Now I recognize that such consolidation has been going on for years, in a calculation pitting the cost of serving outlying subscribers against their value to local advertisers.

But my parents' disappointment resonated with me because, at about the same time, I had opened my home-delivered New York Times to learn the paper was ending television listings for my area, along with accompanying wonderfully droll recommendations. It was described as a cost-cutting move.

I understand the economics, but I also understand something that might matter more.

How, in ultracompetitive times, can a business afford to be seen as reducing value and service?

Doesn't that smack of defeatism? Give me instead a maniacal, refuse-to-lose, never-give-up fighting spirit and competitive fire that could electrify newsrooms, harness their limitless dedication and passion, ignite the fiercest creative fervor in media history and court audiences with quality so wondrous and indispensable that they wouldn't dare turn away.

Before time runs down, why not launch a counteroffensive to preserve serious journalism?

Before time runs down, why not launch a counteroffensive to preserve serious journalism, which has precious value in a confusing world; to recapture domination of the overall information market, where professional journalists lead in expertise and credibility; and to rebuild the business to make more money in more ways than ever before, all in keeping with the highest standards.

The guiding principles would be these:

- Make it better not worse
- Make it astonishingly, irresistibly better
- Make it easier, not harder, to use and enjoy
- Involve everyone from school kids to staff members to senior subscribers in the ultimate group science project of creating the greatest news outlets imaginable.

Last Christmas, I encountered a large sign on the door of a local electronics store. The store had no Nintendo Wii consoles, it sadly reported, and didn't know when any would arrive.

Can you imagine selling products so popular you can't supply enough of them?

Sales of video game consoles, software and accessories rose 43 percent last year, with each category gaining in double digits, according to the NPD Group, a market research firm.

Not many years ago, parents bought their kids board games and baby dolls, at maybe $15 or $20 apiece. Then, a reinvigorated toy and gaming industry seized on emerging technologies to invent games so alluring and coveted that parents almost overnight began shelling out hundreds of dollars for consoles that required an endless diet of $50 game cartridges.

That doesn't mean the $500 newspaper or $50 Web visit is feasible, but it should teach journalists something vital:

The smart response to change and challenge is to embrace arriving technologies to lift your work to new peaks of excitement and quality. Offer people something that's amazing enough, and they'll line up and happily pay the price.

The days of selling out papers over some fabulous story aren't that far behind us. To recapture that momentum, news organizations need to mobilize and unify. But as I visit newsrooms and websites, this preliminary groundwork looks rickety. Too often you find a collection of rival fiefdoms rather than a coordinated campaign. Somebody needs to take charge.

You also need a vision. For most local news organizations, the vision is to become the community's central source of dependable information services in any and all formats.

Think of a mega-mall, with its anchor stores (your website, daily newspaper, cable channel), its boutiques (inserts, magazines, giveaways, niche offerings), its service kiosks (archives, search engines, hosting capacity) and its ease of use (syndication feeds, mobile access, electronic alerts, whatever comes next).

You're reaching multiple audiences in multiple ways with multiple opportunities for information, interaction, commerce and revenue.

But success requires coordination, commitment and, most of all, content and formats that entice the audience. Here, too, news organizations lag. I'd propose launching an all-hands, ground-level brainstorming fury to generate idea after idea after idea. Some will fail, some will work and some may work big. Ideally, all could contribute to a workplace climate elevating creativity and a marketplace surge commanding attention.

To turn specific, below are some sample ideas. Many are already being tried. Others may be nutty or humdrum. Who knows? The point is to kick-start new rounds of thinking with ideas such as:

- A four-section daily paper recognized as the best available guide and overview to the overwhelming information world. Give it less the feel of a one-way pipeline and more of journalists and readers sharing, digesting and discussing news together:

Section 1, a dynamic, definitive guide to the locally relevant information universe, featuring digests, analysis, explanation, listings, links, columns and audience contributions; excerpts and synopses of top content appearing elsewhere; and a well-edited, annotated guide to the best material anywhere concerning international, national, regional and local news, sports, business and arts

Section 2, the most important and interesting news, local, national and foreign, from briefs to full reports, offering breadth and range, pointing ahead not behind, fully updated and differentiated from earlier Web copy

Section 3, an in-depth package, changing from day to day, presenting serious enterprise, investigative, explanatory and watchdog journalism of the highest possible level, not available anywhere else

Section 4, all the expected features from crosswords to comics, plus new ones including reader creations.

- An online information superstructure built around a double home page, with an easy toggle back and forth: one screen for an orderly display of news and other content, the other a portal-type screen offering a master index of anything useful and appropriate for your audience, with more choices, more services and a nontraditional license to experiment
- A renewed commitment to the public interest across all platforms, ranging from increased hyperlocal news to intense coverage of developing and continuing issues to giving voice to the needy, oppressed and silenced: a demonstrated long-view investment in community, service and editing
- A new, more conversational tone, both online and in print, including staff and outside blogs, behind-the-scenes essays from staff members and a higher proportion of analysis and explanation
- Far more easily searchable archives and galleries, with a user-friendly format more like Google or Yahoo! than the primitive systems many news organizations currently use; for example, searches that cluster content by precinct, neighborhood or topic, searches that index advertising or searches programmed to answer questions such as where a movie is playing or when the school board will meet
- Expanded interactive guides to movies, shows, concerts, galleries and other arts, with amazon.com-like reader reviews and interaction
- Calendars of events, searchable and easily subdivided by date, location or theme

- Real-time online traffic and weather blogs, in intensely localized detail
- Contests every day for the funniest, weirdest, most helpful or most outrageous local images, audio and video
- Tournaments, online and in-print, pitting local individuals and teams against one another in solving puzzles, predicting sports or election outcomes, guessing the first day it will snow or anything else
- Online book clubs and discussion groups on local sports, religion, relationships and other meaningful topics
- Ratings for anything you can get away with, from local sermons to sundaes
- Original uploaded programming, in which readers Web-cam their neighborhood news, read political commentary, offer Leno-like stand-up comedy bits on the news and debate key local issues
- Interactive neighborhood centers, for news, debate, exchange, advice, problem-solving and searchable, specialized advertising
- Galleries for local photos, audio and video, and applications that let readers upload their own material and search and reorganize existing content
- A complaint forum, directed toward local government or business, in which editors or audience choose which questions have merit and pose them to local authorities
- A local records center, providing agendas and minutes of every significant meeting in your area; text or links to as many public records as feasible; and your homemade community databases such as local sports stats, crime maps, home values or restaurant menus
- A homework center, where paid or volunteer teachers answer questions and offer advice (without, of course, actually doing anyone's homework)
- Greater capitalization on the treasures of your archive; for example, through creation of cheap software—call it something like localscrapbook.com—that lets readers develop and download scrapbooks featuring every article, photo or other mention of themselves and their families in your library; or publication and sale of special in-depth or feature reports drawing on your archives and research capabilities
- A help-needed feature, a sort of super-classifieds, that lets readers pose questions, seek products, evaluate services and possibly engage in transactions from which you share the profits
- Moderated forums and advice segments for personal finance, health, travel and other subjects
- New products and revenue sources: frequent-visitor points, premium services (such as customized news delivery, conferences featuring star journalists, first crack at ads and coupons, local discounts), neighborhood magazines, daily auctions (lunch with the editor!), grants from nonprofits, vastly upgraded searching services and search-related ads, customized magazine and book-length reports on key topics

- Above all, an unquenchable burst of new energy channeled into brainstorming
- Giving regular awards for good ideas from inside and out
- Unleashing teams of high school and college kids to spark innovation
- Staging regular creativity meetings throughout the news organization and in the community
- Hosting an ongoing online suggestion box with prizes
- Deputizing all staff members to suggest ideas and applications and offering them partial ownership rights and a share of any profits
- And spending some real money: Give $100,000 to three or four of your smartest people and challenge them to design something breathtaking.

Given their base of talent and passion, news organizations still can regain the initiative—if they stop plodding and start to rocket themselves forward.

"Even in hard times," James O'Shea wrote on losing his job as editor of the Los Angeles Times early this year, "wise investment—not retraction—is the long-term answer to the industry's troubles.

"A dollar's worth of smart investment is worth far more than a barrel of budget cuts."

CARL SESSIONS STEPP (cstepp@jmail.umd.edu), AJR's senior editor, teaches at the Philip Merrill College of Journalism at the University of Maryland. He wrote about newsroom transformation in the magazine's October/November issue.

UNIT 3

Players and Guides

Unit Selections

Key Points to Consider

- What are the arguments for deregulation of media ownership? Against deregulation? Which do you think is stronger? Why?

- It has been argued that spectrum scarcity, the driving force behind FCC regulation of electronic media, is no longer an issue. Is there a need for the regulation of the collective reach of media that one organization can acquire? Why or why not?

- For what kinds of media content do you advocate government regulation? For what do you advocate industry regulation? Sex? Violence? Portrayals of minority groups? Anti-American messages? Liberal versus conservative viewpoints? Evangelical Christian messages? Atheist messages? How should the rules regarding objectionable content be enforced?

- How would you define the rules of "ethical practice"? Who, besides the subject of a news story, is affected by such judgments?

Student Website
www.mhhe.com/cls

Internet References

The Electronic Journalist
http://spj.org

Federal Communications Commission (FCC)
http://www.fcc.gov

Index on Censorship
http://www.indexonline.org

Internet Law Library
http://www.phillylawyer.com

Michigan Press Photographers Association (MPPA)
http://www.mppa.org

Poynter Online: Research Center
http://www.poynter.org

World Intellectual Property Organization (WIPO)
http://www.wipo.org

The freedom of speech and of the press are regarded as fundamental rights, protected under the U.S. Constitution. These freedoms, however, are not without restrictions. The media are held accountable to legal and regulatory authorities whose involvement reflects a belief that the public sometimes requires protection.

Regulatory agencies, such as the Federal Communications Commission (FCC), exert influence over media access and content through their power to grant, regulate, and revoke licenses to operate. They are primarily concerned with the electronic media because of the historically limited number of broadcast bands available in any community (called spectrum scarcity). The courts exert influence over media practice through hearing cases of alleged violation of legal principles such as the protection from libel and the right to privacy. Antitrust law has been summoned in attempt to break up media monopolies. Copyright laws protect an author's right to control distribution of her or his "intellectual property." Shield laws granting reporters the right to promise informants confidentiality are the topic of debate in "Why Journalists Are Not Above the Law." The courts have heard cases based on product liability law, in which plaintiffs have—sometimes successfully and sometimes not—sued media companies for harmful acts attributed to a perpetrator's exposure to violent media content. The Federal Trade Commission (FTC) and the U.S. Food and the Drug Administration (FDA) have regulatory controls that affect advertising.

The first two articles in this section contribute differing perspectives on media business practice and access—the "players" of the unit's title. "What's a Fair Share in the Age of Google?" describes tension regarding application of fair use and copyright law to the Internet, noting "there is a growing sense among the 'legacy' media, at least, that Google facilitates a corrosive move away from paying content providers for their work." "Ideastream: The New 'Public Media'" lends insight to the Public Broadcast System (PBS), a nonprofit public television service funded largely by the Corporation for Public Broadcasting. "The Shame Game" addresses reality TV sting operations.

Beyond the reach of legal and regulatory sanction, there is a wide grey zone between an actionable offense and an error in judgment. For example, while legal precedence makes it difficult for public figures to prevail in either libel or invasion-of-privacy cases, it is not necessarily right to print information that might be hurtful to them. Nor is it necessarily wrong to do so. Sometimes a "good business decision" from one player's perspective impedes another's success. Sometimes being "truthful" is insensitive. Sometimes being "interesting" means being exploitive. Some media organizations seem to have a greater concern for ethical policy than do others; however, even with the best intentions, drawing the line is not always simple.

The remaining articles in this unit raise questions of ethical practice. "The Battle over the Battle of Fallujah" explores questions of taste and ethics surrounding distribution of a painstakingly realistic video game created to put gamers inside the 2004 title battle in Iraq. "Distorted Picture" addresses the ethics of altering photographs. Technology such as Photoshop makes it easy to edit photos and often photo editing is done for aesthetic

© The McGraw-Hill Companies, Inc/John Flournoy, photographer

reasons rather than with intent to deceive. What are the limits of acceptable practice? "What Would You Do?" ponders the ethics of investigative experimenters, who "step out of their customary role as observers and play with reality to see what will happen." "The Lives of Others" is about gatekeeping in the context of reality shows such as *America's Most Wanted.*

"The Quality-Control Quandary" discusses immediacy versus accuracy as traditional journalists struggle with acceptable expectations for proofreading and fact-checking prior to online posting. "The Porous Wall" addresses the traditional boundary between news and advertising copy in newspapers and how newspapers come to terms with changing rules as they fight to sustain revenue.

What rules of practice should be applied in balancing the public's right to know against potential effects on individuals and society at large? Which great photograph shouldn't run? Which facts shouldn't be printed? Who owns media channels and makes these decisions? Is it ethical for journalists to cover stories on issues about which they have strong personal views, or does such practice compromise objectivity? Is it fair to become a "friend" to win trust, then write a story that is not flattering, or does not support the source's views or actions? Should the paparazzi be held legally responsible for causing harm to those they stalk, or should that responsibility be borne by consumers who buy their products? What about the well-intentioned story that attempts to right a social wrong, but hurts people in the process?

These are not easy questions, and they do not have easy answers. Media in the United States are grounded in a legacy of fiercely protected First Amendment rights and shaped by a code for conducting business with a strong sense of moral obligation to society. But no laws or codes of conduct can prescribe an appropriate behavior for every possible situation. When people tell us something in face-to-face communication, we are often quick to "consider the source" to evaluate the message. Media-literate consumers do the same in evaluating media messages.

What's a Fair Share in the Age of Google?

How to Think about News in the Link Economy

Peter Osnos

The buzz inside Google is overwhelmingly positive about what the company does and how we will all benefit from the results—including the embattled denizens of newspapers and magazines who increasingly see Google as an enabler of their demise. Barely a decade ago, Google received its first $25 million investment, based on search technology developed by Sergey Brin and Larry Page, the company's cofounders. By the time it went public just five years later, "Google" was a verb. Today it is the dominant force in what has turned out to be the central organizing principle of the Internet's impact on our lives: the search function and the accompanying links, keywords, and advertising that make sense and commerce out of the vast universe of information and entertainment on the Web. Google is as important today as were Microsoft, IBM, and the original AT&T, linchpins of our culture and economy, in the development of modern computation and communications.

By contrast, the great twentieth-century print companies, such as Time Inc., Tribune, and The New York Times Company, are in a battle for survival, or at least reinvention, against considerable odds. Google has become a kind of metaphor for the link economy and the Internet's immense power to organize content. Yet as the global leader among Web-based enterprises, it has also become a subject of debate and controversy, even though its sense of itself is still as benign as the playful tenor of its Manhatttan offices, where the fittings include scooters for zipping around the halls and a lavish free cafeteria.

At lunch there, I was surrounded by an animated crowd that included Brin, Google's thirty-six-year-old cofounder, wearing jeans, a sweater, and a demeanor indistinguishable from the rest of his eager young crew. Google maintains that it is actively working to make journalism and literature truly democratic and, functionally, easier to do. Google's "Office of Content Partnerships" sent me a list of "free tools journalists could use today for nearly every aspect of their work," including Blogger, a platform for publishing online; Google Analytics, for measuring Web traffic; Google website Optimizer; and other tools. The publishers of newspapers, magazines, and books, recognize that Google and the link-referral service it represents have become

inextricable from their audiences' lives, and indispensable to reaching that audience in large numbers.

And yet there is a growing sense among the "legacy" media, at least, that Google facilitates a corrosive move away from paying content providers for their work. Proceeds go instead to those who sell advertising and other services while aggregating and/or lifting material they did not create. It is true that the content providers have submitted to the link economy of their own accord. Still, in a piece last winter, I wrote that the notion that "information wants to be free" is absurd when the referral mechanism makes a fortune and the creators get scraps. That position was excoriated by some bloggers, including one who, in a quote cited on *The New York Times*'s Opinionator blog, called it "sheer idiocy."

Maybe. But only two months later, the Associated Press (clearly acting on behalf of the news organizations that own it) made a similar point and initiated a process that could end in lawsuits. Addressing the Newspaper Association of America, the chairman of the AP's board of directors, William Dean Singleton, CEO of MediaNews, said: "We can no longer stand by and watch others walk off with our work under misguided legal theories."

The full quote from which "information wants to be free" was lifted, by the way, is more ambiguous and complicated than that widely-quoted excerpt. The line comes from the futurist Stewart Brand, who first said it at a programmer's convention in 1984 and elaborated in his book, *The Media Lab: Inventing the Future at MIT,* in 1987, where he wrote:

> Information Wants To Be Free. Information also wants to be expensive. Information wants to be free because it has become so cheap to distribute, copy, and recombine—too cheap to meter. It wants to be expensive because it can be immeasurably valuable to the recipient. That tension will not go away. It leads to endless wrenching debate about price, copyright, 'intellectual property,' the moral rightness of casual distribution, because each round of new devices makes the tension worse, not better.

Brand leaves out another factor—that valuable information is expensive to produce. But two decades later, the battles he foresaw are fully engaged.

An ecosystem in which all stakeholders in the content economy have a fair share. That is one media executive's succinct summary of what is necessary to redress the growing imbalance of power and resources between traditional content creators and those who provide links to or aggregate that material. But the effort to find that formula is complicated because it involves technologies upgrading at warp speed, sweeping changes in popular habits, collapsing and emerging business models, and one of the basic pillars of our democracy—what we have always called a free press.

As this century began, newspapers, especially those in metro areas with dominant positions, were reporting profits of 20, 30, and even 40 percent. *The New York Times* was selling over a billion dollars a year in advertising and *Time* magazine held its seventy-fifth-anniversary gala celebration at Radio City Music Hall, which had been specially redone for the occasion. Fortunes disappeared in the tech bust of 2000–01, which seemed to underscore the fact that Internet-based commerce was in its formative stages. The news products on the Web—CompuServe, Prodigy, and America Online—seemed, on the whole, complementary to newspapers and magazines rather than competitive against them.

Yet the unlimited expanse that the Internet provides and the amazing capacity of Google (and Yahoo and MSN, etc.) to search it, soon began to change everything. Vending services like eBay and Craigslist flourished; sensations like MySpace and YouTube, where users provide the content, were born at the intersection of creativity and engineering; audiences were suddenly huge for essentially brand-new Web news providers online, such as MSNBC and CNN. Sites like The Drudge Report showed the potential of aggregation and, later, The Huffington Post showed the potential for garnering large crowds partly by recycling material created elsewhere.

Significantly, most of the established news organizations reached the same conclusion about how to take advantage of what was happening on the Web. They went for the model that had supported network television for decades—mass audiences attracted by free access that would justify high advertising rates. Virtually overnight, Google et al were delivering hundreds of millions of readers to media companies which, in turn, believed they could monetize those visitors.

This approach contrasted with the one adopted in the 1980s by the emerging cable systems for television. Those companies negotiated subscription fees with the providers of their most popular programming, such as ESPN and dozens of other channels, including some that carried news. (The average cable subscriber, for example, pays 77 cents per month for Fox News, whether they watch it or not.) Most cable networks also have copious advertising, from inexpensive pitches for local establishments to national campaigns. This flow of subscription revenues, combined with advertising, made cable programming a lucrative business—which, ironically, resembles the way newspapers

and magazines operated until they unilaterally decided they were better off giving content away. (There are differences, of course, especially since barriers to a cable system are high, while barriers to launching on the Web are low, even though moguls like Barry Diller at The Daily Beast and others have found themselves investing real money there to get started.)

As the scale of the global economic implosion became clear, accelerating negative trends in circulation and advertising already under way, it became increasingly obvious that the free-content model was not working. News audiences were huge. On September 29, 2008, the day the Bush administration's first bailout proposal was voted down by the House of Representatives and the Dow fell almost eight hundred points, nytimes.com had 10 million visitors and 42.7 million page views. But revenues for The New York Times Company were disappearing so fast that this respected gatherer of news had to beg and borrow just to meet its debt obligations and maintain its news operation while also sustaining morale for the myriad innovations necessary to stay extant. This spring it threatened to shut down *The Boston Globe,* another financially sick newspaper with healthy traffic on its website. Unless new ways of attracting and sharing revenue are devised with the same breathtaking speed with which they have disappeared, the gathering of news by reputable, experienced institutions that are cornerstones of their community and the nation will be irreversibly damaged.

Print journalism bought into the free-news online model. Still, it is hardly surprising that the winners in the transformation of news dissemination, the distributors and aggregators, would become the focus of grievances by those they have trounced, willfully or not. So what is to be done to manage the consequences of this inexorable transformation of news delivery? If there is a simple, all-encompassing answer to that question, I did not find it in discussions with practitioners and pundits on all sides of the problem. But in the haze, I did find a tripartite framework for understanding the major aspects of the issue—let's call them the doctrines of Fair Conduct, Fair Use, and Fair Compensation.

Fair Conduct

On Saturday afternoon, February 7, 2009, SI.com, the website of *Sports Illustrated,* broke a huge story: Alex Rodriguez, the mega-rich Yankees star, had taken performance-enhancing drugs while playing for the Texas Rangers. *Sports Illustrated* released the story on its website rather than in the magazine, according to the editors involved, in an effort to enhance SI.com's standing as a destination for fans increasingly conditioned to getting sports news online. Within hours the story was everywhere, but if you went through Google to find it, what you likely got instead were the pickups that appeared elsewhere, summaries or even rewrites, with attribution. Most galling was that The Huffington Post's use of an Associated Press version of *SI*'s report was initially tops on Google, which meant that it, and not SI.com, tended to be the place readers clicking through to get the gist of the breaking scandal would land.

Traffic on SI.com did go up on that Saturday and for days thereafter, but not nearly as much as the editors had projected. As long as the value of advertising on the Web is measured by the number of visitors a site receives, driving those numbers is critical, and therein lies the dilemma. Why did The Huffington Post come up ahead of SI.com? Because, even Google insiders concede, Huffington is effective at implementing search optimization techniques, which means that its manipulation of keywords, search terms, and the dynamics of Web protocol give it an advantage over others scrambling to be the place readers are sent by search engines. What angered the people at *Sports Illustrated* and Time Inc. is that Google, acting as traffic conductor, seemed unmoved by their grievance over what had happened to their ownership of the story. An *SI* editor quoted to me Time Inc's editor-in-chief, John Huey, noting crisply that, "talking to Google is like trying to talk to a television."

The rules of the road for distributing traffic on the Internet need to include recognition, in simple terms, of who got the story. The algorithm needs human help; otherwise, valuable traffic goes to sites that didn't pay to create the content.

Fair Use

This has to do with how content is gathered, displayed, and monetized by aggregators, not how it is found and distributed. Fair use is a technical term for the standards one must meet in order to use copyrighted material without the permission of rights holders, as in excerpts, snippets, or reviews, and it turns out to be far more flexible than I long had thought. U.S. copyright law sets four main factors to consider in determining what is fair use: whether the quotation of the material is for commercial gain, the nature and scale of the work, the amount being used in relation to the whole, and the impact on the value of the material by its secondary use.

The definition of fair use was central in the lengthy negotiations among book publishers, the Authors Guild, and Google to settle litigation over Google's intention to digitize copyrighted books for search and distribution without paying for them. At the outset, in 2006, Google apparently believed that releasing only "snippets" of the books meant it would prevail in a court test. The publishers and authors argued that once Google had unrestricted access to the content, it would inevitably be widely used in full or large part.

Ultimately, the sides decided not to force the matter to resolution. Instead, in October 2008, Google agreed to pay $125 million to the plaintiffs and to establish a system to pay copyright holder, share advertising revenues that may result, and build a registry for all books that are available.

The book agreement—actually the settlement of several lawsuits—is nearly 150 pages, plus attachments, of excruciatingly complex detail. Debate over the terms ever since they were announced has been fierce and the court has already postponed final comments from interested parties until October 7. He will then look at the criticisms put forward by, among others, the Harvard librarian and lawyers funded by Microsoft who contend that Google is gaining what amounts to a monopoly in the digital book arena. Then, the judge will determine whether to approve the agreement as is, or send it back for further negotiations to satisfy the objections of its critics. He cannot amend the terms himself.

How the logic of publisher-author-Google pact applies to the news business is not clear—except that Google has acknowledged that the right to scan and distribute information has value, which can be shared with the originators of that content. Google's licensing agreement with the AP and other wire services—in which it publishes some AP content on its own servers rather than merely linking to it—may be another illustration of the same idea: pay to play.

But what of the aggregation of links? The Google position is that a link with a sentence or two as a tease is fair use of the material, and the site that generated the content actually is a beneficiary of the traffic. With news, the argument becomes entangled in whether the aggregation enhances or detracts from the value of the original content, and also in determining what amounts to fair use when an aggregator surrounds those links with its own summaries, blogs, and other interpretative embellishments, as some aggregators do. The news organizations also argue that aggregators should pay for that right to aggregate when they sell advertising around the links and snippets.

It would take a mind-bending interpretation of fair use to work these issues out, especially if the case went to trial. Many news providers don't have the time that a case would take (years, probably). And Google, again, may not want to force a final determination of the matter, as in the books case. As the controversy over Google's role in news intensified in the spring, executives from The New York Times Company, The Washington Post Company, and presumably others, met with Google in search of formulas that might balance their respective interests. Every one involved has signed nondisclosure agreements. If progress has been made in these discussions, it has not become public.

Fair Compensation

All of this still leaves the considerable question of monetizing the reading of material on the free-to-access sites that newspapers and magazines offer, now that it seems that online advertising alone will not be enough to support those operations. There are many ideas around for micropayments or subscriptions, memberships or paid sections within a free site, out of which may come a viable business solution or solutions. Based on my own reporting, the answer could be in some combination of individual payments or cable and telephone fees. Americans routinely pay telecom providers (Verizon, Optimum, and AT&T are the ones in my house) to deliver information and entertainment by television, computer, and wireless devices. The goal would be to extend those payments to the originators of news content. Google, it seems to me, might serve as a kind of meter, helping determine what percentage should go to the content originators. Complicated? Yes, but that is the kind of challenge that computers and the engineers who master them are meant to meet.

One of the best statements on this subject came from Jonathan Rosenberg, president for product management at Google, who wrote on a company blog, "We need to make it easier for the experts, journalists, and editors that we actually trust to publish their work under an authorship model that is authenticated and extensible, and then to monetize it in a meaningful way." The book publishers and authors agreement with Google recognized that goal, acknowledging that all information is not equal and cannot be free and endure.

These fairness goals for the internet age are plainly arguable. However, this is not a debate that will end in a vote that determines the outcome by majority rule, which is why predicting where things will go next is so hard. Still, what is known, earnestly but correctly, as accountability journalism—news that orders and monitors the world—is indispensable, and paying for it is vital to society. We now know conclusively that digital delivery is going to be a (or perhaps the) main way people find out what is happening around them, so the burden of responsibility on those who frame the way news is presented is incalculable.

Google is in its adolescence as a company. Cycles in the digital era tend to be short, but Google and the enterprises and services it encompasses are at the pinnacle now. What the company will do with that power is unknown in large part because, like most big institutions, Google limits transparency and is defensive when it comes to criticism.

There is a message in history for Google's leaders: nothing in the realms of business, information, entertainment, or technology remains as it is. Brin and Page stand on the shoulders of Gates and Jobs who followed Watson, Sarnoff, and Paley, who came after Luce and Disney and succeeded Hearst, Edison, and Bell. The next breakthrough innovators are doubtless at work somewhere. Will they help meet society's fundamental demand for news that supports itself in a way that Google and the rest of the digital generation say they want to do, but have not yet done?

Google is an extraordinary company with a nonpareil record of creativity. What a wondrous thing it would be for newsgathering, in a time of mounting crisis, if Google turned out to be as much a source of solutions as it is a part of the problem.

PETER OSNOS, *CJR*'s vice-chairman, is the founder and editor-at-large of PublicAffairs Books and a senior fellow for media at The Century Foundation. His previous *CJR* piece was about the future of books.

Ideastream: *The New* "Public Media"

In Cleveland, a partnership between a public radio station and public television station may be one model for the future of American public media.

M. J. ZUCKERMAN

A short walk from the Rock and Roll Hall of Fame and not far from "The Jake," home of the Cleveland Indians, there's a curious 95-year-old seven-story building—originally a fashionable furniture showroom—which, recently renovated, is the home of ideastream, a re-invention of public broadcasting that is generating a digital pulse of media excitement in the surrounding communities while, nationally, attracting curiosity and some downright envious stares.

An engagingly open structure, with more than 80 feet of windows on the avenue enticing passersby to peer in on live broadcast operations and dance studio rehearsals, the building is the physical manifestation of an elegantly simple concept. This is the vision of two media veterans who placed the mission ahead of all other interests to create an organization whose work is rippling outward into the education community, rejuvenating real estate development, bringing at least a thousand jobs to downtown, increasing public access to government and the arts, providing a center for performing artists to train and exchange ideas, giving rise to a hip tech neighborhood and convening public debate about American ideals.

And those are just the bonuses, the add-on benefits. Originally, when this all began about 10 years ago, the goal was to define a sustaining purpose for public broadcasting in Cleveland. The underlying concept was to merge the resources of public television and public radio. And then things kept percolating. By most accounts, ideastream has not only succeeded in defining a sustaining purpose for public broadcasting in Cleveland, but also demonstrated enduring potential as a hybrid: public media.

Along the way, ideastream's founders struck upon what more than a few leaders in the industry see as one of the most robust models for the future: A multiple media public service organization operating on broadband and built on two critical principles: 1) a commitment to the mission of "strengthening our communities," which is realized by 2) placing the values of partnership ahead of any desire for control.

If this sounds simple, it isn't. Even if you are deeply versed in the pervasive challenges facing public radio and public television, there is likely to be an "Aha!" moment as you come to understand that Jerry Wareham and Kit Jensen—respectively, the CEO and COO of ideastream—have established a *raison d'etre* for public television and public radio that transcends traditional notions of broadcast and simultaneously offers a model that could, in time, remedy what some have called "the flawed business model" of public broadcasting.

Wareham, formerly CEO of television station WVIZ, acknowledges that his "midwestern modesty" is an essential asset, keeping ideastream's partnerships free of control issues and, yet, it is also a quality that innately limits his ability to openly tout the accomplishments he has realized in concert with Jensen. He is the genial host and deal maker, she is the firewall and executor of planning.

Jensen, the former CEO at radio station WCPN, is a serious woman who chooses her words carefully and whose frontier, can-do spirit (she spent nearly 20 years in Alaska, building the state's first National Public Radio station, which for years broadcast the only statewide news content) has been instrumental in shaping ideastream. Jensen recalls arriving in Alaska in 1968 as a period ripe with potential, a time when the federal government was anxious to see Alaska's social, cultural and economic infrastructure developed in support of the oil pipeline to Prudhoe Bay. But she says it took "intentionality" to make the government's interests dovetail with the community's need for honest, broadcast information.

"I had this incredible opportunity to be there and be part of it, so my background is predisposed to possibilities and a little broader view of what broadcast could be and mean to a community," she says. "It was an exciting, and heady time."

She speaks similarly of her work with Wareham in creating ideastream and later overseeing the renovations of the building at 1375 Euclid Avenue, now known as the Idea Center. Though Jensen sees the development of ideastream as mostly the product of "really hard work," she also says, "I think a lot of it is making your own luck. Seeing things as they might be and asking: Why not? I think it's a matter of will, willing it to be and using every asset you can find to bring it about."

Initially, what Wareham and Jensen sought to accomplish, the merger of WVIZ and WCPN, was by itself no small management task. While each organization had outgrown its facilities and recognized the benefits of convergence, both in terms of technology and reducing costs through shared infrastructure and operations, they faced an uphill struggle in making their boards and staffs understand the value of surrendering separate, time-tested identities as traditional programmers and broadcasters to become a single, multiple-media public service organization.

And, as they began to wrap their minds around the challenges inherent in such a merger, the tougher, bedrock issues emerged: lingering 20th century questions facing public broadcasting, made more critical by the digital era's costly rules of engagement:

- Is public television still relevant in an era when 90 percent of American households are wired to receive 500 television channels, which in many cases deliver the type of content formerly available only from the Public Broadcasting System (PBS)?
- How are PBS, NPR, their affiliates and sister organizations to produce competitive, quality programming when the business model for financing public broadcasting—dependence upon the whims of federal, corporate and philanthropic sponsors, supplemented by mind-numbing on-air fund drives— is showing signs of new structural defects and losses in audience?

The answer, in Cleveland, was to create a multiple-media center that is not only about more or better-targeted programming but also about becoming a resource for community interaction, providing a variety of traditional broadcast and extraordinary broadband-related services.

David Giovannoni, whose market analysis of public radio over the past 20 years is widely credited with shaping today's success at NPR, insists that it's a mistake to lump radio and television together. They are separate entities with their own strengths and failures. "There is no such thing as 'public broadcasting,'" he says. "There is public radio and there is public television, and then, arguably, there is something you could call public media."

From the consumer's perspective the merger is seamless. WCPN is still public radio and WVIZ is still public television. *Morning Edition* is there when folks awake and *All Things Considered* brings them home at night; *Sesame Street* inspires children's learning and *The NewsHour* informs adults' ideas. But when you talk to those who have worked with ideastream, they will tell you, again and again, that together, the two stations are doing much more than they could ever have done separately to serve their communities.

The media and technology here runs the gamut: obviously there is television and radio and, certainly, Internet, but also broadband delivering on-demand, digitally stored lesson plans, live accounts from the state legislature and the state supreme court, hi-tech classrooms to help educators learn cutting-edge software to engage their students and a truly stunning state-of-the-art theater adaptable for live performance and/or broadcast. They have done away with separate TV and radio staffs; there is no "newsroom." Instead, they have merged into a single "content staff," charged with finding new ways to embrace and engage various communities— defined with a broad brush as regions, ethnic groups, political interests, technologies, educators, health matters, families, children, religions, and so on—with a digital presence. That's how you compete and remain relevant in a 500-channel environment.

Think of ideastream as a digital community center or a virtual YMCA, seeking to draw together the resources of "heritage institutions"(museums, theaters, colleges, libraries, medical centers, government agencies, etc.) and make them digitally available on-demand to patrons, clients and students. For these and other services they develop, ideastream and its partners receive grants or are paid an operating fee by school districts, government agencies or philanthropies. This is still a not-for-profit organization, but one financed, sometimes directly, by the communities it serves. They call it a "sustainable service model." Skeptics have called it "pay to play."

Ideastream is certainly not the only PBS or NPR affiliate attempting these kinds of initiatives. Wareham and Jensen rattle off the call letters of many affiliates in cities large and small that have inspired, influenced and informed ideastream's efforts. Many of the 355 PBS and 860 NPR stations are examining the benefits of mergers or partnerships, experimenting with new media, working with new ways to produce and distribute content, and becoming more interactive with their communities. Yet ideastream, for now, seems to be ahead of the crowd.

"What Jerry and Kit are doing in Cleveland may well be the model for what other stations should be doing," says David Liroff, a widely recognized visionary of public media. "And they are not alone in this. They just have focused more clearly as a locus and catalyst and convener of civic discussion. And what is truly radical about them is that they mark such a departure from the traditional expectations of what the traditional public television and public radio model should be."

Origins of Public Broadcasting

There seems little doubt that the original lofty goals set out for public broadcasting remain deeply woven into the character of the organization and the aspirations of its leaders. "On a sustaining basis no one is in the space that we're in," says Paula Kerger, President of the Public Broadcasting System.

"At the end of the day, the commercial marketplace simply is not fulfilling what public television originally set out to do, which was to use the power of media to entertain, educate and inspire. They [cable] sometimes entertain pretty well but they don't always hit that educate and inspire part."

While several of the 500 channels—"the vast wasteland" as former FCC Commissioner Newton Minow famously labeled television in 1961—have sought to produce high-minded programming, it rarely survives Wall Street's demands for ever-increasing profits, which require large and loyal audiences, typically built on a formulaic "lowest common denominator" of public interests. Thus, A&E has lowered its once PBS-like standards and now provides prime-time staples such as *CSI Miami* while Bravo touts its lineup as: "Fashion, Comedy, Celebrity and Real Estate."

Although commercial attempts at playing in the PBS marketplace have frequently fallen short, PBS itself, while true to its calling, struggles to maintain its viewership, with the commensurate loss of pledges those viewers provide. Add to that erosion in the financial support it previously enjoyed from business, foundations, governments and universities.

The New York Times wasn't the first to question PBS' future this past February, when it wrote a biting analysis beneath the headline "Is PBS Still Necessary?" According to the article, "Lately, the audience for public TV has been shrinking faster than the audience for commercial networks. The average PBS show on prime time now scores about a 1.4 Nielsen rating, or roughly what the wrestling show 'Friday Night Smackdown' gets." Acknowledging the occasional "huge splash" from a Ken Burns special, the *Times* uses the term "mustiness" to describe PBS's prime-time lineup, noting, "*The Newshour, Nova, Nature, Masterpiece* [Theatre] are into their third or fourth decade, and they look it."

While PBS viewership has slipped from 5.1 million members in 1990 to 3.7 million in 2005, public radio scored dramatic gains in weekly audience, up from about 2 million in 1980 to nearly 30 million today. But NPR, too, is realizing significant losses, according to Giovannoni, whose market research is the gold standard of public radio.

There was a 6 percent decline in listeners to *All Things Considered* and *Morning Edition* between 2004 and 2005, Giovannoni's research found. His most recent report, *Audience 2010,* which "set out to identify what is causing public radio's loss of momentum" found that "our listeners are still listening to radio [but] increasingly not listening to us."

Losses in popularity translate into lost revenues. While listeners and viewers who remain loyal have been willing to pay more in annual subscriptions or membership fees—on the PBS side, an average of $55.04 per subscriber in 1990 rose to $99.84 in 2005—the loss in market share has taken its toll as corporate sponsors follow the audience. And because the federal side of the ledger is light in a good year, the bulk of funding comes from subscribers, corporate sponsors, foundations and state and local government, with the balance coming from colleges, universities, auctions and other activities. For 2005, the last year for which the Corporation for Public Broadcasting (CPB) has reported data, statistics reflect a one-year loss of 6.7 percent in business sponsorships, a 7.1 percent decrease in foundation support, a 3.9 percent cut by states, a 3.7 percent loss in federal grants and contracts, and a meager 0.3 percent rise in subscriber support.

Adding to the difficulty, each year since taking office, the Bush administration has sought to slash spending for public broadcasting operations, most recently seeking a $200 million slice of the $400 million Congress approved for the FY2009 budget. Each year the faithful have rallied, successfully preserving the 10-to-20 percent federal share of the PBS and NPR budgets.

This financial dilemma is as old as public radio and public broadcasting in the U.S.. In January 1967, the landmark Carnegie Commission on Educational Television, created by Carnegie Corporation of New York, completed a two-year study, providing the blueprint for creating public television—to which Congress added, over some objections, public radio—and enacted the Public Broadcasting Act of 1967, creating CPB as the oversight mechanism which, in turn, created PBS in 1969, and NPR in 1970, as the national content producers and parent organizations for stations throughout the nation. Congress rejected the Carnegie Commission's proposal for a 2-to-5 percent excise tax on the sale of television sets—modeled on the British system for funding the BBC—to guarantee the unfettered, financial health of public broadcasting.

Ten years later, a second Carnegie Commission, often called Carnegie II, issued *A Public Trust: The Report of the Carnegie Commission on the Future of Public Broadcasting,* which sought, once again, to secure financial independence for media technology and a more forward looking purpose for public broadcasting.

Carnegie II recognized that new technologies were affecting the media and reinforcing the deeper questions, raised by visionaries such as Marshall McLuhan, regarding media's influence on society, cultural values and democracy. Said the report, "This institution [public broadcasting], singularly positioned within the public debate, the creative and journalistic communities, and a technological horizon of uncertain consequences, is an absolutely indispensable tool for our people and our democracy." Thus, Carnegie II sought to keep the door propped open to future technologies through a strong, independent financing mechanism, noting, "We conclude that it is unwise for us to attempt to chart the future course of public broadcasting as it continues to interact with new technologies. We are convinced, however, that it is essential for public broadcasting to have both the money and flexibility necessary to enable it to chart its own course as it responds to the future."

That idea, too, went nowhere. Not surprising, suggest Liroff, a 28-year veteran of WGBH in Boston and currently Senior Vice President, System Development and Media Strategy at CPB. He says, "It was, to paraphrase McLuhan, as though we were speeding into the future at 90 miles per hour with our eyes firmly fixed on the rearview mirror. The idea of public broadcasting pre-Internet, pre- any of these technologies, was going to be a manifestation of the broadcasting system they knew at the time, dominated, of course, by commercial broadcast." He continues, "This question of what is the role of public broadcasting in the media environment is as relevant today as it was back then except that the answers have to be very different. This is hardly the environment in which this system [of media distribution] was first envisioned."

Increasingly, there is appeal for public broadcasting to expand its traditional role, to grow their portfolios as ideastream has done in order "to provide new services in new, non-broadcast ways," explains Richard Somerset-Ward, an expert on public media and senior fellow at the Benton Foundation, which promotes digital media in communications. "This includes distributing other people's content as well as its own; to open up the possibility of new revenue streams and to become, in general, a community enabler, a go-to organization at the heart of the community, one whose identity is bound up in that of the community," he says.

Ward and others argue that public broadcasting has followed a flawed trickle-up business model: local public broadcasting stations must raise funds which they pay to NPR or PBS to produce programming. This has created enormous challenges, primarily for television where production costs are huge and viewership is decaying.

"The problem with the PBS stations is that they've never been able to contribute enough for PBS to not be almost totally dependent upon sponsorships, which they have been unable to keep up," says Somerset-Ward. "What you need to do is to increase the amount of funding the stations put in and that means optimizing the health of the stations. That doesn't mean an entirely new business plan [for the stations], just augmenting the present one. And the way is open to do that because of digital and all that implies. And Cleveland is the best example of how that can be done."

However that requires an attitude adjustment on the part of broadcasters accustomed to an "I-produce, you-view" model, in which content is tightly control by producers and "pushed" to consumers, says Liroff.

Larry Grossman, the former PBS president, highly regarded as a visionary in public broadcasting, began talking in the 1980s about the need to create "a grand alliance" of "heritage institutions," bringing together public broadcasters, universities, libraries and museums. Today, Grossman remains committed to a top-down approach in which PBS and NPR lead and the stations follow. What is lacking, he says, "is a blueprint and anybody articulating the dream: what is the role of public broadcasting, what should it be going forward?"

Yet, Grossman's vision in the 1980s remains vital today. Explains Liroff, "What Grossman saw more clearly than the rest of us is that public broadcasters and universities and libraries and all the rest are all in the same business and the old business model that makes them look so different is being compromised—in the best sense of that word—in terms of their separate identities by digital technologies, which they all share. So it is just as likely . . . that digital technologies allow these heritage institutions, among others, to begin to extend their services . . . on the Internet in ways, which at least in form, will be indistinguishable one from the other."

Or, put another way, Internet consumers tend to be agnostic about the sources of data; they don't necessarily know or care which museum or library provided the recording of, say, Robert Frost reading "The Road Not Taken"—just that they can access it. Add to that the current steep declines in the cost of digital storage and you have "extraordinary consequences for any individual's ability to call up what they want when they want it," says Liroff.

What all this means is that broadcasters and journalists, who have been trained by competition and regulators, most notably the FCC, to fiercely protect and keep tight reign over their turf, to serve as gatekeepers, must learn to loosen the controls, become more interactive and accepting of "pull" technologies.

But that raises an important question: if traditional broadcasters are expanding their roles to serve as content developers and data distributors on platforms other than broadcast, does the mean that five or ten years from now their primary function could be something other than delivering programming by radio and television?

That seems a distinct possibility, say many observers, including Liroff, Grossman and Somerset-Ward. Yet industry leaders, including Wareham, Kerger and others, are quick to disagree.

"Everyone is quick to write off traditional broadcasting, but it's been around a long time and survived all sorts of predictions of early demise," says Ken Stern, former CEO of NPR. "So I don't think that's going to change."

Stern resigned his post as CEO this March after only 18 months, reportedly in a dispute with his board over NPR's digital future, which he saw combining a strong video presence on the web with Public Radio's traditional radio journalism. "I absolutely agree that the audience is being fragmented and it's important for public broadcasters to meet the audience where it is, so things like podcasting and moving to multiple platforms is the reality," he says. "But the need is to meet the audience across many platforms and not to give up the broadcast platform."

Creating Ideastream

Wareham and Jensen are absolutely sure that they can't recall the first time they discussed merging WCPN and WVIZ. That's probably because they tried dating for a while before contemplating marriage—that is, the broadcast operations, not Wareham and Jensen.

The Idea Center

It was here, at 1375 Euclid Avenue, back in the 1950s, in the studios of WJW, that disc jockey Alan Freed coined the phrase "Rock & Roll." Well, Cleveland still rocks!

All the proof you need is a visit to The Idea Center, home of ideastream, where you will experience a symbiosis of community-based arts and media raised to the highest level of quality. For example: one afternoon last December, Alice Walker and Marsha Norman sat facing each other on the stage of the black box theatre that occupies a three-story space in the center of the building.

This was an event that served multiple purposes. Walker, author of *The Color Purple,* was in Cleveland to promote the Oprah Winfrey musical based on her book, due to open in the spring of 2008. Norman, author of the play *'night Mother',* wrote the libretto for the Winfrey musical.

Walker made a little news by saying this would be her final appearance on behalf of the book, the movie or the musical. But the real show was listening to these two sophisticated ladies light up a corner of downtown Cleveland.

Filling the 300-seat bleachers rising up two stories in front of the floor-level stage were college and high school students as well as several local arts dignitaries, who took turns lining up at the microphones to ask questions. Meanwhile, at a half-dozen schools throughout northeast Ohio, another hundred-plus students watched the event live via broadband and they, too, lined up for a chance to interact

with the two Pulitzer Prize-winning writers. Currently, ideastream is linked via broadband to 115 public schools and 190 private schools, reaching a potential audience of 500,000 students.

On any given day, the black box theater does double duty, serving primarily as a theater for the performing arts sponsored by the Playhouse Square Foundation and also as a live TV studio for WVIZ and PBS. So, on this occasion, the two-hour event was also taped for local broadcast in the spring, when *The Color Purple* is presented at one of the major theatrical stages at Playhouse Square and is being offered to PBS affiliates as one in a series of artist appearances at the Idea Center.

These presentations, and the resulting TV productions, are called "Master Moments," where famous performers speak candidly about their work. Some other recent visitors to the "Master Moments" stage include composer Marvin Hamlisch, actress Chita Rivera and composer/lyricist Adam Guettel.

Many of the student-questions Walker fielded related to fame—How has it changed her life? Does it make writing easier or more difficult?—and with each answer she seemed to become more succinct and focused until, towards the end of the two-hour session, she offered in reply a poem she said she wrote some time ago:

Expect nothing, Virgules Live frugally Virgules On surprise.

In 1997, the stations joined forces to do a series of stories on "urban sprawl," and despite a rough start it pointed the way towards greater cooperation. "It was a really miserable experience," says Wareham, laughing. "The computer systems didn't talk to one another. The radio people thought the TV people were shallow. The TV people thought the radio people were weird. But a funny thing happened. We started getting these phone calls from viewers and listeners: 'Didn't I see or hear something about how to get involved in my community?' And, in spite of ourselves, we had made an impact and that got the attention of our boards." They continued to look for joint projects and, with Wareham and Jensen in the lead, by the fall of 1999 the planning committees of the two boards were in meetings discussing merger.

While Cleveland's economy was and continues to be distressed, the financial motivations for merger related to increased efficiencies realized in staffing, marketing, fundraising and grant seeking. Both were also desperate to replace dilapidated facilities.

"But this did not start out with something being broken. Both broadcast stations were in good shape. Except for their physical location," says Susan Eagan, then with the Cleveland Foundation, which served as a neutral moderator to the discussions. "It was mostly Kit and Jerry looking out ahead and seeing a lot of unrealized opportunities . . . and knowing

that if public broadcasting was not repositioned and aligned with what was going on in the larger marketplace, at some point down the road there could be some significant issues."

Wareham and Jensen argued that the emerging reality, the shift in the marketplace, meant, "Access to programming through broadcast distribution is becoming relatively less valuable than content creation, packaging, marketing and control of intellectual property." In other words, having control of the media delivery system is no longer sufficient to remain a player in the community; content development is of greater importance.

While much of this may seem self-evident today, it wasn't all so clear in 1999 to members of the two boards. To make their case, Wareham and Jensen turned first to Chicago and then to Cinderella.

Network Chicago, a multiple media public service organization operated by Chicago's WTTW was a model very similar to what Wareham and Jensen wanted to create in Cleveland. A 1999 promotional video, which they brought to a meeting of the Cleveland boards, explains, "We can create alliances with cultural, educational and business institutions . . . We can leap beyond the television screen and carry our quality content to radio, print, and the Internet . . . [create] strategic alliances . . . driven by our values." (Unfortunately for WTTW, Network Chicago's business model relied heavily on advertising in a print publication, which did not succeed.)

But the "Aha!" moment in the negotiations, the inspiration that enabled people to understand how this worked, they say, came when Jensen posed the question, *What is Cinderella?* To illustrate the point, she passed around several props including a Disney DVD, an illustrated story book, a Cinderella Barbie, and a volume of the original French fairy tale. Which one of these various media forms is Cinderella? "The right answer was really intellectual property," she says. "We needed an object to illustrate that platforms do not define content, content just exists. Cinderella had presented itself in all these different media in all these periods of time. And now we were facing the need to reinvent how we present our stories. This really worked for people."

From that point forward, parties to the talks say, there was only one essential sticking point: who's in charge? And this provided a defining moment in ideastream's reinvention of public broadcasting.

"When it came to the CEO question it all fell apart because people had their loyalties," says Eagan. The WVIZ board pressed for Wareham; the radio side wanted Jensen. But what happened next was iconic in terms of the ideastream partnership model: Wareham and Jensen wrote a memo saying, if the boards agreed, they would resolve the leadership issue on their own. But until the discussions moved off this point neither of them would have anything further to do with the proposed merger. They took their egos off the table.

"That was a very, very critical moment," says Eagan. "And it set a standard that said, this is not about us, this is what the community is entrusting to us."

The boards bought it. Weeks later, on a Sunday, Wareham and Jensen met over coffee. Each made a long list of what they liked most and least about their jobs. They exchanged documents. They agreed he would be CEO and she COO. The same procedure was followed with other managers at the two stations.

Somerset-Ward and others credit this enduring, almost stubborn, spirit of cooperation as the primary reason for ideastream's success, stemming from the Wareham-Jensen leadership model. "They don't take credit for anything and that, of course, is one of the main reasons why it works," he says. "Everywhere else, public broadcasting stations that I know of, would leap at the opportunity to grab credit. Jerry and Kit understood from the beginning that you couldn't do that, not if you want to be a partner. That is why they have been successful."

On July 1, 2001 ideastream became a reality.

The Listening Project

Wareham is fond of noting how clearly the current mission and approach of ideastream mirrors a key statement of the 1967 Carnegie Commission report, which contends that the underlying purpose of public media is not about technology or distribution: "It is not the location of the studio or transmitter that is most relevant. Rather, what is critical is the degree to which those operating the facilities relate to those they seek to serve."

Toward that goal, Jensen created The Listening Project, which has informed ideastream's programming, content and partnerships since its inception. Every year since 2001, ideastream goes out into the communities it serves, drawing leaders and citizens into a discussion of what matters most to them, how they see their lives, what assets they see in their communities and what public services they see a need for. Ideastream was overwhelmed when nearly 10,000 people took part in 2001. Since then, the number has been held to a more manageable level—1,410 in 2007—who respond to on-air, in-print and online solicitations to fill out a questionnaire. There are also live town meeting discussions open to the public.

This is not the usual market research approach: what do you think of our product and how can we make you use it more? Instead, the key proposition is how to connect to communities in ways that are deemed useful by those in the communities.

Four standard questions are asked each year are: 1) What are the most important assets of the community? 2) What are the most important challenges? 3) Who strengthens those assets and challenges? 4) What could multimedia do to strengthen those assets and [address those] challenges?

What they have heard clearly is that citizens want public media to look into problems and then stay on the topic long enough to lead the way towards some resolution. That means, unlike the normal modus operandi of media, not merely shining a bright light on an issue. Such an approach, The Listening Project finds, only serves to increase public anxiety.

"What the community was really asking us to do was to do the partnership, but then hang in there and be consistent about addressing these challenges and assets," says Wareham. "They wanted us to create community connection and participation. They wanted us to facilitate the process of community members talking with one another." That has given rise to a community advisory board and two new programs, *Sound of Ideas* a daily radio show and *Ideas* a weekly television program, which extend the community dialogue.

In 2001, Doug Clifton, the editor of *The Cleveland Plain Dealer,* asked ideastream to join the newspaper in a project ideal for the new organization. Clifton wanted to do a series of stories, editorials, town meetings and panel discussions examining the departure from Cleveland and the surrounding area of Fortune 500 companies. Wareham and Jensen jumped at the opportunity.

During the next few years, the organizations shared resources and promoted one another's efforts in what was called "the Quiet Crisis," which rapidly became the shorthand by which everyone in the region referred to the economic downturn affecting northeastern Ohio. "It was an effort to document the depth of the decline, assess what the future might hold and look at some solutions," says Clifton. "Although the *Plain Dealer* penetrated the home market very deeply some people would turn to public radio and public TV and that was the audience we were looking for."

Both organizations saw the effort as a success. "The sum of it was greater than its individual parts because it brought together three of the serious institutions in the region who were speaking with one voice," Clifton says.

In addition to anecdotal evidence of success, ideastream can point to:

- Combined 2007 radio and television fund raising campaigns that brought in $1,999,653, up from $1,419,530 in FY 2006, $1,425,575 in FY 2005, $1,632,609 in FY 2004 and $1,490,434 in FY 2003.
- Weekly cumulative audience for the spring Arbitron ratings found WCPN audience increased 32 percent between 2001 and 2005. During the same period, the national audience increased 11.5 percent.
- Weekly cumulative audience for the February Nielsen ratings period found the WVIZ audience declined 6.25 percent between 2001 and 2005 compared with a 13.5 percent downturn regionally.
- In the past five years, public radio and public television stations throughout the U.S. have sought guidance from ideastream; they have taken their story on the road to public broadcast operations in at least nine states.

Partnerships: Inside ideastream
Playhouse Square Foundation Provides a Home

Among the partnerships fostered by ideastream, the most evident is The Idea Center, at 1375 Euclid Avenue, from which all else emanates.

One of Wareham's and Jensen's earliest ambitions for the WVIZ-WCPN merger was to combine their infrastructure operations and develop a new headquarters. After contemplating a number of locations and partnerships, they became enamored with a proposal from Art Falco, Executive Director of Cleveland's Playhouse Square Foundation, which, with 10,000 seats, is the second largest center for the performing arts in the U.S., after New York's Lincoln Center.

Over the past 20 years, Playhouse Square has invested $55 million to obtain and renovate almost one million square feet of commercial real estate in downtown Cleveland in an effort to restore the once-thriving theater district, says Falco. According to one economic impact study, the commercial and theatrical programs enabled by Playhouse Square generate $43 million a year for the local economy.

The building on Euclid Avenue was seedy, run down, and only about 10 percent occupied when the mortgage holder agreed to donate it to the foundation, which hoped to turn it

into auxiliary work space for its performing arts operations. "We needed to create an arts education space," says Falco. "We had these wonderful theaters but we didn't have classrooms and we didn't have a dance studio, we didn't have a . . . theater, we didn't have gallery space."

Knowing that ideastream was in the market, he approached Wareham and Jensen and after some design work the two organizations realized they could realize some big savings by sharing their most costly facility needs: Falco wanted a "black box theater" (unadorned performance space) and ideastream needed a second television studio, but neither needed to have access to it on a daily basis. "We knew that we could build a great education and arts center and they could built a great tech and broadcast facility, but we knew it wouldn't be as good as it would be if we did it together," says Falco.

By sharing their space needs, the two groups reduced their total footprint from 120,000 square feet down to 90,000, and saved $7 million. It also meant that a greater portion of the four upper floors would be available to rent, creating revenue flow to defray their annual operating costs. "It has turned out to be a building that not only served our purposes, but has been characterized as a 'cool' building, where other commercial tenants who have connections with technology and architecture and design want to be located," says Falco. "It's surpassed my expectations."

As has proven true with many of its partnerships, the ideastream-Playhouse Square partnership is a wondrous symbiosis. Their combined capital campaign exceeded its goal, bringing in $30 million. They began moving into the facility in fall of 2005 with the last wave in February 2006. The upper floors are 90 percent occupied, well ahead of schedule.

OneCommunity Provides Reach

The grand symbiotic relationship ideastream has embarked upon, which has drawn national attention—including a Harvard Business School study—and opened vast opportunities for Cleveland, is with OneCommunity.

OneCommunity—formerly OneCleveland—was the vision of Lev Gonick, who became CIO and Vice President, Information Services at Case Western Reserve University in 2001, just as ideastream came into being and the Cleveland community was coming to know about the Quiet Crisis. Essentially, what Gonick sought was to build a regional broadband network at relatively little cost to serve the educational, health and nonprofit communities of northeast Ohio. What he didn't have in mind, until he was approached by Wareham, was someone to provide content to that network and, perhaps more importantly, someone with the community connections to bring together the nonprofit community in Cleveland in support of Gonick's vision.

Toward the end of the 20th century, an estimated $3 trillion-plus was sunk into the streets of the U.S. in the form of fiber optic cable in anticipation of the explosion in broad-band digital service, which halted abruptly when the e-commerce bubble burst. Gonick understood that this fortune in so-called "dark fiber" (unused cable), was everywhere in the country. In 2003, Gonick convinced City Signal Corp. to donate several strands of dark fiber to his nonprofit organiza-tion, for which the corporation got a substantial tax write-off. In September of that year, OneCleveland was incorporated and Scot Rourke, a former venture capitalist and Cleveland native, became its first executive.

If Gonick is the visionary, Rourke is the master builder. Rourke's plan for the nonprofit was to expand the broadband connection well beyond the city of Cleveland. What he pro-posed was that the corporations donating some portion of their dark fiber would not only get a healthy tax write-off, but also, said Rourke, "We are going to build the market for you. We will expose the community to the value of [broadband], we'll do the missionary work and build a market demand for the rest of your fiber."

"Scot has a wonderful concept," says Wareham. "He refers to 'Liberating content held captive by various com-munity institutions, universities, foundations, and nonprofit organizations.'" Adds Rourke: "It's not that they are trying to imprison it, it's that they don't know how to let it out."

Some of the programs enabled by the ideastream-OneCommunity partnership:

Distance Learning enables schools, which pay an annual fee, to have interactive access to live shows and instructional classes presented at the Idea Center.

Voices and Choices enables anyone interested in the eco-nomic issues of the region to log into a dedicated website, study the issues, make choices and contribute to an ongoing dialogue, including community town meetings.

One Classroom is the outgrowth of a $2 million grant from the Cleveland Clinic connecting 1,500 area schools to the OneCommunity network, making rich media content cre-ated by ideastream, including lesson plans and other educa-tional content, available on-demand. In time, this is expected to include digitized content from the many museums and cultural institutions in the region.

Wireless Mesh Network is a work in progress, building on ideastream's FCC licenses to develop a citywide wi-fi network with OneCommunity, Case Western Reserve Uni-versity, the city of Cleveland and area schools.

Rural Health Network, when completed, would create a broadband network for participating medical institutions in Northeastern Ohio to exchange medical data ranging from paper records and MRIs to televised medical exams.

Somerset-Ward says of ideastream and its partnerships: "They are becoming much more than just community broadcast-ers, they are becoming community enablers. And they are doing that by forming partnerships with community institutions. Jerry and ideastream are in a class of their own . . . But it's a model of what communities can do when institutions like schools, uni-versities, and health authorities create partnerships."

Harsh Realities

Perhaps the toughest part of using ideastream as a model is broadband access. Rourke, however, insists that should not be a problem. Dark fiber exists throughout the nation and large telecommunication companies are anxious to build a mar-ket for broadband by getting the attention of consumers—and one way to do that is to donate a couple of strands of fiber to a local nonprofit, with the added benefit of a tax break. "We know we can repeat this pretty much anywhere in the United States by promising that we are going to cre-ate the market and we aren't going to touch the residential customer," says Rourke.

It's a tough challenge for people to cede control in terms of the traditional gatekeeper role played by broadcasters and journalists.

Some observers say that an equally tough challenge is finding people willing to cede control, both in terms of the traditional gatekeeper role played by broadcasters/journalists and a willingness to enter into partnerships in which the tra-ditional objectivity of the broadcaster/journalist might be questioned. Other skeptics have challenged ideastream's partnerships with regional institutions that are sometimes subjects of media scrutiny, such as the Cleveland Clinic, the second-largest employer in the state, which has provided grants to OneCommunity and ideastream.

Unquestionably, partnerships can create the appearance of conflicts of interest for journalists whose stock in trade is perceived objectivity. But the same can be said with respect to advertisers: does *The New York Times,* for example, have a problem covering a scandal at General Motors because it accepts ads from GM?

David Molpus, a veteran reporter with NPR and Executive Editor at ideastream since March 2006, says that there are some legitimate issues to be addressed when working with another organization on content creation. "What are the rules of the game? We've started to work that out and codify it," he explains. "We obviously see that there is one level of coop-eration with another news organization like the *Plain Dealer.* But then there are degrees of variation: What could you do with the university? What could you do with the city library? What could you do with other nonprofits? What could you do with a government agency?"

There was an early dust-up over a perceived conflict of interest, concerning a grant provided to ideastream to do stories about affordable housing by an organization that also provided affordable housing. "There was concern in the newsroom, at that time, that this organization was set-ting some agenda," says Mark Smukler, ideastream's Senior

Director of Content. "But they never did get involved, there was no direct conversation, no proposals, no story ideas. At one point they did place a call to the reporter that was working on it and I told them not do that and they said fine and that was the end of it."

And, as with any merger or change in corporate identity, there were myriad management issues, including heightened staff distress and brain drain. "I have a great deal of admiration for the model and for the people who put it in place," says Mark Fuerst of the Integrated Media Association. "Merging any two organizations is a particularly hard undertaking. There are fears, anxieties and big concessions that have to be made. Kit and Jerry deserve great credit for what they've done."

Neither Wareham nor Jensen is recommending others follow ideastream's lead. "I don't know if our model can be or should be replicated elsewhere," says Jensen. "But the key has to be to work within the resources that the communities provide and with full recognition of the communities' needs."

M. J. ZUCKERMAN is a veteran freelance journalist, author and lecturer, currently on the adjunct staff of the George Washington University School of Media and Public Affairs.

The Shame Game
'To Catch a Predator' Gets the Ratings, but at What Cost?

DOUGLAS McCOLLAM

It was just before 3 P.M. on a Sunday afternoon last November when a contingent of police gathered outside the home of Louis Conradt Jr., a longtime county prosecutor living in the small community of Terrell, Texas, just east of Dallas. Though the fifty-six-year-old Conradt was a colleague of some of the officers, they hadn't come to discuss a case or for a backyard barbeque. Rather, the veteran district attorney, who had prosecuted hundreds of felonies during more than two decades in law enforcement, was himself the target of an unusual criminal probe. For weeks the police in the nearby town of Murphy had been working with the online watchdog group Perverted Justice and producers from *Dateline NBC's* popular "To Catch a Predator" series in an elaborate sting operation targeting adults cruising the Internet to solicit sex from minors. *Dateline* had leased a house in an upscale subdivision, outfitted it with multiple hidden cameras, and hired actors to impersonate minors to help lure suspects into the trap. As with several similar operations previously conducted by *Dateline,* there was no shortage of men looking to score with underage boys and girls. In all, twenty-four men were caught in the Murphy sting, including a retired doctor, a traveling businessman, a school teacher, and a Navy veteran.

Conradt had never shown up at the *Dateline* house, but according to the police, using the screen name "inxs00," he did engage in explicit sexual exchanges in an Internet chat room with someone he believed to be a thirteen-year-old boy (but was actually a volunteer for Perverted Justice). Under a Texas law adopted in 2005 to combat Internet predators, it is a second-degree felony to have such communications with someone under the age of fourteen, even if no actual sexual contact takes place. Armed with a search warrant—and with a *Dateline* camera crew on the scene—the police went to Conradt's home to arrest him. When the prosecutor failed to answer the door or answer phone calls, police forced their way into the house. Inside they encountered the prosecutor in a hallway holding a semiautomatic handgun. "I'm not going to hurt anybody," Conradt reportedly told the police. Then he fired a single bullet into his own head.

Standing outside the house with his crew, the *Dateline* correspondent Chris Hansen said he did not hear the shot that ended Conradt's life, but did see his body wheeled out on a gurney. Discussing Conradt's death over lunch a couple of weeks later, I asked Hansen how it made him feel. Hansen said his first reaction was as a newsman who had to cover the story for his network (Hansen filed a report the next morning for NBC's *Today* show). Hansen said that on a human level Conradt's death was a tragedy that, naturally, he felt bad about. But he understood the true import of my question: "If you're asking do I feel responsible, no," Hansen said. "I sleep well at night."

Others aren't so sanguine. Galen Ray Sumrow, the criminal district attorney of Rockwall County, Texas, who heads the office where Conradt worked as an assistant district attorney, has reviewed evidence surrounding the case and believes it was badly botched. Among the problems he cites are that the search warrant obtained by the Murphy police officers was defective because it had the wrong date and listed the wrong county for service, basic errors that he believes would have gotten any evidence seized from Conradt's home tossed out of court. He is also mystified as to why the police would force their way into Conradt's home when they could have tried to talk him out, or just picked him up at work the next day. "He was here in the office every morning," says Sumrow, who is himself a former police officer and has been prosecuting cases for more than twenty years. "You generally like to do an arrest like that away from the home to avoid things like what happened." A sworn affidavit supporting the warrant also shows that the information about Conradt's online activities was given to the Murphy police by Perverted Justice just hours before they went to arrest him. Why were the police in such a rush to pick up Conradt? Texas Rangers are investigating that question, but Sumrow thinks he knows the answer: "It's reality television," he says. Sumrow says an investigator told him the police pushed things because the *Dateline* people had plane tickets to fly home that afternoon and wanted to get the bust on film for the show. He says investigators also told him that film excerpts show *Dateline* personnel, including Hansen, interacting with police on the scene, supplying them with information, and advising them on tactics. Sergeant Snow Robertson of the Murphy police says accommodating *Dateline's* schedule "wasn't a factor at all."

Rather, he says, the urgency was to keep Conradt from contacting another minor. *Dateline*'s Hansen confirms that he was to fly out that Sunday, but says such plans are always subject to change and that he hadn't even checked out of his hotel. He also denies advising the police during the operation at Conradt's house. "This stuff is not remotely based in fact," Hansen says.

At a town meeting called to discuss the *Dateline* sting operations, several Murphy residents expressed outrage that a parade of suspected sexual predators were lured to their community. Neighbors recounted police takedowns and car chases on their blocks, and some said fleeing suspects tossed drugs and other contraband into their yards. In a statement to the Murphy City Council, Conradt's sister, Patricia, directly implicated *Dateline* in her brother's death. "I will never consider my brother's death a suicide," she said. "It was an act precipitated by the rush to grab headlines where there was no evidence that there was any emergency other than to line the pockets of an out-of-control group and a TV show pressed for ratings and a deadline." She added: "When these people came after him for a news show, it ended his life." In an interview, she was even more direct: "They have blood on their hands," she said, referring to *Dateline,* the police, and Perverted Justice.

In a sense, Conradt's death was a tragedy foretold. In a piece for *Radar* magazine about the show, the writer John Cook quoted an unnamed *Dateline* producer as saying that "one of these guys is going to go home and shoot himself in the head." When I asked Hansen and David Corvo, *Dateline*'s executive producer, if they were reviewing the show's procedures in light of Conradt's death, both said that there was no evidence to suggest that Conradt was aware of *Dateline*'s presence when he shot himself (though a camera crew was apparently on his block for hours before the police arrived), and that there were no plans to alter how the "Predator" series is handled. "I still feel like the show is a public service," said Corvo. "We do investigations that expose people doing things not good for them. You can't predict the unintended consequences of that. You have to let the chips fall where they may."

The reluctance to tinker with the show's formula is no doubt attributable to the fact that since its debut in the fall of 2004, "To Catch a Predator" has been the rarest of rare birds in the television news world: a clear ratings winner. The show regularly outdraws NBC's other primetime fare. It succeeds by tapping into something that has been part of American culture since the Puritans stuck offenders in the stockade: public humiliation. The notion of delighting in another's disgrace drives much of the reality TV phenomenon, and is present in the DNA of everything from *Judge Judy* to *Jackass* to *Borat.* "Predator" couples this with a hyped-up fear of Internet sex fiends, creating a can't-miss formula. The show's ratings success has made it a sweeps-week staple and turned Chris Hansen into something of a pop-culture icon. To date, by the show's own count, it has netted 238 would-be predators, thirty-six of whom have either pleaded guilty or been convicted. Hansen regularly gives talks to schools and parent groups concerned about Internet sex predators, and he was even summoned to Washington to testify before a congressional subcommittee investigating the problem, where he and *Dateline* received effusive praise for their efforts.

When the comedian Conan O'Brien filmed a bit to open this year's Emmy Awards that showed him parading through the sets of hit shows of every network, his last stop was a "Predator" house where Hansen confronted him and O'Brien gave a spot-on rendition of the sweaty, shaky dissembling that most of the show's targets display.

All that is a long way from where "To Catch a Predator" started. The *Dateline* producer Lynn Keller says she first contacted the Perverted Justice group about the possibility of doing a show in January or February of 2004. Perverted Justice had already worked with several local television stations, including one in Detroit, where Chris Hansen knew one of the producers and had talked with him about a sting operation the station had filmed using Perverted Justice's online expertise to lure targets. *Dateline*'s first sting house was set up in Bethpage, Long Island, about an hour outside of New York City. Hansen recalls being nervous that no one would show up and that he might have to explain to the network why he had blown a bunch of money on a flop investigation. "We thought we might get one person," Keller recalls. They needn't have worried. Before he could even reach the house for the first day of filming, Hansen got a frantic call from Keller that the first target was inbound. Hansen beat him there by just fifteen minutes.

The Long Island sting netted eighteen suspects in two and a half days. Eight months later, the show set up a sting house in Fairfax, Virginia (at a home belonging to a friend of Hansen's in the FBI), and snared nineteen more men, including a rabbi, an emergency-room doctor, a special-education teacher, and an unemployed man claiming to be a teacher, who memorably walked into the house naked. The third show, filmed in early 2006 in southern California, drew fifty-one men over three days. But even as the stings expanded and ratings soared, critics inside and outside the network raised serious questions about whether "To Catch a Predator" was erasing lines that even an increasingly tabloid newsmagazine show should respect.

To begin with, the show has an undeniable "ick" factor. The men (and to date they are all men) are mostly losers who show up packing booze and condoms. It is also undeniably compelling television. Each show follows a similar pattern: after asking the mark to come in, the decoy disappears to change clothes or go to the bathroom. Then, in a startling switcheroo, Hansen appears from off-stage and directs the man to take a seat. The men almost always comply, concluding that Hansen is either a cop or a father. The marks then proffer comical denials about what they are doing at the house, which never include their intent to have sex with a minor. Hansen then produces some particularly salacious details from their Internet chat with the decoy ("But you said you couldn't wait to pour chocolate syrup all over her and lick it off with your tongue"). The mark then switches gears to say he has never done anything like this before and was just kidding around or role playing, which in turn cues Hansen to say something like, "Well, you're playing on a big stage, because I'm Chris Hansen from *Dateline NBC,*" at which point cameras enter from off stage like furies summoned from hell. The mark, now fully perceiving his ruin, usually excuses himself, often pausing to shake hands with Hansen—the cult of celebrity apparently transcends even this awful reality—then exits into the waiting arms of police outside who swarm him as if he had just shot the president.

The police busts are the emotional capper to the encounter, one that highlights the show's uncomfortably close affiliation with law enforcement. On the first two "Predator" stings, the show didn't involve arrests, an omission that garnered complaints from viewers and cops alike. Though certain individuals from the initial episodes were subsequently prosecuted, the lack of police involvement from the outset made it hard to make cases that would stick. "The number one complaint from viewers was that we let them walk out," says Keller. Starting with the third show and in the five subsequent stings, police were waiting to take down the suspects. In our interview and in his congressional testimony, Hansen is careful to refer to those arrests as "parallel" police investigations, as if they just happened to be running down the same track as *Dateline,* but the close cooperation is always evident. At a time when reporters are struggling to keep law enforcement from encroaching on news gathering, *Dateline,* which is part of NBC's news division, is inviting them in the front door—literally. Hansen tried to deflect this criticism of the show by saying that the volunteers from Perverted Justice serve as a "Chinese wall" between the news people at *Dateline* and the police.

But as we've learned from recent corporate scandals, such Chinese walls are often made of pretty thin tissue. In the case of "To Catch a Predator," Perverted Justice does most of the groundwork preparing the shows and roping in the men. Initially, *Dateline's* responsibility was to cover the group's expenses, procure the house and outfit it with hidden cameras and, of course, supply Chris Hansen and airtime. However, after the third successful "Predator" show, Perverted Justice hired an agent and auctioned its services to several networks. NBC ended up retaining the group for a fee reported in *The Washington Post* and elsewhere to be between $100,000 and $150,000. Hansen would not confirm an amount but said he saw nothing wrong with compensating the group for its services, likening it to the way the news division will sometimes keep a retired general or FBI agent on retainer. "In the end I get paid, the producers get paid, the camera guy, why shouldn't they?" says Hansen.

On the surface that certainly seems reasonable, but it ignores a few relevant points. First, Perverted Justice is a participant in the story, the kind of outfit that would traditionally be covered, not be on the news outlet's payroll. "It's an advocacy group intensely involved in this story," says Robert Steele, who teaches journalism ethics at The Poynter Institute. "That's different from hiring a retired general who is no longer involved in a policy-making role." Second, it is clearly a no-no, even at this late date in the devolution of TV news, to directly pay government officials or police officers. Yet in effect that's what *Dateline* did in at least one of its stings. The police in Darke County, Ohio, where *Dateline* set up its fourth sting in April 2006, insisted that personnel from Perverted Justice be deputized for the operation so as not to compromise the criminal cases it wished to bring against the targets. After some discussion, NBC's lawyers agreed to the arrangement, which the network shrugs off as less than ideal but an isolated circumstance.

Further, though Hansen and *Dateline* reject allegations that they are engaging in paycheck journalism by paying Perverted Justice—arguing for a distinction between paying a consultant and paying a source for information—the line looks a little fuzzy. For example, Xavier von Erck, who founded Perverted Justice, says via e-mail that the operation had come to a point where it could "not bear any further costs relating to the shows. Hence, we obtained a consulting fee." In turn, local law enforcement groups have stated that without the resources provided by Perverted Justice they couldn't afford to do the criminal investigations they've mounted in conjunction with the "To Catch a Predator" series. See the problem? But for NBC's deep pockets, no "parallel" police actions would take place. And are they really parallel? One lawyer I spoke with, who asked not be identified because her client's case is still pending, claims the man was entrapped and said she has every intention of subpoenaing members of *Dateline's* staff to testify if the case goes to trial. "They are acting as an arm of law enforcement and are material witnesses," the lawyer said. "They definitely crossed a line."

There is also the question of whether the series is fair to its targets. Let's concede up front that this is an unsympathetic bunch of would-be perverts. But are they really that dangerous? Hansen himself divides those snared in the probes into three groups: dangerous predators, Internet pornography addicts, and sexual opportunists. But by Hansen's own calculation fewer than one in ten of the men who show up at a sting house have a previous criminal record.

But the image projected by the "Predator" series is clearly meant to inflame parental fears about violent Internet sex fiends. The show has invoked the specter of famous child abduction cases like Polly Klaas. The very term "predator" calls to mind the image of the drooling, trench-coated sex fiend hanging out at the local playground with a bag full of candy. Reading through the chat transcripts posted on the Perverted Justice website, however, it seems clear that a lot of the men snared aren't hardcore predators. Many express doubts about what they're doing and have to be egged along a bit by the decoys, many of whom come off as anything but innocent children. Consider a few of these exchanges. In the first, the mark (johnchess2000) is talking to someone he believes is an underage girl (AJ's Girl). She has agreed to let him come over to watch a movie:

johnchess2000: anything you want me to wear or bring?

AJ's Girl: hmm

johnchess2000: wow your thinking for a long time

AJ's Girl: lol sowwy

AJ's Girl: u beter bring condoms

johnchess2000: wow. condoms???

johnchess2000: wow. your thinking big huh? ;0

johnchess2000: ;)

AJ's Girl: :">

johnchess2000: wow so you like me that much? :)

AJ's Girl: maybe

johnchess2000: maybe?? why did you say condoms?

AJ's Girl: :"> i duno

johnchess2000: haha. be honest

johnchess2000: you must like me a lot then huh?

AJ's Girl: yea

AJ's Girl: ur cute

Or this exchange between Jason, a twenty-one-year-old fireman and the decoy, a girl he thinks is thirteen:

jteno72960: so what kinda guys u like

katiedidsings: hot fireman 1s

jteno72960: ok what else is sexy to you

katiedidsings: tats

jteno72960: i have 2 inside my arm

jteno72960: will u kiss them for me?

katiedidsings: ya

jteno72960: what about on the lips

katiedidsings: ya

jteno72960: i love to kiss

katiedidsings: me 2

jteno72960: really what else

katiedidsings: i dunno watevr u wantd 2 do

jteno72960: well what have u done

katiedidsings: evry thing

katiedidsings: wel not evrything

katiedidsings: but alot of stuff

jteno72960: well what did u like

katiedidsings: from behind

Or this last exchange between Rob (rkline05) a twenty-year-old from Ohio, and *Dateline's* online decoy "Shia," who poses as an underage girl. After days of chatting, Rob expresses doubts about their age difference and about a sexual encounter, but Shia dismisses his concerns and reassures him:

rkline05: but idk about everything we talked about

shyshiagirl: why not

rkline05: well you sure you wana do all that

shyshiagirl: yeaa why not

rkline05: idk i just wasnt sure you wanted to you are a virgin and all

rkline05: you sure you want it to be me that takes that

shyshiagirl: yea why not. ur cool

rkline05: i just. . . you really sure i feel weird

about it you being so much younger than me and all

shyshiagirl: ur not old. dont feel weird

Rob came to the *Dateline* sting house and later pleaded guilty for soliciting a minor online.

Entrapment is a legal term best applicable to law enforcement. Perverted Justice says it's careful not to initiate contact with marks, nor steer them into explicit sexual banter. But as these chats and others make clear, they are prepared to flirt, literally, with that line. Under most state statutes passed to combat online predators, the demonstrated intent to solicit sexual acts from a minor is sufficient to land you in jail regardless of whether the minor is a willing participant. So, as a legal matter, the enticements offered by the decoys are of little importance to the police, or to issue advocates like Perverted Justice. But journalistically it looks a lot like crossing the line from reporting the news to creating the news.

Dateline has run afoul of this distinction before. Famously, in 1993, several producers and correspondents were fired for rigging a General Motors truck to explode in a crash test. More recently the program took heat for bringing Muslim-looking men to a NASCAR race to see what might happen (the program never aired). "Predator" seems to fall somewhere between those two examples. Perhaps its most direct counterpart in recent journalistic history is the famous sting operation mounted by the *Chicago Sun Times*. In 1978 the paper set up the Mirage Tavern in Chicago and snared a host of city officials for seeking bribes from the "owners," who were actually undercover reporters. The Mirage was controversial in its day, but it seems tame by comparison to the *Dateline* stings. Al Tompkins, who teaches the ethics of television journalism at the Poynter Institute, draws a clear distinction between the Mirage and "Predator." Mirage, he notes, was targeted at public officials who were known to be abusing the power of their offices for personal enrichment. "It was a legit question whether you could have covered the story any other way," Tompkins says. "You couldn't go through law enforcement because you didn't know if police were involved in the corruption." Tompkins, who has watched the *Dateline* series, says it looks more like a police prostitution sting than a news investigation.

Dateline has argued that "Predator" serves a genuine public good, but it could be argued that, in fact, *Dateline* is doing the public a disservice. When Attorney General Alberto Gonzales gave a speech about a major initiative to combat the "growing problem" of Internet predators, he cited a statistic that 50,000 such would-be pedophiles were prowling the Net at any given moment and attributed it to *Dateline*. Jason McLure, a reporter at *Legal Times* in Washington, D.C., (where I was formerly an editor), asked the show about the number. *Dateline* told him that it had gotten it from a retired FBI agent who consulted with the show. When the agent was contacted he wasn't sure where the number had come from, terming it a "Goldilocks" figure—"Not small and not large." He added that it was the same figure that was used by the media to describe the number of people killed annually by Satanic cults in the 1980s, and before that was cited as the number of children abducted by strangers each year in the 1970s. *Dateline* has now disowned the number, saying solid statistics about Internet predators are hard to find, but that the problem seems to be getting worse, a sentiment echoed by lawmakers in Congress.

But actually there isn't much evidence that it is getting worse. For example, many news reports have cited a Justice Department study as saying that one in five children is approached online by a sexual predator. But as Radford Benjamin of *The Skeptical Inquirer* pointed out, what that 2001 study actually said was that 19 percent had received a "sexual solicitation" online, about half of which came from other teens and none of which led to a sexual assault. According to the study, the number of teens aggressively solicited by adults online was about 3 percent. A more recent study by the Crimes Against Children Research Center at the University of New Hampshire found that the number of kids getting unwanted sexual advances on the Internet was in fact declining. In general, according to data compiled by the National Center for Missing and Exploited Children, more than 70 percent of sexual abuse of children is perpetrated by family members or family friends.

That doesn't mean Internet sex predators don't exist, but *Dateline* heavily skews reality by devoting hour after hour of primetime programming to the phenomenon. As Poynter's Tompkins notes: "Is there any other issue that's received that much airtime? The question is whether the level of coverage is proportional to the actual problem."

The answer, it seems, is no, and the explanation of why *Dateline* has seized on this mythical trend to anchor its venerable news show is that reality TV has so altered the broadcast landscape that traditional newsmagazine fare—no matter how provocative—just doesn't cut it anymore. "Reality programs came in and newsmagazines no longer looked so great," says

one former producer for NBC News. While newsmagazines are cheap compared to other primetime shows, they don't have the potential to be gigantic hits like *Survivor or American Idol.* For that reason, the producer notes, the entertainment divisions at the networks never really liked newsmagazines, which they had little hand in producing and for which they received no credit. At NBC, the former producer says, Jeff Zucker, formerly the president of the network's news and entertainment group and now the c.e.o. of its television operations, regularly put the squeeze on *Dateline,* maintaining that the network needed its time slots to either develop new programming or schedule hit shows. "About the only thing they really want newsmagazines to do now is crime," says the former producer. "If it's not crime, they don't think they can sell it. The traditional investigative reporting on shows like *Dateline,* or *48 Hours,* or *Primetime Live* is no more." (A notable exception, he says, is *60 Minutes.*)

Dateline's executive producer David Corvo prefers to see the change as a setting aside of older journalistic conventions to focus on new kinds of issues. The "Predator" series, he says, is just another form of enterprise journalism, one suited to the Internet age. But the distinction between enterprise and entertainment can be a difficult one. *Dateline* hasn't so much covered a story as created one. In the process it has further compromised the barrier between reporters and cops that is central to the mission of journalism. If humiliating perverts and needlessly terrifying parents is the best use that newsmagazines can make of hours of primetime television, then perhaps they should be allowed to die and the time given over to the blood sport of reality programming. At least no one would dare to call it news.

Douglas McCollam is a contributing editor to *CJR*.

The Battle over the Battle of Fallujah
A *Videogame So Real It Hurts*

Dan Ephron

Peter Tamte was months away from completing his dream project—turning the largest urban battle of the Iraq War into a videogame—when it all seemed to fall apart. The 75 employees of one of his companies, Atomic Games, had worked on the endeavor for nearly four years. They'd toiled to make Six Days in Fallujah as realistic as possible, weaving in real war footage and interviews with Marines who had fought there. But now relatives of dead Marines were angry, and the game's distributor and partial underwriter had pulled out of Tamte's project. On May 26, he got on the phone to Tracy Miller, whose son was killed by a sniper in Fallujah, and tried to win her over by arguing that the game honors the Marines. Miller listened politely, but remained skeptical. "By making it something people play for fun, they are trivializing the battle," she told NEWSWEEK.

Tamte is not above triviality. A second company he runs, Destineer, makes games with titles like Indy 500 and Fantasy Aquarium. But the 41-year-old executive says he's now attempting something more serious: a documentary-style reconstruction that will be so true to the original battle, gamers will almost feel what it was like to fight in Fallujah in November 2004. At his studio in Raleigh, N.C., Tamte has been helped by dozens of Fallujah vets who have advised him on the smallest details, from the look of the town to the operation of the weapons. And he's staked the fate of his company on the success of the $20 million project. "If for some reason it doesn't work, we'll have to think about making some very significant changes to the studio," he says.

Can something as weighty and complex as war be conveyed by the same medium that produced Mario Brothers and Grand Theft Auto? Mostly, videogames are associated with mindless entertainment or gratuitous violence or both. For Tracy Miller and other skeptics, the idea that animated shooters can communicate the heroism and sacrifice of Fallujah is deeply misguided.

But efforts to document war in new ways have always garnered skepticism and controversy. The first published photographs of dead American servicemen—including a 1943 shot showing three bodies sprawled out on Buna Beach in New Guinea—prompted a public outcry. The effect of television footage beamed from Vietnam directly to the living rooms of Americans was hotly debated throughout the war. Miguel Sicart, an expert on videogames at the IT University of Copenhagen, says it took decades for people in television and film to figure out how to convey the experience of war (and for audiences to get accustomed to the new media). If videogames can overcome stigmas, he says, their interactive technology gives them an advantage. "You can almost occupy the actual space of Fallujah and explore the environment in a videogame," Sicart says. "For someone interested in the events there, that can be very powerful."

Tamte says he got the idea to make a videogame of the Fallujah battle from Marines who fought there. Starting in 2003, he worked closely with members of the Third Battalion, First Marine Regiment, to make training simulators based on games he'd helped develop. A year later, those same Marines ended up at the center of the Fallujah battle, code-named Operation Phantom Fury. When they came home, Tamte says, several were already contemplating how they could turn their experience into the kind of game they themselves would want to play.

One of those Marines was Eddie Garcia, a sergeant from the Bronx who had suffered shrapnel wounds on the first day of the fighting. He says even before he left the hospital, he was e-mailing Tamte about Fallujah. "I mentioned that since we'd already made one game together, why not make another?" After he recovered, Garcia began regular brainstorming sessions with Tamte and his designers, showing them unclassified maps and photos from his deployment. Garcia had been stationed just outside Fallujah for months before the battle. Notes he kept about every meeting and mission helped bring the experience to life for Tamte and Atomic creative director Juan Benito. The vision of a game that would reenact the first days of Fallujah began to take shape.

Atomic's sprawling office feels almost like a shrine to Phantom Fury, with photos of the fighting pinned to walls and scattered on desks. Graphic designers, still trying to perfect the game, study the posters to help re-create the precise look of Fallujah: the pockmarked cinder blocks and the sagging electric lines. On a recent day, in a studio attached to the entry hall, an Atomic employee was interviewing Jason Arellano, a former

Marine sergeant who had been clearing insurgents in a home when a grenade exploded near him and a bullet struck his groin. "As we pushed further and further into the city, we became aware of a more well-trained or disciplined fighter," he said into the camera for a clip that might be inserted in the game. It's not unusual to hear Atomic employees talking about something as technical as the specific properties of an AT-4 shoulder-fired rocket.

Capt. Read Omohundro, who led a Marine company in Fallujah and lost 13 men there, acts as a kind of quality-control manager for Six Days. "I'll say to them, no, that guy has to be facing the other way. This piece of ammunition doesn't blow up so fast, it only detonates this much. You can't be standing next to it when it goes off or you'll become a casualty." In Atomic's conference room, Omohundro recently described to artists and designers what Fallujah looked like when tanks kicked up dust and debris. "It's not sand like at the beach," he said. "It's that talcum-powder crap. It gets into everything. It just hangs around and you're waiting forever for it to go away."

Omohundro says many of his troops would play shooter games on their Xboxes or other consoles after patrolling all day in Iraq. "It seems pretty natural to me that these guys would want to have their war documented in a videogame." But on April 9, when Atomic showed a 30-second promotional clip at a publicity event put on by the game's distributor, Konami, Fallujah relatives responded immediately. "The war is not a game, and neither was the Battle of Fallujah," the group Gold Star Families Speak Out said in a statement. "For Konami and Atomic Games to minimize the reality of an ongoing war and at the same time profit off the deaths of people close to us by making it entertaining is despicable."

Konami is a Japanese company that distributes and underwrites mostly family-oriented games with names like Dance-DanceRevolution and Karaoke Revolution. Two weeks after the publicity event, Konami's Los Angeles–based executives told Tamte in a conference call that the company was ending its involvement with Six Days. Atomic would have to find a new distributor. (Konami would not return NEWSWEEK's calls.)

Tracy Miller, whose son, Cpl. Nicholas Ziolkowski, was killed Nov. 14, was among the Gold Star family members behind the letter. Ziolkowski had been attached to Omohundro's Bravo Company. He and other snipers had taken up position at the Grand Mosque in downtown Fallujah that morning. Dexter Filkins, a *New York Times* reporter who embedded with Bravo Company, wrote that Ziolkowski had removed his helmet to get a better look in his scope when a bullet caught him in the head.

Miller, an academic adviser at Maryland's Towson University, believes Atomic genuinely wants to honor the Marines who fought in Fallujah. She thinks Six Days is the kind of game her son would have liked to play. Still, Miller says any game about the battle would be distasteful. "I think they're bending over backwards to contact people to make sure what they do isn't going to offend anyone," she told NEWSWEEK. "But I think that it's probably impossible not to offend people with a game." Miller teaches a popular course on the 1960s, including the antiwar movement. She worries that Six Days, precisely

because it aims to re-create the Fallujah battle so realistically, will further desensitize youngsters to the horrors of war. And she's concerned that insurgents will learn about the operational procedures of American troops.

There's another aspect of the game that could be troubling to relatives. Though parents often want to know the precise details of a child's death, seeing the circumstances even loosely replicated in a videogame—where a player can affect the outcome—might be painful. It potentially raises agonizing questions for the parents, not just about how a tragedy unfolded, but how, with the tiniest shift in circumstances, it might have been avoided. To ease these concerns, Atomic has vowed not to use the Marines who died in Fallujah as characters in the game (though the circumstances of their deaths might be portrayed). In an e-mail to the Fallujah families dated May 22, John Farnsworth, Atomic's studio director and an Army Reserve lieutenant colonel, wrote: "I have the highest regard for our troops in uniform and their families, for their brave willingness to sacrifice for liberty, country, family and friends. Out of respect, we have not included any fallen Marine in the interactive reenactments."

For skeptics, the idea that a game can communicate sacrifice is deeply misguided.

That gesture is significant to the families. For documentarians, it's where Six Days begins to fall short. How can a game document a battle if it doesn't identify the fallen? And how can the portrayal be accurate if a player can manipulate the events? David Waddington, an assistant professor of education at Concordia University in Montreal who has written articles about the ethics of videogames, says they cannot convey important aspects of real life, including complex characters. "You do have characters in a videogame in some sense, but . . . character development isn't very robust. So you don't sympathize with characters very much." Though he hasn't previewed Six Days, Waddington thinks Atomic might have generated unrealistic expectations by billing it as something more than a game. "I'm not convinced Six Days in Fallujah as a first-person shooter game is a legitimate form of documentation."

But since videogames are a relatively new medium, the debate about what they can and can't get across is still open. Sicart in Copenhagen also writes about the ethics of videogames. He concedes that games don't do a good job of accurately portraying a sequence of actual events. But he says they can convey the feeling of being there—of occupying the space and having to make decisions—better than television and maybe even movies. "The real goal is not to document the action sequentially but to understand how and why it unfolds and how it felt to the people who were there," he says. "If players understand the emotions of a serviceman in combat, then they are already understanding the real power of Fallujah."

Tamte is now negotiating with a few other potential investors. He says Atomic needs several million dollars to complete the game and millions more to market and distribute it. "We have a lot of people who are interested in the project," he says. "But I'll feel better when we sign something and the checks start coming." Tamte concedes he had not given enough thought to the feelings of the Fallujah families and should have reached out to them earlier in the process. But he says their perceptions have been shaped mostly by the word "game"—which doesn't quite do justice to his project. "We're trying to do something that hasn't been done before, and naturally people use the points of reference they understand," Tamte says. "It's hard for anyone to envision it until it's actually created." Opponents of the project hope that time never comes.

With **Dina Maron** in Washington.

Distorted Picture

Thanks to Photoshop, it's awfully easy to manipulate photographs, as a number of recent scandals make painfully clear. Misuse of the technology poses a serious threat to photojournalism's credibility.

SHERRY RICCHIARDI

If photo sleuths in Ohio hadn't noticed a pair of missing legs, Allan Detrich still would be cruising to assignments in his sleek blue truck, building his reputation as a photographer extraordinaire at the Toledo Blade. In April, the veteran shooter was forced out of the newsroom in disgrace, igniting a scandal that swept the photojournalism community. Coworkers were mystified about why a highly talented, hard worker who had garnered a slew of awards would cheat.

Detrich says that for a time, he felt like the most "reviled journalist in the country." Internet forums buzzed about his misdeeds, and photographers attacked him for sullying the profession. Some even sent hateful e-mail messages. "I wasn't the first to tamper with news photos and, unfortunately, I probably won't be the last," he says. "I screwed up. I got caught."

In his case, he says, he was seduced by software that made altering images so easy that "anyone can do it."

With new technology, faking or doctoring photographs has never been simpler, faster or more difficult to detect. Skilled operators truly are like magicians, except they use tools like Photoshop, the leading digital imaging software, to create their illusions.

Detrich, who had worked for the Blade since 1989, manipulated most of the images while alone in his truck, using a cell phone or WiFi for quick and easy transmission to the photo desk. There was little reason for him to return to the newsroom to process images. Until April 5, no one challenged the veracity of his photographs.

The photographer's downfall underscores a disturbing reality: With readily accessible, relatively inexpensive imaging tools (Photoshop sells for around $650) and a low learning curve, the axiom "seeing is believing" never has been more at risk. That has led to doomsday predictions about documentary photojournalism in this country.

"The public is losing faith in us. Without credibility, we have nothing; we cannot survive," says John Long, chairman of the ethics and standards committee of the National Press Photographers Association. Long pushes for stricter newsroom standards with missionary zeal and believes all journalists are tarnished when someone like Detrich falls from grace.

On June 2, Long, who built a distinguished career in photography at the Hartford Courant before retiring earlier this year, preached to an audience at NPPA's photo summit in Portland, Oregon. If the self-described purist had his way, news photographers would take a vow of abstinence in regard to photo altering; editors would enforce zero-tolerance policies. "The problem is far greater than we fear," Long told the group that afternoon.

There are no statistics on the number of rule-breakers, but indicators within the profession do not bode well for the cherished precept of visual accuracy.

During an NPPA ethics session in Portland, a group of some 50 photographers and photo managers were asked for a show of hands if they believed they had ever worked with peers who routinely crossed ethical boundaries. Nearly every arm flew into the air. "That was a scary thing to see," says Long, who was on the panel. Ethical breaches were the topic of conversation at coffee breaks and during presentations at the photo summit.

Many of the offending photos and illustrations discussed in Portland appear in a rogues' gallery posted by computer scientist Hany Farid (www.cs.dartmouth.edu/farid/research/tampering).

Among the dozens he highlights are Time and Newsweek covers, a Pulitzer Prize-winning photo, images in the Charlotte Observer and Newsday, and a famous portrait of Abraham Lincoln that was discovered to be less than accurate.

The Dartmouth College professor uses the term "digital forensics" to describe pioneering methods to detect image altering. Although not a cure-all, these tools could provide help in the future, says Farid. He predicts that scandals over photo forgeries are "absolutely going to get worse." That notion is underlined by the attention being paid to the problem by media organizations and at conferences.

In August, visual communications expert David Perlmutter will serve on a panel titled "Seeing is Not Believing: Representations and Misrepresentations" at the Association for Education in Journalism and Mass Communication gathering in Washington, D.C. Perlmutter poses the question: "Is the craft I love being murdered, committing suicide or both?"

The Toledo Blade's descent into photo hell began with a telephone call.

On April 4, Ron Royhab, the paper's executive editor, returned home to find a message requesting he phone back, no matter how late. He punched in the number and listened in stunned silence to the voice on the other end. There were suspicions that a photographer had altered a news photo that had run prominently on the Blade's front page four days earlier. The caller was Donald R. Winslow, editor of News Photographer magazine, an NPPA publication.

"I was speechless; I couldn't collect my thoughts. I felt like someone had punched me in the stomach," recalls Royhab. "I got off the phone and thought, 'Not at my newspaper. It can't be!'"

By noon the next day, Detrich, 44, was being questioned in the newsroom. He admitted altering the photograph but said it was for his personal use, a copy he intended to hang on an office wall. He claimed he had mistakenly transmitted the wrong version on deadline. He told Photo District News, "that's not something I would do."

The paper's editors decided to review all of the photos that Detrich, twice named Ohio Photographer of the Year and a Pulitzer Prize finalist in 1998, had submitted for publication this year. They didn't like what they found. By April 7, he had resigned. If he had not, he would have been fired, says Royhab.

The episode began on March 30, when Bluffton University's baseball team played for the first time since five of its athletes had been killed in a bus accident earlier that month. Photographers jostled for position as players knelt in front of banners bearing the names and uniform numbers of the dead.

When similar photos appeared in Cleveland's Plain Dealer, the Dayton Daily News and Ohio's Lima News the following day, a pair of legs clad in blue jeans was visible from behind one of the banners hanging from a fence. In Detrich's version, there was only grass under the banner, although he shot from roughly the same angle. Ohio photographers brought the mysterious disappearance to Winslow's attention.

A review of Detrich's original digital files revealed that he had habitually erased unwanted elements in photos, including people, tree limbs, utility poles, electrical wires, light switches and cabinet knobs. In some instances, he added tree branches or shrubbery. In one sports shot he added a hockey puck; in another he inserted a basketball.

Detrich submitted 947 photographs for publication from January through March of 2007. Editors found that 79 clearly had been doctored. The paper apologized to readers and Detrich posted a mea culpa on his website (www.detrichpix.typepad.com/allandetrich_picturethis). The investigation found that Detrich had altered photos as far back as 2002. The Blade noted that no evidence of tampering was discovered on Detrich's award-winning photos, and there were no alterations in earlier years, when he was shooting on film and editing and processing in the newsroom.

In the May issue of News Photographer, Winslow ran a report on the situation at the Blade and labeled Detrich a "serial digital manipulator," the most prolific to surface in newspaper history.

As for the legs, it turned out they belonged to freelancer Madalyn Ruggiero, who was shooting in Bluffton for the Chicago Tribune and had positioned herself behind the fence in search of a different angle.

Brian Walski had covered war in the Balkans, famine in Africa and conflict in Kashmir before he made a fateful decision while on assignment in Iraq for the Los Angeles Times. The Chicago native was fired via satellite phone on April 1, 2003, after it was discovered he used his computer to combine two images, taken seconds apart, into a composite that ran on page one of the Times on March 31. The subject was a British soldier helping Iraqi civilians find cover outside Basra.

After the photos appeared, an employee at the Hartford Courant noticed that several Iraqis in the background appeared twice (see Drop Cap, May 2003). The Courant, which like the Times is owned by the Tribune Co., had also published the picture.

In an e-mail to the newspaper's photo staff, Walski, who had been with the Times since 1998 and had won Photographer of the Year honors in California, wrote: "This was after an extremely long, hot and stressful day but I offer no excuses here. . . . I have always maintained the highest ethical standards throughout my career and cannot truly explain my complete breakdown in judgment at this time. That will only come in the many sleepless nights that are ahead."

Colin Crawford, the L.A. Times' assistant managing editor for photography, calls Walski "incredibly experienced and talented" and says there was no hint of wrongdoing before the lapse. A review of his work found no other evidence of tampering.

"It's hard for me to get into the head of someone who is risking his life every day," says Crawford, who acknowledges the pressures Walski was under on the battlefield. Still, "I can't imagine in my wildest dreams why he would ever do it." After leaving the Times, Walski started Colorado Visions, a commercial photo business.

In another war-zone episode, Adnan Hajj, a Lebanese freelancer on assignment for Reuters, was fired for doctoring images during the August 2006 conflict between Israel and Hezbollah in Lebanon. In one photo, Hajj darkened and cloned plumes of smoke rising from buildings the Israelis bombed in Beirut, amplifying the devastation. In another, he altered the image of an Israeli F-16 fighter jet to make it appear that it was firing several missiles instead of a single flare, as the original photo of the plane shows.

This time, bloggers acted as sheriff. According to news reports, Charles Johnson, who runs a blog called Little Green Footballs (www.littlegreenfootballs.com/weblog) sounded the alarm about the Beirut photo. Another conservative political blog, The Java Report (www.mypetjawa.mu.nu), drew attention to the phony missiles.

Bloggers also played a role in uncovering a USA Today misstep. (Disclosure: My husband, Frank Folwell, is a deputy managing editor who oversees photography and graphics for USA Today.) On October 26, 2005, WorldNetDaily.com reported that the newspaper pulled a photograph of Condoleezza Rice from its website after a blog called The Pen (www.fromthepen.com)

Back in Action

In early May, the message board for SportsShooter.com lit up after the headline "Detrich Rises From the Dead" appeared. Photographer Allan Detrich, who resigned from the Toledo Blade in April after an investigation showed he had doctored more than 79 images, was back.

The avid storm chaser had covered a tornado that leveled Greensburg, Kansas, on May 4, killing 12. Several news outlets interviewed Detrich, including Fox News Channel and CNN, and his pictures were shown on the air. The president of Polaris Images, a New York photo agency, saw the broadcasts and offered to distribute the Greensburg photos.

Some on SportsShooter.com were outraged by the turn of luck for a photographer ostracized one month earlier. Others took a more practical view. "Sad but true, it seems like the only people upset about this are the photographers. [They] liken what he did to a deadly sin, while the average person sees it as a simple mistake that should be forgiven," said a respondent from Cedar Park, Texas. That is what Detrich is counting on.

After he left the newspaper, he found it difficult to go out of the house, "I felt everybody would be looking at me, saying, 'That's the guy.' " Now he has moved on.

"I have apologized and admitted I was wrong. I'm being up-front with people if they ask about it. I can't do more than that," Detrich says. "I'm not going to sit back and sulk for the rest of my life. I am going to let my images speak for themselves."

—S.R.

revealed it had been manipulated, giving the secretary of state a menacing stare. The blog used the original version of the Associated Press photo to show the image had been doctored.

The altered photo circulated on other blogs, drawing a firestorm of public protest. USA Today explained in an editor's note that "after sharpening the photo for clarity," a portion of Rice's face was brightened, "giving her eyes an unnatural appearance." The distortion violated the paper's editorial standards, the note said.

One of the most ballyhooed examples of photo manipulation was Time magazine's June 27, 1994, cover. Time darkened the skin and added a five o'clock shadow to a mug shot of O.J. Simpson, making him look more sinister. On its December 1, 1997, cover, Newsweek glamorized Bobbi McCaughey, the Iowa mother of septuplets, by straightening her teeth. The magazine superimposed Martha Stewart's head on a model's body for the March 7, 2005, cover, when Stewart was released from prison.

The credit explaining the super-imposed photo of Stewart appeared inside the magazine. Since then, Newsweek's attribution policy has changed. When a photo illustration runs on the front of the magazine, the credit also appears on the cover, says Simon Barnett, Newsweek's director of photography. That provides "an additional layer of information, so if anyone is in any doubt whatsoever, it's there to confirm what they see as being an illustration," he wrote in an e-mail interview.

As for news photos, "We do nothing beyond what has traditionally been done in the photographic darkroom," says Barnett, who took over as photo director in July 2003.

Barnett says the advent of Photoshop has increased the push to create flawless magazine covers. "As digital technology has evolved, art directors at major magazines have forgotten how and when to say 'enough.' This tweaking and buffing and polishing down to the last pixel has frequently had the consequence of changing the photograph into something that at a minimum is plastic, and at worst inaccurate," says Barnett, who counts himself among a minority that appreciates the natural imperfections that real photography brings. "It adds to authenticity," he says.

Time's readers are accustomed to finding the credit for covers on the table of contents, says spokesman Daniel Kile. If the photograph has been altered, the image is clearly labeled a "photo-illustration." That was the case on March 15, when Time illustrated a story, "How the Right Went Wrong," on the cover with a photo of Ronald Reagan crying. The inside credits noted: "Photograph by David Hume Kennerly. Tear by Tim O'Brien." (See "Finding a Niche," April/May.)

But no matter how pure the intention, NPPA's John Long doesn't buy attribution as a substitute for authenticity. "No amount of captioning can ever cover for a visual lie or distortion. If it looks real in a news context, then it better be real," says Long, who maintains there should be the same respect for visual accuracy that there is for the written word in journalism.

Long points out that some photos are doctored with the sole intent of doing harm. In February 2004, a photograph showing Democratic presidential candidate John Kerry with actress Jane Fonda at a 1971 anti-Vietnam war rally swept the Internet. Two photos, taken a year apart, were merged into one and carried a phony AP credit line.

Ken Light, who took the original Kerry photograph sans Fonda, raised a key question in a March 11, 2004, New York Times article about faked images: "What if that photo had floated around two days before the general election and there wasn't time to say it's not true?" The story noted that image tampering did not begin in 1989, with John Knoll's creation of Photoshop.

On the cusp of the digital revolution in 1991, ethicist Paul Lester documented the history of forgeries in a book, "Photojournalism: An Ethical Approach." He noted that Hippolyte Bayard made the first known counterfeit photograph more than 160 years ago, and during the Civil War soldiers were instructed to play dead and corpses were moved for dramatic impact. In World War I, photos were forged for propaganda purposes, including one of Kaiser Wilhelm cutting off the hands of babies.

Lester included a classic example from 1982 often cited as the beginning of the steep challenge for photojournalism in the digital age. When National Geographic employed what was considered computer wizardry to squeeze together Egypt's pyramids of Giza for the perfect cover shot, tremors shot through the photo community. Many bemoaned the onset of an era when tampering with photos would be effortless.

In his book, Lester quoted Tom Kennedy, photo director at the Geographic from 1987 to 1997, who laid down new rules for the magazine. Technology no longer would be used to manipulate elements in a photo simply to achieve a more compelling graphic effect, Kennedy said. As for the pyramids, "We regarded that afterwards as a mistake, and we wouldn't repeat that mistake today."

Writing for the New York Times in 1990, acclaimed photo critic Andy Grundberg predicted, "In the future, readers of newspapers and magazines will probably view news pictures more as illustrations than as reportage, since they will be aware that they can no longer distinguish between a genuine image and one that has been manipulated." History has given weight to his prophecy as photo managers search for answers.

"Fundamentally, there is only so much you can do. You hope and pray and respect your staff. . . . You trust that they're not going to do this kind of thing," says the L.A. Times' Crawford, who, like many others interviewed for this story, sees setting clear, strict policies as critical for quality control. He believes that, despite the Walski incident, the Times has had a solid system in place. "You do the best you can, talking to your staff and making sure they understand what your ethics are," he says.

Since the Detrich episode, the Toledo Blade is spot-checking more photos and scheduling more one-on-one time with photographers to go over their work. "With the ability to send electronically, it is easy to feel isolated from the rest of the photo department, so we will try harder to establish a sense of team," says Luann Sharp, the Blade's assistant managing editor for administration.

Santiago Lyon, the AP's director of photography, oversees the wire service's vast army of 300 shooters plus 700 others operating on a freelance or contract basis. The AP handles about three-quarters of a million images a year, leaving ample potential for error.

Lyon has turned to the Poynter Institute, NPPA, the White House News Photographers Association and other media groups for guidance as he updates and fine-tunes the wire service's standards.

"We're looking at their ethical guidelines and our own and coming up with wordage and phraseology more in tune with the changing world out there," says Lyon, who attended Photoshop training sessions for about 200 AP photographers and photo editors throughout the U.S. in 2006. At each stop, he hammered home the guidelines for responsible use of imaging tools and repeatedly stressed that "credibility is the most important thing we have at the AP and journalism in general."

Lyon says a handful of photographers have been fired for tampering with pictures over the years. He views the core of experienced photo editors at AP's editing hubs around the globe as a first line of defense for detecting phony images.

There are certain clues photo monitors look for. According to experts, the most common signs are differences in color or shadows, variations in graininess or pixilation, blurred images or elements in the photo that are too bright or much sharper than the rest.

Dartmouth College professor Farid is developing computer algorithms, or mathematical formulas, that can detect altered images. Lyon and Farid have met to discuss possibilities for the future, and Lyon has had the professor analyze old photos the AP had on file and knew had been altered to test the reliability of the detection software. It worked in all but one case, Lyon says.

But for now, the method is too cumbersome, given that the AP receives between 2,000 and 3,000 pictures each day. "To work for us, that type of process would have to be instantaneous, or close to it," says Lyon.

Farid doesn't promote his detection software as a magic formula. "The technology is getting better and better. It's getting easier to manipulate, and it is affordable. Everybody has it. At least we might slow [the forger] down, make it more challenging, more difficult," says the computer scientist, who likens the scramble for improved safeguards to an arms race.

"I guarantee you there will be people out there developing anti-forgery detection software or software that makes better forgeries," says Farid.

Beyond stopping cheaters, there also is the thorny issue of defining the limits of what is and is not acceptable. Photo editors commonly say that the only appropriate techniques with Photoshop are those analogous to what was acceptable in the traditional darkroom. That might ring hollow to a generation of photographers who have always processed images on computers and transmitted them to the photo desk from the nearest Starbucks. Still, one rule is clear: Removing visual content from a photo or adding it crosses the divide.

Lyon warns that using words to describe visual nuances in guidelines is very complicated. "How do you define the correct use of tonal differences—lightening or darkening aspects of a picture in a way that accurately reflects what the photographer saw?"

In an attempt to clarify standards, Kenny F. Irby, the Poynter Institute's photo expert, confessed in a September 2003 report that he had "dodged" (to lighten) and "burned" (to darken) elements in his pictures throughout his career. He maintained there was nothing sinful about his actions because he did not take those techniques to extremes.

Irby listed notables such as Gordon Parks and W. Eugene Smith among the many great photojournalists who employed the same techniques. When, then, do photographers slip into the abyss?

On August 15, 2003, Patrick Schneider of the Charlotte Observer was suspended for three days without pay for excessive adjustments in Photoshop. The North Carolina Press Photographers Association stripped Schneider of the awards he had won for the photos in question. Its investigation found that details such as parking lots, fences and people had been removed from pictures.

At the time, Schneider told Irby, "I used the tools that for decades have been used in the darkroom, and now, in Photoshop, I do them with more precision. My goal is to bring more impact to my images, to stop the readers and draw their attention."

The award-winning photographer was fired in July 2006 for an image of a firefighter on a ladder, silhouetted against a vivid sunlit sky. The Observer explained in an editor's note that in the original, the sky was brownish-gray. Enhanced with photo-editing software, the sky became a deep red, and the sun took on a more distinct halo. In the judgment of his bosses, Schneider had violated the paper's rules.

While the photo establishment buzzes over scandals like those of Schneider and Detrich, others ask, "So what?"

The Toledo Blade's Royhab was surprised when some readers questioned the ruckus raised over Detrich's misdeeds and asked what was wrong with changing the content of a photograph in a newspaper. "The answer is simple: It is dishonest," Royhab wrote in an April 15 column.

On SportsShooter.com, a website run by USA Today photographer Robert Hanashiro, some attacked Detrich for his duplicity while others defended his right to stay in journalism. That did not sit well with Bob DeMay, chairman of the board of the Ohio News Photographers Association and an acquaintance of Detrich's.

"I find it very scary that some people didn't find fault at all," says DeMay, photo editor at the Akron Beacon Journal. "There used to be an old saying, 'Pictures don't lie.' Well, they do now. Once that seed of doubt is put in somebody's mind, it's frightening."

Like many others, DeMay sees the troubled state of newspapers playing into the equation. Pushed to the limits by layoffs and hiring freezes, many photo departments have fewer bodies to do more work. Three photo staffers at the Beacon Journal were laid off last year, taking a toll on quality, says DeMay. As travel budgets are slashed, there is more reliance on freelancers who file photos from a distance, without the backstop of newsroom accountability or ethics codes. And the competition for newspaper space has never been fiercer, increasing the pressure for dramatic images.

There also has been a cultural change in how photo departments operate. In the past, photographers often worked together in the darkroom; there was more collaboration and more oversight from photo desks. Today, it is common to transmit images from the field via laptop computers, with only occasional newsroom visits.

Opportunities for misdeeds are boundless, warns Larry Gross, coeditor of the book "Image Ethics in the Digital Age." Once photographers step over the line, there is very little they can't do, and, if they are skilled enough, they may leave little or no trace, says Gross. Years ago, editors could ask for the photo negative to make comparisons, but digital images can be changed so that there's no original left, no way to track back to an initial state. Adding to the angst of photo watchdogs, new and better versions of Photoshop are on the horizon, which is likely to widen the scope of fakeries.

NPPA's Winslow wonders if the ethics quandary in photojournalism is akin to the problem professional baseball has with steroids. "Are there lots of people doing what Detrich did without editors and managers realizing the extent of the problem?" he asked in his May article. "Or do they suspect, but do nothing about it?"

Not everyone sees a dim future. Author David Perlmutter believes that, by some standards, this is the golden age of photojournalistic ethics.

"If you are caught faking a picture today, you are fired. Fifty years ago, it was just part of the business. Now most people have gone to journalism school and learned ethics. Newsrooms are taking these things more seriously. Standards are higher than ever," Perlmutter says. "On the other hand, it has become so much easier to get away with the crime."

Senior contributing writer **Sherry Ricchiardi** (sricchia@iupui.edu) has written about coverage of the war in Iraq and the Virginia Tech massacre in recent issues of *AJR*.

The Quality-Control Quandary

As newspapers shed copy editors and post more and more unedited stories online, what's the impact on their content?

CARL SESSIONS STEPP

Sunrise approaches on a Friday morning, and the St. Louis Post-Dispatch website is being updated early—from Mandy St. Amand's bathroom.

St. Amand, the Post-Dispatch continuous news editor, has balanced her laptop on the toilet lid and, while drying her hair and prepping for the office, is reworking homepage headlines.

Not surprisingly, no copy editor is handy at 5:30 A.M., so St. Amand's work goes online unchecked by a colleague. She estimates that between 40 and 50 Post-Dispatch staffers can post directly to the site, often remotely and without a second read—a growing, troubling trend in these days of never-ending news cycles and ever-dwindling editing corps.

A similar if less dramatic effect follows on the print side, where buyouts and layoffs over several years have cut the number of Post-Dispatch copy editors from more than 40 to about 21. The inevitable result, not only at the Post-Dispatch but at newsrooms nationwide, is that fewer editors scrutinize copy, and they often spend less time per item than they would have just a few years ago.

Together, these developments raise unprecedented questions about the value—and the future—of editing itself. Already at many news organizations, journalists and readers alike have noticed flabbier writing, flatter headlines, more typos. How far can you cut editing without crippling credibility? How do you balance immediacy and accuracy? How much does fine-tuning matter to the work-in-progress online ethos?

"When you think about the assembly line that was a newsroom, it's changed," says Post-Dispatch Editor Arnie Robbins. "In the world we live in now, readers expect immediacy, and we have to deliver. But we also have to be careful."

At ground level, these concerns fuel another trend: developing ways to maintain reasonable quality control now that the end-of-the-line copy desk can no longer process everything. Interviews and visits by AJR make clear that newsrooms are lurching toward new ways, from "buddy editing" (where you ask the nearest person to read behind you) to "back editing" (where copy is edited after posting) to "previewing" (where

copy goes to a holding directory for an editor to check before live posting).

For now, though, progress is slow, and the risks seem scary.

Bill McClellan, a Post-Dispatch columnist since 1983, has one of the news organization's most familiar bylines. But he recently experienced a "brain cramp" and called Missouri a blue state, even though it has gone Democratic only twice in the past eight presidential races. The error zipped past editors and ended up in print.

McClellan won't blame the copy desk, which he says is "astoundingly good," and regularly calls to check things like song lyrics he's tangled. "Nine times out of 10 the copy desk catches things," he says, "and the red-blue error was the tenth."

But, he adds, "You never do more with less. You do less with less. You have fewer copy editors, more mistakes get through."

Reporter Adam Jadhav remembers writing that a woman had lost her right arm in a car crash. Six paragraphs later, he called it her left arm. Like McClellan, Jadhav takes full responsibility for his errors. Still, he says, "I'd like to think that a reasonably worked copy desk could catch them."

"Obviously in the future there are probably going to be fewer and fewer reads," Editor Robbins says. "There is concern there, and there is some risk there. However, I think it is manageable."

Can good editing endure amid all the changes?

Mandy St. Amand, by now operating from the newsroom rather than the bathroom, thinks about the question. "I really wish I had a wise-sounding, beard-stroking answer," she says. "But I don't."

Post-Dispatch Managing Editor Pam Maples is leading a newsroom tour, pointing out physical and operational alterations aimed toward Journalism 2.0.

In the center, a glass office has been dismantled, creating space for a 9:30 A.M. stand-up news huddle—earlier, faster-paced and more Web-oriented than before. A homepage editor presides. For the first agenda item, she turns to a dry-erase board where the phrase "top mods" appears in all caps. What should fill the modules atop the website?

The newsroom now has two early-morning reporters, often hustling on traffic and weather stories. Their goal is to start the process of moving at least 20 items a day through the top Web positions. The nine editors also discuss tomorrow's printed paper, but they project urgency to get moving online.

"Anything that happens, our assumption is it goes online," Maples says. "It puts a demand on editors and how they manage their people and how they think. Deadline is always."

Maples and Robbins have graciously let AJR into their newsroom at a bad time: the week after the paper laid off 14 people in the newsroom, including several editors. Four other rounds of layoffs or buyouts have taken place since 2005. A news staff of about 340 five years ago is about 210 today, Robbins calculates. Some 40 pages of space per week have been lost in the newspaper, which is introducing a narrower page width that could cost another 5 percent of newshole.

These challenges are not unique to St. Louis, but the Post-Dispatch seems a symbolic place to examine their impact on editing. It is a 241,000-circulation, middle-American, blue-collar institution, founded in 1878 by Joseph Pulitzer, the editing giant famous for preaching "accuracy, accuracy, accuracy."

Even today, four years after the Pulitzer family sold the paper to Lee Enterprises (see "Lee *Who?*" June/July 2005), a visitor is reverently shown a vacant but still furnished office, last occupied by a Pulitzer family member, where portraits of multiple generations of the family peer down. As you enter the paper's downtown lobby, the founder's words thunder from the front wall: "Always remain devoted to the public welfare."

The ghost of Joseph Pulitzer, it seems, haunts the Post-Dispatch, and perhaps newspaper journalism itself. Can "accuracy, accuracy, accuracy" survive "cuts, cuts, cuts"?

Post-Dispatch staffers warm to the challenge.

"We have a brand," says Deputy Metro Editor Alan Achkar. "People expect from the St. Louis Post-Dispatch a level of quality and accuracy. If we don't have good, responsible journalism that people can bank on, we don't have anything."

But maintaining quality takes more and more effort.

"For the Internet, speed is king," Achkar says. "You often worry that we're just slapping stuff online without properly vetting it. . . . It's added work. Sometimes you feel that no one wants to acknowledge that putting out a newspaper—even a thinner one—is a monumental task."

Top editors acknowledge that, by policy, cutbacks have fallen disproportionately on editors. Saving reporting jobs is the priority.

"People on the street, you try to protect as much as possible," Robbins says. "That's not to minimize the importance of editing and design at all. But ultimately you have to make tough decisions. Reporters on the street do separate us from other places."

So, the assigning editors and copy editors who are left adapt.

These days, says Frank Reust, a Post-Dispatch copy editor for 10 years, editors find themselves hovering somewhere between "comfortably rushed" and "always having to railroad stuff."

That means more rapid copy editing and sometimes, especially for wire stories, fewer reads. For online copy, says designer and Web producer Joan McKenna, "we are forgiven for mistakes. Speed is much more important than anything else."

The fallout so far seems noticeable but not calamitous. More than one reporter mentioned increased reaction from readers pointing out errors, mostly small. For example, a sportswriter's post confusing the names of two St. Louis Rams coaching prospects was flagged in the comments section and fixed within minutes.

Editors also express some larger concerns.

For instance, Reust sees less creative time applied to the "accuracy and tone" of headlines. He also worries that writers and editors brainstorm less. "The general time devoted to good writing is almost nonexistent now," he says.

Jean Buchanan, the paper's assistant managing editor for projects, sees that too. Writers sometimes can't get an editor's attention when they need it, and less time goes into those vital ingredients of enterprise and investigations, "rooting around for potential stories, requesting information that might lead to a story, meeting with small groups of reporters talking about what they are seeing."

Reid Laymance, the assistant managing editor for sports, spends more time on hands-on editing and less on planning. His editors have less time to develop "extras" like charts or breakout boxes. Down a copy editor since he took over last spring, "we're not as much editors as we used to be," he says. "Our guys have become processors. Getting the game in by 8 o'clock, making sure the headline fits, that's all we have time for."

Director of Photography Larry Coyne offers a good news/bad news example. With today's digital cameras, it isn't uncommon for photographers to shoot a thousand exposures on an assignment, many times more than they previously would have. Online galleries allow far more photos to run. But Coyne has three-and-a-half photo editors today instead of the five-and-a-half of about three years ago, so collaboration and editing can suffer. "There is more emphasis on quantity and getting them out," he says, "and less on feedback with photographers."

In fairness, it must be emphasized that not one of these editors comes across as whiny or bitter. They seem candid about their plight but determined to succeed. "Every time there's a reduction in staff," copy editor Reust says, "there is a period where you feel the load is just too much to handle. Then two months down the road you're thinking, 'We can handle things.'"

Patrick Gauen, the self-described "cops and courts editor" and a veteran police reporter, looks back over his 24 years at the paper and says, "A lot of what is changing—the platform stuff—really doesn't matter to me. It gets to the public one way or the other. . . . I feel like I still have the time I need. Our adequacy of editing is still good."

"There are so many balls in the air at once and some of them are going to drop. You try to understand which ones are breakable and try not to let those go."

—Patrick Gauen

He lives by something he once heard: "There are so many balls in the air at once and some of them are going to drop. You try to understand which ones are breakable and try not to let those go."

General assignment reporter David Hunn echoes that balanced sentiment. "The most serious stories I write" get attentive editing, he says, but the rush to post online is "kind of like the Wild West. . . . If anything is clear to me right now, it's that we are feeling our way as we go—and as a whole doing a pretty good job of it."

Editors being editors, though, they tend to see themselves in a code orange world, their equivalent of an earthquake zone or hurricane corridor, bracing for the Big One.

"What will wake us up," says Enterprise Editor Todd Stone, "is going to be the first big lawsuit where somebody really gets creamed. It's going to happen. And I'd bet you about 10 bucks it will be because of a lack of editing vigilance."

At the Washington Post, another paper that has lost editors, A-section copy desk chief Bill Walsh has the same worry.

"I keep fearing a disaster of some kind. I think it is only a matter of time," says Walsh, a nationally known blogger and author. "Doing more with less is always going to mean a compromise in quality. Three sets of eyes are always better than two."

Last year, the Post's ombudsman at the time, Deborah Howell, made a public pitch for editing. Reporting that the Post had lost 40 percent of its copy editors since 2005, Howell wrote that they are "the last stop before disaster."

On Walsh's combined national-foreign copy desk, seven editors now work where 12 once did. Where a typical piece of copy formerly got careful reading from an assigning editor, copy editor, slot editor and an editor looking at page proofs, today there tends to be one less layer, with the slot editor just taking a "glance," Walsh says.

Front-page and other sensitive stories still get extra edits, but Walsh acknowledges, "We're probably spending on average less time with stories, although that is not universally the case. I can't say we are doing as good a job with a rim read and a half-assed slot read as we were with more people looking at every story."

To help compensate, Walsh adds, the Post has succeeded in improving flow so copy reaches his desk earlier. It is also stressing that assigning desks must polish stories as much as possible before moving them.

Forty miles up I-95, the Baltimore Sun offers its version of the same tale.

The Sun, too, features its founder's words on the lobby wall, A.S. Abell's 1837 exhortation to serve "the common good."

But like other newsrooms, the Sun has fewer editors' eyes trained on that common good. John E. McIntyre, the director of the copy desk since 1995, counted about 54 copy editors several years ago, 48 about a year ago and 34 as of January, for news, features and sports.

However, McIntyre points out a "grim advantage" for the Sun and other papers. For print, at least, there is less copy to edit. The paper, he says, has lost about a third of its staff in the past few years and almost that much newshole.

"The size of the paper has been cut back to the point at which we have just about enough copy editors to manage it," he says. "It's the only reason we are not slapping basically unread copy into print."

Still, McIntyre sees worrisome signs, like "minor errors in fact and slack writing," fewer minutes for making headlines shine and, of course, less attention to online postings.

"That scares the bejeezus out of me," says McIntyre, who writes a blog about language called You Don't Say (http://weblogs.baltimoresun.com/news/mcintyre/blog). "I would rather have people on the staff catch my errors than readers."

Like editors elsewhere, McIntyre pledges to maintain quality. "The Sun has a reputation for the accuracy and clarity of what it publishes, and we are going to find a way to uphold the paper's standards."

McIntyre, a charter member and former president of the American Copy Editors Society (ACES), believes in documenting to management the vital contributions editors make.

A man given to unusually natty dress for a newsroom, who sips tea from a real cup during an interview, he offers an earthy defense of the editor's role. It is, he says, "to save the paper's ass."

He keeps a file of great prepublication catches by editors. Not long ago, he says, a veteran reporter and an assigning editor let through a piece of libelous work. "Were it not for the copy editor," McIntyre declares, "the biggest decision on the afternoon after publication would have been how many zeroes to put on the settlement check."

ACES and its current president, Chris Wienandt, have boosted efforts to promote and defend editing.

"Everyone is trying to cut costs, and editors and copy editors are relatively invisible jobs," says Wienandt, the business copy chief of the Dallas Morning News. "There is still this perception that we are proofreading drones.

"But the work of the copy editor involves the most-read work in the paper—the headlines. Editors are guardians of credibility, and without credibility we really haven't got a leg to stand on. Imagine a manufacturing company that didn't have a quality-control department. They would be in hot water pretty quick if things started going out defective."

128

"Imagine a manufacturing company that didn't have a quality-control department. They would be in hot water pretty quick if things started going out defective."

—Chris Wienandt

Wienandt and other ACES board members have collaborated on several editorials on the organization's website (www.copydesk.org), scolding those like Tribune Co. owner Sam Zell, who complained that layers of editing delay publication.

If stories are posted too quickly, the ACES editorial countered, they are "more likely to contain errors . . . be unethical, or present an actual legal problem. . . . If credibility evaporates, so will sales."

ACES also attacked the idea of outsourcing editing. "You simply can't duplicate the collective wisdom of a locally based copy desk," another editorial argued. To diminish local editing would jeopardize quality and undermine "the key selling point to an industry that more than ever needs selling points."

W hat then is the future of editing?
Will Sullivan, the Post-Dispatch's 28-year-old interactive director, appreciates the concerns of veteran colleagues but also welcomes a future of new thinking and tools.

He envisions that editing will become "more of a barnraising . . . an everyone-is-an-editor model," where "the concept of news is a wiki" and a story becomes "a kind of rolling document" moving through a continuous editing process.

Better training can spread editing skills to writers and producers, he says. New tools, from automated step-savers like spell-check to simplified photo-editing software, can add speed and quality. Merging staffs can promote efficiency, for example, by assigning the same section editor to manage features on the Web and in print.

During this time of transition, several practices seem increasingly common:

- bringing copy editors in earlier to help with online copy and to expedite flow
- using floating, "quick-hit" editors to handle stories as they break
- expecting writers and assigning desks to move copy earlier
- enforcing the perhaps neglected principle that writers should be better self-editors
- encouraging "buddy editing," where a writer or poster doesn't wait for the copy desk but asks a colleague for a second read
- using "preview" directories as a holding point for material about to go live online, so an editor can look over it first

- creating protocols for Web editing, such as posting a note whenever something new goes onto the Web, to trigger an editor's check
- systematizing "back editing," so that even after being posted, all copy gets edited as soon as possible

Repeatedly, Post-Dispatch editors and reporters underline the importance of constant coaching and communicating to help solve problems early rather than dump them on editors late.

"The shift in responsibility has moved to the front end with the reporter and the originating editor more than ever," says Adam Goodman, deputy managing editor for metro and business news. "You can't rely on somebody catching things down the road as much as we used to. . . . It needs to be camera-ready when the reporter sends it."

Deputy Managing Editor for News Steve Parker tracks every published correction. ("It's kind of like being a prison guard," he jokes.) From 2002 to 2005, the annual number sat in the 800s. Then it began drifting downward, to 771 in 2006, 636 in 2007, and 546 last year.

Partly, Parker acknowledges, the drop reflects a declining newshole and volume of copy. But in 2006, the paper also developed a set of "verification guidelines" to reduce errors and spread accountability. They range from the basics ("Ask the subject to spell his/her name. . . . Just before ending the interview, recheck the spelling") to avoiding hoaxes ("Remember that IDs can be faked") to double-checking graphics ("A finished copy . . . must be provided to the reporter or originating editor before it is published").

In addition, Managing Editor Maples says, it becomes essential to recognize when you truly must take your time.

She cites high-profile breaking stories where the newsroom delayed or withheld postings while discussing thorny issues. When area police made a surprise discovery of two missing teenage boys, one of whom had been gone for four-and-a-half years, the Post-Dispatch held an early report because it was based on only one source. A television news operation broke the story, beating the paper by a few minutes. The Post-Dispatch also withheld other information because a reporter's online research was putting it in doubt. It turned out to be incorrect, but other outlets used it.

Last year, a Post-Dispatch stringer witnessed a shooting at a Kirkwood, Missouri, city council meeting. The stringer saw two people get shot, by someone whose voice she recognized, before she took cover under a chair. Reached on her cell phone, she identified both victims and the shooter. After a quick, intense debate involving key editors, the paper's website went with the names but not their conditions or other sensitive details.

By contrast, the paper last year apologized for a "journalistic breakdown" over a feel-good Easter story about a woman's past of "victimization . . . followed by recovery." Multiple details—including the woman's name, marriage, children and various dramatic incidents—were challenged after publication.

To Maples, the broad lesson is that "we have to keep talking about the balance between immediacy and standards . . . We can't slow down, but it should not be 'publish at all costs.'"

Reporters want the help. "If we have to wait six more minutes," says 24-year veteran reporter Tim O'Neil, "let's get it out correctly. The number of times I might grouse about being edited is outweighed by the times people have saved my tail."

Mandy St. Amand, the continuous news editor, once worked at the Associated Press and still believes, "Get it first, but first get it right."

But she recognizes, too, that changing times will test that venerable credo.

"I think there is a trade-off," she concludes. "The editing overall in terms of polishing has waned, but the sense of urgency and excitement has increased. I guess whether that's a fair trade-off will be decided by the readers."

CARL SESSIONS STEPP (cstepp@jmail.umd.edu), AJR's senior contributing editor, teaches at the Philip Merrill College of Journalism at the University of Maryland.

Why Journalists Are Not above the Law

GABRIEL SCHOENFELD

To hear some tell it, the fundamental freedom of the press promised by the First Amendment of the U.S. Constitution is in peril today as perhaps never before. In his four decades representing the media, says Floyd Abrams, one of the country's leading First Amendment lawyers, the work of reporting has "never been as seriously threatened as it is today." Norman Pearlstine, until recently the editor-in-chief of Time Inc., warns that today's situation "chills essential news-gathering and reporting." William Safire, the longtime columnist for the *New York Times,* says "the ability of journalists to gather the news" is "under attack." Nicholas Kristof, also a *Times* columnist, says "we're seeing a broad assault on freedom of the press that would appall us if it were happening in Kazakhstan."

The source of the problem, according to these and other concerned observers, is the American government, in the form of the White House and the Justice Department. Both are threatening to prevent journalists from doing their work by depriving them of the right to rely on confidential sources of information: the lifeblood of the journalistic profession and the prime avenue through which the public learns about impending shifts in policy, about official wrongdoing, and about much else besides.

Overstated or not, such worries reflect continuing reverberations from a number of recent cases. The most prominent involves Judith Miller, a reporter for the *New York Times* who had gathered information about the leak of an undercover CIA officer's name in possible violation of the Intelligence Identities Act. In his effort to uncover the leaker, the government's special counsel, Patrick Fitzgerald, brought Miller before a grand jury in 2005 to answer questions about what she had learned.

Declining to disgorge her confidential sources, and citing her First Amendment rights as a journalist, Miller refused to testify. In July 2005, the judge presiding over the process held her in contempt. She spent the next 85 days in the Alexandria City jail before finally naming her source: I. Lewis "Scooter" Libby, chief of staff to Vice President Dick Cheney.[1]

The spectacle of a reporter from our country's premier newspaper going to prison for almost three months was only the most visible example of the heavy hand of government. Another journalist, a video blogger by the name of Josh Wolf, is currently sitting in a California jail for declining to turn over to a grand jury video clips of an anarchist riot in San Francisco. And there are similar cases elsewhere that have stirred fears among reporters over the increasing legal hazards of their work—not to mention the alarm of those like Floyd Abrams who are convinced that the public's fundamental access to vital news is being impaired by an overreaching officialdom, bent on protecting itself from legitimate scrutiny.

With such apprehensions on the rise, Congress has come under increasing pressure to establish an official reporter's privilege—analogous to the attorney-client, the priest-penitent, and the husband-wife privilege that already exist in law—exempting a journalist from having to disclose his sources in any federal criminal investigation or trial. Today some 31 states have formally created such a "shield law," while everywhere else, with the exception of Wyoming, reporters enjoy a more qualified privilege as a matter of common law. Only the federal system remains without such a statute—a deficit that a coalition of news organizations and First Amendment activists now seeks to rectify in the new Congress.

A number of prominent Republicans, including Senators Arlen Specter and Richard Lugar, have long championed such a law. The new chairman of the Judiciary Committee, Patrick Leahy of Vermont, and a bevy of other Democrats including Charles Schumer of New York and Christopher Dodd of Connecticut, are also firmly behind it. With bipartisan support in place, and with the Democrats now in charge, the prospects for passage of such a bill are better than they have been for a generation.

In its modern form, the issue of a reporter's privilege is exceptionally nettlesome, and has been so ever since the Supreme Court ruling in *Branzburg v. Hayes* (1972). That ruling brought together a number of then-recent cases. Paul Branzburg, a reporter for the Louisville *Courier-Journal,* had witnessed people manufacturing and using illegal narcotics. More or less at the same time, two other journalists, a Massachusetts television reporter and a reporter for the *New York Times,* were also believed to have witnessed behavior that appeared to be illegal. All three were summoned to testify before grand juries. All three, citing the First Amendment, declined to answer questions about their confidential sources. All three were held in contempt.

Presenting the same set of legal issues, the three cases were combined and made their way up to the Supreme Court. Its majority decision, written by Justice Byron White, held that the First Amendment did not offer a privilege for journalists that "other citizens do not enjoy," and the Court emphatically declined to create one.

White's ruling was crystalline in its logic and seemingly absolute in its conclusion. But it did not put an end to controversy. For one thing, nothing in White's ruling barred Congress from establishing a reporter's privilege as an act of law. For another thing, the 5–4 decision of the Court was itself deeply muddied by a concurring opinion, written by Justice Lewis Powell, which even Powell's colleagues called "enigmatic."

While adding his name to White's decision, Powell undercut its central premise by suggesting that courts should operate on a case-by-case basis, the better to strike "a proper balance between freedom of the press and the obligation of all citizens to give relevant testimony with respect to criminal conduct." Leaving unspecified the ground rules for this balancing act, Powell's opinion had the effect of plunging lower courts into confusion. Today, five of the twelve circuits in the federal system have relied on *Branzburg* to compel journalists to provide confidential information; another four, basing themselves on Powell's inscrutable words, have granted journalists a qualified privilege.

This confusion has only added fuel to the latest push for a shield law. But is such a privilege warranted? And is it desirable?

I n considering those questions, one might profitably turn to another case now before the courts. This one, too, involves Patrick Fitzgerald and Judith Miller, and centers on the disclosure of sensitive government material. In contrast to the Scooter Libby affair, this case is surprisingly low-profile; and again in contrast to the Scooter Libby affair, it is of exceptional national importance.

In December 2001, federal law-enforcement officers were preparing to raid the offices and seize the assets of the Holy Land Foundation and the Global Relief Foundation—two Chicago-based Islamic "charities," both of which were linked to terrorist organizations abroad. Evidently, on the eve of the raid, Miller and another *Times* reporter, Philip Shenon, acting on confidential information from a source inside a federal grand jury, telephoned officials of the two foundations and asked them questions that had the effect of tipping them off to the impending operation, thereby potentially if not actually nullifying its value and imperiling the law officers carrying it out.

Given this breach of closely held information, Fitzgerald, acting in his capacity as U.S. attorney in Chicago, opened an investigation. Among other things, he issued a subpoena for the telephone records of the two *Times* reporters during the period in which the leak was thought to have occurred. The *Times*

strenuously resisted, and for the last four or five years the matter has slowly moved through the courts. This past August, a three-judge federal panel ruled against the *Times*. "We see no danger to a free press" in so ruling, wrote one of the panel's members. "Learning of imminent law-enforcement-asset freezes/searches and informing targets of them is not an activity essential, or even common, to journalism." In December, the Supreme Court, declining to hear an appeal, let stand the decision of the three-judge panel.

The *Times,* for its part, has steadfastly insisted that no damage was done by its reporters' actions. According to an attorney for the paper, the pair were merely "conducting their journalistic duties by getting reaction to an ongoing story." The *Times* editorial page has blasted the Supreme Court's December action as "the latest legal blow to the diminishing right of journalists to shield informants." Citing the public interest in the "dissemination of information," it has seized the occasion to argue yet again that the "privilege granted to journalists to protect their sources needs to be bolstered with a strong federal shield law."

But the *Times* is wrong. For here is an instance, one of many in the recent past, where it is hardly clear that the public interest resides in promoting the "dissemination of information." To the contrary, where protecting the country from terrorism is at stake, the public interest may rather reside in *narrowing* access to information, and not in broadcasting it to terrorist fundraisers and to the public at large. Although the two reporters have not been charged with any crime, and although there is no evidence that either of them acted with malicious intent, a convincing argument can be made that in ferreting out secret information from a grand jury, and in placing telephone calls to criminal suspects on that basis, they endangered us all.

C onsiderations like these have, in fact, informed recent congressional debates over whether to enact a shield law. Thus, a bill considered by the Senate Judiciary Committee in 2005 made a point of excluding from any such privilege information that posed "imminent" harm to national security—a very narrow exclusion that was duly subjected to withering criticism by the Justice Department. The following year, a bill introduced by Lugar and Specter appeared to take Justice's concerns into account, broadening the array of unprotected categories to include, among other things, any information necessary to government in fulfilling its obligation to "prevent significant and actual harm" to national security.

A parade of Senators have pronounced themselves satisfied with this compromise, hailing it as a way of ensuring the flow of information to the public while also safeguarding genuine secrets. But a moment's reflection exposes the defect in this reasoning. For what exactly constitutes "significant and actual harm" to national security, and how would a court, of all institutions, go about determining it?

The military, diplomatic, and intelligence machinery of the U.S. government, acting under the authority of presidential executive orders and employing criminal sanctions enacted by Congress, classifies an immense volume of information. It also keeps a careful account of what it is doing—tabulating, for example, 14,206,773 "classification decisions" in fiscal year 2005 alone.[2] Three primary categories are in use—top-secret, secret, and confidential—of which the overwhelming share is "secret." According to official definitions, the disclosure of "top-secret" or "secret" material "could reasonably be expected" to cause either "exceptionally grave" or "serious" damage to the United States, while disclosure of "confidential" material "could reasonably be expected" to cause only "damage." By passing a shield law that requires prosecutors to demonstrate "significant and actual harm" before compelling a journalist to testify, Congress would effectively dismantle this entire classification system without erecting any safeguards in its place.

To begin with, while leaving statutes on the books that ostensibly criminalize leaks of *all* classified documents, the exception would almost automatically free journalists who come into possession of "confidential" information from the possibility of ever being subpoenaed—on its face, mere "damage" would not qualify as "significant" harm. But even "secret" and "top-secret" material might also not fall under the exception, since "actual" harm is virtually impossible to prove, hinging almost always on an evaluation of actions taken in secret by an adversary about which we may not ever learn. It is for this very reason that the rules of the classification system do not speak of actual harm, safeguarding instead information that could "reasonably be expected" to injure our national security.

A shield law, in other words, would effectively immunize one large category of leakers at a stroke, and perhaps immunize almost all leakers, dramatically intensifying the flow of even the most sensitive secrets into the public domain. Every bureaucrat with a private agenda would feel free to contact a Judith Miller or an even more prolific collector of leaks like the *New Yorker*'s Seymour Hersh to relay classified national-defense information without any apprehension of ever being arrested or prosecuted on the basis of something that might one day be disclosed by a reporter in a court proceeding.

Protecting national secrets is already a problematic venture. Some of the most notorious leaks of the past several years have been not of the confidential but of the secret and top-secret variety. Thus, in 2005, the *Washington Post* revealed a highly classified network of clandestine CIA prisons in Europe for al-Qaeda captives. That same year, the *New York Times* disclosed the existence of a highly classified National Security Agency program of government surveillance of al-Qaeda suspects.[3] In 2006, the *Times* revealed a highly classified program monitoring al-Qaeda financial transactions; most recently, it published the contents of a highly classified memo revealing administration misgivings about the prime minister of Iraq, a leak described by one government official as among the most damaging in recent memory. And this is not even to take account of leaks from the criminal-justice system like police and FBI investigative reports, surveillance tapes, and grand-jury transcripts (as in the Holy Land Foundation case) that are not marked with a classification stamp.

Such leaks have proliferated, even though *Branzburg* is on the books and the shadow of Judith Miller's imprisonment has supposedly given pause to informants considering whether they can trust a reporter. This hardly suggests that journalists are in desperate need of a shield law to induce leakers to impart information to them. On the contrary, such a law would only unleash a great tidal wave of leaks, to be followed inevitably by an equally destructive backwash of litigation.

In the case of each such contested leak, courts would be asked to weigh whether the disclosed information caused "significant and actual harm" to national security, which in every instance the press would deny, claiming (a) that the information at issue, even if secret or top secret, was improperly classified and (b) that disclosure of this information provided a vital service to the public weal. The main effect of a shield law would thus be to the draw the judicial branch into the very heart of foreign-policy decision making, requiring judges to evaluate matters that they lack either the expertise or the experience to assess. As a result, the confusion that now exists among the various federal circuit courts would not be cleared up; it would be deepened.

A nd even that is not the end of it. Any legislation in this area would ineluctably have to specify exactly who is worthy of being shielded. Anticipating this very problem, Justice White observed in *Branzburg* that, sooner or later, administering a constitutional privilege for reporters would necessitate defining "those categories of newsmen who qualified for the privilege." But such a procedure, he noted, would itself inevitably do violence to "the traditional doctrine that liberty of the press is the right of the lonely pamphleteer who uses carbon paper or a mimeograph just as much as of the large metropolitan publisher who utilizes the latest photocomposition methods."

The Lugar-Specter bill already does precisely this sort of violence. It defines the term "journalist" as a person who, "for financial gain or livelihood," is engaged in the news business "as a salaried employee of or independent contractor" to a news agency. This definition, with its emphasis on monetary compensation, no doubt applies to many journalists. But it excludes many more. And it takes a large first step toward erecting a system of federally recognized or federally licensed journalists.

In the Internet age, the functional equivalent of the lonely pamphleteer is the lonely blogger, working at home in front of his computer screen. Internet blogs have become a major force in the dissemination of news and opinion; one has only to recall the role played by the website PowerLine.com in unmasking the fraudulent documents employed by Dan Rather and CBS in their 2004 election-eve coverage of the military service of George W. Bush. In the Lugar-Specter version of a shield law, bloggers would be ineligible for membership in the new privileged caste.

Nor would they be alone. As Justice White stressed in *Branzburg,* freedom of the press is not a right "confined to newspapers and periodicals" but rather a "fundamental personal right" that attaches to all of us. Any effort to restrict this personal right to a few select professionals will collide with the reality that "[t]he informative function asserted by representatives of the organized press . . . is also performed by lecturers, political pollsters, novelists, academic researchers, and dramatists."

Herein, continued White, lies the difficulty in crafting a shield, for almost any author "may quite accurately assert that he is contributing to the flow of information to the public, that he relies on confidential sources of information, and that these sources will be silenced if he is forced to make disclosures before a grand jury."

The proposed shield legislation attempts to surmount this difficulty by excluding amateurs and many other categories of purveyors of information from its reach—thereby violating the spirit if not the letter of the First Amendment. Even worse, however, is that it would *include* under its protection all sorts of highly dubious *professional* journalists: American reporters in the employ of Al Jazeera, the pan-Arab broadcasting company, for example; American journalists working in, say, the Washington bureau of the Chinese Communist party's *People's Daily;* journalists for extremist domestic publications like the Nation of Islam's *The Call,* or the Liberty Lobby's avowedly racist *Spotlight,* or Lyndon LaRouche's crackpot *Executive Intelligence Review.* So long as they were drawing a salary, they too could receive immunity for any leaked confidential information they collected or published.

So where does that leave us? When all is said and done, do we really want to retain a system that on occasion can imprison journalists merely for going about their daily work? Is there perhaps some alternative, short of enacting a shield law, that would avoid that untoward result?

A better question is this: do we need such an alternative? Despite what newsmen and their lawyers incessantly tell us, our current laws governing confidential informants do not require journalists to go to prison *ever.* On the contrary, this is always a choice they make of their own free will. Like every journalist who has dealt with a confidential informant, Judith Miller made a series of such choices, each of her own volition, before she was led away to her cell. They are worth reviewing.

In the first place, as she went about gathering information about the leak of an (allegedly) undercover CIA officer, Miller was under no obligation to promise her contacts in or out of government that she was prepared to violate U.S. law to protect their identity. In seeking to gain their trust and cooperation, she might have chosen to promise something less—that, for example, she would never disclose their identity unless she herself were subpoenaed. Such a promise might well have sufficed to elicit the information she was pursuing while avoiding any suggestion that she was ready to go to prison to keep her word.

Many confidential informants would readily accept such terms, as Miller's own case eventually proved. For after she was hit with a contempt citation, I. Lewis Libby, the man who turned out to be her principal source, offered to sign letters freeing her of any obligation to observe promises of confidentiality she had made. What this suggests is that an absolute promise, one that holds the potential of dragging a reporter into conflict with the law, is likely to be necessary only under extraordinary circumstances.

The Justice Department has its own highly restrictive internal guidelines that sharply limit the circumstances in which it will subpoena reporters. Historically, indeed, such subpoenas have been rare; the Justice Department has issued only 12 over the past 15 years.[4] Ours is thus not a hostile environment for journalists but a congenial one, assuring them that they need incur the risk of offering an absolute promise of confidentiality only when the information at stake is worth the highest price in terms of the public's right to know. There was certainly no information of such value in the Miller fiasco. Whatever she learned from Libby, she wrote about only in her notebook; neither she nor, evidently, her editors ever thought it sufficiently important to be printed in the pages of the *New York Times.*[5]

Confronted by a subpoena to a grand jury, and having failed to quash that subpoena, Miller still could have chosen to avoid jail merely by following the law of the land, fulfilling her obligation as a citizen to tell the grand jury what she knew about a possible crime. This she declined to do. But despite the plaudits she earned from many for keeping her promises, it is debatable whether this act of civil disobedience on her part was either honorable or wise. For what Miller was defying was the will not only of the special counsel or of the Supreme Court but of the highest power in a democracy, namely, the American people.

At the time Miller was incarcerated, the American people acting through their elected representatives had had decades to contemplate establishing a testimonial privilege for journalists. Up until then, and indeed up until this moment, they have declined to bestow such a privilege on a profession they do not hold in particularly high esteem. Successive Congresses have considered the idea of a shield law only to reject it; and as I have tried to show, they have had good reasons for rejecting it. It was proper that Miller should have been cited for contempt, for she was being contemptuous of a grand-jury process that is the cornerstone of our criminal laws.

Once again, Justice White cut to the essence. "[I]t is obvious," he wrote in *Branzburg,* "that agreements to conceal information relevant to commission of crime have very little to recommend them from the standpoint of public policy." Historically, White pointed out, citizens not only are forbidden to conceal a crime, they have a positive "duty to raise the 'hue and cry' and report felonies to the authorities." Concealment, even of a crime in which one is oneself not a participant, is itself a crime—misprision of a felony—punishable by a statute enacted by the very first Congress and still on the books. Covering up a crime, wrote White, "deserves no encomium, and we decline to afford it First Amendment protection by denigrating the duty of a citizen, whether reporter or informer, to respond to grand-jury subpoena and answer relevant questions put to him."

The claim that Miller, or any other journalist in similar circumstances, had no choice but to go jail is, therefore, specious in the extreme, a rationalization put forward by spokesmen of the establishment media in their own effort to gain and maintain their privileges and powers. These they require not in order to report the news but rather, it would appear, to ratify their self-proclaimed position as the arbiters and shapers of American opinion. In the performance of that role, they fancy, their exalted position should place them beyond the reach of American law.

A free press is a vital component of our democracy, but it is not the only component. The same preamble of the Constitution that speaks of securing "the blessings of liberty to ourselves and our posterity" also speaks of insuring "domestic tranquility" and providing "for the common defense." At a moment when the United States faces the present danger of assault by Islamic terrorists and is struggling to protect itself from falling victim to a second September 11, a murmuration of over-zealous, self-interested, and mistaken advocates is striving to shield the press's freedom of movement at the expense of many if not all of the competing imperatives of a system based upon the rule of law. By acquiescing in this hubristic folly, Congress would do a disservice both to the First Amendment and to the security of the American people.

Notes

1. Shortly thereafter, Libby was indicted, not for any violation of the Intelligence Identities Act but for allegedly lying to the FBI during the course of the investigation.

2. A "classification decision" is the bureaucracy's label for the creation of a classified fact. Of this gigantic number, only 258,633 were brand-new classified facts; the remainder were "derivative," that is, based upon a paraphrase or a restatement of an original decision to classify something. A widely recognized problem is that a significant fraction of what the government classifies or retains as classified is actually misclassified or over-classified. The solution has been an orderly and timely process to *de*classify records: in 2005, some 29,540,603 pages of historical records were declassified. A "record" is defined by law "as a book, paper, map, photograph, sound or video recording, machine-readable material, computerized, digitized, or electronic information, regardless of the medium on which it is stored, or other documentary material, regardless of its physical form or characteristics."

3. For a discussion of this case, and the broader framework of laws governing the publication of national-defense information, see my "Has the *New York Times* Violated the Espionage Act?" in the March 2006 COMMENTARY.

4. A different set of issues is presented by the fact that, in the aftermath of *Branzburg,* the press has been hit with a growing number of subpoenas for source material arising out of *civil* litigation, including in two high-profile cases. In 2004, five reporters were held in contempt by a federal judge for refusing to testify about their sources in a case brought by Wen Ho Lee, the Los Alamos atomic scientist who pleaded guilty to a charge of mishandling secret documents but then sued the government for violating his privacy rights. The case was dropped when the five news agencies involved agreed to contribute $750,000 to a settlement with Lee to avoid having their reporters testify. In a libel case brought against Nicholas Kristof by Stephen J. Hatfill, who had been named by Kristof as a suspect in the post-9/11 anthrax attacks, a federal magistrate judge ruled that the *Times* could not refuse to identify Kristof's confidential sources. That case is still moving through the courts.

5. As we now know, for its own partisan reasons the *Times* was wildly overstating the significance of the leak, which had its origins not (as the paper alleged) in a White House plot to discredit its critics but in the careless talk of a ranking official at the Department of State named Richard Armitage.

GABRIEL SCHOENFELD is the senior editor of *Commentary.* Correspondence on his "Dual Loyalty and the 'Israel Lobby'" (November 2006) appears on page 3.

What Would You Do?

The Journalism That Tweaks Reality, Then Reports What Happens

DANIEL WEISS

On a Friday morning last January, a group of Washington, D.C., commuters played an unwitting role in an experiment. As they emerged from the L'Enfant Plaza metro station, they passed a man playing a violin. Dressed in a long-sleeved T-shirt, baseball cap, and jeans, an open case for donations at his feet, he looked like an ordinary busker. In reality, he was Joshua Bell, an internationally renowned musician. The idea was to gauge whether Bell's virtuosic playing would entice the rushing commuters to stop and listen.

The experiment's mastermind was *Washington Post* staff writer Gene Weingarten, who had dreamed it up after seeing a talented keyboardist be completely ignored as he played outside another metro station. "I bet Yo-Yo Ma himself, if he were in disguise, couldn't get through to these deadheads," Weingarten says he thought at the time. Ma wasn't available to test the hypothesis, but Bell was.

For three-quarters of an hour, Bell played six pieces, including some of the most difficult and celebrated in the classical canon. Of 1,097 passersby, twenty-seven made donations totaling just over $30. Seven stopped for more than a minute. The remaining 1,070 breezed by, barely aware of the supremely talented violinist in their midst.

When Weingarten's account of the experiment ran in the *Post's* magazine three months later, readers followed the narrative with rapt attention that contrasted starkly with the indifference of the commuters. The article was discussed on blogs and other forums devoted to classical music, pop culture, politics, and social science. Weingarten said he received more feedback from readers than he had for any other article he had written in his thirty-five-year career. Many were taken with the chutzpah of disguising Joshua Bell as a mendicant just to see what would happen. Others were shocked that people could ignore a world-class musician. Still others argued that the results were insignificant: rerun the experiment outdoors on a sunny day, they said, and Bell would draw a massive crowd.

I was one of those rapt readers, but I wasn't quite sure what to make of the piece's appeal. Was it just a clever gimmick or was there something more profound going on? At the same time, the story felt familiar. Indeed, Weingarten's experiment was a recent entry in a journalistic genre with deep, quirky roots.

Working on a hunch that begs to be tested or simply struck with an idea for a good story, journalistic "experimenters," for lack of a better term, step out of their customary role as observers and play with reality to see what will happen. At their worst, these experiments are little more than variations on reality-TV operations that traffic in voyeurism and shame. At their best, they manage to deliver discussion-worthy insights into contemporary society and human nature. The very best, perhaps, serve up a bit of both. In any case, the growing number of journalists and news operations who do this sort of thing are heirs to a brand of social psychology practiced from the postwar years through the early seventies. During this period, considered by some the golden age of the discipline, experiments were bold and elaborately designed and frequently produced startling results. Many were conducted outside the laboratory and often placed subjects in stressful or disturbing situations.

These experiments also have roots in forms of investigative, immersion, and stunt journalism that have been practiced for more than a century. In 1887, while working on an exposé of asylum conditions, muckraker Nellie Bly demonstrated that one could feign insanity to gain admission to a madhouse—and when she began to insist that she was in fact perfectly sane, doctors interpreted her claims as delusions. In so doing, Bly anticipated psychologist David Rosenhan's classic 1972 experiment in which "pseudopatients" claiming to hear voices were admitted to psychiatric hospitals and then kept for an average of several weeks despite reverting to sane behavior.

It's difficult to pinpoint when the genre shifted, but by 1974, when New York City's WNBC-TV asked its viewers to call in and pick the perpetrator of a staged purse snatching from a lineup of suspects, the journalistic experiment had attained its modern form. The station was flooded with calls and, after fielding over 2,100, cut the experiment short. The results: respondents picked the correct assailant no more frequently than they would have by guessing.

Over the last decade, as best-sellers such as *The Tipping Point* and *Freakonomics* have lent social science a sheen of counterintuitive hipness and reality television has tapped into a cultural fascination with how people behave in contrived situations, journalistic experimentation has become increasingly common. In addition to *The Washington Post Magazine,* it has been featured in *The New York Times, Harper's,* and *Reader's Digest.* Its most regular home, however, has been on network-television newsmagazines.

ABC's *Primetime* has staged a series of experiments in recent years under the rubric "What Would You Do?" which enact provocative scenarios while hidden cameras capture the reactions of the public. Chris Whipple, the producer who conceived the series, refers to it as a *"Candid Camera* of ethics." Starting with a nanny verbally abusing a child, the series has gone on to present similar scenarios: an eldercare attendant ruthlessly mocking an old man; a group of adolescents bullying a chubby kid; a man viciously berating his girlfriend, seeming on the verge of violence; etc.

The sequences tend to begin with the narrator pointing out that many pass right by the incident. Several witnesses are confronted and asked to explain why they didn't step in. One man, who gave the fighting couple a long look before continuing on his way, reveals that he is an off-duty cop and says he determined that no laws were being broken, so there was nothing for him to do. The focus shifts to those who did intervene, and the camera lingers over the confrontations, playing up the drama.

These experiments are, in a sense, the flip side of the reality-TV coin: rather than show how people act in manufactured situations when they *know* they're being watched, they show us how people act when they don't. And the experiments have clearly appealed to viewers. From the first minutes of its first hour, when its ratings doubled those of the previous week, "What Would You Do?" has been a success. After appearing periodically in 2005 and 2006, ABC ordered five new hours that were scheduled to air last November before the writers' strike put them on hold. It is, Whipple says, highly "watchable" television.

In the world of print, *Reader's Digest* has come closest to making such experiments a franchise. Over the last two years, the magazine has pitted cities around the world against each other in tests of helpfulness and courtesy, to determine which city is most hospitable. The first round used the following three gauges to separate the rude from the solicitous in thirty-five cities: the percentage of people who picked up papers dropped by an experimenter; the percentage who held the door for experimenters when entering buildings; and the percentage of clerks who said "Thank you" after a sale. When the scores were tallied, it was clear that *Reader's Digest* had hit the counterintuition jackpot: the winner was New York City. According to Simon Hemelryk, an editor with the UK edition of *Reader's Digest* who came up with the idea for the tests, the press response was "totally, totally mad." Hundreds of media outlets picked up the story. David Letterman presented a tongue-in-cheek, top-ten list of the "Signs New York City Is Becoming More Polite."

The notion that New Yorkers are more polite than commonly believed was also at the center of a 2004 experiment conducted by *The New York Times.* Reenacting an experiment originally performed by graduate students of social psychologist Stanley Milgram at the City University of New York in the early seventies, two *Times* reporters asked riders on crowded subway cars to relinquish their seats. Remarkably, thirteen of fifteen did

so. But the reporters found that crossing the unspoken social boundaries of the subway came at a cost: once seated, they grew tense, unable to make eye contact with their fellow passengers. Jennifer Medina, one of the reporters, says that she and Anthony Ramirez, her partner on the story, found the assignment ludicrous at first. "It was like, 'What? Really? You want me to do what?'" she says. "We made so much fun of it while we were doing it, but we got so much feedback. It was one of those stories that people really talked about." And papers around the world took notice: within weeks, reporters in London, Glasgow, Dublin, and Melbourne had repeated the experiment.

I n these journalistic experiments, the prank always lurks just beneath the surface and is clearly part of the genre's appeal. During ABC *Primetime's* experiments, there always comes the moment when host John Quiñones enters and, with a soothing voice and congenial smile, ends the ruse. *These people are actors. You have been part of an experiment.* And in that moment, no matter how serious the scenario, there is always the hint of a practical joke revealed, a touch of "Smile, you're on *Candid Camera!"*

Sometimes the experiment is overwhelmed by the prank. Last year, *Radar Magazine* sent a reporter to snort confectioner's sugar in various New York City locales. The idea was to test anecdotal evidence from a *New York Times* article that cocaine use was growing more publicly acceptable. (The results: public snorting was actively discouraged at the New York Public Library's main reading room, but not at a Starbucks or *Vanity Fair* editor Graydon Carter's Waverly Inn.) Carter's own *Spy Magazine* pulled a classic prank/experiment in the late eighties when it sent checks of dwindling value to moguls in an attempt to determine who was the cheapest millionaire. (Donald Trump reportedly cashed one for just thirteen cents.) Even *Borat* was, in a sense, an extended experiment in the extremes to which a Kazakh "journalist" could push pliant Americans, and was anticipated by one of *Primetime's* "What Would You Do?" episodes in which a taxi driver goes off on racist or homophobic rants, baiting riders either to defy him or join in.

If Medina, the *Times* reporter, was made uneasy by the whiff of "stunt" in the subway experiment, she is not the only one. Even Weingarten, whose Joshua Bell experiment was a monumental success, looks at the genre slightly askance. Asked whether he plans to conduct similar experiments in the future, he replies: "If I can think of one this good, there's no reason I'd quail at it. But, you know, you also don't want to go off and be the stunt writer. I would need to feel as though the next thing I'm doing was of equal sociological importance. And this wasn't just a lark. We had something we wanted to examine, and it was the nature of the perception of beauty."

The appeal of the best journalistic experiments, indeed, runs much deeper than their entertainment value. Medina came to see her role in the subway experiment as that of a "street anthropologist or something, which is essentially what [reporters] are supposed to be doing every day." And Weingarten received over one hundred messages from people who said that his piece on the Bell experiment made them cry. (One testimonial from an online chat Weingarten had with readers: "I cried because I find it scary and depressing to think of how obliviously most people go through daily life, even smart and otherwise attentive people. Who knows what beautiful things I've missed by just hurrying along lost in my thoughts?") In essence, many readers imagined themselves as actors in the story. Weingarten set out to chronicle an experiment; he ended up writing a deeply effective profile of his own readers. "What Would You Do?" asks *Primetime*—and that, on some level, is the question that all such journalistic experiments ask. Would you walk by the famous violinist? Would you give up your seat on the subway? Would you protect a woman from an abusive boyfriend?

In that quirky, postwar "golden age" of the discipline that informs today's journalistic experimenters, researchers captured the public imagination with bold, elaborately choreographed experiments that frequently drove subjects to extreme behavior or confronted them with seemingly life-or-death situations.

Stanley Milgram, the designer of the subway-seat experiment, was one of the most creative social psychologists of that era. His infamous obedience experiment, first performed in 1961, in which subjects were instructed to shock a man in a separate room every time he gave an incorrect answer on a memory test, showed that normal people were capable of great cruelty. Sixty-five percent of the subjects went to the maximum—450 volts—despite the test-taker's cries of pain and pleas to be released due to a heart condition. By the end, the test-taker no longer responded at all, having presumably passed out or died. (In reality, the test-taker was an actor and his protests tape-recorded.) Even more unsettling was Stanford professor Philip Zimbardo's 1971 prison experiment, in which college students randomly assigned to play the role of guards in a mock prison terrorized those playing inmates. Slated to run for two weeks, it was terminated after six days, during which several "prisoners" came close to nervous breakdown.

Given the dramatic nature of these experiments, it's little wonder they've provided such inspiration to journalists. Bill Wasik, an editor at *Harper's,* started the flash mobs trend in 2003 as an homage to Milgram, whom he considers as much performance artist as scientist. Flash mobs were spontaneous gatherings in which participants showed up at a given location for a brief period and did something absurd, such as drop to their knees en masse before a giant Tyrannosaurus Rex at Toys "R" Us. In a piece published in *Harper's,* Wasik explained that he saw the mobs as a Milgram-esque test of hipster conformity. Like a hot new indie band, he hypothesized, the mobs would rapidly gain popularity before being discarded as too mainstream and, ultimately, co-opted by marketers, which is more or less what happened.

Wasik argues that the popular resonance of experiments by Milgram and others of the golden age derives from the compelling narratives they created. "It's like a demonstration whose value is more in the extremes that you can push people to and the extremes of the story that you can get out of what people do or don't do," he says. "Milgram could have done an authority experiment in which he got people to do all sorts of strange things that didn't seem to be simulating the death of the participant." Many contemporary social psychologists credit researchers from this fertile era with cleverly demonstrating how frequently human behavior defies expectations. But others, such as Joachim Krueger of Brown University, argue that the experiments were designed in ways that guaranteed unflattering results. "You could call it a 'gotcha psychology,'" he says.

Due in part to the rise of ethical concerns, contemporary social psychologists rarely do experiments that take place outside the laboratory or that involve deception or stressful situations. This has left journalistic experimenters as a sort of lost tribe of devotees of the golden-age social psychologists. Unlike investigative journalism, these experiments have largely flown under the ethical radar. This may be because of the fact that, while some journalistic experiments may be frivolous, they are on balance innocuous. However, as experimenters increasingly tackle sensitive topics, they have begun to draw some heat. In 2006, conservative bloggers accused *Dateline* of trying to manufacture a racist incident by bringing a group of Arab-looking men to a NASCAR race. And, last November, these same bloggers ripped an experiment by *Primetime* in which same-sex couples engaged in public displays of affection in Birmingham, Alabama, for attempting to provoke homophobic reactions. (As of press time, the same-sex segment had not yet aired, but according to the Fox affiliate in Birmingham, which broke the story, Birmingham police received several complaints from people disgusted by the sight of two men kissing in public.)

But what of the oft-cited "rule" that journalists should report the news rather than make it? Michael Kinsley, who conducted a 1985 experiment while at *The New Republic* to determine whether the Washington, D.C., elite actually read the books they act like they have, rejects the premise. "If you've got no other way to get a good story," he says, "and you're not being dishonest in what you write and publish, what's wrong with it?" Kinsley's experiment involved slipping notes deep into fashionable political books at several D.C. bookstores, offering $5 to anyone who called an intern at the magazine. In five months, not a single person claimed the reward.

Journalistic experiments have been criticized far more consistently for their scientific, rather than ethical, shortcomings. Robert Cialdini, an Arizona State University social psychologist, believes strongly in the value of communicating psychological insights via the media, but he has found that journalists don't always value the same material that he does. For a 1997 *Dateline* segment on conformity, he conducted an experiment showing that the number of people who donated to a New York City subway musician multiplied eightfold when others donated before them. A fascinating result, but even more fascinating to Cialdini was that people explained their donations by saying that they liked the song, they had some spare change, or they felt sorry for the musician. These explanations did not end up in the finished program. "To me, that was the most interesting thing, the fact that people are susceptible to these social cues but don't recognize it," says Cialdini. "I think that's my bone to pick with journalists—they're frequently interested in the phenomenon rather than the cause of the phenomenon."

Others are frustrated by the premium journalists place on appealing to a mass audience. Duncan Watts, a Columbia University sociologist, designed an experiment for *Primetime* to test Milgram's small-world theory—commonly known as "six degrees of separation"—that people divided by great social or geographical distance are actually connected by a relatively small number of links. In the experiment, two white Manhattan residents competed to connect with a black boxer from the Bedford-Stuyvesant neighborhood of Brooklyn using the fewest links, then the boxer had to connect with a Broadway dancer. All three connections were made using at most six links. Watts says that after the segment aired in late 2006, he received an e-mail from its producer, Thomas Berman, saying that its ratings had been poor. (An ABC spokeswoman insists that the network was satisfied with the ratings.) "One of the limitations of this model is that it's crowd-driven, it's about entertainment," says Watts. "It's a bit of a Faustian bargain."

Another quibble that some social psychologists have with these journalistic experiments is the use of the word "experiment" to describe them in the first place. To a dyed-in-the-wool researcher, an experiment involves comparing a control group with an experimental one, in which a single condition has been varied so that any changes in the outcome can be clearly attributed. Practically no journalistic "experiment" meets this standard, but many golden-age experiments didn't either, strictly speaking. In addition, practically every journalistic experiment includes a disclaimer that its results are decidedly unscientific.

Wendell Jamieson, city editor at *The New York Times* who assigned the subway-experiment story, chafes at calling the exercise an "experiment," pointing out that it was conducted in connection with another article about the original experiment. "It's just a fun way to take a different approach to a story," Jamieson says, comparing it to when he was at the New York *Daily News* and sent a reporter to Yankee Stadium during a subway series dressed in Mets regalia. "It's tabloid trick two-hundred and fifty-two." Bill Wasik, the *Harper's* editor who started flash mobs, points out that using the word "experiment" is a way for journalists to appropriate the "alpha position" of science, lending their endeavors a sort of added legitimacy. "The piece is wearing a lab coat," Wasik says of his own article, which repeatedly describes flash mobs as an experiment, "but it's not entirely scientific by any means."

Perhaps no media outlet has tried harder to achieve uniformity in conducting its experiments than *Reader's Digest*. Detailed instructions for how to conduct its "studies" are distributed to researchers in more than thirty cities around the world to ensure that their results will be comparable. For the courtesy tests, researchers were told how long dropped papers were to be left on the ground, how far to walk behind people entering buildings to see whether they would hold the door, and what sort of demeanor to adopt when speaking with clerks who were being tested to see whether they would say "Thank you." Nonetheless, despite all the careful planning, New York City's courtesy title may need to be affixed with an asterisk. Robert Levine, a social psychologist at California State University, Fresno, did a series of helpfulness experiments in the early nineties in which New York City placed dead last out of thirty-six United States cities. While this doesn't necessarily contradict the *Reader's Digest* result, in which New York was the only U.S. city tested among a global selection of cities, Levine points out that all the *Reader's Digest* New York tests were carried out at Starbucks, yielding a potentially skewed sample. What if Starbucks employees and customers are simply more courteous than New Yorkers as a whole? "I'm not saying they screwed up," says Levine, "but that was certainly a flag that was raised for me."

So maybe journalists can and should be more careful in how they design experiments, but that debate, in many ways, is beside the point. The best examples of the genre are undeniably good journalism, and the lesser lights, for the most part, amount to innocuous entertainment. Indeed, my hope is that some enterprising reporter is even now hatching a plan to find out whether Joshua Bell really would draw such a big crowd outdoors on a sunny day in D.C.

DANIEL WEISS is a freelance writer based in New York City.

The Lives of Others

What Does It Mean to 'Tell Someone's Story'?

Julia Dahl

On March 22, *America's Most Wanted* told my story. I wasn't the fugitive, or the victim, and it shouldn't have been my story. It should have been Tyeisha's. But as the producer from AMW told me, "Girls die in ditches every day. The reason Tyeisha stands out is because she was profiled in *Seventeen* magazine." I met Tyeisha Martin at a Red Cross shelter in Henry County, Georgia, on a sunny September afternoon in 2005. She was barefoot, wearing a tank top and Capri jeans, waiting in line to get a tetanus shot. I was living in a small town nearby called McDonough, south of Atlanta. I'd moved there a year earlier from New York City with my boyfriend. We were both writers, still thinking we might be able to publish the novels we'd written in grad school. I knew I wanted to write for a living, but I'd left my job at a women's magazine certain I'd never go back. I didn't like what I'd been able to write in that world. Every time I put together an article, it felt like I was building a little lie. Whether it was culled from quotes e-mailed through a publicist, like the cover story I did on the movie star; or built upon crude stereotypes, like the "profile" of the three beauty queens who lived together in Trump Place; or the time I followed the rules of a dating book and neatly concluded that it's better to just be yourself if you want to meet a guy. My instincts as a writer were nowhere in these stories. They weren't little windows on the human condition, they didn't wrestle with questions about the world; they passed the time on the Stair-Master, at the dentist, by the pool.

I justified it plenty. I told myself that Joan Didion had started at *Vogue*. I told myself it meant something that I could make it in the glossies. That I was successful. The problem was that I didn't feel successful. I decamped to Georgia, in part, to get some perspective on all this. But still, I wanted to write. So when *Seventeen* called and asked me to do a story for its Drama section about a young girl in Tennessee who'd been drugged and raped by her cousin, I said yes. Hell, yes. I did stories like this for two years. I went to Birmingham, Alabama, to learn about twelve-year-old Jasmine Archie, who died, according to police reports, after her mother poured bleach down her throat and sat on her chest until she stopped breathing. I went to Wythe County, Virginia, and knocked on the door of the home where fourteen-year-old Nakisha Waddell had stabbed her mother forty-three times and buried her in the backyard. I wrote about

two teenage lesbians who murdered one's grandparents in Fayette County, Georgia. The stories were still formulaic, but instead of chasing publicists and trailing beauty queens, I got to read trial transcripts, track down family members, and hang out in county jails. Each story was an adventure, and, at least initially, the reporting felt like the kind of work I imagined a "journalist" would do.

Tyeisha was an accident. I was in Virginia reporting Nakisha's story when Hurricane Katrina hit, and my editor called to ask if I knew anybody in New Orleans. They wanted to profile a teenage evacuee. I said I might know someone—a girl I knew from the local coffee shop had been headed to Tulane—but I'd have to get back to her.

I promptly forgot about it. There was no easy way to find this girl, since I didn't even know her last name, and I was tired from the reporting trip. Sitting for hours with Nakisha's grandmother had been mentally exhausting. This was the second Drama piece I'd done, and I knew what *Seventeen* wanted was brief and uncomplicated. I wouldn't be able to tell how the old woman's hands shook, or how cigarette smoke was stitched into every fiber in her trailer. Or that hanging in the back hallway where Nakisha stuck a knife in her mother's throat was a plaque that read: "This house shall serve the Lord."

When I got home, I needed to get out of myself, so I went to the Red Cross shelter at the local church where my boyfriend's mom, a nurse, was helping tend to the hundreds of suddenly homeless people from New Orleans. That's when I saw Tyeisha, standing in the middle of a group of boys. Tall, bored, beautiful. I remembered the editor from *Seventeen* and I approached her. She agreed to be profiled. Over the next several days, as she waited for FEMA money in a Days Inn near Atlanta and tried to decide where to go next, Tyeisha told me about her life. She'd dropped out of school in the ninth grade and had a baby at seventeen (she was nineteen when we met). When Katrina hit, she had a GED, a job at a linen factory, and though she and her daughter, Daneisha, were living at her mother's house, Tyeisha dreamed of getting her own place.

On the evening of August 28, 2005, when residents were bracing for the storm, Tyeisha took her daughter to the little girl's father's apartment; he lived on the third floor and she thought two-year-old Daneisha would be safer there. Tyeisha spent the

140

night with her sister, Quiana, and Quiana's boyfriend, Chuck. Before dawn, the water broke down their front door. Tyeisha was terrified as the water rose; she couldn't swim, and thought she was about to die. But Chuck and Quiana helped her, and the three of them climbed out a window and found a wooden door to float on. After several hours of paddling through the filthy water, they found a three-story house that had been abandoned, kicked in a window, and spent the night.

The next morning, the three refugees climbed up to the roof, and at the end of the day were lifted to safety by an Army helicopter. After several sweltering days in the gym at the University of New Orleans, they boarded a bus to Atlanta, where Quiana had friends. Through a series of fortunate coincidences, Tyeisha got in touch with her mother, who had Daneisha and was in Dallas. Her on-again, off-again boyfriend was in Texas, too. Tyeisha decided that's where she should be.

On Friday, September 16, 2005, I dropped Tyeisha off at the Atlanta Greyhound station. She bought a ticket to Dallas and set off for the fifteen-hour ride. Six months later, Tyeisha was dead. She was found in a ditch beside a rural road in Fort Bend County, Texas. She'd been shot in the back of the head.

I learned about Tyeisha's death from Quiana, who called me one night in March 2006 and whispered, "Tyeisha's gone." When she hung up, I went to my computer and found an article in the Texas paper: there was a sketch, and though her features were exaggerated, it was clearly Tyeisha. The article said the body they'd found had tattoos: *Daneisha, RIP Larry.* I remembered those tattoos. I'd asked about them as we sat on a bench outside the church. Larry was Tyeisha's father, who had died, she said, about a year before Katrina hit.

I called the number in the paper and asked to speak to the detective in charge. I explained that I hadn't seen or heard from Tyeisha in months, but I told him what I knew: that she'd survived Katrina, and that she'd apparently gone to Texas to be with her mother, daughter, and boyfriend. He asked me to fax him a copy of the article I wrote for *Seventeen.* He said they didn't have many leads. I gave him Quiana's number, and he promised to call me back. I called *Seventeen,* thinking that if the editors would allow me to write about her death, I could finance a trip to Texas. I could help find her killer. The impulse was a combination of personal outrage (I'd never known anyone who'd been murdered), curiosity, and ambition. I knew the victim and already had the family's trust. I began having visions of writing the *In Cold Blood* of the Katrina diaspora. But there was a new editor on the Drama section, and she didn't sound terribly excited about the idea. She said she'd talk to the editor-in-chief and get back to me.

Days passed. My editor called and said they might want to mention Tyeisha's death in the next issue, but that they didn't want a story about it. "It might be too morbid for the readers," she told me. In my three years covering crimes for *Seventeen,* I had written about four female murderers, about stabbings and suffocation and gunshots to the head. The editors I'd worked with talked a lot about what their readers "wanted." Those readers' attention spans were short, apparently, and their eyeballs had to be hijacked with big, red letters and shocking graphics. When my story about Nakisha ran, "She killed her mom" was

splashed in red letters across the first page; pictured below was a hunting knife "similar" to the one she'd used, and opposite was a grainy yearbook snapshot of Nakisha with stab marks Photoshopped all around her. I called to complain. My editor was polite, but said they knew what was needed to grab the readers' attention in this "media-saturated" environment.

Of course, I was as culpable as the editors at *Seventeen.* I did the reporting that revealed nuance and uncertainty, and then did what I was told and turned in simplistic, straightforward stories with immutable lines between cause and effect. So why didn't Tyeisha's unsolved death make the cut? It occurred to me that the story didn't fit the fiction of the magazine. The rigid code that dictated a certain number of pages be given to fashion, celebrities, and make-up also assured that lines didn't get crossed. Tyeisha's story had been one of triumph over tragedy. To have her escape Katrina and six months later be found by a roadside in rural Texas was just too complicated.

But I didn't push. I dashed off pitches to various other publications I thought might be interested in her story: *Texas Monthly,* the *Christian Science Monitor, The New York Times.* No one bit. So I let go. Quiana and I talked every few days, then every couple of weeks. The case went nowhere.

Six weeks later, I got a call from *America's Most Wanted.* Karen Daborowski, a producer, had read about Tyeisha in the *Houston Chronicle* and said they wanted to do a segment on her death. "Maybe we can find her killer," she said. I had not watched *America's Most Wanted* in years. In fact, had you asked me about the show the day before Karen called, I probably would have said it had been pulled by Fox a long time ago. But what I remembered as a mildly creepy combination of *Unsolved Mysteries* and *A Current Affair* had been airing nonstop every Saturday night since 1988. The show was still hosted by a man named John Walsh, who'd been thrust into the spotlight in 1981 when his son, Adam, was kidnapped and murdered. To date, it has helped catch a thousand fugitives.

So I agreed to the interview. But the interview turned into a request to travel with the producers and a crew to Texas. "We want the story to be about you," said Karen. "About your bond with Tyeisha and how you cared enough to find her killer." Calling my fleeting relationship with Tyeisha a bond was a stretch, but in my mind, Karen was asking how much I was willing to do to help Tyeisha. The story of her death deserved to be told, and if I couldn't convince *Seventeen* or any other publication of that, I figured I could get in front of a camera and help someone else tell it. I didn't think about what it meant, journalistically, to become an advocate for someone I'd written about. Having had no formal training in the craft I practiced, I navigated articles and the people involved by my gut, and I felt I owed Tyeisha this much. It also didn't occur to me that I'd become to Karen what Tyeisha had been to me: a subject. Just as I'd asked Tyeisha to relive Katrina beneath a magnolia tree so I could write an article about her for *Seventeen,* Karen was asking me to be a character in her own television report about Tyeisha.

On October 13, 2006, I met Karen and Sedgwick Tourison, another producer, at the American Airlines terminal at Baltimore's BWI. We landed in Dallas around noon and drove to a Whattaburger restaurant near the airport to meet Dave Barsotti and Tom Overstreet, the local camera and audio guys. We all said hello, then Dave dropped a mini-microphone down my blouse, tucked a battery pack into my pants, and told me to get in the driver's seat of the rented Jeep Cherokee. As I drove, Tom aimed his camera at me and Sedg prompted me to talk about what I was doing.

"I'm driving," I said, lamely.

"To . . ." steered Sedg.

"I'm driving to visit Tyeisha's mom, Cabrini, and her daughter Daneisha," I said.

We exited the freeway and made our way into Cabrini's apartment complex. As the crew unloaded the equipment, I wondered how I would greet Cabrini. The woman's daughter had been murdered not six months before, and here I was waltzing in with cameras and lights and four more strangers to poke at her pain. The point, obviously, was to find Tyeisha's killer. I hoped Cabrini knew that. Karen gave the word, and I walked down the outdoor hallway toward Tom, who had his camera positioned on his shoulder, and knocked on the door. Quiana opened it, looking gorgeous, just liked I remembered her. We hugged and I stepped toward Cabrini, who was wearing a T-shirt with a picture of Tyeisha on it. I wasn't sure if I should hug her or shake her hand, but she came toward me with her arms open, and I was glad. The crew flipped on the lights, wired everyone up, and we started talking on-camera, first about Katrina, then about what Cabrini remembered of Tyeisha's arrival in Texas. Tyeisha didn't want to stay in Dallas a day longer than she had to. "She was like, 'Mama, it's all old people around here,'" said Cabrini. So she took Daneisha and left for Houston, where her boyfriend lived. For the first time in her entire life, Tyeisha got her own apartment. Her own furniture. "She was so excited," said Cabrini. "She said, 'Mama, there's no rules. I can wake up when I want.' I said, 'Lord, I wouldn't want to live where there's no rules.'" In February, Tyeisha stopped calling. On March 9, 2006, six months to the day after I met her, her body was found in a grassy ditch at the bend of a county road.

We woke up early the next morning and met downstairs at the hotel for breakfast. Sedg laid out the day's schedule, which began with an hour of them filming me typing on my laptop in my room. Sedg wanted more shots of Quiana and me, so we picked her up and drove to a nearby park. Quiana was six years older than Tyeisha, and more articulate and outgoing. Life hasn't been easy for her. She is twenty-nine, and has four children. She had an emergency hysterectomy just a few months before Katrina hit. The storm washed away her home and separated her from her mother, sister, and children. She settled in Atlanta with her boyfriend, but they broke up. And then her sister was murdered.

When the cameras were ready, we said our lines. I asked her about the last time she talked to her sister, and she said it had been weeks and that she'd begun to worry. We repeated this sequence several times so they could film us from different angles. Quiana didn't seem to mind. I remembered what she said to me months ago, when she called and told me about the murder: "I don't want to see my sister on *Cold Case Files* in five years. I want somebody caught."

After we dropped off Quiana, Sedg and Karen told me they wanted some *Sex and the City* shots of me, so we stopped at an upscale strip mall to do more filming. Trailed by Tom and his camera, I dutifully walked into a boutique and gazed at racks of clothing I couldn't afford. Karen assured me that they needed shots like this to "set me up" as a former New York City magazine writer. They thought it important to play up the "fish out of water" angle: big-city girl gets caught up in a small-town murder. The whole thing was false, and I reminded Karen that I hadn't been on staff at a women's magazine since 2002. But in the language of reality television, three years of my life are boiled down to a shopping trip in order to facilitate a story arc.

That night we flew to Houston, and the next morning we showed up at the Fort Bend County sheriff's station. Inside, Detective Campbell—who Sedg had warned me was "all business"—opened his case file, and pulled out color photographs of the crime scene. There she was: lying in the grass, her skinny legs sticking out from under a yellow tarp. She had on the same blue jeans and belt she was wearing when I met her. The grass around her body was long and lush, green and damp. I wondered if it rained on her while she laid, eyes wide open, in the clover. She was found just a few feet off the road, and according to Campbell, had been shot there. There were minimal wounds other than the fatal bullet wound, which Campbell said suggested that she had been killed by someone she knew. Campbell told us that when he visited her apartment, "it was organized and homey. Like she was focused on raising a child." He showed us birth certificates and FEMA correspondence. She'd kept her papers in a shoebox. "She was doing all the things she should," he said. "She was setting up her future."

The big Texas sky was crowded with clouds in every shade of gray as we drove past fields of cows and ducks, past an old country homestead with a gated family cemetery in the front yard, past Trav's Roadhouse, to the bend in the road where Tyeisha was murdered. A house sat just a few hundred yards away, but Campbell interviewed the people there, and they didn't hear the gunshot. "The TV was probably on," he said. As Tom and Dave set up the shot, I stepped onto the grass, half expecting to feel some sort of ghostly presence. The sun shone through the clouds, but I tried to imagine the road at night. I tried to see her in her last moments. I tried to feel her fear. But I couldn't. All I could do was what I was doing, standing before the cameras to make sure she was not forgotten.

Months went by. And then a year. Occasionally, I would get a phone call from Karen, saying they were planning to air the show soon, but then she'd drop out of contact for a couple of months. At one point, it had apparently been slated to run as part of a special Hurricane Katrina hour in late 2007, but then she told me it was "so strong," they wanted it to anchor another episode. Tyeisha had been dead more than two years when the segment finally aired on March 22, 2008.

I was back in Georgia that weekend, visiting my boyfriend's family. We got take-out BBQ from a local rib shack and gathered in front of the TV. Before each commercial break, they teased my segment: "Coming up: a magazine writer leaves behind the glitzy New York fashion world in a quest for justice." I covered my face as they pasted my voice over clips of Sarah Jessica

Parker adjusting her skirt on the street and cringed at the reenactments. The "Julia" in the segment had a big apartment with leather couches, and the "Tyeisha" was much more conservative than the tattooed girl with messy, maroon-tinted hair extensions I'd met in Georgia. They flashed images of the real Tyeisha on the screen, but my face was the most prominent. The piece even ended with John Walsh giving me a "personal thanks" for being involved.

To me, the compelling story is still Tyeisha's. How, like thousands of her friends and neighbors in New Orleans, she was torn from her support system, separated from the people who looked out for her. She'd tried to rebuild a life for herself and her child in a new state and instead became the victim of a brutal murder. But no one else seemed particularly interested in that story. According to the Centers for Disease Control, homicide is the second leading cause of death for black women between ages fifteen and twenty-four, but even to *America's Most Wanted,* Tyeisha's tale was only worth telling in relation to me.

I suppose I knew that the press tends to illuminate the exceptions, the extremes. The plight of the family with septuplets instead of the more common burden of unexpected twins; the detained immigrant with the amputated penis instead of the thousands with untreated depression. The impulse is understandable, and certainly an oddball story can draw attention to a worthy issue, but what of the issues inside the more common stories? By their very nature, such issues—like mental illness in immigrant communities, or the high murder rate among young black women—are more intransigent, harder to untangle and fit into a facile narrative. I imagine that maybe Jill Leovy, a reporter at the *Los Angeles Times,* was thinking this way when she created The Homicide Report, a blog on the paper's website that attempts to report on every single homicide in Los Angeles County; last year, there were 324. As the explanatory page puts it, "only the most unusual and statistically marginal homicide cases receive press coverage, while those cases at the very eye of the storm—those which best expose the true statistical dimensions of the problem of deadly violence—remain hidden."

It remains to be seen whether my appearance on *America's Most Wanted* will lead to the capture of Tyeisha's killer. Two months after the show aired, there are no promising leads, but I believe I did the right thing, as a human being and as a journalist, when I realize that had I walked out of that Georgia church ten minutes later, or turned left instead of going straight out the door, Tyeisha Martin—not yet twenty years old, mother, sister, daughter, hurricane survivor—would have died not only too soon, but in silence.

JULIA DAHL is a writer who lives in Brooklyn.

A Porous Wall

As news organizations, in their struggle to survive, blur the line between editorial and advertising, does credibility take a hit?

NATALIE POMPILIO

The latest fissure in the wall between editorial and advertising came in April, when the Los Angeles Times ran a front-page advertisement that could easily have been confused for an actual news article. Placed prominently in the left-hand column below the fold, an ad for the police drama "Southland" carried NBC's peacock logo and was labeled "advertisement," but it was written in story form as if a reporter had accompanied the police officer who is the show's main character on a ride-along.

Many in the Times' newsroom balked, including Editor Russ Stanton. A circulated petition decried the ad as deceptive and said it made "a mockery of our integrity and our journalistic standards."

The newspaper's publisher responded that the ad netted a premium rate and was part of the effort to ensure the survival of his publication, which has cut hundreds of jobs in the last year and whose parent company, Tribune Co., has filed for bankruptcy.

Is this a sign of things to come or simply a misstep as newspapers seek to redefine themselves as economically viable?

"There's so much economic pressure, it seems everything is on the table," says Andy Schotz, chairman of the Society of Professional Journalists' ethics committee and a general assignment reporter for the Herald-Mail in Hagerstown, Maryland. But "we have to be vigilant about maintaining the integrity of the news side. A struggling economy is not a reason to loosen the standards."

There was a time when advertisements on the front page of a newspaper were anathema, when the separation between marketing and editorial was as vigorously defended as the separation between church and state. "We were all so pristine," recalls Geneva Overholser, director of the School of Journalism at the USC Annenberg School for Communication and former editor of the Des Moines Register. The attitude, she says, was "no one from advertising should ever darken the newsroom."

Those days seem to be gone, as remote as newsrooms thick with cigarette smoke and loud with the clatter of typewriter keys. Even Overholser says, "I long ago gave up the idea of front-page ads as sin."

Front-page and section-front advertisements are more common, with even the most respected publications putting prime news real estate up for sale (see "No Longer Taboo," June/July 2007). Sponsored content, online and in print, is growing. Advertisers are crossing lines with their marketing techniques, packaging selling points as news to increase their product's credibility while possibly hurting journalists'.

While many experts agree the beleaguered news industry has to change its ways in order to survive, the question is how to do so while maintaining credibility and standards.

"Now, when newspapers are desperately trying to figure out what their future is, it's time to figure out what the principles are," Overholser says. "The rule is you don't try to deceive or fool readers. That's deeply offensive and breaks the bond with readers. That's not about the wall breaking down. That's about principles. It's about credibility."

Bob Steele, the Poynter Institute's Nelson Poynter Scholar for Journalism Values, says the idea of a solid Berlin Wall-type structure between advertising and editorial is outdated. He's long seen it as more of a picket fence: Each side has clearly delineated roles and principles, but "you can talk over the picket fence. If there's a gate, you can go back and forth," he says.

Skip Foster, former editor and now publisher of the Star in Shelby, North Carolina, says a different game is afoot when marketing and advertising decisions directly affect the number of newsroom bodies left to cover the news. While the L.A. Times ad may have stirred up a controversy, he says, at least it took a chance with something new.

"If we're not goofing up occasionally, we're probably not testing that line as we should," he says. If "we don't start trying some crazy things and [won't] be willing to fail and look stupid, I don't think we're going to make it."

He believes it's time to question those who simply want to maintain the status quo when talk comes to the dividing line between news and ads: "Did we have the line in the right place in the first place?" he asks. "How movable is that line? Is the line in a different place online and a different place in print?"

This is not the first time print organizations have made short-term news decisions that may not be in the long-term interest of the publication, he says. Some papers, his included, used to mock the old TV adage "If it bleeds, it leads." Now he finds his front page playing to the idea. "And not feeling bad about it, either. If it's what people want and we can benefit from it, there aren't many win-wins out there," he says. "Having a long-term view is a lot harder when you don't know what the long term's going to be or if the long term includes your presence as a news organization."

The Star hasn't dabbled in much front-page advertising—"we're probably holding out for too high a price," Foster says—but he's willing to consider it. The "right" advertisements will be clearly labeled with some design oversight so it's not messing up the page, but otherwise it's " 'you know it when you see it' type stuff," he says.

"If somebody comes to us willing to pay the premium rate to do something that doesn't fit into my initial set of standards, I'll listen," he says. "We're not going to do anything that's masquerading as news, but the rest is gray."

The bottom line is not to deceive: One newspaper publisher, who didn't want to be quoted by name, so as not to alienate his marketing department, described how one major local business not only wanted to sponsor a column related to its industry but also have one of its own writers produce it. Why not, the business argued, as another nearby newspaper is already doing the same thing? The publisher declined the column—and the ad revenue.

Kelly McBride, ethics group leader at Poynter, says she constantly gets questions on this issue. "Every major metro market is debuting new products meant to generate more revenue, and there's questions about all of it," she says.

She's written about one TV station that put a fast-food company's cup in prominent places on its anchors' desks during newscasts, and she participated in a panel discussion with bloggers whose independence was marred by the many handouts they received. She recently took a call from someone who knew of a newspaper that has a nightlife column that is editorially driven in print but is an advertisement online.

"It's going to become increasingly murky what is independent journalistic judgment and what is influenced by an advertiser with an ulterior motive."

—Kelly McBride

"I see the business imperative to find new sources of revenue and new ways to make money. What worries me is the cost to credibility," she says. "You can't tell me that people are not confused. I believe the audience is savvy, but I also believe the more things we throw at them, the more confusing it gets. The ultimate result of all of this is in the audience's mind. It's

going to become increasingly murky what is independent journalistic judgment and what is influenced by an advertiser with an ulterior motive."

More than one person interviewed for this article noted the growing number of advertisements packaged as news copy and wondered if publications should accept them. Weekend newspaper inserts have featured an advertisement for the so-called "Amish fireplace," an electric heater. The full-page ad is designed to look like a news story, complete with bold headline, subheads, photos and a byline. The word "ADVERTISE-MENT" appears in small print at the center of the top of the page.

SPJ's Schotz notes that ad designers will "push as far as they can" unless pushed back. In one case, a reader called Schotz's newsroom about an ad, wondering if reporters knew whether its claims were true. "I put him in touch with our advertising department," Schotz says. "We're used to how a newspaper is put together and what is what, but many people aren't necessarily as sophisticated."

At his own newspaper in Hagerstown, Schotz dislikes the placement of so-called "sticky ads"—the removable promo stickers that are now appearing on front pages. When, after a long illness, a local politician died, his name was stripped across the front—but the sticky ad was stuck over the all-important verb in the headline—"DIES".

"You can't have two pieces of information in the same physical spot," Schotz says. "You can't have a news headline and an ad and expect they won't interfere with each other."

Sponsored content is another vexing issue facing journalists in the 21st century. For the last two years, Citizens Bank has sponsored a column in the Philadelphia Inquirer. The bank's trademark green outlines the column and its logo appears prominently on the front page of the business section. The column is written by veteran business reporter Mike Armstrong.

Inquirer Editor William K. Marimow says the sponsorship brings in "a significant amount of revenue" but his only real complaint about the advertising element of it is that it takes away from the newshole.

"It's probably symbolically annoying to some of us, but in my view it has no effect on what Mike Armstrong writes or doesn't write," Marimow says. "When Citizens Bank does something great, we're going to report it, and if they do something awful, we're going to report it."

Could other columns receive sponsorship? "As long as something does not intrude with the news, it's something I'll consider," Marimow says.

Armstrong says that while it may sometimes be awkward—"who else has a column that has an ad wrapped around it in this country?"—the sponsorship has no effect on what he writes. He still addresses banking issues, as do other reporters in the business section. In some ways, he says, the choice of sponsor may have made the project easier on him: Citizens Bank is owned by the Royal Bank of Scotland and doesn't make much news in Philadelphia.

"If they were a bailout bank, it would be a little uncomfortable," Armstrong says, "but I would need to be writing about it."

He doesn't even notice the ad anymore. "It's like wallpaper," he says. But readers notice it, and sometimes they are confused. "I've gotten calls from readers asking for the name of the branch manager in their neighborhoods," he says. "I say, 'I don't work for the bank.'"

In some ways, allowing the bank to put its logo on the business page is simply a placement issue, similar to the way a clothing store might ask that its ad go in the features section or a law firm might want its ad near the legal notices, says Robert Niles, editor of Online Journalism Review and a blogger for Knight Digital Media Center.

"If a sponsor wants to say, 'I want my ad to appear every day on page A2,' and it runs opposite someone else's column, we've given them placement," Niles says. "It's only a baby step to say, 'This column is presented by.' It's not 'produced by.' It's not 'created by.' It's just 'sponsored by.'"

"For the advertiser, control of the day-to-day coverage isn't as important as there being coverage of the thing that is important to them."

—Robert Niles

When Niles worked at the Rocky Mountain News, the online weather page was sponsored by the outdoor gear company REI. There's little doubt that REI wasn't able to control what temperatures were reported. "For the advertiser, control of the day-to-day coverage isn't as important as there being coverage of the thing that is important to them," Niles says. "They're smart enough to know that if they control the everyday coverage, the public will know and ignore it. It's no good to publish something that nobody reads."

Dallas Mavericks owner Mark Cuban said as much last year in a post on blogmaverick.com. In the December missive, Cuban proposed creating a "beat writer cooperative." Funded by major sports leagues, the cooperative would employ at least two writers in each sports market. The owners would benefit with increased, in-depth coverage of their teams. The newspapers would benefit because the writers would answer only to the editors they were writing for.

In an e-mail interview with AJR, Cuban explained that control of content wasn't what mattered.

"Newspaper coverage helps build awareness and commitment to a team. Whether it's positive or negative," he wrote. "The suggestion that there is a theme of control means that you believe that there cannot be any trust or contractual agreement between media and teams. That is just not the case. It would be incredibly easy to do a document of understanding saying, 'you write what you want to write. We won't have any say in the matter. Even if we get mad at you over what you

wrote, we won't interfere. On the flip side, since we are contributing financially to your survival and hoped for success, we expect that you cover the team at minimum, on a daily basis during our season, and at least x times per week in the off season.'"

Such an agreement could improve sports coverage, according to Cuban.

Reporters and columnists in today's climate are so worried about keeping their jobs that they might hold back negative coverage so as not to affect their access to their teams. A cooperative would "provide some level of stability to the business of sports reporting [and] it could actually open the door for better reporting. Regardless of whether that coverage is positive or negative," Cuban wrote.

"Either you trust your reporters to do their job and for editors and publishers to attempt to be impartial in the stories they choose, regardless of pressure from any outside source, or you don't."

—Mark Cuban

"Either you trust your reporters to do their job and for editors and publishers to attempt to be impartial in the stories they choose, regardless of pressure from any outside source," he concluded, "or you don't."

Given all the entanglements, transparency may be the best way for news organizations to stay credible. "Anything that is sponsored by anything needs to be clearly labeled," Overholser says. "To me, transparency is the last strong ethic standing."

Readers have to know an organization's ethics policies—and be reminded of them again and again and again. McBride says that if she were editor of the Inquirer, for example, she might end each Citizens Bank-sponsored column with a tagline like, "Our standards for editorial independence can be found here," with an accompanying link.

"Full disclosure is a bare minimum," McBride says. "You also need to write policy and best-practices issues for your public and let them comment upon it."

What's worrisome, she says, is the fact that not everyone will hold to the same high standards. And that, she adds, "will undermine everything that we do. Their stink will wash off on us."

Fred Brown, a former SPJ president and vice chair of the organization's ethics committee, believes one of the mistakes the L.A. Times made with its front-page ad was not discussing the placement with everyone involved and invested in the product's credibility.

"If you're going to have standards that apply to your particular media outlet, everyone should have a say in what those standards are," Brown says. "That discussion needs to happen in the newsroom. Let the marketers in on the discussion, too. The problem is, reporters don't understand the marketing side, and the marketers don't understand the reporting side. Their goal should be the same, but their methods are different."

Brown recently worked to revise SPJ's ethics handbook. Someone asked about including the L.A. Times case as an example. He didn't think that was such a good idea.

"If you're going to have a good ethics case study, there ought to be two sides to that," he says. "In this case, one side would be, 'We have to survive,' but that's not an ethics question."

NATALIE POMPILIO (nataliepompilio@yahoo.com), a former reporter for the Philadelphia Inquirer and New Orleans' Times-Picayune, is a Philadelphia-based writer.

From *American Journalism Review,* June/July 2009, pp. 32–37. Copyright © 2009 by the Philip Merrill College of Journalism at the University of Maryland, College Park, MD 20742-7111. Reprinted with permission.

UNIT 4

A Word from Our Sponsor

Unit Selections

Key Points to Consider

- What is the difference between media that appeal to older versus younger adults? Males versus females? If an advertiser wanted to sell a product to you, specifically, where should she put her dollars?

- Is it worth it for you to pay more for television, magazines, newspapers, radio, and/or the Internet with fewer or no advertising messages? Why or why not?

- What is your take on how Nielsen Media Research data are collected and how those data are used?

- If ratings and sales figures indicate that the public is attracted to lowbrow content, should media owners give media consumers what they want? Why or why not?

- How do you respond to product placement in entertainment media? Do you notice it? Do you have objections to it? To what degree do you think it affects consumer behavior?

- Which do you predict is more likely: (a) Niche media will replace true mass-mass media or (b) the most popular niche media formats will become the new mass-mass media (survival of the biggest sellers)? Why?

Student Website
www.mhhe.com/cls

Internet References

Advertising Age
   http://adage.com
Citizens Internet Empowerment Coalition (CIEC)
   http://www.ciec.org
Educause
   http://www.educause.edu
Media Literacy Clearing House
   http://www.frankwbaker.com/default1.htm

Advertising is the major source of profit for newspapers, magazines, radio, and television, and advertising tie-ins are a common element in motion picture deals. While media writers have the potential of reflecting their own agendas and social/political viewpoints as they produce media messages, they depend largely upon financial backing from advertisers who have other interests to protect. Advertisers use media as a means of presenting goods and services in a positive light. They are willing to pay generously for the opportunity to reach mass audiences, but unwilling to support media that do not deliver the right kind of audience for their advertisements.

Mass advertising developed along with mass media; in fact, commercial media have been described by some as a system existing primarily for the purpose of delivering audiences to advertisers. The price for selling commercial space is determined by statistical data on how many and what kinds of people are reached by the media in which the ad is to appear. In 2008–2009, a 30-second spot on *Grey's Anatomy* sold for $327,000 (down from $419,000 in 2007–2008), on *Sunday Night Football* $435,000 (up from $358,000). A 30-second spot during the 2009 Super Bowl ran about $3 million, an all-time high even in a tough economy. The Super Bowl is the most watched television program in the United States, with about 100 million U.S. viewers. In a local market, an ad on a daytime program that reaches about 10,000 viewers might cost as little as $50 or $60, and slots between midnight and 5:00 AM in some markets sell for even less. The American Association of Advertising Agencies and Association of National Advertisers statistics report 18 minutes of each hour (30%) during prime time television is devoted to commercials; half-hour programs may include as much as 12 minutes of ads.

As the number of media choices increases and audiences diffuse, advertising agencies have largely adjusted their media-buying focus from quantity to quality of potential consumers who will be exposed to a single ad. According to a recent study by Marian Azzaro, professor of marketing at Roosevelt University in Chicago, advertisers would need to buy 42 percent more time on the three major networks than they did 10 years ago to reach the same number of consumers. The current focus of many agencies is niche advertising, with particular interest in ratings/circulation data split by age, gender, ethnic background, and income factors that determine how a given consumer might respond to a product pitch. The outgrowth of niching is seen in media products from the Food Network and Home & Garden Television, to magazines targeted to narrowly defined interests (e.g., *Golf*), to ads on the Web, in video games, over cell phones, on "airport TV," and in classrooms on Channel One. Google sold $21.1 billion in ads in 2008, compared to $16.4 billion in 2007 and $10.5 billion in 2006.

Sometimes, product pitches creep directly into entertainment media, where they can strike below the level of consumer awareness. Market research finds viewers 25 percent more likely to shop at Sears after viewing *Extreme Makeover: Home Edition,* which features Sears Kenmore appliances and Craftsman tools. Coke is on the judges' desk on *American Idol,* Doritos and Mountain Dew are presented to challenge winners on *Survivor.*

© Janis Christie/Getty Images

BMW donated 32 Mini Coopers to be demolished in the production of *The Italian Job* and reported a 20 percent spike in Mini Cooper sales following the movie's 2003 release. Pepsi-Cola financed the 2005 snowboarding documentary *First Descent,* about five snowboarding icons to "build buzz by association" with Mountain Dew. The Mountain Dew logo appears in subtle places, such as on the boarders' helmets. Products or logos may also be inserted into already filmed movies and television programs—not a new practice—but one attracting new attention, as technological advances make it easier to do so, and as VCRs, DVRs, and TiVo allow consumers to bypass traditional commercial messages.

This section begins with articles about advertising and new media. Aside from addressing its title question, "How Can YouTube Survive?" lends insight into new media business models and marketing strategies in general: "The fact that most people over the age of 30 doubt that online businesses can survive by offering free services is irrelevant, because most people under the age of 30 are demanding them. . . . And while many see this as a selfish, unrealistic attitude, the onus is on businesses to get themselves out of this mess because the digital medium exercises unstoppable power." "The Secrets of Googlenomics" describes AdWords, the "data-fueled, auction-driven recipe for profitability" by which Google sells online advertising. Google generates enormous profits. YouTube does not.

"But Who's Counting" includes discussion of panel-based audience measurement services designed to provide headcount figures for Web views that parallel Nielsen ratings for television.

Advertisers are subject to federal agency rules that regulate their content. For example, until recently, the Federal Drug Administration tightly restricted advertising of prescription drugs. The Federal Trade Commission monitors deceptive advertising. However, from a media literacy standpoint, analyzing the truth and values communicated by advertisements themselves is only part of understanding advertising's impact. It is important to understand the gatekeeping role financial backers have in overall media content. Most advertising account executives admit their unwillingness to be associated with media that create negative publicity. All of them put a premium on reaching certain advertiser-desirable groups; media targeted to the interests of those audiences proliferate, while those attractive to other audiences do not. In light of current trends, some critics contend true "mass-mass" media may no longer be considered commercially viable.

Unit 4 also contains articles about traditional media in a new media landscape. "Online Salvation?" describes the challenges facing newspapers, which once competed with TV, but now also have to compete with the Internet for readership and advertiser support. "Old Media Strikes Back" analyzes the evolution of Hulu as an example where "the old-media guys fought back." Hulu draws fewer viewers than YouTube but generates a profit. From an old-media perspective, it is proof that traditional business models will thrive online because in the end they provide salable content. "A Fading Taboo" is about selling front page space for advertising. "Nonprofit News" looks at the future of news media supported by philanthropic foundations and trusts. "Open for Business" takes a position that consumers will pay for niche-specific specialized information and the future of news media lies in "deciding what you can sell to those willing to pay . . . to underwrite the cost of producing original work that might remain free and be of interest to more than a select few." "The Massless Media" concludes that mass and niche media can and will coexist: "Although much changes in the media over time, there are some eternal truths. Most outlets crave two things, money and impact, and the easiest path to both is the old-fashioned one: grow your audience. Ambitious niches will always seek to become larger, and in so doing attract a more diverse audience."

How Can YouTube Survive?

It's wildly popular—and thought to be losing hundreds of millions of dollars a year. Now questions are being asked about the future of YouTube. Rhodri Marsden investigates a mystery of digital-age "freeconomics."

It must surely rank as the most mundane business launch in history. Jawed Karim, one of the founders of YouTube, shuffles timidly in front of a video camera while standing in front of a group of elephants at San Diego zoo, with precious little idea of what he was starting. "The cool thing about these guys," he says, nervously gesturing behind him, "is that they have really long trunks. And that's pretty much all there is to say."

This 19-second video clip, uploaded to the brand-new website later that day, 23 April 2005, may have been insubstantial, but it certainly wasn't inconsequential. Within 18 months, Karim and his partners Steve Chen and Chad Hurley had sold YouTube to Google for $1.76bn, and in doing so became one of a select band of online entrepreneurs who managed to grab our attention—and keep it.

Innumerable jaded web entrepreneurs will tell you how easy it is to get thousands of people to glance at a site, but how tortuous it is to get people to stick around or even come back again the following day. Not only do you have to fulfil a desire that people didn't even realise that they had, but it has to be done with such style and panache that your service becomes indispensable. While the internet may have dismantled many of the traditional barriers to reaching us, the general public, if your idea is anything less than sensational, we will flatly ignore it.

But YouTube was sensational. Prior to its launch, creating a videoclip for someone else to watch online was an arcane and deeply frustrating procedure of digitisation, encoding and embedding that was way more trouble than it was worth—not least because incompatible technologies meant that many people wouldn't be able to watch it. But from humble beginnings in a room above a pizzeria in San Mateo, California, Hurley, Chen and Karim made the process simple, they made it relatively quick, and above all else, they made it free.

By mid-2006, the site was fizzing with activity as we started using our YouTube channel as a jukebox, a blogging service, a promotional tool for our bands, a home video vault, a repository of famous film and television moments—sometimes with the blessing of the copyright owners, more often without it—and just occasionally, it provided an unexpected route to stardom. YouTube entered the lexicon and became synonymous with online video; the former Secretary of State for Local Government, Hazel Blears, dropped the phrase "YouTube if you want to" into an attack on Gordon Brown's style of Government.

Blears making a feeble joke about YouTube is just one small measure of its phenomenal success. But while its staggering popularity is without question—some 345 million visitors worldwide descend upon the website every month—it is haemorrhaging cash. The question of exactly how unprofitable it is continues to be the source of fierce debate online; back in April, analysts at Credit Suisse estimated that its operating losses for this year would reach $470m, while San Francisco-based IT consultants RampRate were more optimistic, but still put the figure at just over $174m. Google isn't rushing to put an end to speculation over the scale of the debt. One thing is abundantly clear from both studies: Google isn't making money by letting everyone and their aunt share videos with each other for free. And the news last week that founder Steve Chen was leaving YouTube to work on other projects at Google kicked off another flurry of rumours as to its possible fate.

Music, television, sport, gaming: the flow of free entertainment to our computer screens seems almost the result of a magical process, and there's been little need for us to consider the costs that might have been incurred by those making it all happen. It's broadly accepted that YouTube will receive around $240m of revenue from advertising this year, but that sum doesn't even cover their general overheads and the cost of acquiring premium video content (such as TV shows) from copyright holders. In addition, there are the huge fixed costs from the supply side—data centres, hardware, software and bandwidth—that have to cope with the 20 hours of video clips that we upload to YouTube every minute of every day. Again, no-one knows the true total of these costs—the Credit Suisse and RampRate reports put it between $83m and $380m this year—but Google's Chief Financial Officer, Patrick Pichette, would only reveal one thing: "We know our cost position, but nobody else does." Or, in other words, we're not telling you.

This typifies the slightly secretive but ultimately sanguine position of Google even as phrases like "financial folly" are bandied about to describe the YouTube business model. With Google's overall profits reaching some $1.42bn for the first quarter of this year alone, the king of online search is certainly in a position to support a loss-making venture that also happens to be the third-most-popular website on the internet. (Google, naturally, is the first.) But Keith McMahon, senior analyst for the Telco 2.0 Initiative, a research group that studies business models in the digital economy, believes that YouTube is not the albatross around Google's neck that it's widely imagined to be. He sees the search company as deriving massive indirect benefits from operating YouTube and believes that estimates of its losses obscure the true picture.

"There are many urban myths surrounding the way that companies extract value from the internet," he says. "Google's spin-off benefits from owning YouTube include the accumulation of our data and strengthening of their network design—and the more time people spend watching online video, the more advertisers will pour into marketing on the internet as a whole. There's no doubt that Google can afford YouTube."

McMahon also believes that by keeping quiet about YouTube's hidden benefits and by allowing the misconception of it as a deeply unprofitable business to circulate, things work very nicely in Google's favour when it comes to negotiating with copyright holders in the world of TV, movies and music. Copyright holders can't demand money that isn't there, and it would certainly take no more than a hint of profitability at YouTube for lawyers to descend, threatening court cases and demanding higher royalties. In the new, topsy-turvy world of online economics, it seems astonishing that losses on paper have actually made YouTube a more powerful online force.

But while Google's pockets may be deep enough to operate a phenomenally popular online service at no cost to its users, what about the countless other internet startups whose operations scarcely extend across a dingy office, let alone several continents? With the free model slowly establishing itself, how can businesses sustain their activities? Sadly, the most common answer is: they can't. The traditional way to generate revenue and offset losses has been to sell some form of advertising space on the website. But an increasing number of industry commentators believe that the internet advertising model is broken—and what better proof than YouTube itself, whose advertising revenues don't even cover their overheads, and who might be dead in the water if it wasn't for their multinational sugar daddy?

In a piece this year for the insider's technology blog, TechCrunch, entitled "Why Advertising Is Failing On The Internet," Eric Clemons, Professor of Operations and Information Management at the University of Pennsylvania, argued that the way that we're using the internet has shattered the whole concept of advertising. We need no encouragement to share our opinions online regarding products and services and offer them star ratings; as a result, we're much more likely to look for personal recommendations from other customers than wait for a gaudy advert to beckon us wildly in the direction of a company website or online store. He claims we don't trust online advertising, we don't need online advertising, but above all we don't want online advertising.

There's certainly a huge weight of evidence to support the latter theory; extensions for web browsers that block advertisements from displaying on the screen have proved to be incredibly popular, and we seem increasingly resentful of attempts by companies to compromise our free online experience by pushing marketing messages in our direction. Spotify, the online jukebox launched this year, has won countless plaudits for its innovative, free and legal approach to online music, but you don't need to look far online before finding users who bitterly complain about the brief audio adverts that play every 20 minutes, interrupting the flow of the new Kasabian album. One comment on a story about the possible expansion of YouTube's advertising is typical: "If advertising is made one iota more intrusive, I shall use other video sites instead."

Small wonder that YouTube only dare feature advertising in less than 5 percent of the videos on the website, along with a few subtle ads in the sidebar of their search results. But while Google continues to finesse its YouTube model, with click-to-buy links and sponsored competitions, it's contended by Professor Clemons that no matter how innovative the advertising industry might become, "commercial messages, pushed through whatever medium, in order to reach a potential customer who is in the middle of doing something else, will fail."

If this is true, it obviously has implications for Google, even though they're sitting very pretty at the moment as the overwhelmingly dominant force in online advertising. But other companies dependent on ad revenue aren't so fortunate. Joost, another ad-funded online video service, announced last week that it would be reinventing itself as a provider of white-label—generic—video for other businesses, and would be cutting jobs in the process.

"In these tough economic times," said its chairman Mike Volpi, "it's been increasingly challenging to operate as an independent, ad-supported online video platform."

But even taking the effects of the recession into account, Keith McMahon is unsurprised. "All those startups have burned through their initial venture capital money, and they've seen that the business model that they were originally planning for—this landgrab for advertising—just isn't there any more." As a leader in The Economist entitled "The end of the free lunch" put it earlier this year, "Reality is asserting itself once more . . . Silicon Valley seems to be entering another 'nuclear winter'."

We are uninterested, verging on contemptuous, of the marketing strategies that were supposed to pay for us to enjoy online services for free. We've become totally unwilling to pay for them directly, either; we simply figure that someone, somehow, will pick up the tab. Rupert Murdoch recently announced plans to "fix" the current newspaper business model by charging for access to News Corporation's newspaper websites, stating that "the current days of the internet will soon be over," but Chris Anderson, the editor of Wired magazine, spends 288 pages in his new book "Free: The Future of a Radical Price" explaining why this is ultimately impossible. He contends that information wants to be free, and that there's an unstoppable downward pressure on the price of anything "made of ideas," adding that the most worrying long-term problem for internet businesses is that the Google Generation are now growing up simply assuming that everything digital is free. They've internalised the economics of the free model "in the same way that we internalise Newtonian mechanics when we learn to catch a ball."

In other words, the fact that most people over the age of 30 doubt that online businesses can survive by offering free services is irrelevant, because most people under the age of 30 are demanding them. On messageboards and forums across the internet you can see them calling for record companies, film studios, newspapers and television channels to come up with a solution that will extend their entertainment utopia, and quick; if they don't, well, they'll find a way around it. And while many see this as a selfish, unrealistic attitude, the onus is on businesses to get themselves out of this mess because the digital medium exercises unstoppable power. However much Rupert Murdoch and others may wish to control it, it's Anderson's contention that the beast is way, way too slippery.

Anderson, along with other digital visionaries, tends to display a sunny optimism that new business models will inevitably step into the breach, while leaving speculation about what those models might actually be to others. But while Anderson says it's "head spinning—and exhilarating—to watch an industry reinvent itself in the face of a new medium," those working in the online economy aren't quite so thrilled. The news regarding YouTube's losses have caused such consternation because people simply can't believe that the third-most-popular website on the web is unable to stand alone and turn a profit. And suddenly, the magical web, whose supposed capacity to revolutionise business has attracted and continues to attract waves of ambitious entrepreneurs, may slowly be revealing itself as an arena in which only a few large companies can survive.

This was illustrated by a tale recounted by the publisher of the Dallas Morning News, James Moroney, who recently told the US Congress about Amazon's proposal for licensing his newspaper's content to be read on Amazon's e-reading device, the Kindle: he was informed that 70 percent of revenue would go to Amazon, with only 30 percent to the Morning News for providing the content. It seems both unhealthy and deeply disappointing that Amazon, Microsoft, Google and the like are beginning to wield so much power; it's even something over which even Google CEO Eric Schmidt has expressed concern.

But Keith McMahon says that we shouldn't be surprised. "Remember in the 1980s when the home computer boom started? The country was full of young kids coding games and selling them on cassette," he says. "But from that rose a gaming industry that's controlled by a small number of very wealthy organisations. Cottage industries that can't survive on their own will either fail, or get swallowed up."

McMahon's message to online businesses is essentially one that's remained the same ever since humans first started making transactions: business is business. For all the cries of foul by entrepreneurs or copyright holders in the face of "unfair" behaviour by multinational corporations or websites such as The Pirate Bay, if you can't find the money to make your business work, that's the end of your business. Because ultimately, the market can't be fought.

YouTube's lack of profitability other than as part of a colossal global multinational may signal the end of a dream that has somehow managed to extend past the bursting of the dotcom bubble back in 2001, and the options for new online ventures seem to be as follows: either produce something that people are willing to pay for, or come up with an idea for a free service that's so ingenious that a benevolent multinational is willing to take it off your hands. But remember: that trick of making a home video of yourself in front of a few elephants has already been done.

Online Salvation?

The embattled newspaper business is betting heavily on Web advertising revenue to secure its survival. But that wager is hardly a sure thing.

PAUL FARHI

Even the most committed newspaper industry pessimist might begin to see a little sunshine after talking to Randy Bennett. Yes, the print business is "stagnant," acknowledges the Newspaper Association of America's new-media guru. And yes, he says, newsrooms are under pressure. But—and here comes the sun—newspapers have staked out a solid position on the Internet, he says. Internet revenue is growing smartly: In 2003, Bennett points out, newspapers collected a mere $1.2 billion from their online operations; last year the figure was nearly $2.7 billion. "We're growing at a double-digit rate," he says.

This is the kind of news that soothes beleaguered publishers and journalists. As print circulation and advertising swoon, the newspaper industry, and news providers generally, have looked for a lifeboat online. Newspapers were the first of the mainstream media to extend their traditional news franchises into the world of pixels, giving them an important "first mover" advantage. websites run by local newspapers typically remain the most popular sources of news and the largest sources of online advertising in their local communities.

Predictions about where the Internet is headed are, of course, hazardous. A dozen or so years after it began to become a fixture in American life, the Internet is still in a formative stage, subject to periodic earthquakes and lightning strikes. Google didn't exist a decade ago. Five years ago, no one had heard of MySpace. Facebook is just four years old, and YouTube is not quite three. Washington Post Executive Editor Leonard Downie Jr. compares the current state of the Internet to television in the age of "Howdy Doody."

Even so, a few dark clouds are starting to form in the sunny vista. Consider a few distant rumbles of thunder:

- After years of robust increases, the online newspaper audience seems to have all but stopped growing. The number of unique visitors to newspaper websites was almost flat—up just 2.3 percent—between August 2006 and August 2007, according to Nielsen/NetRatings. The total number of pages viewed by this audience has plateaued, growing just 1.8 percent last year.
- Newspaper websites are attracting lots of visitors, but aren't keeping them around for long. The typical visitor

to nytimes.com, which attracts more than 10 percent of the entire newspaper industry's traffic online, spent an average of just 34 minutes and 53 seconds browsing its richly detailed offerings in October. That's 34 minutes and 53 seconds per month, or about 68 seconds per day online. Slim as that is, it's actually about three times longer than the average of the next nine largest newspaper sites. And it's less than half as long as visitors spent on the Web's leading sites, such as those run by Google, Yahoo! and Microsoft.

Many news visitors—call them the "hard-core"—linger longer online, but they're a minority. Greg Harmon, director of Belden Interactive, a San Francisco-based newspaper research firm, estimates that as many as 60 percent of online newspaper visitors are "fly-bys," people who use the site briefly and irregularly. "Everyone has the same problem," says Jim Brady, editor of washingtonpost.com. The news industry's continuing challenge, Brady says, is to turn "visitors into residents."

- As competition for visitors grows, news sites are rapidly segmenting into winners and losers. In a yearlong study of 160 news-based websites (everything from usatoday.com to technorati.com), Thomas E. Patterson of Harvard University found a kind of two-tier news system developing: Traffic is still increasing at sites of well-known national brands (the New York Times, CNN, the Washington Post, etc.), but it is falling, sometimes sharply, at mid-size and smaller newspaper sites.

"The internet is redistributing the news audience in ways that [are] threatening some traditional news organizations," concluded Patterson in his study, produced for the Joan Shorenstein Center on the Press, Politics and Public Policy. "Local newspapers have been the outlets that are most at risk, and they are likely to remain so."

Patterson suggests that some of the declines at newspaper sites may be due to increased competition from local broadcast stations, particularly TV. Although they got a late start on the Internet, local TV stations are beginning to catch up, thanks to copious video news clips and strong promotional capabilities.

"A lot of papers are close to maxing out their local audiences," Patterson said in an interview. "It's hard to know where more readers will come from. . . . They have to figure out how to deal with a pretty difficult future."

In other words, for many, that first-mover advantage has vanished.

Most ominous of all is that online ad growth is beginning to slow. Remember those confidence-building double-digit increases in online advertising revenue? They're fading, fast. In the first quarter of this year, the newspaper industry saw a 22 percent gain in online revenue. Not exactly shabby, but still the smallest uptick (in percentage terms) since the NAA started keeping records in 2003. In the second quarter, the industry rate slipped again, to 19 percent. The third quarter promises even less, considering what various companies have been reporting lately. E.W. Scripps Co. saw a 19 percent increase. The Washington Post Co. said its online revenue was up 11 percent in the period, the same as Gannett's. Tribune Co. saw a gain of 9 percent. McClatchy was almost in negative territory, with a weak 1.4 percent increase for the quarter and the year to date.

All of which begins to hint at one of the deeper economic challenges facing online news providers. Even as advertisers move from traditional media to new media, a big question lingers: Can online ad revenue grow fast enough to replace the dollars that are now being lost by the "old" media? And what happens if they don't?

At the moment, the Internet has a long way to go. Newspapers collected $46.6 billion from print advertisers last year; they took in another $11 billion in circulation revenue in 2004, the last time the NAA compiled the total. Even with the double-digit increases online, that's more than 20 times what they're generating from the Internet. Among the industry's most cutting-edge publishers, the Internet still accounts for only a fraction of the overall pie. The leading online newspaper company, the New York Times Co., derives only about 11 percent of its revenue from the Web. This fall, MediaNews Group, which publishes 57 daily newspapers, including the Denver Post and the San Jose Mercury News, touted plans to increase its share of Internet revenue to 20 percent—by 2012.

Philip Meyer, author of "The Vanishing Newspaper" and a former journalist and University of North Carolina journalism professor, believes that it's "in the interest of both newspapers and advertisers to shift content to the Internet." Advertisers get narrower target audiences for their products, he notes, and greater accountability, since they can monitor consumers' behavior. "Newspapers can at last grow their businesses without being held back by the variable costs of newsprint, ink and transportation," he said in an e-mail interview. "In the recent past, newspaper owners have preferred to cut fixed costs, like editorial staff, which gives a quick boost to the bottom line but weakens their hold on the audience. Using technology to cut the variable costs is a better strategy even though the payoff takes longer."

Shedding the big overhead costs of the old media is certainly an attraction of the new one. The problem is, an Internet visitor isn't yet as valuable as a print or broadcast consumer. The cost of reaching a thousand online readers—a metric known in advertising as CPM, or cost per thousand—remains a fraction of the print CPM. The price differential can be as much as 10-to-1, even though many newspaper websites now have online audiences that rival or exceed the number of print readers.

Some of this disparity is a result of the witheringly competitive nature of the Web. Unlike the print business, in which newspaper publishers generally enjoy near-monopoly status, the online news world is littered with entrants—from giants like MSNBC.com and AOL.com, to news aggregators like drudgereport.com, to blogs by the millions. This makes it tough for any online ad seller to do what newspaper publishers have done for years—keep raising their ad rates. "Ultimately, it comes down to supply and demand," observes Leon Levitt, vice president of digital media for Cox Newspapers. "And there's an awful lot of supply out there."

Harvard's Patterson offers a more intriguing, and perhaps more unsettling, theory about why it's hard to squeeze more money out of online advertisers: Web ads may not be as effective as the traditional kind. "I'm not sure [advertisers] are convinced yet about how terrific a sales tool [a Web display ad] is," he says. "The evidence isn't strong yet that it can drive people into a store the way a full-page newspaper ad can. They're less confident about what they're getting online." Moreover, unlike their here-and-gone counterparts on the Internet, print subscribers still stay around long enough to see an ad. Some 80 percent of print readers say they spent 16 or more minutes per day with their newspaper, according to Scarborough Research.

These dynamics could change, perhaps as stronger news sources emerge on the Web and weaker ones disappear. But even if the newspaper industry continued to lose about 8 percent of its print ad revenue a year and online revenue continued to grow at 20 percent a year—the pace of the first half of 2007—it would take more than a decade for online revenue to catch up to print.

Journalists, or indeed anyone with an interest in journalism, had better pray that doesn't happen. Because online revenue is still relatively small and will remain so even at its current pace, this scenario implies years of financial decline for the newspaper industry. Even a 5 percent decline in print revenue year after year might look something like Armageddon. Newspapers were already cutting their staffs before this year's advertising downturns. A sustained frost of similar intensity would likely lead to even more devastating slashing. The cuts could take on their own vicious momentum, with each one prompting a few more readers to drop their subscriptions, which would prompt still more cuts. Some daily papers would undoubtedly fold.

Some remain confident that these dire scenarios won't come to pass. "I don't foresee [print dying] in my lifetime," says Denise F. Warren, chief advertising officer for the New York Times Co. and its websites. "I'm still bullish on print. It's still an effective way to engage with the audience." On the other hand, she adds, "The business model will keep evolving."

Yes, says Phil Meyer, but it may evolve in ways that render many daily newspapers unrecognizable to today's subscribers: "You want a prediction?" he says. "There will be enough ads for ink on paper to survive, but mainly in niche products for specialized situations."

Adding It up

Here is how much print and online ad revenue newspapers have attracted in recent years:

Year	Print Total $Mill	Print Total %change	Online Total $Mill	Online Total %change	Print and Online Total $Mill	Print and Online Total %change
2000	$48,670	5.10%				
2001	$44,305	−9.00%				
2002	$44,102	−0.50%				
2003	$44,939	1.90%	$1,216		$46,156	
2004	$46,703	3.90%	$1,541	26.70%	$48,244	4.50%
2005	$47,408	1.51%	$2,027	31.48%	$49,435	2.47%
2006	$46,611	−1.68%	$2,664	31.46%	$49,275	−0.32%
2007						
Quarter						
First	$9,840.16	−6.40%	$750.04	22.30%	$10,590.20	−4.80%
Second	$10,515.23	−10.20%	$795.68	19.30%	$11,310.90	−8.60%

Source: Newspaper Association of America.

Question: Do you see a smart online business model for traditional media that will permit newspapers and other publications to continue to do deep reporting and attract talented journalists?

Craig Newmark: Not yet. While there are people working on it . . . no one's figured it out yet.

—From an online Q&A with Craigslist founder Newmark, posted on nytimes.com on October 10.

To restore the industry's momentum online, executives like Denise Warren suggest the key may simply be more. More new editorial features that will attract new visitors and keep the old ones engaged on the site for longer.

The Times, for instance, expanded three "vertical" news and feature sections last year (real estate, entertainment and travel) and this year is fleshing out similar sections on business, health and technology. In early December, the paper will launch a Web version of its fashion and luxury goods magazine, called T. The paper has also stopped charging for its op-ed columns, after having determined that it could attract more readers—and hence more advertising dollars—by removing the "pay wall" that blocked unlimited access. (The Wall Street Journal is also considering doing away with online subscriptions and moving to a free, ad-supported model, the Journal's new owner, Rupert Murdoch, said in mid-November.)

Washingtonpost.com has added more blogs, more video and special features, like a religion and ethics discussion called On Faith. In June, it started a hyper-local site-within-the-site called LoudounExtra.com that focuses on exurban Loudoun County in Virginia. Coming next summer: a complete redesign of the site. With so much movement, Brady isn't concerned about traffic slowing down. "I'm not worried that people's interest in the Internet has peaked," he says. "There's a whole generation coming up that uses the Internet a lot more."

Cox Newspapers is focusing on its papers' local markets with freestanding niche offerings that target specific demographic groups underserved by the main newspaper, such as young mothers and pet owners and local sports fans, says Leon Levitt. The idea is to assemble a larger, geographically concentrated online readership bit by bit, with as many as seven to nine specialized publications, he says.

Harvard's Patterson has a simpler idea: Just play the news better online. His study of news sites found "substantial variation" in how local sites display news, with some pushing blogs, ads and "activity lists" over breaking news. "If local news is downplayed, local papers are conceding a comparative advantage in their competition with other community sites for residents' loyalties," the study concluded. "If national and international news is downplayed, local papers may increase the likelihood that local residents will gravitate to national brand-name outlets."

The news may be the primary product, but the way the news is served online needs to be updated, too, says Mark Potts, a Web-news entrepreneur and consultant. He says newspaper-run sites are falling behind the rest of the industry in their use of technology. "For the most part, once you get past the bigger papers, newspapers are not up to date" online, he says. "They've got some video, a podcast, some blogs, yes, but mostly . . . they're just pasting the newspaper up on the screen. That was barely OK five years ago." Potts ticks off the tools that news sites usually lack: social networking applications, database-search functions, mapping, simplified mobile-device delivery technology, services that let readers interact with one another, etc. His one-word description for the state of newspapers online: "Stodgy."

On the ad side, traditional news organizations are starting to join, rather than trying to fight, some of the Internet's giants. In recent months, major newspaper companies have struck alliances with Yahoo! and Google in an attempt to pair newspapers' strength in selling local advertising with the search engines' superior technology and national reach. (See The Online Frontier, page 42.)

In the first phase of a multipart alliance, some 19 newspaper companies that own 264 daily papers have linked their online help-wanted advertising to Yahoo!'s HotJobs recruitment site. When an advertiser seeking to hire, say, a nurse, in St. Louis buys an ad through the St. Louis Post-Dispatch, the newspaper places the ad on its site, which is co-branded with HotJobs and automatically linked to HotJobs' national listings. As a result, the advertiser gets his message in front of both local job candidates and others across the country. HotJobs, in turn, gets a local sales agent—the Post-Dispatch—to sell more listings. Although the partners have revealed few financial details about the arrangement, revenue from such ads is split between the newspaper and Yahoo!, with the newspapers taking a majority of each dollar generated.

In a second phase of the alliance that is now being tested, publishers such as McClatchy, Lee Enterprises, Media General, Cox and others will attempt to do something similar with display ads. Using Yahoo!'s search capabilities and technology, the companies hope to marry national and local display ads to their visitors' interests. People interested in, say, pickup trucks (as identified by tracking software and registration questionnaires), would likely see national ads for Ford, and perhaps for local Ford dealers, when they logged on to a newspaper's site. Such highly targeted advertising would command much higher CPMs than plain old banner ads, says Cox's Levitt.

While it's still too early to declare victory, the general scheme of the partnership has drawn praise from Wall Street. Deutsche Bank analyst Paul Ginocchio has estimated that some members of the consortium could see online ad growth rates of 40 percent for the next two years, thanks in large part to revenue generated by the Yahoo! tie-in.

However, other publishers have declined to join the Yahoo! consortium, in part out of concern that newspapers may be giving away too much to Yahoo! and leaving readers little reason to visit the newspapers' own sites. For example, Gannett and Tribune Co. are developing a display advertising network of their own.

Another group of publishers, including Hearst, E.W. Scripps and the New York Times Co., have turned to Google. Under an experimental program that was expanded this summer, Google is running auctions that enable thousands of smaller advertisers to bid on ad space—size, section and date of their choosing—on some 225 newspaper websites. The newspapers are free to accept the offer, reject it or make a counteroffer (Google says more than half the bids have been accepted). The process is streamlined by Google's technology, which automates billing and payments.

A little less cooperation might help, too. Some argue that news providers made a huge strategic mistake when they decided to make their content available to others online. "Free riders" like Yahoo.com, MSN.com, Google and AOL.com have built massive franchises—far larger than any traditional mainstream news site—in part by posting news stories created and paid for by others. These days, of course, anyone can assemble a series of links and headlines to become a "news" site. The Shorenstein Center put it bluntly in its recent study of news on the Internet: "The largest threat posed by the Internet to traditional news organizations . . . is the ease with which imaginative or well positioned players from outside the news system can use news to attract an audience."

"It's a terribly unfair deal," says Randy Siegel, the publisher of Parade, the weekly newspaper magazine. "Newspapers need to negotiate a more equitable share with search engines that are making billions of dollars by selling ads around newspaper content without the costs of creating that content. . . . The book industry and the movie industry don't give their content away."

Arkansas Publisher Walter Hussman Jr. knows he sounds like a man from another century when he says it, but he thinks newspapers shouldn't be free, online or off. He rues the day that the Associated Press, which is owned by the newspaper industry, agreed to sell stories to the Yahoo!s and AOLs of the world. Free or bargain-priced news, Hussman says, cheapens everyone's news. Free, he says, "is a bad business model."

Hussman has an idea that's so old and abandoned it seems almost new: Make people pay for the news they want, even in the Internet age. Hussman obviously is swimming upstream with this notion. Not long after the New York Times stopped charging for its op-ed columns under the now-jettisoned Times-Select initiative, the Sacramento Bee dropped subscription fees for Capitol Alert, the paper's website for political news.

The newspaper Hussman publishes, the Arkansas Democrat-Gazette in Little Rock, is one of the few that charge a fee ($4.95 a month) for full access to its site. The site has a modest base of 3,000 subscribers, but Hussman says walling it off protects a more lucrative franchise: the newspaper. He believes it's no coincidence that the Democrat-Gazette's print circulation is growing—about 2,000 daily in the latest six-month period that ended in September—at a time when so many others are sliding.

But what about the ad revenue that the newspaper is giving up with such a restricted website? Hussman says ad rates are so low online that they often don't cover the cost of producing original journalism. Example: An online gallery of photos from a local high school football game might generate 4,000 page views. If an advertiser paid $25 for each thousand views—a premium figure, by the way—the photo feature might generate $100, barely enough to pay the photographer for his work.

"I know what I'm saying is going to sound too simplistic to some people, but it seems to be working," he says. "The reason I advocate this is not some ideological or esoteric reason or because of pride of authorship. I'm basing this on experience."

Hussman sees an industry that generates nearly $60 billion a year in print ad sales and subscription fees, and that supports the expenditure of roughly $7 billion a year on newsgathering operations, and worries about it all slipping away in an era in which news is so abundant—and so free. "It would be wonderful if someone could figure out a way" to do all that online, he says before concluding, "but I just don't see it now."

PAUL FARHI (farhip@washpost.com) is a *Washington Post* reporter who writes frequently about the media for the *Post* and *AJR*. He has written about the San Francisco area's news blues, hyperlocal news websites and the business magazine *Portfolio* in recent issues of *AJR*.

The Secrets of Googlenomics

Sure, it rules the world of search, but the real engine of Google's enormous success lies in its secret sauce: a data-fueled, auction-driven recipe for profitability that the rest of us need to start learning from fast.

STEVEN LEVY

In the midst of financial apocalypse, the gadflies and gurus of the global marketplace are gathered at the San Francisco Hilton for the annual meeting of the American Economics Association. The mood is similar to a seismologist convention in the wake of the Big One. Yet surprisingly, one of the most popular sessions has nothing to do with toxic assets, derivatives, or unemployment curves.

"I'm going to talk about online auctions," says Hal Varian, the session's first speaker. Varian is a lanky 62-year-old professor at UC Berkeley's Haas School of Business and School of Information, but these days he's best known as Google's chief economist. This morning's crowd hasn't come for predictions about the credit market; they want to hear about Google's secret sauce.

Varian is an expert on what may be the most successful business idea in history: AdWords, Google's unique method for selling online advertising. AdWords analyzes every Google search to determine which advertisers get each of up to 11 "sponsored links" on every results page. It's the world's biggest, fastest auction, a never-ending, automated, self-service version of Tokyo's boisterous Tsukiji fish market, and it takes place, Varian says, "every time you search." He never mentions how much revenue advertising brings in. But Google is a public company, so anyone can find the number: It was $21 billion last year.

His talk quickly becomes technical. There's the difference between the Generalized Second Price auction model and the Vickrey-Clark-Groves alternative. Game theory takes a turn; so does the Nash Equilibrium. Terms involving the c-word—as in *clicks*—get tossed around like beach balls at a summer rock festival. Clickthrough rate. Cost per click. Supply curve of clicks. The audience is enthralled.

During the question-and-answer period, a man wearing a camel-colored corduroy blazer raises his hand. "Let me understand this," he begins, half skeptical, half unsure. "You say that an auction happens every time a search takes place? That would mean millions of times a day!"

Varian smiles. "Millions," he says, "is actually quite an understatement."

Google is an economy unto itself, a seething laboratory of fiduciary forensics.

Why does Google even *need* a chief economist? The simplest reason is that the company is an economy unto itself. The ad auction, marinated in that special sauce, is a seething laboratory of fiduciary forensics, with customers ranging from giant multinationals to dorm-room entrepreneurs, all billed by the world's largest micropayment system.

Google depends on economic principles to hone what has become the search engine of choice for more than 60 percent of all Internet surfers, and the company uses auction theory to grease the skids of its own operations. All these calculations require an army of math geeks, algorithms of Ramanujanian complexity, and a sales force more comfortable with whiteboard markers than fairway irons.

Varian, an upbeat, avuncular presence at the Googleplex in Mountain View, California, serves as the Adam Smith of the new discipline of Googlenomics. His job is to provide a theoretical framework for Google's business practices while leading a team of quants to enforce bottom-line discipline, reining in the more propellerhead propensities of the company's dominant engineering culture.

Googlenomics actually comes in two flavors: macro and micro. The macroeconomic side involves some of the company's seemingly altruistic behavior, which often baffles observers. Why does Google give away products like its browser, its apps, and the Android operating system for mobile phones? Anything that increases Internet use ultimately enriches Google, Varian says. And since using the Web without using

Anatomy of an Auction

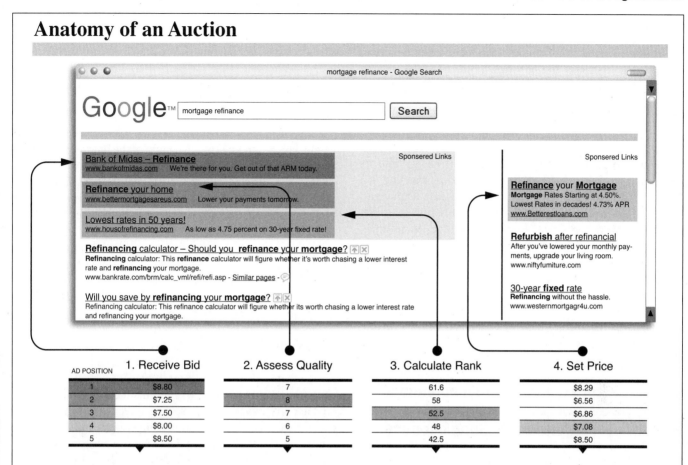

AD POSITION	1. Receive Bid	2. Assess Quality	3. Calculate Rank	4. Set Price
1	$8.80	7	61.6	$8.29
2	$7.25	8	58	$6.56
3	$7.50	7	52.5	$6.86
4	$8.00	6	48	$7.08
5	$8.50	5	42.5	$8.50

Every time you do a Google search, up to 11 ad spots are auctioned off simultaneously, just in time to show up on the results page. Here's how it works.

Receive Bid

Bank of Midas selects keywords like *mortgage refinance* and places bids on them. To help advertisers set smart bids, Google provides an estimated minimum bid needed to get on the first page of search results. Besides keywords, advertisers can connect their ads to specific dates, times, and geographic locations. But the highest bid doesn't guarantee an ad will appear at the top of page.

Assess Quality

Google also scores ads—like this one for Better Mortgages Are Us—on a quality scale of 1 to 10. The score is based on relevance (how well the ad matches a user's query), the quality of the landing page that the ad links to (the value of its content and how quickly it loads), and the ad's past click-through rate (or, if it's new, the rate of a similar ad), along with other criteria Google won't reveal.

Calculate Rank

The order in which the ads will be displayed is determined by a simple formula: Rank = bid × quality score. An above-average quality score, like the 7 earned by House of Refinancing, can compensate for a lower bid.

Set Price

In a twist on a classic second-price auction, the cost of each ad is tied to the bid of the advertiser ranked one notch down, using the formula below. (Here, BetterestLoans' price hinges on NiftyFurniture's bid and quality.)

$$P_1 = \frac{B_2 Q_2}{Q_2}$$

P_1 - Price paid by the advertiser
B_2 - Next-highest-placing ad's bid
Q_2 - Quality score of next-highest-placing ad
Q_1 - Advertiser's quality score

—Joanna Pearlstein

Google is like dining at In-N-Out without ordering a hamburger, more eyeballs on the Web lead inexorably to more ad sales for Google.

The microeconomics of Google is more complicated. Selling ads doesn't generate only profits; it also generates torrents of data about users' tastes and habits, data that Google then sifts and processes in order to predict future consumer behavior, find ways to improve its products, and sell more ads. This is the heart and soul of Googlenomics. It's a system of constant self-analysis: a data-fueled feedback loop that defines not only Google's future but the future of anyone who does business online.

When the American Economics Association meets next year, the financial crisis may still be topic A. But one of the keynote speakers has already been chosen: Googlenomist Hal Varian.

Ironically, economics was a distant focus in the first days of Google. After Larry Page and Sergey Brin founded the company in 1998, they channeled their energy into its free search product and left much of the business planning to a 22-year-old Stanford graduate named Salar Kamangar, Google's ninth employee. The early assumption was that although ads would be an important source of revenue, licensing search technology and selling servers would be just as lucrative. Page and Brin also believed that ads should be useful and welcome—not annoying intrusions. Kamangar and another early Googler, Eric Veach, set out to implement that ideal. Neither had a background in business or economics. Kamangar had been a biology major, and Veach's field of study was computer science.

Google recruited its own chief economist, UC Berkeley professor Hal Varian, to serve as in-house high priest of Googlenomics.

Google's ads were always plain blocks of text relevant to the search query. But at first, there were two kinds. Ads at the top of the page were sold the old-fashioned way, by a crew of human beings headquartered largely in New York City. Salespeople wooed big customers over dinner, explaining what keywords meant and what the prices were. Advertisers were then billed by the number of user views, or impressions, regardless of whether anyone clicked on the ad. Down the right side were other ads that smaller businesses could buy directly online. The first of these, for live mail-order lobsters, was sold in 2000, just minutes after Google deployed a link reading SEE YOUR AD HERE.

But as the business grew, Kamangar and Veach decided to price the slots on the side of the page by means of an auction. Not an eBay-style auction that unfolds over days or minutes as bids are raised or abandoned, but a huge marketplace of virtual auctions in which sealed bids are submitted in advance and winners are determined algorithmically in fractions of a second. Google hoped that millions of small and medium companies would take part in the market, so it was essential that the process be self-service. Advertisers bid on search terms, or keywords, but instead of bidding on the price per impression, they were bidding on a price they were willing to pay each time a user *clicked* on the ad. (The bid would be accompanied by a budget of how many clicks the advertiser was willing to pay for.) The new system was called AdWords Select, while the ads at the top of the page, with prices still set by humans, was renamed AdWords Premium.

One key innovation was that all the sidebar slots on the results page were sold off in a single auction. (Compare that to an early pioneer of auction-driven search ads, Overture, which held a separate auction for each slot.) The problem with an all-at-once auction, however, was that advertisers might be inclined to lowball their bids to avoid the sucker's trap of paying a huge amount more than the guy just below them on the page. So the Googlers decided that the winner of each auction would pay the amount (plus a penny) of the bid from the advertiser with the next-highest offer. (If Joe bids $10, Alice bids $9, and Sue bids $6, Joe gets the top slot and pays $9.01. Alice gets the next slot for $6.01, and so on.) Since competitors didn't have to worry about costly overbidding errors, the paradoxical result was that it encouraged higher bids.

"Eric Veach did the math independently," Kamangar says. "We found out along the way that second-price auctions had existed in other forms in the past and were used at one time in Treasury auctions." (Another crucial innovation had to do with ad quality, but more on that later.)

Google's homemade solution to its ad problem impressed even Paul Milgrom, the Stanford economist who is to auction theory what Letitia Baldrige is to etiquette. "I've begun to realize that Google somehow stumbled on a level of simplification in ad auctions that was not included before," he says. And applying a variation on second-price auctions wasn't just a theoretical advance. "Google immediately started getting higher prices for advertising than Overture was getting."

Google hired Varian in May 2002, a few months after implementing the auction-based version of AdWords. The offer came about when Google's then-new CEO, Eric Schmidt, ran into Varian at the Aspen Institute and they struck up a conversation about Internet issues. Schmidt was with Larry Page, who was pushing his own notions about how some of the big problems in business and science could be solved by using computation and analysis on an unprecedented scale. Varian remembers thinking, "Why did Eric bring his high-school nephew?"

Schmidt, whose father was an economist, invited Varian to spend a day or two a week at Google. On his first visit, Varian asked Schmidt what he should do. "Why don't you take a look at the ad auction?" Schmidt said.

Google had already developed the basics of AdWords, but there was still plenty of tweaking to do, and Varian was uniquely qualified to "take a look." As head of the information school at UC Berkeley and coauthor (with Carl Shapiro) of a popular book called *Information Rules: A Strategic Guide to the Network Economy,* he was already the go-to economist on ecommerce.

At the time, most online companies were still selling advertising the way it was done in the days of *Mad Men.* But Varian saw immediately that Google's ad business was less like buying traditional spots and more like computer dating. "The theory was Google as yenta—matchmaker," he says. He also realized there was another old idea underlying the new approach: A 1983 paper by Harvard economist Herman Leonard described using marketplace mechanisms to assign job candidates to slots in a corporation, or students to dorm rooms. It was called a two-sided matching market. "The mathematical structure of the Google auction," Varian says, "is the same as those two-sided matching markets."

Varian tried to understand the process better by applying game theory. "I think I was the first person to do that," he says. After just a few weeks at Google, he went back to Schmidt. "It's amazing!" Varian said. "You've managed to design an auction perfectly."

"All of a sudden," CEO Eric Schmidt says, "we realized we were in the auction business."

To Schmidt, who had been at Google barely a year, this was an incredible relief. "Remember, this was when the company had 200 employees and no cash," he says. "All of a sudden we realized we were in the auction business."

It wasn't long before the success of AdWords Select began to dwarf that of its sister system, the more traditional AdWords Premium. Inevitably, Veach and Kamangar argued that *all* the ad slots should be auctioned off. In search, Google had already used scale, power, and clever algorithms to change the way people accessed information. By turning over its sales process entirely to an auction-based system, the company could similarly upend the world of advertising, removing human guesswork from the equation.

The move was risky. Going ahead with the phaseout—nicknamed Premium Sunset—meant giving up campaigns that were selling for hundreds of thousands of dollars, for the unproven possibility that the auction process would generate even bigger sums. "We were going to erase a huge part of the company's revenue," says Tim Armstrong, then head of direct sales in the US. (This March, Armstrong left Google to become AOL's new chair and CEO.) "Ninety-nine percent of companies would have said, 'Hold on, don't make that change.' But we had Larry, Sergey, and Eric saying, 'Let's go for it.'"

News of the switch jacked up the Maalox consumption among Google's salespeople. Instead of selling to corporate giants, their job would now be to get them to *place bids in an auction?* "We thought it was a little half-cocked," says Jeff Levick, an early leader of the Google sales team. The young company wasn't getting rid of its sales force (though the system certainly helped Google run with far fewer salespeople than a traditional media company) but was asking them to get geekier, helping big customers shape online strategies as opposed to simply selling ad space.

Levick tells a story of visiting three big customers to inform them of the new system: "The guy in California almost threw us out of his office and told us to fuck ourselves. The guy in Chicago said, 'This is going to be the worst business move you ever made.' But the guy in Massachusetts said, 'I trust you.'"

That client knew math, says Levick, whose secret weapon was the numbers. When the data was crunched—and Google worked hard to give clients the tools needed to run the numbers themselves—advertisers saw that the new system paid off for them, too.

AdWords was such a hit that Google went auction-crazy. The company used auctions to place ads on other websites (that program was dubbed AdSense). "But the really gutsy move," Varian says, "was using it in the IPO." In 2004, Google used a variation of a Dutch auction for its IPO; Brin and Page loved that the process leveled the playing field between small investors and powerful brokerage houses. And in 2008, the company couldn't resist participating in the FCC's auction to reallocate portions of the radio spectrum.

Google even uses auctions for internal operations, like allocating servers among its various business units. Since moving a product's storage and computation to a new data center is disruptive, engineers often put it off. "I suggested we run an auction similar to what the airlines do when they oversell a flight. They keep offering bigger vouchers until enough customers give up their seats," Varian says. "In our case, we offer more machines in exchange for moving to new servers. One group might do it for 50 new ones, another for 100, and another won't move unless we give them 300. So we give them to the lowest bidder—they get their extra capacity, and we get computation shifted to the new data center."

The transition to an all-auction sales model was a milestone for Google, ensuring that its entire revenue engine would run with the same computer-science fervor as its search operation. Now, when Google recruits alpha geeks, it is just as likely to have them focus on AdWords as on search or apps.

The across-the-board emphasis on engineering, mathematical formulas, and data-mining has made Google a new kind of company. But to fully understand why, you have to go back and look under AdWords' hood.

Most people think of the Google ad auction as a straightforward affair. In fact, there's a key component that few users know about and even sophisticated advertisers don't fully understand. The bids themselves are only a part of what ultimately determines the auction winners. The other major determinant is something called the quality score. This metric strives to ensure that the ads Google shows on its results page are true, high-caliber matches for what users are querying. If they aren't, the whole system suffers and Google makes less money.

Google determines quality scores by calculating multiple factors, including the relevance of the ad to the specific keyword or keywords, the quality of the landing page the ad is linked to, and, above all, the percentage of times users actually click on a given ad when it appears on a results page. (Other factors, Google won't even discuss.) There's also a penalty invoked when the ad quality is too low—in such cases, the company slaps a minimum bid on the advertiser. Google explains that this practice—reviled by many companies affected by it—protects users from being exposed to irrelevant or annoying ads that would sour people on sponsored links in general. Several lawsuits have been filed by would-be advertisers who claim that they are victims of an arbitrary process by a quasi monopoly.

You can argue about fairness, but arbitrary it ain't. To figure out the quality score, Google needs to estimate in advance how many users will click on an ad. That's very tricky, especially since we're talking about billions of auctions. But since the ad model depends on predicting clickthroughs as perfectly as possible, the company must quantify and analyze every twist and turn of the data. Susan Wojcicki, who oversees Google's advertising, refers to it as "the physics of clicks."

During Varian's second summer in Mountain View, when he was still coming in only a day or two a week, he asked a recently hired computer scientist from Stanford named Diane Tang to create the Google equivalent of the Consumer Price Index, called the Keyword Pricing Index. "Instead of a basket of goods like diapers and beer and doughnuts, we have keywords," says Tang, who is known internally as the Queen of Clicks.

The Keyword Pricing Index is a reality check. It alerts Google to any anomalous price bubbles, a sure sign that an auction isn't working properly. Categories are ranked by the cost per click that advertisers generally have to pay, weighted by distribution, and then separated into three bundles: high cap, mid cap, and low cap. "The high caps are very competitive keywords, like 'flowers' and 'hotels,'" Tang says. In the mid-cap realm you have keywords that may vary seasonally—the price to place ads alongside results for "snowboarding" skyrockets during the winter. Low caps like "Massachusetts buggy whips" are the stuff of long tails.

As the amount of data at the company's disposal grows, the opportunities to exploit it multiply.

Tang's index is just one example of a much broader effort. As the amount of data at the company's disposal grows, the opportunities to exploit it multiply, which ends up further extending the range and scope of the Google economy. So it's utterly essential to calculate correctly the quality scores that prop up AdWords.

"The people working for me are generally econometricians—sort of a cross between statisticians and economists," says Varian, who moved to Google full-time in 2007 (he's on leave from Berkeley) and leads two teams, one of them focused on analysis.

"Google needs mathematical types that have a rich tool set for looking for signals in noise," says statistician Daryl Pregibon, who joined Google in 2003 after 23 years as a top scientist at Bell Labs and AT&T Labs. "The rough rule of thumb is one statistician for every 100 computer scientists."

Keywords and click rates are their bread and butter. "We are trying to understand the mechanisms behind the metrics," says

Qing Wu, one of Varian's minions. His specialty is forecasting, so now he predicts patterns of queries based on the season, the climate, international holidays, even the time of day. "We have temperature data, weather data, and queries data, so we can do correlation and statistical modeling," Wu says. The results all feed into Google's backend system, helping advertisers devise more-efficient campaigns.

To track and test their predictions, Wu and his colleagues use dozens of onscreen dashboards that continuously stream information, a sort of Bloomberg terminal for the Googlesphere. Wu checks obsessively to see whether reality is matching the forecasts: "With a dashboard, you can monitor the queries, the amount of money you make, how many advertisers you have, how many keywords they're bidding on, what the rate of return is for each advertiser."

Wu calls Google "the barometer of the world." Indeed, studying the clicks is like looking through a window with a panoramic view of everything. You can see the change of seasons—clicks gravitating toward skiing and heavy clothes in winter, bikinis and sunscreen in summer—and you can track who's up and down in pop culture. Most of us remember news events from television or newspapers; Googlers recall them as spikes in their graphs. "One of the big things a few years ago was the SARS epidemic," Tang says. Wu didn't even have to read the papers to know about the financial meltdown—he saw the jump in people Googling for *gold*. And since prediction and analysis are so crucial to AdWords, every bit of data, no matter how seemingly trivial, has potential value.

Since Google hired Varian, other companies, like Yahoo, have decided that they, too, must have a chief economist heading a division that scrutinizes auctions, dashboards, and econometric models to fine-tune their business plan. In 2007, Harvard economist Susan Athey was surprised to get a summons to Redmond to meet with Steve Ballmer. "That's a call you take," she says. Athey spent last year working in Microsoft's Cambridge, Massachusetts, office.

Can the rest of the world be far behind? Although Eric Schmidt doesn't think it will happen as quickly as some believe, he does think that Google-style auctions are applicable to all sorts of transactions. The solution to the glut in auto inventory? Put the entire supply of unsold cars up for bid. That'll clear out the lot. Housing, too: "People use auctions now in cases of distress, like auctioning a house when there are no buyers," Schmidt says. "But you can imagine a situation in which it was a normal and routine way of doing things."

Varian believes that a new era is dawning for what you might call the datarati—and it's all about harnessing supply and demand. "What's ubiquitous and cheap?" Varian asks. "Data." And what is scarce? The analytic ability to utilize that data. As a result, he believes that the kind of technical person who once would have wound up working for a hedge fund on Wall Street will now work at a firm whose business hinges on making smart, daring choices—decisions based on surprising results gleaned from algorithmic spelunking and executed with the confidence that comes from really doing the math.

It's a satisfying development for Varian, a guy whose career as an economist was inspired by a sci-fi novel he read in junior high. "In Isaac Asimov's first *Foundation Trilogy,* there was a character who basically constructed mathematical models of society, and I thought this was a really exciting idea. When I went to college, I looked around for that subject. It turned out to be economics." Varian is telling this story from his pied-à-Plex, where he sometimes stays during the week to avoid driving the 40-some miles from Google headquarters to his home in the East Bay. It happens to be the ranch-style house, which Google now owns, where Brin and Page started the company.

There's a wild contrast between this sparsely furnished residence and what it has spawned—dozens of millionaire geeks, billions of auctions, and new ground rules for businesses in a data-driven society that is far weirder than the one Asimov envisioned nearly 60 years ago. What could be more baffling than a capitalist corporation that gives away its best services, doesn't set the prices for the ads that support it, and turns away customers because their ads don't measure up to its complex formulas? Varian, of course, knows that his employer's success is not the result of inspired craziness but of an early recognition that the Internet rewards fanatical focus on scale, speed, data analysis, and customer satisfaction. (A bit of auction theory doesn't hurt, either.) Today we have a name for those rules: Googlenomics. Learn them, or pay the price.

Senior writer STEVEN LEVY (steven_levy@wired.com) wrote about the *Kryptos* sculpture at CIA headquarters in issue 17.05.

But Who's Counting?

No one really knows how many people visit websites. A San Francisco startup and Google are both working to change that.

JASON PONTIN

I n August 2006, when Roger McNamee invested in Forbes, he did so in part because its Web audience was thought to be huge. McNamee is a founder of Elevation Partners, a Silicon Valley private-equity firm that counts Bono of the rock band U2 as one of its managing partners; it specializes in big, bold investments in media and technology. Onstage at EmTech, Technology Review's annual conference, he said, "Look: I'm not investing in Forbes for its dead-trees business."

At the time, Jim Spanfeller, the chief executive of Forbes .com, claimed that more than 15 million readers around the globe had visited his site in February, making Forbes the world's leading business site. He supported his boast with research from ComScore Media Metrix, one of the two leading suppliers of third-party traffic data for the Web. The numbers seemed safe enough: Forbes.com's internal server logs showed even greater Web traffic. It was embarrassing, therefore, when ComScore announced that it had changed the methods it used to estimate worldwide audiences, and that little more than seven million people had visited Forbes.com in July. That placed Forbes's online audience below those of Dow Jones (whose sites include WSJ.com) and CNN Money (whose sites include Fortune). Bitchy press accounts suggested that McNamee had been overcharged—if not actually robbed—for his investment, which was variously reported at between $250 million and $300 million.

More than two years later, McNamee claims he always knew there were broad discrepancies between what the internal server logs of Forbes.com showed and what third parties reported. "To be a headache, it would have to be surprising," he says. Instead, he suggests, he invested with no very precise idea of Forbes.com's audience: "I looked at every indicator that was out there. They were all bad. In the end, I had to think about it differently. I invested in Forbes because I thought the market was underserved, and because they had made fewer mistakes than anyone else." (To this day, McNamee declines to say how much he paid for how large an equity stake.)

People still can't agree on how many readers visit Forbes .com. "According to ComScore, we have six to seven million visitors [per month]; our own logs say 18 to 20 million," says Spanfeller. But while the difference between third-party and internal measurements is, for a variety of reasons, particularly striking in the case of Forbes, confusion about the size of online audiences is universal.

No one really knows how many people visit websites. No established third-party supplier of audience measurement data is trusted. Internal Web logs exaggerate audiences. This matters to more people than investors, like McNamee, who worry that they have no way to evaluate new-media businesses. The issues involved are technical, and occluded by ugly jargon, but they concern anyone anxious about the future of media as print and broadcast television and radio shrink in importance.

Happily, a California startup and Google are working to measure Web audiences in new and better ways.

The Price of Journalism

Why care about something as arcane as dodgy audience measurement? Here's why: where content is free, as it is on most websites, the only thing that will pay for quality journalism—or, really, anything valuable at all—is advertising. For most new-media businesses, "display" or banner advertising is the main source of operating revenues. But the general inability to agree on audience numbers is stunting the growth of display advertising.

Every year, advertisers spend billions of dollars online; eMarketer, a research firm, predicts $25.7 billion in 2009 in the United States alone. Marketers study Web audiences to help them decide which sites to spend money on: they try to divine the number of people who visit a site every month, demographic details about those visitors, the length of time they stay on the site, the number of pages they view, and the relationship, if any, between the ads they see and the way they behave. The people who actually buy ads—media buyers and planners at advertising agencies—use this information to choose appropriate sites for campaigns. Finally, publishers use the data to set advertising rates.

However, the correlation between the size of Web audiences and their value to advertisers is not direct. In print, the relationship between audience size and advertising spending is simple, because the prices of ads derive largely from a publisher's audited statement of circulation; media planners buy the total audience. Online, it's more complicated because the currency of display advertising is ad impressions, or the number of times a specific ad is served to a particular part of a website. "Audience numbers don't affect my buying decisions very much," explains David L. Smith, the chief executive and founder of Mediasmith, an interactive-media planning and buying agency whose clients include the National Geographic Channel and Sega. "If we were buying the total audience of a site, it would be different. But most of the time we buy packages of impressions."

Jim Spanfeller, who is a past chair and current board member of the Interactive Advertising Bureau (IAB), the industry association that represents sellers of online advertising, agrees with Smith that unreliable audience measurement doesn't directly affect ad spending, at least at larger sites: "If you're an established site like Forbes.com, you're selling on an ad-impression basis. The problem arises when an agency is thinking about moving money from one medium, like print or television, onto the Web." Then, Spanfeller says, media planners can't show their clients whether Web audiences replicate or complement the audiences that advertisers are reaching through traditional media. "We need believable numbers so that we can do cross-media comparisons," he says. Additionally, bad audience measurement "hurts smaller sites with more targeted audiences that don't have a lot of impressions"—the class of sites that Spanfeller, like many digerati, says occupies "the long tail."

Thus, the real consequence of the audience measurement problem is a chilling effect on the transfer of advertising from older media to new. Meanwhile, another form of online advertising is growing quickly—but it's not the ads publishers sell. The numbers clarify. Spending on "keyword" or search advertising (the sponsored links that appear near search results on Google.com and other search sites) grew 21 percent in 2008, mostly at the expense of print, local television and radio, and Yellow Pages advertising; it now constitutes 45 percent of all online advertising. That's because the effectiveness of keywords is unambiguous: advertisers pay directly for click-throughs or purchases. There's no need to appeal to anything so disputed as the size or composition of Web audiences. This growth in keyword advertising has mainly benefited the search firms. By comparison, the display advertising that media companies sell grew only 4 percent the same year.

Four percent growth might sound all right to some, but it occurs at the same time that advertising revenues in print are falling rapidly. For instance, ad spending in newspapers will decline from $50.8 billion in 2007 to $45 billion by 2012, according to Borrell Associates, a research firm. Even Forbes is sweating. As a private company, it does not disclose its revenues, but the number of ad pages in its magazine has been shrinking since 2000. At the same time, the company's online advertising revenues are reported to be between $55 million and $70 million, a figure Spanfeller did not dispute. That's not so much for a publication with an audience of 20 (or even seven!) million. In the glory days of print advertising, publications with much smaller audiences earned as much or more: Red Herring, which I once edited, earned more than $50 million in print advertising revenue in 2000, and its circulation was only 350,000 readers, according to Ted Gramkow, the magazine's former publisher.

Display advertising was meant to fund the great shift of readers to new media. It's not happening. For more than 100 years, advertising paid publishers and underwrote their production of great journalism; now, those ad monies are being funneled to search firms that create nothing but code. As Roger McNamee says: "Getting this right is absolutely necessary for publishers to be able to continue to do interesting things."

Panel Discussion

What's wrong with existing methods of measuring Web audiences? Lots.

ComScore and Nielsen Online, a division of the Nielsen Company, are the established leaders in the field of audience measurement and the sale, to advertisers, agencies, and publishers, of the data that audience measurement produces.

These third-party audience measurement firms exist because the internal logs of publishers are notoriously unreliable in quantifying user activity on a given site. "When publishers use their log files, there are many limitations," David Smith says. He says that the limitations of using these internal logs (a practice sometimes called "census measurement") include, in ascending order of impact, overcounting individuals with multiple computers or Web browsers; counting "mechanical visits" by Web "bots" and "spiders" (for example, when Google crawls the Web to estimate the popularity of sites) as visits by real people; and overcounting individuals who periodically flush out the "cookies" of code that sites stash on browsers so that returning visitors can be recognized.

To create more-accurate audience numbers, ComScore and Nielsen Online rely on a methodology inherited from television audience research: the panel. Nielsen, for instance, has recruited nearly 30,000 panelists for its flagship product, called Netview. Panelists agree to have their Web browsing monitored through interviews and through "meters," or spyware, installed on their personal computers.

But what worked with television doesn't work nearly so well with the Web. "Panels are always problematical," says Spanfeller, "but on the Web they're super-problematical.

Panels undercount by one-third to one-half." In short, publishers simply can't accept that their audiences are as small as panel-based measurements suggest they are.

Among the problems with panel-based audience research, according to both Spanfeller and Smith, is that it tends to undercount people who look at sites at work, because most companies' information technology managers won't install strange spyware on their computers. Sometimes, panelists lie to interviewers. Also, both say, there is a straightforward "sampling error" (what statisticians consider the misprisions that derive from sampling too small a portion of a general population): with as few as 30,000 panelists, the audiences of smaller sites are often grossly underestimated or missed entirely.

A final problem with panel-based measurements is that at the moment, neither Nielsen nor ComScore has itself been audited by an independent party. Who knows, both Spanfeller and Smith asked darkly, how valid the firms' reporting methods really are?

Nielsen defends its panels. "I guarantee you, if our numbers were higher than the publishers' server data, we wouldn't be having this argument," says Manish Bhatia, the president of global services at Nielsen Online. Bhatia notes that Nielsen does sell products, such as SiteCensus, that install software tags on publishers' websites and measure server logs. "In combination with panels, they're useful," he says. "But panels are more reliable, they provide demographic information, and they tell you what people do after they've seen an online ad."

For its part, ComScore also concedes that server logs have their place: they disclose which Web pages a publisher served, and when. But like Nielsen, the company insists that only panels provide an accurate measurement of audiences and their demographic makeup. "Servers don't measure people," says Andrew Lipsman, director of industry analysis at ComScore.

Why are Nielsen and ComScore so wedded to panels? According to David Smith, "The incumbents have a huge amount of money invested in their methodologies—and getting them to admit they have a problem isn't easy."

Roger McNamee is more blunt. "I understand why Nielsen is so bad," he says. "But why isn't there anything better? There's a huge market opportunity for any venture capitalist who is willing to fund a system that audits actual traffic."

"What we need is a third-party Omniture," says Spanfeller, referring to the website analytics software that many publishers (including Technology Review) use to log their own traffic.

Measure for Measure

Recently, I visited Quantcast, a San Francisco-based startup that is hoping to provide just such a service. Founded in 2005 and funded with $26 million, mainly from Polaris Ventures and Founders Fund, the company wants its service, which launched in 2006, to overthrow traditional panel-based Web audience measurement.

Konrad Feldman, the company's youthful, redheaded, British-born chief executive and cofounder, met me at the company's headquarters overlooking the Yerba Buena Gardens and the Moscone Center. In a large conference room with a cement floor, decorated according to the precepts of venture-capitalist high minimalism, he asked whether Technology Review was "quantified"—that is, whether its online visitors were tracked by the startup's software tags. After we confirmed that our site had been quantified for some time, he opened his laptop and searched for our URL at Quantcast.com.

An elegant dashboard of audience information was swiftly served: TechnologyReview.com, it said, had 342,000 "global people" and 205,000 "U.S. people." These numbers, which measured monthly visitors to our site, were not so low as those reported by traditional third-party audience measurement firms, but they seemed suspicious: throughout 2008, Omniture reported around 650,000 unique visitors to TechnologyReview.com every month. But we also learned that 32 percent of TechnologyReview.com's readers earned more than $100,000 a year and that 24 percent had postgraduate degrees, which seemed about right. (A peek at Forbes.com, which is not quantified but whose numbers the startup had extrapolated, showed that the business site had 4.9 million "U.S. people," who were richer than TechnologyReview.com's readers, although not as highly educated. Because Forbes was not quantified, Quantcast didn't supply Forbes.com's total worldwide audience.)

Quantcast's service, like that of existing audience measurement firms, begins with panels—or, more precisely, panel-like data in the form of "reference samples," provided to the company by third parties such as market research firms, Internet service providers, and toolbar companies, among other sources. These statistical methods create a basic model of U.S. Web traffic. But when publishers install Quantcast's tags on their servers, Quantcast gets more details; the startup adjusts for spiders and bots, people with multiple computers, and cookie flushers. The two methodologies are combined using something Quantcast calls its "mass inference algorithm," created with the aid of two Stanford University mathematicians and refined by the seven mathematically minded PhDs who work at the company. This algorithmic analysis of panel research and server-based measurement is unique in Web audience measurement (although Nielsen more coarsely combines the two methodologies with a service called VideoCensus, which tracks online video viewing). The resulting audience information, says Feldman, is much more reliable than anything offered by ComScore or Nielsen.

"Publishers and advertisers have used panel-based research for nearly 75 years," says Feldman. "So there's obviously an established way of doing things. But equally, there's a pretty clear recognition in the marketplace that something has got to change."

Because Quantcast's audience information is free (where ComScore's and Nielsen's measurements are not), the company hopes to make money by charging publishers who enroll in Media Planner, a service launched last May that helps media planners spend their clients' cash. Although Media Planner is wholly free for now, Quantcast wants to expand the service so that it can finely describe demographic subsets within websites' audiences, a utility for which the company believes the sites themselves will pay. Feldman explains this tricky idea: "You have a sales force at TechnologyReview .com, and they can't possibly speak to everyone who might value your audience. But if you can expose that audience to buyers, then you can create a way whereby buyers can discover the parts of your audience they find particularly valuable." Feldman says that Media Planner allows media buyers to find appropriate audiences, "but it's the publishers that should pay, as they're the ones getting higher rates for their audience segments." More ambitiously, Feldman hopes Quantcast's audience data, in combination with ad impressions, will create a new currency for advertisers, advertising agencies, and publishers that will make display ads more effective and therefore more valuable.

Feldman and his cofounder, Paul Sutter, the company's president, do not approach the problem of audience measurement as veterans of media. Feldman, a computer scientist, was the cofounder of Searchspace (now Fortent), which developed software to help financial-services firms detect money laundering and the financing of terrorists. Sutter founded the network optimization company Orbital Data (later acquired by Citrix) as an expert on high-performance computer architectures, a background that has proved useful as Quantcast processes the thousands of terabytes of data it has collected.

When the founders first conceived the company, Sutter says, "we just asked the most simple, kindergarten questions, and it soon became clear that the language that media buyers and planners were speaking was nothing like the language of Internet advertising, with its cost-per-clicks and so forth. Media planners liked to talk about audiences, demographics, and lifestyles. So the answer was quantcasting, which means just reaching the people you want to reach." Today, the company claims that 85,000 broadly defined "publishers" have elected to be directly measured by Quantcast, including the Disney-ABC Television Group, NBC, CBS, MTV Networks, Fox, BusinessWeek, and Time's SI.com and CNNMoney .com.

Quantcast is not the only company with the bright idea of replacing panel-based audience measurement. Last June, Google announced a new service, Google Ad Planner, which uses the company's detailed knowledge of Web traffic to provide interested parties with a more accurate understanding of Web audiences. Wayne Lin, Ad Planner's product manager, demonstrated the service to me when I visited the Google-Plex in Mountain View, CA. Because Google owns Double-Click, one of the two dominant systems for serving ads, Web audience data can be combined with the ad-serving system so that media planners know which sites are best suited for which ads. The combination should be powerfully attractive for media planners and marketers, says Lin.

How do media planners regard the two new audience measurement services? "We use Quantcast now at Mediasmith, but they are not complete enough yet to be a total solution," says David Smith, who briefly advised the startup during its formation. The difficulty, according to Smith, is that the site's audience information won't be really useful—let alone a new currency—until more publishers elect to be quantified. Jim Spanfeller agrees. "They're to be commended for working hard on the problem," he says. "But it's very much a chicken-and-egg thing."

As for Google's Ad Planner, Smith says, "the agencies will never stand for it." Smith, like everyone I spoke to, argued that media planners will resist Google's audience information because no one wants one company to be so dominant in online advertising: were Ad Planner to be widely adopted, Google would be selling keywords through its search advertising network, AdWords; selling banner advertising through its display advertising network, AdSense; serving those ads through DoubleClick; and advising media planners on where to spend their advertising dollars.

Ad Planner also lacks a number of important features that an advertising agency might expect from an audience measurement service. According to Smith, it offers neither very detailed demographics nor a full explanation of its methodologies. Patrick Viera, TechnologyReview.com's own digital strategist and West Coast advertising manager, said disdainfully when I asked his opinion: "Yeah, I looked at it. It doesn't do anything you want. It's just a tool for selling AdSense."

Still, says Smith, there's demand for something new. "Publishers have to use third-party measurements, but third parties [such as ComScore and Nielsen] may underestimate audiences, and the truth is probably somewhere in between. That's why new companies like Quantcast have a chance."

Growing Pains

But neither Quantcast nor Google nor improved products from ComScore and Nielsen Online could, by themselves or in combination, fix display advertising and thereby ensure the future health of media.

Whatever audience measurement tools are adopted, they will themselves have to be validated by an independent party. Quantcast, ComScore, and Nielsen Online (but not Google) are all in the process of being audited by the Media Rating Council (MRC), which was established by the U.S. Congress in the 1960s to audit and accredit the ratings of broadcasters. Accreditation will smooth disputes about the different audience measurement methodologies, according to George Ivie, the chief executive of the MRC: "It will help bring the numbers closer together; and it will explain and make transparent the differences between the census and panel systems."

In addition to the disagreements about the size of Web audiences, though, online advertising suffers from deep structural problems that must be addressed before media planners and their advertising clients will spend really large sums. These are various and dauntingly technical, but according to David Smith, they all involve, in one way or another, the absence of commonly accepted, automated means to create, sell, serve, and track the performance of online ads.

Fixing all that will take years, as will the adoption of undisputed audience measurement methods. "This industry is only 13 years old," says Smith. "It grew rapidly with few standards for six years. Then it collapsed, with very little research and development for four years, and has just been getting back to the right kind of R&D and standards in the past three."

Still, by any estimate, the general confusion about Web audiences is the reason why the online medium has matured in so ungainly a fashion. "It's an amazing topic," wrote Roger McNamee in a conversation using the messaging service of the social network Facebook. "You could see it coming a mile away. Unfortunately, the remedy is not yet obvious."

JASON PONTIN is the Editor in Chief and Publisher of *Technology Review*.

Old Media Strikes Back

Daniel Lyons

As the worlds of technology and media collide, the same contest keeps getting played out over and over again: lumbering old-media companies take on nimble new-media upstarts, and usually the new-media guys win, since it's easier for them to figure out the content business than it is for the content companies to figure out the techie stuff involved in launching an Internet business. Apple outfoxed the music companies and now in effect controls their business. Google reaps billions by selling ads that run next to content created by others—while some of those creators, newspapers and magazines, teeter on the edge of the tar pit. In video, Google figured it could work the same trick again, so in late 2006 it spent $1.65 billion to acquire YouTube, a site that had built a huge audience by dishing up user-generated videos and pirated clips from movies and TV shows. YouTube wasn't bringing in any money, but Google believed it would figure something out. Meanwhile, Apple was trying to lure movie and TV studios into the iTunes store, just as it had done with music labels.

But this time the old-media guys fought back. In 2007, a few months after Google bought YouTube, NBC Universal and News Corp. announced they would jointly build their own Internet video site. Conventional wisdom among Silicon Valley pundits was that the site, called Hulu (named after a Chinese word that means "holder of precious things"), would be an epic disaster—or "Clown Co.," as they dubbed it. Old-media guys didn't "get" the Internet, detractors said, and partnerships between bitter rivals never work.

Hulu, founded by NBC and Fox, has become a better moneymaker than Web darling YouTube. The moral: Better content wins.

But guess what? Unlike YouTube, Hulu had legal access to great content—shows from NBC, Fox and others. And it had great technology—a clean, simple user interface and a smart search engine. Today, just one year after its launch, Hulu has gained the upper hand. "The empire is striking back," says Arash Amel, analyst for researcher Screen Digest. Amel estimates that while Hulu attracts far fewer visitors per month than YouTube (8.5 million versus 89.5 million), in financial terms Hulu is actually doing better. He estimates that last year Hulu took in $65 million in U.S. ad revenue and cleared $12 million in gross profit, while YouTube generated $114 million in U.S. revenue but had no gross profit. This year Amel estimates Hulu's revenue will grow to $175 million in the U.S. and that YouTube will take in slightly less. (Neither company confirmed these figures; Amel developed revenue estimates on his own.)

YouTube has lots of content, but from the perspective of advertisers much of it is utterly worthless. Nobody wants to tout their brand amid user-generated videos that could turn out to be almost anything, Amel says. He reckons only 3 to 4 percent of YouTube's video streams go out with an advertisement attached, while at Hulu the figure is 80 percent. YouTube says Amel's estimates are too low, but won't provide the actual figure. YouTube also insists that advertisers aren't scared off by user-generated content, though YouTube now is striking deals to add more TV shows and movies to its mix.

Perhaps the smartest move Hulu's founders made was looking outside for talent. They recruited a former Amazon division chief, Jason Kilar, to be Hulu's CEO, and a 28-year-old former Microsoft researcher, Eric Feng, to oversee development. Feng, who was living in Beijing, assembled an eight-member team in China that banged out the initial Hulu code in two months, and the site went live four months later, in March 2008. Much of the code writing still gets done in Beijing, where Hulu employs 30 engineers. The rest takes place at headquarters in Los Angeles.

Hulu's team is trying new approaches to advertising that they hope will be more palatable to viewers, and more effective as well. One idea: a viewer can choose to see ads interspersed throughout a show, or can watch a single long advertisement up front. (But either way you can't skip through the ads.) Another example: a carmaker lets the viewer choose to see an ad for a pickup truck, a crossover SUV or a sports car—so the viewer gains some control, and the advertiser doesn't waste a pickup-truck ad on someone who wouldn't be caught dead in one. Hulu also has taken a unique approach to distribution, striking deals with nearly 30 affiliates (these include MySpace, Yahoo and MSN) that run Hulu videos on their sites. The idea is to bring content to the audience, rather than forcing the audience to come to the main site to watch shows.

Hulu insists it's not really competing with YouTube. In fact, its real victim might be cable companies. Why pay $100 per month for a cable subscription when you can get so much great stuff online at no cost? Movies and TV shows are flooding onto the Internet, not just through Hulu but through upstarts like Veoh and Joost, as well as established players like CBS, which operates TV.com, and ABC, which offers TV shows on ABC .com. The lesson in all this? Fun as it may be to watch someone's kitten playing with a piece of string, last night's episode of "The Office" makes for a more compelling experience. Turns out those old-media guys still know something about how to capture an audience—and make money from it. "We've come a long way from Clown Co.," says Jean-Briac Perrette, the president of NBC Universal Digital Distribution and a board member of Hulu. They have indeed.

A Fading Taboo

Paper by paper, advertising is making its way onto the nation's front pages and section fronts.

Donna Shaw

Sometimes they snake across the bottom of the page as relatively unobtrusive six-column strips. Sometimes they catch the eye more forcefully as right-corner boxes. And sometimes they scream for attention as in-your-face fluorescent stickers plastered across a newspaper's masthead.

Whatever the shape, size or hue, the long-unfashionable page-one advertisement is gaining grudging acceptance from many editors, page designers and even reporters. As the industry struggles to identify innovative sources of revenue, newspapers not only are launching audacious online ventures (see "Rolling the Dice", page 40, and "*Really* Local," April/May) but also are dangling fresh enticements for advertisers in their old-fashioned print editions.

Page-one ads may net premium prices, but they're distasteful to many journalists who believe they violate the purity of page one and the sacred wall between news and business. From a design standpoint, they can detract from the flow and order of a page. They also eat up space that otherwise could be devoted to stories, particularly in an era of dwindling newsholes.

Among newspapers that recently have published page-one ads are the Wall Street Journal, San Francisco Chronicle, Philadelphia Inquirer and Hartford Courant. Others, such as USA Today and many other Gannett papers, have published them for years (see "Out Front," July/August 1999). Still others—the New York Times, Los Angeles Times, Boston Globe and Minneapolis' Star Tribune, for example—are experimenting with ads on section fronts but so far have kept page one off-limits.

"I don't think anyone in journalism is happy about them, but personally, and here at the paper, we felt we should do it," says Robert J. Rosenthal, managing editor and vice president of the San Francisco Chronicle, which debuted front-page ads on April 18. He sees them as part of the evolution toward the multimedia newsroom, adding, "If the business model supports good journalism, then I'm in favor of it."

As ads creep onto front pages and section fronts, designers are working to minimize how distracting—and sometimes garish—they may appear. "I think that most people in the newsroom realize the [financial] environment we're working in," says Chris Clonts, assistant design director for news at the Star Tribune, which began running section-front ads early this year (so far none on page one). He thinks the ad department also realizes that changing ad placement "will require some hand-holding" for journalists.

Gene Patterson, former chairman of the Poynter Institute and former editor of the St. Petersburg Times, sees the page-one ad as a sign of painful economic times for newspapers. "I find the section-front ads to be acceptable; I find the page-one ads repugnant," he says. "But if they are done tastefully and held down in size, I think perhaps we have to accept them. . . . We have to police it and monitor it and be guided by taste, but I don't think the advertisers want to ruin us. We are their vehicle, after all, and I think we can work with them to achieve compromises."

Others want to hold the line. Gene Roberts, a former managing editor of the New York Times and executive editor of the Philadelphia Inquirer, says front-page ads are just another in a series of industry mistakes triggered by short-term thinking. "It's one more in this kind of death by a thousand cuts that the newspaper business seems to be administering to itself," says Roberts, a journalism professor at the University of Maryland, which houses AJR. "In the long run, the big necessity is to get and maintain readers, and I think without question that front-page ads work against readership."

Roberts says newspapers didn't move away from front-page ads years ago because page one was a holy shrine. They did it because "the front page is what you have to lure readers into the rest of the paper."

What editors hear from their publishers, he says, is, "If you don't do this and you don't do that to keep the profit level up, we're going to have to cut you again." The editors translate that as, " 'Well, if I fight front-page ads I might in effect be inviting a buyout or a layoff of my staff.' "

Page-one placement can spark visceral reactions not only from journalists but also from readers. Take the case in March of the fluorescent advertising stickers (for a motor oil company and a carpet-and-flooring company) pasted atop the front page of the Hartford Courant. Reader Representative Karen Hunter received several indignant comments on her blog. "That is disgusting to have advertising on the front page of my newspaper," wrote one woman. Said another: "This has got to stop." One reader took it further, accusing the Tribune Co., the Courant's parent, of "absolutely whoring for advertising. . . . It screams, 'We're desperate!' It screams, 'Ethics be damned!' "

Hunter says the newsroom isn't crazy about the trend. She's heard complaints, but says her colleagues believe there isn't anything they can do to halt it. "I think they understand it . . . we're struggling like lots of other papers."

Not that front-page ads are all that new. But at most papers, they've been out of vogue for a while. Among the reasons the ads began to disappear: the advent of professional standards among journalists and heightened competition among publishers.

Kevin G. Barnhurst, a professor and head of the department of communication at the University of Illinois at Chicago, says that in 18th century newspapers "there was not a sharp distinction between ads and editorial matter." What's more, the blurring of news and ads didn't really disturb readers of that era. "People didn't say, 'Oh, here's advertising, here's editorial matter,' because it was all the stuff of news," Barnhurst says.

Nor did early American newspapers offer much in the way of page design. As ads and stories trickled in, they simply were dropped onto the page, starting with the first column. The newspapers generally were four pages; front and back were filled first. So the newest material went inside. "You didn't want the latest stuff on the back page or the front page—you wanted it on the inside where it wouldn't smear on people's clothes," Barnhurst says.

Michael Schudson, a professor of communication at the University of California, San Diego, says that during that era, "page one and page four were almost entirely ads, and a lot of page three was ads." News started to appear on page one in the first half of the 19th century, "but it was still common at that point for there to be a lot of advertising on the front page."

That approach began to change later in the 19th century as newspapers became more competitive, according to Schudson and Mitchell Stephens, a journalism professor and news historian at New York University. When major cities such as New York, Chicago, Philadelphia and Boston each had several newspapers, and publishers relied heavily on street sales, they began splashing more news out front as a way to lure readers.

Then, around 1914, a confluence of events portended the fading popularity of the front-page ad. "The American newspaper was at its absolute height in penetration," and journalists "were feeling their most muscular and able to define themselves as a profession," Stephens says. It was 1914 when Walter Williams—who six years earlier had founded the world's first journalism school at the University of Missouri—wrote "The Journalist's Creed." The American Society of Newspaper Editors was founded in 1922 and adopted a canon of ethics a year later; the Society of Professional Journalists approved its first ethics code in 1926.

"In the 1920s, there's a growing self-consciousness of journalists being in a profession and wanting to distinguish themselves as a profession," Schudson says. Journalists' efforts to codify their increasingly lofty ethical goals—about unbiased truth and "freedom from all obligations except fidelity to the public interest," as the ASNE canon states—distanced newspapers from their commercial origins.

None of this might have mattered so much to publishers, but it happened to coincide with another important development: Prospering financially, the publishers were shedding their partisan affiliations. They gambled that a less biased approach would elevate their standing in the community—and create an opportunity to profit from that standing. "So the commercial interest of publishers and owners converged with the professional aspirations of news workers," Barnhurst says, "and that's the moment, by the 1920s and 1930s, when what you would call the modern newspaper emerged, and that's when the model of page one emerged"—a model that did not include so many ads out front.

But today, with fewer newspapers to choose from, increasing competition from the Internet and decreasing reliance on street sales, the model is changing again. "Newspapers are in big, big trouble," Stephens says, "and I think if I were in a newsroom right now, I'd be more worried about whether I'm putting together an interesting read, a read that justifies the expense . . . and I'd worry less about the particular arrangement of the advertisers."

Barnhurst has a similar view. "There is a notion out there that somehow commerce is dirty—the sacred is what the journalist does and the profane is what the advertiser does," he says. "In fact, this is a profound confusion." What gives a town life, he suggests, is its Main Street businesses, which need to be "rubbing shoulders" with the commercial activity of the local newspaper.

ASNE Executive Director Scott Bosley says that while his organization has no official position on front-page ads, "it's not earth-shattering new ground in my view . . . it's a change, obviously, for people in this era." He recalls that when he was editor of the Journal of Commerce from 1991 to 1995, "we had a quarter-page ad on page one forever." (The Journal is available now in electronic format only.) The ad, Bosley notes, "was not the favorite thing of layout people or even of me, because sometimes it seemed intrusive."

Bosley believes most editors have arrived at the decision to accept page-one ads in consultation with their publishers, as opposed to being ordered to run them. He also thinks editors understand there's a bottom line that must be reached, and they have to help figure out how to get there. "I think we've come to the point where a lot of newspapers have realized that there's not just revenue but enhanced revenue from selling those positions, and in the market we're in, we need revenue," Bosley says.

John Kimball, senior vice president and chief marketing officer for the Newspaper Association of America, believes the challenging economic climate for newsrooms necessitates more flexibility, but he strongly rejects the notion that the page-one ad is compelled by a sense of desperation. "That just really, really drives me nuts, because that is far from reality. . . . To think that we are somehow in this death spiral, I just don't understand that," he says. He can see why that view prevails in newsrooms that have endured repeated cuts and reduced circulation, "but that's not an industry that's fighting for its life—that's one that's going through transition."

The primary impetus for the page-one ad, Kimball says, is that advertisers are increasingly demanding "new and unique and different ways to creatively use the newspaper. I think not necessarily coincidental to that is the fact that newspapers are looking for options for new revenue streams."

Advertisers want "creative shapes, things you might not have seen 10 to 15 years ago, but are exciting and fresh," Kimball says. "What's that somebody said, 'Pain helps make you focus?' When business is great, it's easy to do things the way you've always done them; when it's not so great, you look for new opportunities."

Those options include the six-column strip across the bottom of a page; the "jewel box," a rectangular, two- or three-column ad; and the "stair steps" or "cascading stairs," an ad that steps up from the left to the right of a page. More controversial are the "watermark" or "shadow" ads that appear behind sports agate or stock tables, because such ads are not separated from news content.

Will page-one ads net more business for advertisers than those inside the paper, making it worth the additional cost for them? It's too soon to tell. "We do have clients who are interested in them," says Bob Shamberg, chairman and chief executive of Newspaper Services of America, a Chicago-based firm that places newspaper ads for more than 50 clients, including Sears Holdings, Home Depot and Rite Aid. "Over time, once an advertiser gets experience with it, then they'll decide what it's worth." But if they get the same response as an interior ad, "then obviously it doesn't merit a premium."

Newspaper executives are tight-lipped about how much they're charging for page-one ads, but it's clear they cost significantly more than those inside the paper. Page one is "a premium location, so probably it's as much as the traffic would bear," says Miles Groves, a media economist and consultant in Washington, D.C.

"It is an expensive ad," says Anne Gordon, former managing editor of the Philadelphia Inquirer, which started running page-one ads on April 15. (Gordon left the Inquirer in early May to become a partner at Dubilier & Co., a private investment firm for which she oversees media, technology and entertainment companies.) She agrees that advertisers are waiting to gauge their effectiveness, and says editors wrestled with surrendering that special page-one space. "The reality of it is we spent a long time talking about it and considering it—18 months," she says.

Ultimately, Gordon adds, the Inquirer decided "we needed to be supportive of our advertisers" while maintaining enough control to make the ads palatable: "It needed to be a more dignified advertiser than, say, a mattress company." So the paper has a one-year contract with the University of Pennsylvania Health System for a page-one ad every Sunday, and is expanding that to Monday as well. The Inquirer also has been using those fluorescent stickers atop the front page. Editors assigned an Inquirer reporter to write a story explaining the economic necessity of violating the "sacred province of news."

The paper has received a handful of complaints from readers, Gordon says, but in most cases, "I think people read past this."

It's another manifestation of the Inquirer's more aggressive approach to attracting advertising dollars under its new ownership. When a local group led by former PR and ad executive Brian Tierney bought the paper last year (see "Life with Brian," August/September 2006), Tierney trumpeted his belief that former owner Knight Ridder hadn't done enough to court advertisers. In announcing that it would sell page-one ads, the Inquirer also said it would publish a new business column sponsored by Citizens Bank. The column is boxed in green, the bank's color, and the bank also has been running ads elsewhere on the business section front.

At the San Francisco Chronicle, Rosenthal says only a few readers have called to complain about his paper's page-one, lime-green boxes for utility Pacific Gas and Electric Co. "We created a couple of info boxes next to it to deal with it, so I don't think it looks that bad, personally," he says. His opinion was reinforced when he asked some friends for their views. "They didn't see it," Rosenthal says. "Journalists are very much aware of it, but I think the general public doesn't think of it as a bad thing."

He does point out one possible pitfall: There may come a day when a newspaper has to publish a negative story about a page-one advertiser, so "there's a potential for embarrassment if an advertiser . . . does something inappropriate."

At the Star Tribune, Clonts says reader reaction to section-front advertising has been minimal. One exception is a design known as the spadea, an advertising flap that wraps halfway around the front of a section, obscuring the editorial content. Clonts says it provokes "heavy and aggressively negative reader reaction. When a spadea runs, we know the following day we will get reader calls. Sometimes a few, sometimes dozens." (A 2006 study sponsored by the NAA notes that while few readers like them, 75 percent notice them, and about four in 10 usually notice what's being advertised.)

Designers tasked with making page-one ads blend with the overall look and feel of the page generally aren't thrilled about them, but they're learning to adjust. At the Star Tribune, the deputy managing editor for visuals and presentation, Cory Powell, works with the advertising department "to ensure section-front ads are as clean, simple and attractive as possible," Clonts says. The designers also have discovered that as pages get narrower, the page-one ad does have some benefits, because it works with both horizontal and vertical layouts.

"Drawing pages for the 52-inch web was easyish," Clonts says. "It got harder for the 50 and gets [harder] still for the 48. To put an ad on the front . . . to some extent simplifies things because you have to pare the elements of your fronts down to the essentials." And as the web narrowed, "the page got a lot more vertical, and things that worked best on that page tended to be vertical." He says the six-column strip ad helps square off a page, giving a design team more flexibility.

Occasionally, though, Powell will suggest that an ad be redrawn to make a page look better, Clonts says, and he'll be told it's not possible—like the time the ad department came up with a six-column strip filled with distracting automobile logos. This is what the client wants, the ad department replied. So it ran.

Denise Covert, a copy editor and page designer at the Daytona Beach News-Journal, works on regional publications that are inserted into the mainsheet. In an e-mail interview, she wrote that on some of the regional section fronts and also on the mainsheet's local front, "there are occasional front-page ads, usually 2 by 4. It works if you have a columnist or something that can easily square off with it on the bottom, but it can be a pain for some centerpiece treatments."

She adds: "In all, my personal opinion is that they're OK as long as they're not too distracting. Distracting means they are a) oddly shaped, b) garishly colored, c) black and white on a color front—we get that fairly often—or d) inconsistent, appearing some weeks and not others, so they're impossible to plan around."

Ultimately, though, newspapers may be worrying too much about ad placement. "For me, the bottom line is: Put some better stories on the top of that front page. Don't give me the same story I saw 20 hours ago" online, says NYU's Stephens. "Give me good stories, and I don't care what you put in that little ad on the bottom of the front page."

The Courant's Hunter is pragmatic, too. "I'd rather see ads inside the paper," she says. "But reality has changed."

AJR contributing writer **DONNA SHAW** (shaw@tcnj.edu) wrote about hyperlocal websites in the magazine's April/May issue.

Nonprofit News

As news organizations continue to cut back, investigative and enterprise journalism funded by foundations and the like is coming to the fore.

CAROL GUENSBURG

Since 1993, the Henry J. Kaiser Family Foundation has funded journalism training on health issues, including funneling up to $50,000 to a handful of fellows each year to support reporting projects. But, dismayed by cuts in newsroom staffing, newsholes and airtime—and the sketchy reporting that can result—foundation officials began kicking around other ways to ensure solid coverage of topics they consider crucial.

One possibility: a nonprofit health news service of their own. Matt James, senior vice president for the California-based foundation, remembers running the idea past longtime editor Bill Kovach, founding director of the Committee of Concerned Journalists and an adviser to Kaiser's media fellows program. James chuckles, a little uncomfortably, recalling the start of Kovach's generally encouraging response during a meeting last May. "He basically said, 'Five years ago . . . I would have told you to go to hell and shown you the door.'"

These days, foundations and philanthropists are finding a warmer reception.

Beleaguered journalists who once clung solely to the business model of paid advertising and circulation now recognize the urgency of developing new revenue sources for labor-intensive newsgathering. For some, foundations hold increasing promise as allies in meeting the public's information needs—beyond superficial headlines and celebrity sexploits—so long as there are safeguards for editorial independence.

"The fact of the matter is philanthropic institutions have provided millions of dollars over the years to help journalists do their work. Journalists have an unfortunate habit of not acknowledging that," says Charles Lewis, head of the nonprofit Fund for Independence in Journalism. From 1989 through 2004, he served as founding executive director of the Center for Public Integrity, which "raised and spent $30 million [on journalism projects] in the years I was there."

New forms of nonprofit, grant-funded news operations are proliferating. The lineup includes the Pulitzer Center on Crisis Reporting (see "Funding for Foreign Forays," page 32), Brandeis University's Schuster Institute for Investigative Journalism, MinnPost.com (see Drop Cap, page 14) and at least two state-level health news sites (see "Healthy Initiatives," page 31). The Washington Independent, freshly minted in January, joined the Center for Independent Media's network of four related sites in Colorado, Iowa, Michigan and Minnesota. And there are many more in the mix.

The highest-profile newcomer is ProPublica (propublica.org), an investigative news operation that opened shop in Manhattan in January (see "Big Bucks for Investigative Reporting"). California philanthropists Herbert M. and Marion O. Sandler dreamed up the project—which they're bankrolling at $10 million annually for at least three years—and hired former Wall Street Journal Managing Editor Paul E. Steiger as editor in chief. He and Managing Editor Stephen Engelberg, a former investigative editor at the New York Times, eventually will oversee a staff of about 25 reporters, editors and researchers charged with producing public interest stories of "moral force," as the website proclaims. These will be offered free to select news outlets, whose own staffs may join in the newsgathering, as well as being showcased on ProPublica's site.

The Sandlers, who made $2.4 billion when they sold the Golden West Financial Corp. savings and loan in 2006, have given millions to Democratic Party causes over the years, according to news accounts. That—and donors' often heightened emotional investment in money they've earned—prompted Slate media critic Jack Shafer to question Herbert Sandler's role as Propublica chairman (slate .com/id/2175942/). Even though the couple pledged not to interfere with editorial content, Shafer recommended that Sandler guarantee at least 10 years' funding and then resign his position, "so he'll never be tempted to bollix up what might turn out to be a good thing."

Some prominent media leaders and innovators have called for even more philanthropic support to ensure journalism's vital watchdog role.

Geneva Overholser, writing in "On Behalf of Journalism: A Manifesto for Change" (annenbergpublicpolicycenter.org/Overholser/ 20061011_JournStudy.pdf), urged a greater role for nonprofits in assisting news media. Her 2006 treatise advanced journalist Lewis' suggestion that foundations and philanthropists create a "Marshall Plan" to create more public-minded forms of news coverage. Grantmakers could "increase support for nonprofit media organizations" and "foster new nonprofit media models," wrote Overholser, a Missouri School of Journalism professor. She also recommended steps for corporations, journalists, government and the public.

Jan Schaffer, executive director of the interactive journalism incubator J-Lab, introduced a "Citizen Media" report (kcnn.org/research/ citmedia_introduction/) last February by writing that community foundations should "be alert to real possibilities for building community capacity" by supporting citizen media. "Journalism alone will not suffice," she elaborated in a phone interview. "I think foundations and philanthropies will play a role in supplementing that information landscape."

Dan Gillmor, in a September 17 op-ed published in the San Francisco Chronicle (sfgate.com/cgi-bin/article.cgi?file=/c/a/2007/09/17/ED1OS4OIU.DTL) and timed for a Council on Foundations' conference there, urged community foundations to "put the survival of quality local journalism squarely on their own agendas." Gillmor—who in January launched the Knight Center for Digital Media Entrepreneurship at Arizona State University's Walter Cronkite School of Journalism—suggested measures such as paying the salary of a local investigative journalist or providing seed funding for a network of local blogs and media sites, adding journalism training for participants.

And Alberto Ibargüen, president and CEO of the John S. and James L. Knight Foundation, publicly addressed those San Francisco conferees with a like-minded appeal, warning: "If the citizens are unaware, then the democracy is in peril." Knight and the council will cohost a seminar February 20 and 21 on communities' information needs in a democracy. Up to 200 community-foundation representatives will meet in Coral Gables, Florida, to consider media trends, the digital revolution, gaps in coverage and how these might be filled.

Foundations see their growing involvement as compensating for newsrooms' diminished coverage of civic issues. They're stepping in because "the traditional news business is not investing as much as it needs to . . . in getting reporters out to cover stories," Kaiser's James pointedly notes. "We as nonprofits have a duty to figure out: Is there a role for us, in increased training, in direct partnerships with news organizations or even [in] creating a new news service to fill that void?

"What we're talking about is supporting real journalism, not advocacy," adds James, whose foundation already partners with National Public Radio, USA Today, the Washington Post and other news media on public opinion research projects. "We're big believers in the role of journalism in democracy. We believe it's important for nonprofits to find ways to support it."

With newspaper revenue tanking as classified and retail advertisers migrate to the Web and Wall Street tightens its grip, journalists are casting about for financial lifelines. Foundations have the wherewithal to throw some: By law, they must spend a minimum 5 percent of their net assets each year on charitable causes. In 2005, U.S. foundations granted $158 million for media and communications, the Foundation Center reports, though it doesn't break down whether the payouts went for journalism per se or marketing or research dissemination. Nor does that figure necessarily reflect spending on journalism-related education.

Journalism's funders include those affiliated with legacy news media—such as Annenberg, Scripps, Tribune, Reynolds, Gannett—plus longtime supporters like Carnegie, Ford and the Pew Charitable Trusts. (AJR has received support from the Freedom Forum, Ford, Knight, Pew and Carnegie.)

Knight, the leading journalism funder overall, announced more than $21 million in journalism grants in 2006 and more than $50 million in 2007, though some of these are multiyear grants and won't be paid out all at once. "There are years when we are not the largest [journalism] grantmaker," Eric Newton, its vice president for journalism initiatives, said in an e-mail interview. Since the foundation's start in 1950, it has invested nearly $300 million in U.S. and global journalism—emphasizing mid-career training in the 1980s, journalism education in the 1990s and digital media innovation in the current decade.

Knight has contributed to journalism philanthropy in another fundamental way. Shortly after joining the foundation in 2001, Newton—former managing editor of the Newseum and, before that, the Oakland Tribune—helped pull together an informal group of program officers from legacy media foundations and others interested in journalism. Participants included the Bill & Melinda Gates Foundation, which in November announced a three-year, $1.7 million grant to the International Center for Journalists to support Knight health fellowships in sub-Saharan Africa.

"We think all foundations should care about the information needs of communities in a democracy," Newton says.

Done right, the journalism-funder relationship benefits both parties as well as the public they aim to serve. It supplies important news resources, and it satisfies a grantmaker's mission—maybe even bringing a touch of prestige. Done wrong, the association raises concerns about editorial objectivity and whether it has been compromised by a funder's agenda.

It's instructive to look at, or listen to, NPR, perhaps the most successful model of nonprofit journalism. The privately supported membership organization derived a third of its revenue from grants, contributions and sponsorships in 2005. Its biggest revenue share (39 percent) came from programming fees paid by member stations, which conduct their own fundraising.

"We're always engaged in very constructive discussions with the world of philanthropy," says NPR President Kevin Klose, who describes himself as an active participant. The conversations emphasize editorial control, "the starting point for us. . . . One of the reasons why we are attractive to foundations and to corporate sponsorship is because of the integrity and independence of what we do. They wish to align themselves with that set of values."

They probably don't mind that their names, and information they care about, reach 26 million pairs of ears.

Klose says he engages with the foundation world not just to gain financial support. "It's also important to us," he explains, to learn "what people are thinking about. These are often very socially aware organizations that track issues naturally of interest to news organizations."

A sturdy firewall separates NPR's news and business operations. Barbara Hall spent more than 14 years on its fund-raising side, serving as vice president of development through late August 2006. (Near the end of her run her group generated more than $50 million a year, excluding a $230 million bequest from Joan B. Kroc in 2004.)

Over that time, Hall saw a shift in funders' strategies. "The best gift any nonprofit can get is unrestricted support. But the trend we've seen with foundations, and increasingly with individuals, is wanting to designate their support for specific issues and topics," says Hall, who left to head development for the Phillips Collection, an art museum in Washington, D.C. While "most foundations understand that news organizations are not advocacy groups," she adds, "now they're being very focused on what they're supporting and its impact."

"Funders may have their own interests—they often do," Klose says, but they can't dictate story focus. "We're very interested in philanthropic support of a whole range of activities: coverage of foreign news, coverage of children, family and education. We have a foreign desk, a national desk, a political desk. That's what people fund."

By designating funding, a grantmaker aims to raise the visibility of an issue or area and expand public knowledge.

Big Bucks for Investigative Reporting

When its imminent launch was announced last fall, Pro-Publica brought a double-barreled blast of attention to nonprofit news media. It wasn't just the premise of an independent newsroom devoted to investigative reporting, an endangered species in an era of down-sizing; it was the promise of $10 million-a-year backing to ensure hard-hitting stories that would be given away to other news outlets.

Founders Herbert M. and Marion O. Sandler committed that chunk of their personal fortune—burnished by the 2006 sale of their Golden West Financial Corp. savings and loan to the Wachovia Corp.—to support the stated mission of "producing journalism that shines a light on exploitation of the weak by the strong and on the failures of those with power to vindicate the trust placed in them."

Additional one-time grants are coming from the John D. and Catherine T. MacArthur Foundation ($250,000) and the Atlantic Philanthropies and JEHT Foundation ($25,000 each).

ProPublica's editor in chief is Paul E. Steiger, who led the Wall Street Journal to 16 Pulitzer Prizes while serving as managing editor from 1991 until last May. As his managing editor, Steiger tapped Stephen Engelberg, a managing editor at Portland's Oregonian who'd earlier been an investigative editor for the New York Times. They'll direct a staff of about 25 reporters, editors and researchers based in a Manhattan newsroom and doing stories of national import.

By mid-November, ProPublica had received roughly 400 résumés "from essentially every major news organization in the country," says General Manager Richard Tofel, who worked with Steiger at the Wall Street Journal and most recently was a vice president of the Rockefeller Foundation.

The organization, which launched in January, will gear up during early 2008, regularly spotlighting others' investigative reports on its website (propublica.org) while developing its own projects.

Steiger says he has spoken with representatives of leading newspapers, magazines and television news outlets about carrying ProPublica projects. With those that are "90 percent done, we'll be looking for a collaborator who can give the most impact and visibility," Steiger says. "For collaborations that we might start at an early stage, we'll be looking at where there would be mutual advantage" for another news outlet to join in the reporting and editing. ProPublica will publish the work on its own site, in some cases simultaneously with the news organization.

As Michael Miner observed in the Chicago Reader, this approach probably cuts out news organizations—especially those far from population centers—with the fewest resources to keep the powerful in check.

Editorial independence will be crucial not just to ProPublica but to the news organizations disseminating or partnering on its stories. And it may be a challenge to overcome newsrooms' preference for stories they've produced internally.

For example, Philadelphia Inquirer Editor William K. Marimow says he's "agonized a lot about ProPublica." Though he's confident that, "with Paul at the helm, they'll do great work," Marimow expressed concern about a news organization ceding any editorial control. "When it comes to investigative reporting, it's my belief that top editors need to take responsibility from the get-go," he says. "A hybrid project creates diffuse responsibility."

—C.G.

The Carnegie Corp. of New York, for instance, gave NPR $200,000 last year to support education coverage. It began subsidizing that around the 2000 election, says Susan Robinson King, vice president of external affairs and director of the journalism initiative at Carnegie. Back then, NPR "had one reporter who sometimes covered education. . . . They were able with our money to hire a producer and really increase the level of reporting."

Dynamic social forces affect nonprofit journalism as readily as commercial news operations. Shifts in the economy boost or deflate endowments. Developments in research, demographics or regional politics, changes in leadership or board structure—all can affect attitudes and funding priorities. No wonder only a quarter of all grants get renewed.

I absorbed these lessons as founding director of Journalism Fellowships in Child and Family Policy from early 2000 through mid-2005. The professional development program, based at the Philip Merrill College of Journalism at the University of Maryland, awarded competitive fellowships for all-expense-paid conferences featuring expert briefings and skills training. Select fellows also received project support of up to $25,000 for six months. They contributed to scores of outlets, including NPR, the Chicago Tribune, the Austin American-Statesman, Reuters, Salon, Mother Jones,

Reader's Digest, Portland's Oregonian, the Milwaukee Journal Sentinel, the Village Voice, WBUR-FM in Boston and Pacific News Service.

Ruby Takanishi, president of the Foundation for Child Development, a private philanthropy in New York, helped conceive the program and make sure it was funded generously. Her goal was to invest in journalists, particularly young ones who might have a more lasting impact in shaping the news, and "really improve the depth of reporting" on child and family policy, she says. Initially there was no limit to what fellows might explore in conference briefings or their own research: the impact of welfare reform on families, harsh "zero-tolerance" policies that criminalized youth, brain research on toddlers, the growing reliance on grandparents for foster care.

The expansive approach began to narrow after four years. The foundation had been concentrating its other funding on three subjects—children of immigrants, education from pre-kindergarten through third grade and an index of child well-being—and "some very strong voices on our board" wondered why these weren't getting more coverage from the news media, Takanishi recalls. The board decided the fellowship program's training and projects should be more clearly aligned with those issues for any future grants. At the time, we had a multiyear grant good through mid-2005.

I'd come out of newspapers, editing and reporting mostly on the features side. I tried to equate the tightening scope as something

Healthy Initiatives

Carol Gentry doesn't think "it's any mystery why health care is bubbling up so early" as the focus of at least two non-profit, state-level news services. "People don't understand how it works," says Gentry, founding editor of the year-old FloridaHealthNews.org. "It's hard to get good coverage, particularly at the local and state level."

There's another basic reason. "It's where the money is," explains Carol DeVita, a researcher at the Urban Institute's Center on Nonprofits and Philanthropy. The news services largely are supported by so-called "conversion" foundations, created when nonprofit hospitals were sold to for-profit providers. Dozens of states have required that proceeds from charitable assets be redirected to support community health—through efforts such as clinics, immunization programs and research.

The Kansas Health Institute, an independent, nonprofit policy and research organization in Topeka, in January 2007 introduced the online KHI News Service to cover state health policy. It has four staff journalists with newspaper backgrounds. It features daily spot news stories and a weekly centerpiece. A recent one examined whether a proposed tobacco tax increase could provide reliable funding for health reform.

Vice President for Public Affairs Jim McLean says the free service primarily reaches legislators, government staffers and lobbyists, though it's also intended for consumers. KHI stories have been picked up by the Topeka Capital-Journal (where McLean was a managing editor) and assorted small papers. McLean hopes to increase distribution this year by introducing story budgets to help editors plan.

The institute gets its funding mostly from philanthropy, with some project-based funding from state and federal agencies. The editorial staff works independently, McLean emphasizes, and "there's no advocacy mission at all."

Florida's independent online news service covers a wide range of state and local health issues. Launched in March 2007 primarily as a news aggregator, the St. Petersburg-based FloridaHealthNews.org tracked health care bills when the Legislature was in session and posted original stories. Until mid-December, it had one paid staffer, part-time Managing Editor Pat Curtis, as well as a paid intern. Gentry has signed up a Tallahassee correspondent and is recruiting stringers around the state. She herself didn't start drawing a paycheck until mid-December, instead logging volunteer hours while reporting on health full time for the Tampa Tribune. She resigned from the paper in late November, after the Florida Health Policy Center—a partnership of eight foundations—approved $183,000 in new grants. The center had provided seed money of $59,200 for the news service's first year.

Gentry says she'll "outsource the fundraising, the marketing, the advertising. We want, as much as we can, to have a firewall between the newsroom and the business side. . . . That's the most important thing, that people can trust us as journalists."

A decade ago, the Oakland-based nonprofit California HealthCare Foundation introduced a health news aggregation site, California Healthline. Now, it may add experienced journalists to produce "in-depth health care reporting in partnership with media organizations," says David Olmos, a former Los Angeles Times reporter and editor who in the fall stepped down as the foundation's communications director. He's researching the project, which might entail partnering with newspapers, public radio and television stations or other news organizations. Like ProPublica, the new nonprofit news outlet for investigative reporting, its services "almost certainly would be free," Olmos says.

Its mission would be "tackling some larger issues that are not sufficiently covered in California," which Olmos describes as "a proving ground or laboratory for some of the health efforts" relevant nationwide.

Both he and Gentry say these niche news services may serve as templates for other areas of coverage, such as education or the environment. Says Olmos: "It's going to be really important that these start-up ventures are thoughtful."

—C.G.

---

akin to the challenge of producing stories for the ad-driven annual dining guide or cruise travel section or the fall prep sports guide. With some effort, you could come up with fresh, worthwhile stories for the dedicated space. But there was a crucial difference: While it was relatively easy to develop briefings and story ideas for covering immigrants and early education, there was no guarantee of real estate or airtime in others' newsrooms.

Our program's compressed focus, combined with industry-wide newsroom cuts in staffing and newsholes, made the fellowships a tougher sell. In the end, my advisory board, my boss at the college of journalism and I decided to seek a final, yearlong grant—which we got—and then put the program to rest.

Most of the former fellows who'd gotten project support said their work wouldn't have proceeded as quickly—or at all—without financial assistance and guidance. Their comments dovetail with those of other journalists who've received fellowships elsewhere—from the Alicia Patterson Foundation, Kaiser and the New America Foundation, to name a few. Funding enabled them to report on issues they cared about passionately. And it's important work, judging from some stories' impact and honors.

Out of my program alone, for instance, reporting by Barbara White Stack of the Pittsburgh Post-Gazette ultimately led the Pennsylvania Superior Court to rule that child-welfare dependency courts should be open to the public. Eric Eyre of the Charleston Gazette, reporting with then-colleague Scott Finn, exposed the high social costs of school consolidation in rural West Virginia. That project, which documented schoolchildren's hours-long bus rides, slowed the consolidation movement and won the Education Writers Association's grand prize in 2003.

Over the years, newsroom leaders and staff repeatedly told me that outside funding from various nonprofit programs validated their journalistic ambitions for projects while delivering vital budget relief.

"It's made a huge difference here. The majority of the long-term investigative projects that we do here would not have been possible" otherwise, says Eyre, a nine-year veteran of the Gazette. The privately owned paper circulates 48,000 copies daily and 74,000 on Sunday. Eyre also won a 2006 Kaiser Media Fellowship in health, which equipped him to do a project on poor oral health in his state.

Funding for Foreign Forays

With backing from one of journalism's pedigreed families, the Pulitzer Center on Crisis Reporting opened in early 2006 to promote foreign affairs coverage in U.S. media.

The center provides travel grants to journalists—mostly freelancers but also news organization staffers—to do in-depth stories about war-torn, exploited or overlooked lands and people. For instance, it helped send a reporter and photographer from North Carolina's Fayetteville Observer to Afghanistan to chronicle U.S. soldiers' rebuilding efforts there at "Fort Bragg East." It has subsidized stories exploring government corruption in Colombia, Maoist activity in India and an American-led effort to save a Mozambique national park devastated by civil war. It has awarded at least 40 grants to date, with most ranging from $3,000 to $10,000.

"I knew from my own experience that if you got a small grant that got you somewhere, you could turn it into something important," says Jon Sawyer, the center's director. He'd reported from five dozen countries while working in the St. Louis Post-Dispatch's Washington bureau from 1980 through 2005. In that last year, as his paper and other Pulitzer holdings were being sold to Lee Enterprises (see "Lee Who?" June/July 2005), Sawyer proposed the center.

He found a backer in Emily Rauh Pulitzer, once his former chain's principal shareholder. "There's [been] a terrible diminution of quality and a strong cutting back of information about what's going on in the rest of the world," says Pulitzer, a center trustee. "That's incomprehensible, because as the world gets smaller, we need to understand more about it."

She put up $250,000 annually for four years to launch the center and another $250,000 to support educational outreach. Other initial donors include David Moore—a grandson of the first Joseph Pulitzer and a longtime Pulitzer Inc. director—and his wife, Katherine.

The initiative started out as "a modest idea," Sawyer says, but it has quickly grown in scope and reach. The Pulitzer Center is an independent division of the World Security Institute—itself a sponsor of journalism and scholarship—which provides office space in Washington, D.C., staff resources and plenty of synergy. The institute produces "Foreign Exchange," a weekly global affairs program for public television. Pulitzer is the primary supplier of its "In Focus" slice-of-life video segment. Pulitzercenter.org features grantees' blogs from the field. The center also set up a channel on YouTube, whose editors in December featured Pulitzercenter.org at the top of their "News and Politics" page and praised its videos as "some of the most moving journalism you'll find on this site."

Sawyer speaks enviously of the financing of ProPublica, a lavishly funded new investigative reporting enterprise (see "Big Bucks for Investigative Reporting," page 29), even though it's clear he's mastering the art of the deal. He assembled multiple supporters for a Palm Beach Post series last November on "Heroes of HIV" in the Caribbean. First, Pulitzer sponsored reporter Antigone Barton's fellowship with the International Center for Journalists to spend three weeks reporting in Haiti and the Dominican Republic. Then Sawyer arranged for Barton to get a National Press Foundation fellowship to the International AIDS Society conference in Sydney, Australia, which included a week's training on HIV. With part of a $102,000 grant from New York's MAC AIDS Fund, the center hired a videographer and Web producer to accompany Barton to the Caribbean. Three of their videos appeared on "Foreign Exchange"; all are on the Pulitzer website, along with interviews and other materials. "He is extremely resourceful," Barton says of Sawyer. "He had a vision of what this could be."

Pulitzer grantees' work has been carried by the Post-Dispatch, Smithsonian magazine, NPR, the New York Times, the Washington Times, the Christian Science Monitor and other outlets. But if Sawyer and Associate Director Nathalie Applewhite believe in an idea, they'll approve funding even without a news organization's prior commitment.

They invested $13,000 to help Utah-based freelance reporter Loretta Tofani travel several times to China for a project on how the lack of safety precautions led to sometimes fatal injuries and illnesses in almost every Chinese industry that exports to the United States. Tofani—who won a Pulitzer Prize reporting for the Washington Post before joining the Philadelphia Inquirer and spending years as its China correspondent—had lined up a news outlet, but that fell through with a change in management. She offered the nearly complete project to the Salt Lake Tribune, which accepted it overnight with the proviso that Tofani localize the story. Tofani says she gladly spent the next month "running all over the state and talking with people about work conditions in the factories they were using."

In October, the Tribune published a four-part series, "American Imports, Chinese Deaths." Editor Nancy Conway says she's "glad that we had the opportunity to work with Loretta and to publish the stories," for which she paid $5,000. The only drawback, says Conway: "It would have been better if we had been in on the story from the beginning."

Sawyer agrees. He wants newsrooms "to be as closely involved as they can be. We're not competing with anybody. We're trying to partner with everybody."

—Carol Guensburg

Colleague Ken Ward received an Alicia Patterson fellowship to examine the coal industry—in December 2005, a month before the deadly Sago mine collapse. He delayed starting the fellowship while contributing breaking stories, then used it to produce a Gazette series on U.S. mine safety and a Washington Monthly article on the Bush administration's mine safety policies. Investigative Reporters and Editors honored Ward's series with a medal—its highest award—and the PBS documentary series "Exposé" focused on Ward's work in a program originally broadcast in November.

"We were pretty happy for them to do this," Ward says. "It certainly made us look good."

Editors in some other places endorse training but decline grant support for newsroom projects. If a story is important enough, they say, they'll find money for it in the budget. They don't want the merest hint of outside influence. Nor do they want to be constrained by a donor's funding scope.

In 2006, as editor of the Lexington Herald-Leader in Kentucky, Marilyn W. Thompson wanted her paper to undertake a major project examining Republican Sen. Mitch McConnell's political fundraising practices and suggestions of influence peddling. When she realized her lean newsroom budget alone wouldn't cover it, Thompson got her Knight Ridder bosses' enthusiastic approval to seek a grant from the nonprofit Center for Investigative Reporting. The California-based center provided $37,500 to underwrite the salary of reporter John Cheves, who took an unpaid six-month leave of absence to do the project, as well as to cover expenses.

Just before the October publication of Cheves' four-part series, "Price Tag Politics," McConnell staff members complained of liberal bias—at the center. They cited center board and staff members' donations to Democratic candidates or causes. They called it "a known liberal entity, but what they seized on was the underlying funding," Thompson remembers. In particular, the McConnell camp objected to involvement by the Deer Creek Foundation of St. Louis, which had funded groups seeking campaign finance reform. McConnell had led the fight against the bipartisan measure in Congress and in court. He was the lead plaintiff in McConnell v. Federal Election Commission, an unsuccessful U.S. Supreme Court challenge to the 2002 law.

By the time the McConnell complaints surfaced, both the newsroom's ownership and leadership had changed. In June, the paper had been acquired by McClatchy; in July, Thompson had gone to the Los Angeles Times as national investigations editor. McClatchy officials "brought me in on several conference calls" before deciding to reimburse the funder, Thompson says. Now an investigative reporter for the New York Times, Thompson says she was disappointed by the decision. Cheves' work—published that October—was excellent and error-free, she says, and "no one likes the suggestion that their reporting was in any way biased."

That was precisely why McClatchy's vice president for news, Howard Weaver, returned the center's grant. "I'm not uncomfortable with the journalism, and I'm certainly not uncomfortable with the journalist," the Herald-Leader quoted Weaver as saying at the time. "I just think that the relationship [with the outside groups] was sufficiently unorthodox that we don't need to do it."

The incident made a lasting impression at the center. While there always has been "a complete firewall" between editorial and fundraising, since then "we have made the case more strenuously to funders that we would prefer general operating support as opposed to project-specific support," says Christa Scharfenberg, the center's associate director. (Funding for the McConnell project had come from money Deer Creek had designated for campaign finance coverage.)

And in mid-December, the center's board voted to offer the executive director job to Robert J. Rosenthal, former managing editor of the San Francisco Chronicle. He accepted. "We decided the organization was ready to grow and evolve," Scharfenberg says. "We wanted an experienced, highly regarded journalist at the helm, which we think also will deflect concerns about the journalistic integrity of the organization."

Takanishi of the Foundation for Child Development believes foundations and journalists have "a shared future" because of the public's right to know. She also encourages "more critical coverage of philanthropy. . . . It exists in the public trust, so it should be open for examination." But "how do foundations, by making grants, [best] support journalism?" she muses. "How does journalism cover philanthropy? It's sort of biting the hand that feeds you."

Edward Wasserman, the Knight Professor of Journalism Ethics at Washington and Lee University in Lexington, Virginia, agrees that foundation handouts can put recipients at a disadvantage. "Who's going to do the story on the Knight Foundation?" he asks rhetorically, noting his own endowed teaching position. The funder does "a good but not infallible job. The news organizations that should be reporting on them can't," at least not impartially. "Most of the people in media have one eye out for where the money might be coming from."

The plight is a familiar one in many newsrooms, though with different players. Is there "any real difference between advertiser influence and donor influence on editorial sanctity? There shouldn't be," says Lewis, of the Fund for Independence in Journalism. A journalist in residence at American University, he maintains that nonprofit journalism ventures can "basically ensure transparency and credibility, sometimes more so than a commercial outlet does."

To preserve newsgathering integrity, nonprofits "must disclose their donors," Lewis says. "I happen to think it's important to have some discretion about whose money you accept. There are some other schools of thought about that," he acknowledges. "Make sure, to the extent possible, that the journalist inside the nonprofit newsroom doesn't have substantial interaction with the donors"—a condition he couldn't follow as both editor and publisher at the Center for Public Integrity, he admits.

Wasserman says he's especially uneasy with "an almost direct line between funder and news organization," a structure emerging in health news services. "I could very readily see that this opens the door for various trade coalitions to bankroll reporting that could in itself be perfectly OK, but, in terms of subject matter, would have a tilt toward topics of greatest interest to the funders: biofuels coverage funded by Archer Daniels Midland. You get into a murky area pretty quickly."

But Missouri's Overholser is less wary of foundations developing their own news media outlets. "There are a lot of ways to do journalism in the public interest," says Overholser, who also chairs the Center for Public Integrity's board and serves on a handful of other nonprofit journalism boards. "The only key here is transparency. . . . An educated consumer should be able to see who put [a report] together, who funded it, what are the underlying goals. . . . I welcome partisan information, as long as it's labeled. What worries me is deceit, when we get people playing on the public stage who don't acknowledge their money is coming from the left wing or the right wing. . . . We need to have some reliable sources whose goal is to be nonpartisan, to report whatever they find—no matter how unsettling to their funders."

Overholser, like others interviewed for this story, expresses confidence that nonprofit news operations will flourish. She believes these may even bolster their for-profit counterparts.

"I never for a moment think nonprofits are going to supplant commercial media," she says. "The existence of nonprofits can strengthen the journalism done by commercial media. Nonprofits can be more fearless, in some ways, because they don't have to worry" about offending the powerful or risking popularity.

CAROL GUENSBURG (carol.guensburg@verizon.net) is senior editor for the *Journalism Center on Children & Families,* a University of Maryland professional program—and a nonprofit. It receives primary support from the Annie E. Casey Foundation. Guensburg spent 14 years as an editor and reporter for the *Milwaukee Journal Sentinel* after working for three other papers.

From *American Journalism Review,* February/March 2008, pp. 26–33. Copyright © 2008 by the Philip Merrill College of Journalism at the University of Maryland, College Park, MD 20742-7111. Reprinted with permission.

Open for Business

**If you want readers to buy news, what, exactly, will you sell?
The case for a free/paid hybrid.**

Michael Shapiro

In the dark winter and spring of 2009, as dispatches from the news business grew ever more grim, as Jim Romenesko's posts took on the feel of casualty reports, newsrooms across the land began to feel like the Emerald City when the Wicked Witch soars overhead, trailing smoke and sending everyone scurrying not for cover, but for an answer, to the Wizard. So it was that in the midst of this gloomy time help appeared, and not merely the illusion of a wizardly hand. It came from Walter Isaacson and from Steven Brill, who were quickly joined by a determined chorus that, no longer willing to stand idly by as its trade died, took up a call that was clear, direct, and seemingly unassailable in its logic: *make the readers pay.*

They envisioned a happy time in which people so loved, or at least appreciated, what journalists did that they would pay to listen, watch, and read online. Excited by the prospect of compensation commensurate with their best efforts, news people raced to find evidence to support this encouraging talk. Suddenly, Peter Kann, dismissed as hopelessly un-Webby when he placed *The Wall Street Journal* behind a paywall in 1996, was being touted in retirement as a man so prescient about revenue streams that Rupert Murdoch, who had taken over Dow Jones with thoughts of bringing that wall down, was now preaching the wisdom of charging for access. People pointed to the money that came from subscribers to such sites as *Congressional Quarterly, Consumer Reports,* and *Cook's Illustrated* as evidence that Isaacson, who had made his case first at a speech this winter at the Aspen Institute and then on the cover of *Time,* had been right. Readers not only would pay, but were already paying. They paid for information and for access to newspaper websites, too—in places like Little Rock, Albuquerque, and Lewiston, Idaho. They paid by the year, the month, the week. Perhaps they might even pay by the story—a micropayment, like for a song on iTunes.

But then, as often happens when euphoria is built on hope born of despair, the good feelings began to recede. The readers-will-pay chorus was ever more drowned out by the voices of the doomsayers, the apostles of information-wants-to-be-free.

Paid content, they insisted, was an illusion. Take a closer look at the sites that charge, they argued, and you will see flaws in your logic: for one, many of them cater to audiences of narrow interest—lobbyists compelled to follow legislation through every subcommittee; business people whose firms cover the costs, so that they might make a buck at the expense of their competitors; lovers of the best, kitchen-tested recipe for Yankee pot roast. And as for those few newspapers that had gotten away with charging for Web access, note that almost all were small, or the sole purveyors of news for hundreds of miles around. These voices were joined by those who saw in the vanishing of the American newspaper a necessary death—much like the Israelites wandering the desert for forty years, waiting for those wed to the old ways to die out.

And so it went, variations on familiar themes that tended to leave little room for the clutter of a middle ground. The back and forth produced a stalemate on the difficult question of whether it was possible, or reasonable, to expect people to pay for news that they had come to believe should be free.

But it obscured the big questions that, logic suggested, would have to come next: If you were going to charge, what, precisely, were you going to sell? And if you sold something new, would that alter, or even revolutionize, the nature of the news?

One

In the beginning, there was the 900 number.

The service had been around for decades when, in 1987, AT&T allowed businesses leasing 900 numbers to charge for calls. People started to pay—for sports scores, news, weather, and stock quotes. Men also paid, sometimes quite a lot, to listen to women talk dirty. The change in dialing habits revolutionized the *idea* of the phone call. The telephone was no longer merely a device that allowed for remote conversation at minimal cost. It became a vehicle for running a business—you could make money with a phone, so long as you sold what people wanted to buy.

That lesson was not lost with the coming of the Internet. Even as people fretted about whether anyone would figure out a way to make a buck online, the pornographers, ever on the vanguard, shifted technologies and began charging not merely for a voice, but for a peek. Others took notice, with higher aspirations. Even as the early apostles of Web culture extolled the virtues of every-man-a-publisher, content did, in fact, go on sale.

Some of it sold. Much didn't—or at least not enough, in the news business, to make up for all the potential lost advertising revenue that has always been the financial backbone of the industry. Slate charged for access for about a year, only to reverse itself in 1999. The *Los Angeles Times* charged for CalenderLive, only to drop the fee in 2005, after twenty-one months of declining page views and modest revenue. *Variety* and Salon took down their paywalls, as did many of the handful of small newspapers that had charged—among them the *Creston* (Iowa) *News Advertiser,* the *Newton* (Iowa) *Daily News,* and the *Aiken* (South Carolina) *Standard,* whose page views tripled after its wall came down in 2007. *The New York Times* ended Times-Select in 2007, having calculated—at that time—that it could more than make up for the $10 million in lost revenue with the advertising generated by all the many new visitors to its site.

Still, there were holdouts, and the titan among the paid-content stalwarts was and remains *The Wall Street Journal,* which continues to charge subscribers $100 annually. While the number of subscribers has grown steadily to its present one million, they pale in comparison to the 20 million monthly unique visitors to *The New York Times,* which, for the moment, remains entirely free—but may not be for much longer.

The sense among the free-content advocates, though, is that the *Journal,* great as it is, is an outlier, a publication not written for a general audience but for the world of commerce. The same was being said of other specialized online publications that cater to people with a financial stake in the news they provided. The growing online presence of the trade press, in the view of the believers in free content, meant only that people already conditioned to spending hundreds or thousands of dollars a year for the brand of news that served their particular needs were now logging on, and not waiting for the newsletter to arrive.

Besides, walled-off content meant content that was not searchable, which meant that it did not draw the great flows of online traffic in a world where the hyperlink had become the coin of commerce and notice.

Sites like CQ.com—which boasted a multitude of databases, brought in about 43 percent of *CQ*'s annual revenue (somewhere between $50 million and $100 million; the company is privately held and will be no more precise about earnings), and had a large editorial staff (CQ Inc. employs more than 165 people)—while admired for the work they produced, were nonetheless relegated to the fringe because they were not part of the greater, link-driven conversation. And hadn't *CQ* subsequently started a free site, CQ Politics, which, while it generated less than 2 percent of the company's revenue, did attract an average of 450,000 uniques a month, ensuring that *CQ* was not left out of Washington's overheated political conversation?

The criticism was much the same for those sites that sold news whose value was not necessarily fungible—politically or financially, either in money earned (the business-to-business press) or in money well spent (*Consumer Reports*). These sites sold news that mattered only because everyone in particular slivers of the online world was talking about it. These were the sites that had occupied small pockets of Chris Anderson's Long Tail, his theory about the rise of niche businesses online. Places like Orangebloods.com.

Orangebloods is a site that, depending on the time of year, has between eight thousand and ten thousand subscribers paying $9.99 a month, or $100 annually, for steady updates about all known thought regarding the University of Texas football team. The site covers practices and assesses the team's strengths and potential worries, but the least important thing it does is cover games. Everyone covers games, the reasoning went, and everyone *watches* games. So instead, Orangebloods found a niche within a niche: it reports and sells what no one else can provide, which is year-round coverage of Longhorns recruiting. Its reporters fan out across the state, and sometimes across the nation, meeting, observing, and collecting footage of leading high-school football players. They then pour all this into the Orangebloods site along with information about those potential Longhorns' size, speed, bench-pressing capacity, and GPAs, all the while offering interviews, commentary, starred rankings, and candid assessments of the Longhorns' chances of securing a commitment: *Solid verbal!*

Orangebloods is one of the 130 paid college-football sites that are part of Rivals.com, which Yahoo bought in 2007 for $100 million. Rivals is run by Bobby Burton, who in the early 1990s, as an undergraduate at Texas, worked in the football team's film library, converting film to video and then editing the footage so that coaches could study, say, tendencies on third and long. Burton took that passion—he uses the word often—to the *National Recruiting Advisor,* a newsletter that reported on recruiting and augmented its service with updates on, yes, a 900 number.

The business went through several iterations—free, then paid, then failing—before re-emerging in 2001. By then Burton had abandoned the idea of using citizen journalists to do his reporting for him, having determined that he needed professionals. In time, the combined editorial staff at Rivals grew to over three hundred and, as the site's reputation grew among the college-football cognoscenti, its subscriptions rose to its present 200,000; Orangebloods is among the most popular.

And that popularity, that desire to subscribe, says its editor, Geoff Ketchum, is as much about the news it reports as it is about the talking and ruminating with an audience that cares beyond all apparent reason about Longhorn football. They make full use of the site's message board, offering lengthy and deeply-felt opinions, and talk with one another with such familiarity that when one subscriber's child was diagnosed with cancer, his online friends raised money for treatment.

"We're like heroin for UT football fans. We've got all the nuts that exist. We cover what the people want to pay for."

—Geoff Ketchum

"We're like heroin for UT football fans," Ketchum says. "We've got all the nuts that exist." He says this with the affection of someone who recognizes his own. "We don't cover all the sports," he adds. "We cover what the people want to pay for."

Two

But would the people pay for news aimed not at the few but at the many? As zealots on either side of the pay divide duked it out, Nancy Wang ran the numbers. The news was not good. For either side.

Wang, who with her husband, Jeff Mignon, runs a Manhattan media consulting firm, crunched nine different scenarios for newspapers of two different approximate sizes—100,000 paid circulation and 50,000. (Here her base scenario was for a most typical American paper, which has 50,000 circulation, publishes seven days a week, charges $17 a month for print subscribers, has a website with 250,000 unique visitors, and online revenues of $700,000.) The analysis, Wang says, were based on real numbers, but were intended as projections of potential, not actual, revenue.

Her conclusions, which were reported in March 2009 by the Newspaper Association of America, essentially boiled down to this: once a newspaper put all its content behind a paywall, online subscriptions dropped dramatically and those subscriptions did not come close to making up lost advertising revenue. The advertising projections, she explains, were based on "very conservative," pre-recession numbers. "It's hard to say that putting in a paid model for content would pay on its own," she says.

But her results were not all that encouraging for the free-content crowd, either—those who advocate an advertising-only model despite the fact that revenue for online ads, though rising, is a fraction of what it is for print.

The online scenario that worked best, she concluded, was a compromise—combining free and paid content, at a percentage of 80 to 20, free to paid. But, she cautions, "there has to be something that people are willing to pay for."

Could that "something" be local news? Wang built her analysis on numbers from the NAA, the media buyers AdPerfect and Centro, as well as from Borrell Associates, a Virginia consulting firm whose president, Gordon Borrell, had for years preached that publishers were wrong if they continued to believe that local news as currently constituted would sell.

Borrell had begun his career as a reporter for *The Virginian-Pilot,* and so came to his conclusion with an understanding and empathy for the work reporters do. The problem, as he saw it, was that newspapers assumed they could continue to sell what he regarded as a tired and tedious product in a new medium simply because they had done so well selling it in an old one.

Borrell had issued his first comprehensive study on paid content shortly after the 9/11 attacks, a time when the public was devouring news, and so a moment when the prospect of online revenue would be running high. He surveyed nearly 1,900 online-newspaper readers and discovered that while people were willing to register for sites—a necessity in attracting advertisers—and might be willing to pay for some news, they were not about to start paying for general online news they had become accustomed to getting for free. He had thought at the time that they might, one day.

But now, eight years later, he saw no evidence of that happening. Readers simply did not value local news enough to pay for it. Borrell found only about 12 percent of most markets went to the Web for local news.

They still bought newspapers, though in diminishing numbers, and quite often not with the same imperative that drove Borrell's one-time newsroom colleagues. While journalists envision people tossing out the coupons to get to the news, many readers perform the ritual in reverse—tossing the news to get to the coupons, a practice confirmed by an NAA study that found that fully half of all readers bought local papers for the ads. Such, Borrell concluded, was the fate of a product that, in the eyes of its intended audience, was "not that compelling."

But wait. Hadn't the industry been pinning its hopes for well over a generation on local news, on bringing to suburban readers targeted versions of the traditional mix of local politics, cops, fires, courts, and the occasional strange doings that used to fill the big-city papers that everyone in town read? And hadn't the mix grown to include dispatches on schools and zoning and features of local interest? And hadn't some of that work been of consequence, hadn't it won awards and allowed publishers to speak of their "watchdog" role and to suggest, channeling Jefferson, that their work kept the citizenry informed and enlightened? *Not that compelling?*

Or did Borrell have a point? Was it possible that the self-satisfaction with which news organizations regarded themselves and their role had been undermined and diluted? The news purists had been warning for years of the danger of a culture in which publishers cheapened the value of their content with cutbacks intended to satisfy investors and media analysts. But no one had paid them much mind, because even in a diminished state the product still sold. If you could do it on the cheap, why not?

Lack of competition was good for profits but turned many dailies into vanilla approximations of themselves.

But it was not just the shareholders' fault. Competition, the catalyst that drove journalists, that fueled their anxiety, fear, ruthless streaks—qualities of personality that propelled them to succeed—had been vanishing for decades. Fewer newspapers in fewer towns found themselves in direct competition for stories, and while this helped make a good many papers very profitable (Exhibit A: Gannett), it also had the effect of rendering many newspapers into vanilla approximations of themselves. The papers weren't necessarily bad; they looked good and read well enough. But it was hard to imagine anyone standing on a street corner shouting, "Extra! Extra! Read all about it!" when the headline screamed ZONING DISPUTE.

The problem with the content, however, did not stop there. Stories were ever more routine, in the subject and in the way they were told—so much so that news, as defined and presented, had for years been an ongoing object of parody in, most famously, *The Onion.*

The pity of it was that in the decades that preceded the recent downsizing of content, newspapers had been stretching the definition of news in ways that made papers of the more distant past seem hopelessly narrow. *Front Page* romanticism aside, readers of, say, the *St. Louis Star* in 1942 would have had no sense of the dark and frightened mood in town in the first winter of World War II, because the paper did not consider such matters news. A generation later, everyone, it seemed, had an investigative team, as well as education, immigration, and health-care reporters, and a local columnist or two. The best writing was no longer necessarily on the sports pages and there was no shortage of FOIA requests. The definition of news expanded, as did the way news was told.

But then, over a stretch of years long enough that it was hard to notice, the reports that came back from once-proud-and-lively newsrooms were that it was getting very hard to, say, sniff out local corruption or capture the zeitgeist of a community when your beat had expanded from three towns to ten, and when the unspoken but well-understood directive from above was to feed the beast, in print and, in time, online. Newspapers still produced admirable work, but the appearance of another plaque on the newsroom wall tended to obscure the fact that while great work was still being accomplished, a good deal of what was otherwise being done was of diminishing value and allure.

So for Borrell, editors and publishers and owners who rallied to the cry of paid content were working under the misapprehension that what they had given away or sold very cheaply would suddenly be regarded as having value by readers whose needs had been sadly undervalued for a long time.

But Borrell still believed that there was money to be made in the news business—online and in print. Print was the place for display advertising, and for all those coupons and end-of-summer ads. Free online access brought the readers—the eyeballs—advertisers wanted. As for paid content, Nancy Wang and Jeff Mignon had for some time been preaching the virtues of a hybrid approach of mixing paid and free online content to the fifty or so news organizations of various sizes they consulted for, and the result, she says, was almost always the same: the young, Web-savvy people would get excited by the possibilities, and their older, more tradition-bound editors, she says, would scream, "NO!"

The resistance, she explains, was not a function of blind stubbornness, but rather a fear that that which they hold sacred was about to be diluted in the name of making a buck. And they were not altogether wrong.

It was at this moment in the conversation that publishers and editors were forced to confront a difficult choice: if a newsroom had a finite number of reporters, and if that newsroom needed a new revenue stream to make up for declining circulation and lower ad rates, it needed to report something that people wanted enough to pay for. Not all people. Just some, with the money and the willingness to pay.

That, in turn, meant *not* devoting the time, the staff, and the money to report on what was presumably of interest to everyone. It meant making the choice to provide content that was exclusive to paying customers. It meant satisfying the core readership at the expense of those unwilling, or perhaps unable, to prove their loyalty with a check or money order.

Something had to go, if you were going to stay in business. But if you were going to start selling news, you had decide what you could offer that people might buy.

And so once the conversation moved past the arguments about the *idea* of paying, and it became ever more apparent that news organizations would do well to charge for *something,* the word heard most often was "value."

Three

Peter Fader was such a fan of TimesSelect—the opinion-oriented section that *The New York Times* briefly put behind a paywall—that had the price doubled he would gladly have paid it. TimesSelect represented value for Fader, a quality, he says, that always eclipses price when a purchase is being considered. Fader is a professor of marketing at the Wharton School at the University of Pennsylvania. He explains that pricing "is a trade-off attitude." Economists, Fader says, often make the mistake of building projections upon the supposition that people are rational beings. But people, he says, will perform the irrational act of paying for all kinds of things that they can otherwise get for nothing.

They will, for instance, pay 99 cents for songs on iTunes that can be downloaded for free because Apple makes the transactional experience not only legal, but easy, attractive, and accessible. People will also pay for subscriptions. They will, for example, willingly allow their bank accounts to be dunned $17 a month for Netflix even though weeks may pass without a rental or download. No matter, Fader says; those subscribers have fallen into an "electronic trance" in which they refuse to cancel because they anticipate renting one day, real soon.

Perhaps the best and most alluring analogy for selling news online is cable television. TV used to be free and in some places still is. But cable transformed the idea that the medium came without cost by making it into a medium that provided a wide choice of occasionally terrific content that was exclusive to those who paid for it.

The transformation did not come instantly, and despite all the new channels, the experience of watching cable TV is often as it was in the old five channels-plus-UHF days: *Nothing's on.* But cable offers lots of choices, on a sliding scale, and Fader says people will continue to pay for the promise of value because whatever disappointments they might have experienced—for instance, a weeper on Lifetime—have been outweighed by, say, *The Sopranos.*

New technologies arrive with lamentations for the institutions and traditions and old technologies sure to die out. It was that way with television—*the death of movie theaters!* And with FM radio—*the end of live concerts!* But new technologies do not replace the old, they merely take a place at their side. Grand and aging movie palaces became multiplexes, and owners did such a brisk business that people decided it was worth spending an extra $1.50 to pre-order tickets on Fandango. So it is that Fandango sells what once came without cost, but which now represents admission denied to someone else.

That, in a sense, is also the calculus for success at *Congressional Quarterly,* which sells information that is available elsewhere at no cost but at considerable hassle. If you are, for instance, a lobbyist who needs to know the status of a particularly worrisome piece of legislation, *CQ* can sell you, through its BillTrack database, the full text and an analysis of the bill, its status in committee, a profile of that committee, a district-by-district breakdown of the members of the committee, a dollar-by-dollar breakdown of those members' campaign contributors—in short, everything a clever lobbyist needs to know *before* that information comes to another clever lobbyist for the opposition. This is what Robert Merry, *CQ*'s president and editor-in-chief, calls "information paranoia," a particularly virulent affliction in Washington.

CQ sells access to thirty-five different databases. It has four niche verticals—homeland security, health, a budget tracker, and its political money line. It does give some information away for free. So do *The Wall Street Journal*—a story at a time—and the *Financial Times*—a limited number of stories each month, before the paywall goes up. But these are, from a marketing standpoint, the journalistic equivalent of movie trailers on Fandango: *If you loved our report on this stimulus package, you'll want to see . . .*

Merry thinks of *CQ* as a pyramid. At its base are the many visitors to CQPolitics who pay nothing but who do deliver eyeballs. At the top are those so ravenous for particular slices of news they can use that they will pay $10,000 or more a year for access. In other words, *CQ* sells various products for various media to audiences who differ not by geography or income but by need. It was doing so well before analysts like Wang and Mignon began preaching the virtues of the "hybrid" model to their sometimes-reluctant clients.

The Wall Street Journal will soon expand its existing free-for-a-single-story "hybrid" model into one that includes micropayments. *The New York Times* is considering such revenue streams as metered payments (like those at the *FT*) and premium content memberships that presumably would cater to the paper's most loyal readers. It is one thing for the *Times*, the *Journal*, and the *FT* to impose fees on some of their content because their content is so highly regarded by so many. But what of those general news publications that have done away with so much of their original coverage of anything that is not local, and have diminished even that? Are they doomed? Or can they save themselves by redefining their content, and by extension, news?

General news has long been predicated on the idea that people's primary interest in news was defined by where they lived. But that was never completely so. The ethnic press, for instance, is as much about where you are from as about where you landed. Similarly, magazines are now almost exclusively defined by the particular interests of their readers. (The demise of the general-interest magazine offers a powerful and emotional parallel to the fate of the general-interest newspaper: a generation ago it seemed impossible to envision an America without *The Saturday Evening Post, Life,* and *Look.*)

Yet most newspapers still represent a model defined by borders. This makes for a relatively easy business to run when most readers lived in one place—a small town or a city. With the post-World War II exodus to the suburbs, however, the urban newspaper model built on cops, courts, fires, and politics was essentially picked up and transplanted not to one locality but to many disparate places where, it was assumed, readers had little interest in the goings-on across the town line, and the ever more remote downtown. Gone was the big-city paper; in its place came the regional daily.

But now, *The Washington Post,* for one, has begun to embrace the idea of defining itself not as the newspaper of Washington, the physical entity, but as Washington, the idea—just as *The Wall Street Journal,* which the *Post*'s new editor, Marcus Brauchli, used to run, is not about Wall Street, a district in lower Manhattan. In a memo to her staff last December, the *Post*'s publisher, Katharine Weymouth, wrote of the paper as "being about Washington, for Washingtonians and those affected by it." The latter phrase is key. It suggests that the paper is both acknowledging the physical boundaries of a portion of its coverage—"the indispensable guide to Washington"—while expanding beyond them. It means that Washington is, in a sense, everywhere—in every tax dollar, FAA hearing, wherever Washington's institutions and influence reach. A new and different hyper-local.

If this succeeds, what's to stop, say, the *Detroit Free Press* from augmenting its definition of Detroit as a municipality with Detroit as an idea—say, all things automotive? There is news in cars, lots of it. And there are people who need to know it, not all of them residents of greater Detroit. One wonders what the denuded *San Jose Mercury News,* a paper that had been a model of the regional news organization, might have become had it positioned itself as the definitive source of tech news for a readership well beyond Silicon Valley.

Once a news organization sees itself as something more than in service of a place, it puts itself in a position to tap into one of the emotional imperatives that sustain the niche sites. Geoff Ketchum's Orangebloods, for instance, is not limited to resident Texans. Regardless of where they live, his core readers have proven themselves willing to pay for the knowledge his site offers so that they can remain a part of a conversation. "Newspapers can't entice us into small payment systems," argues the media thinker Clay Shirky, "because we care too much about our conversation with one another. . . ." Newspapers, as presently defined, cannot. But if Orangebloods can, why can't a vertical on what is otherwise a general news site?

Those conversations can be inclusive (pay $9.95 a month and become an Orangeblood) or exclusive (CQ BillTrack), but what they have in common is that each, in a sense, represents what might best be called a Community of Need. The need is for the news that fuels a particular conversation. So long as there is something new to report.

Niche sites succeed, in large measure, by staking out a line of coverage that represents precisely the kinds of stories that newspapers decided to abandon years ago because so many readers found them so tedious: process stories. The relentless journey of a bill through a legislative body—*cloture vote!* Tracking a running back as he decides between Baylor and Texas. But process stories are stories that, by their nature, offer an endless source of developments; there is always something new happening, even if to those on the outside of the conversation, it is news of little value. Robert Merry wonders, for instance, why so many newspapers abandoned their statehouse bureaus when those capital cities were awash in money, lobbyists, legislators, and eager-beaver aides who'd be willing to pay quite a lot for information that might give them an edge. They did so because most readers said the stories were boring—and that was true for most readers, but not all.

But there is an important caveat: such projects do not succeed if they're done on the cheap. They require reporters whose primary responsibility is to supply the endless news that feeds those relatively few readers' needs. The need is for news. Not opinion. (Bobby Burton is not alone in believing the *Times* erred in what it chose to place behind its TimesSelect paywall, which was not news but the opinions of its famous columnists.) The problem with opinion is that the Web has made everyone a columnist precisely because it costs nothing to offer a point of view. Nor does it cost very much, or sometimes nothing at all, to fill a site with well-intentioned work, and opinion, provided by citizen journalists. But as Burton discovered in the early days of Rivals, those amateur journalists may have wise and clever things to say, but when he wanted to regularly break news he went out and hired people who knew how to do it—and he pays them between $30,000 and more than $150,000 a year.

Orangebloods is only as good as its next scoop; because if its stories begin appearing with any frequency someplace else— and perhaps, for free—the compact that Ketchum has with his readers is in jeopardy. Which is why there is nothing passive or reactive about the site's approach to its work. That, however, has not always been the case for general news that has traditionally defined itself by default: it's news because it's always been news. This, in turn, has created a culture of news in which the operative verb, far too often, is *said,* a culture in which all a reporter needs to do is listen and record.

As a result, too much of what fills the news pages is, as is often said, stenography. And because it can be done quickly, and at great volume, and with relatively little effort, it endures. The timing could not be more dispiriting, given that the generation in power in journalism now came to the field with a sense of journalism's possibilities, and broadened the idea of what news could be. But this generation also came of age at a time of growing newsroom prosperity.

This expanded sense of what the content could be made newspapers fatter; new sections appeared; nothing had to go, save for those process stories that no one wanted to read. Not a tough choice. Not like now, when the redefinition of news may mean deciding what you can sell to those willing to pay, and, by extension, what you will give up in the rest of the day's report so that you can redeploy your shrinking staff.

Inevitably, this raises an existential issue: What are newspapers for? Do they exist to serve narrow bands of interest? Or are there issues that transcend the paying niches, journalistic responsibilities that we should worry might well be overlooked and ignored in the interests of satisfying those who foot the bill?

It is not enough to simply hope that editors and publishers will retain their nobler instincts, not when times are tough. But, at the risk of sounding cynical, there is every reason to believe that they might continue offering stories of consequence for a larger, and perhaps unpaying audience for another reason—because it might be good for business. There are stories that transcend demographic borders. They are stories that are universal in their appeal, and infectious in their presentation. Not all novels, after all, are written for niche audiences; some speak to people who, on the surface, have nothing in common with one another. And as it is with novels, and movies, and television shows that attract wide followings, there are stories that capture the eye and the imagination, and which lure readers who might stick around, or even come back, and bring advertisers with them. The burden rests on the news organization to do what news people have always done: find those stories.

Transform the everyday work of journalism from a reactive, money-losing proposition into a more selective enterprise.

So it is that journalism's crisis offers an opportunity to transform the everyday work of journalism from a reactive and money-losing proposition into a more selective enterprise of reporting things that no one else knows. And choosing, quite deliberately, to ignore much of what can be found elsewhere.

People will pay for news they deem essential, and depending on the depth and urgency of their need, they will pay a lot. Their subscriptions, in turn, might well help to underwrite the cost of producing original work that might remain free and be of interest to more than a select few.

Those subscriptions will not save newspapers. They alone will not pay for the cost of reporting. No one revenue stream will—not online or print advertising, or alerts on handheld devices, or new electronic readers that display stories handsomely. The hope is that they *all* will.

The means of distributing the news will change, but what is clear and unchanging is people's desire to know things, to be told a story, and to be able talk about it all with other people— for such things matter.

Extra! Extra! Read all about it!

MICHAEL SHAPIRO, a contributing editor to CJR, teaches at Columbia's Graduate School of Journalism. His most recent book is *Bottom of the Ninth: Branch Rickey, Casey Stengel, and the Daring Scheme to Save Baseball From Itself.*

The Massless Media

With the mass media losing their audience to smaller, more targeted outlets, we may be headed for an era of noisy, contentious press reminiscent of the 1800s.

WILLIAM POWERS

One day last June, as a hot political summer was just warming up, a new poll was released. This one wasn't about which candidate voters favored for the White House. It was about which news channels they were choosing with their TV remotes.

"Political polarization is increasingly reflected in the public's news viewing habits," the Pew Research Center for the People and the Press reported.

Since 2000, the Fox News Channel's gains have been greatest among political conservatives and Republicans. More than half of regular Fox viewers describe themselves as politically conservative (52%), up from 40% four years ago. At the same time, CNN, Fox's principal rival, has a more Democrat-leaning audience than in the past.

It's no surprise, of course, that Fox News viewers are more conservative than CNN viewers. But it is rather surprising that even as the network's audience is growing in sheer numbers, it is also growing increasingly conservative. The months following the poll offered further evidence of the ideological sorting of cable-news viewers. During the Democratic National Convention, in July, CNN came in first in the cable ratings, prompting a Fox spokesman to say, "They were playing to their core audience." Weeks later, during the Republican National Convention, Fox News played to its core audience and scored ratings that beat not only CNN and the other cable channels but even the broadcast networks—a historical first. When election day came around and George Bush won, it wasn't hard to predict that Fox News would again be the cable ratings victor: the conservative candidate took the prize, and so, naturally, did the news channel favored by conservatives.

Committed partisans on the left and the right have always had ideological media outlets they could turn to (*The Nation and National Review*, for example), but for most Americans political affiliation was not the determining factor in choosing where they got their news. The three national networks, CBS, NBC, and ABC, offered pretty much the same product and the same establishment point of view. That product was something you shared with all Americans—not just friends, neighbors, and others like you but millions of people you would never meet, many of them very unlike you.

For some time now Americans have been leaving those vast media spaces where they used to come together and have instead been clustering in smaller units. The most broad-based media outlets, the networks and metropolitan newspapers, have been losing viewers and readers for years. But lately, thanks to the proliferation of new cable channels and the rise of digital and wireless technology, the disaggregation of the old mass audience has taken on a furious momentum. And the tribalization is not just about political ideology. In the post-mass-media era audiences are sorting themselves by ethnicity, language, religion, profession, socioeconomic status, sexual orientation, and numerous other factors.

"The country has atomized into countless market segments defined not only by demography, but by increasingly nuanced and insistent product preferences," *Business Week* reported last July, in a cover story called "The Vanishing Mass Market." To survive in this environment even old mass-media companies have had to learn the art of "niching down." Though national magazines have produced targeted sub-editions for years, the slicing grows ever thinner. Time, Inc., the granddaddy of print media for the masses, has launched a new women's magazine just for Wal-Mart shoppers. Radio now has satellite and Web variants that let listeners choose their taste pods with exceptional precision. The fast-growing XM Satellite Radio has not just one "urban" music channel but seven, each serving up a different subgenre twenty-four hours a day.

Some niches are so small they're approaching the vanishing point. There are now hundreds of thousands of bloggers, individuals who publish news, commentary, and other content on their own idiosyncratic websites. Some boast readerships exceeding those of prestigious print magazines, but most number their faithful in the double and triple digits. Find the one who shares your tastes and leanings, and you'll have attained the ne plus ultra of bespoke media: the ghostly double of yourself.

To sensibilities shaped by the past fifty years, the emerging media landscape seems not just chaotic but baleful. Common sense would suggest that as the vast village green of the broadcast era is chopped up into tiny plots, divisions in the culture will only multiply. If everyone tunes in to a different channel, and discourse happens only among like minds, is there any hope for social and political cohesion? Oh, for a cozy living room with one screen and Walter Cronkite signing off with his authoritative, unifying "That's the way it is."

It's instructive to remember, however, that the centralized, homogeneous mass-media environment of Cronkite's day was really an anomaly, an exception to the historical rule. For two centuries before the arrival of television America had a wild, cacophonous, emphatically decentralized media culture that mirrored society itself. And something like that media culture seems to be returning right now.

When primitive newspapers first appeared in seventeenth-century London, they were just official bulletins about the doings of the monarchy. Royally sanctioned and censored, they had no ideology other than that of the throne. The first real American newspaper, the *Boston News-Letter*, came straight from this mold. It was put out by an imperial official, the postmaster of colonial Boston, and stamped with the same seal of governmental approval worn by its British predecessors: "Published by Authority."

That timid approach didn't last long in America, however. In 1721 a Boston printer named James Franklin, older brother of Benjamin, founded a paper called the *New England Courant*, which brashly questioned the policies of the colony's ruling elite. The very first issue attacked Cotton Mather and other worthies for their support of smallpox inoculations. The paper was on the wrong side of that argument, but the real news was that it made the argument at all. The *Courant* was "America's first fiercely independent newspaper, a bold, antiestablishment journal that helped to create the nation's tradition of an irreverent press," Walter Isaacson writes in his recent biography of Benjamin Franklin (whose first published writings appeared in his brother's paper).

Franklin's paper set the tone for the evolution of the media in this country. Outspoken newspapers played a crucial role in the Revolutionary War, and when it was over the leaders of the young republic consciously used public policy to nurture a free press. As the Princeton sociologist Paul Starr notes in his recent book, *The Creation of the Media: Political Origins of Modern Communications*, the United States dispensed with the European tradition of licensing papers and policing their content. Congress even granted American publishers lower rates for postal delivery, a valuable subsidy that made starting up and running a paper more economical.

Such policies, combined with the freewheeling ethos that had already taken root in the press, set off a wild journalistic flowering in the nineteenth century. By the 1830s newspapers were everywhere, and they spoke in a myriad of voices about all manner of issues. Alexis de Tocqueville, who was accustomed to the reined-in newspapers of France, marveled at all the variety.

> The number of periodical and semi-periodical publications in the United States is almost incredibly large . . . It may readily be imagined that neither discipline nor unity of action can be established among so many combatants, and each one consequently fights under his own standard. All the political journals of the United States are, indeed, arrayed on the side of the administration or against it; but they attack and defend it in a thousand different ways.

In this the media reflected the political scene. The nineteenth century was a time of intense national growth and fervent argument about what direction the country should take. Numerous political parties appeared (Democratic, Whig, Republican, Free Soil, Know-Nothing), and the views and programs they advocated all found expression in sympathetic papers. In fact, the parties themselves financially supported newspapers, as did the White House for a time. Starr notes that according to a U.S. Census estimate, by the middle of the nineteenth century 80 percent of American newspapers were avowedly partisan.

This partisanship was not typically expressed in high-minded appeals to readers' better instincts. As Tocqueville wrote, "The characteristics of the American journalist consist in an open and coarse appeal to the passions of his readers; he abandons principles to assail the characters of individuals, to track them into private life and disclose all their weaknesses and vices." When Martin Chuzzlewit, the central character of the Dickens novel by the same name, arrives in the New York City of the early 1840s, he is greeted by newsboys hawking papers with names like the *New York Slabber* and the *New York Keyhole Reporter*. "Here's the *New York Sewer*!" one newsie shouts. "Here's the *Sewer*'s exposure of the Wall Street Gang, and the *Sewer*'s exposure of the Washington Gang, and the *Sewer*'s exclusive account of a flagrant act of dishonesty committed by the Secretary of State when he was eight years old."

Partisan and scandalously downmarket, the nineteenth-century media nonetheless helped forge a sense of national identity.

Yet even though the media of this period were profuse, partisan, and scandalously downmarket, they were at the same time a powerful amalgamator that encouraged participatory democracy and forged a sense of national identity. Michael Schudson, a professor of communication and sociology at the University of California at San Diego and the author of *The Sociology of News* (2003), says that the rampant partisanship displayed by newspapers "encouraged people to be attentive to their common enterprise of electing representatives or presidents." Commenting that "politics was the best entertainment in town in the middle of the 19th century," Schudson compares its effect to that of sports today. "Professional baseball is an integrative mechanism even though it works by arousing very partisan loyalties," he says. In other words, newspapers helped pull the country together not by playing down differences and pretending everyone agreed but by celebrating and exploiting the fact that people didn't. It's the oldest American paradox: nothing unifies like individualism.

We tend to think of the rise of the modern mass media as primarily a function of technology: the advent of television, for example, enabled broadcasters to reach tens of millions of Americans, but the cost of entry was high enough to sharply limit the number of networks. However, technology was only one of several factors that determined the character of the media establishment that arose in the United States after World War II. Beginning in the nineteenth century the idea of objectivity began to cross over from science into business and popular culture. As the historian Scott Sandage notes in his new book, *Born Losers: A History of Failure in America*, a whole new industry rose up in nineteenth-century New York when a handful of creative entrepreneurs discovered they could gather "objective" information about businesses and people (the precursor of modern-day credit ratings) and sell it to other businesses for a profit. Soon journalists, including the muckrakers of the Progressive Era, were embracing a similar notion of objective, irrefutable fact. When the Washington journalist Walter Lippmann wrote in the 1920s that "good reporting requires the exercise of the highest of scientific virtues," and called for the founding of journalistic research institutes, he was, as Starr notes, codifying a standard of disinterested inquiry that would influence generations of journalists to come.

At the same time, a federal government that had once used policy to encourage the growth of a free press now faced a very different challenge. Unlike newspapers, the public airwaves were a finite resource, and someone had to decide how to dole it out. The solution was a federal regulatory structure that sought to ensure fairness but could never offer the ease of access or the expressive freedom of the press. (Not that the networks necessarily wanted the latter; in order to pull in the large audiences that ad buyers demanded, all strove for a safe neutrality that offended no one.) For these reasons, although the broadcast media reached more people, the range of content they offered was actually more constricted than that of the print media that preceded them.

Finally, the political culture of the 1940s and 1950s discouraged extremism. The two major political parties of that period certainly had their differences, but they shared a basic set of beliefs about the country's priorities. Politics hewed to the center, and the media both reflected and reinforced this tendency. The centrist, "objective" networks and large newspapers didn't just *cover* the political establishment; they were an essential part of it. The anchormen who appeared on television and the columnists of the great papers were effectively spokesmen for the ruling postwar elite. (On occasion literally so: Lippmann, the great proponent of objectivity, worked with his fellow reporter James Reston on a famous speech by Senator Arthur Vandenberg; both journalists then turned around to write about the speech for their respective papers.)

That establishment consensus exploded in the 1960s and 1970s, with Vietnam and Watergate, but the mass media hung on for a few decades, a vestigial reminder of what had been. The Reagan era and the end of the Cold War dealt the old politico-media structure the final blows. In the 1990s partisan politics really took hold in Washington, and again the news media followed suit. The demise of the postwar consensus made the mass media's centrism obsolete. Long-simmering conservative resentment of the mainstream media fueled the rise of Rush Limbaugh and Fox News. Their success, in turn, has lately inspired efforts on the left to create avowedly liberal radio and cable outlets.

Socially, too, our fragmented media are to this era what James Franklin's newspaper was to the 1720s and the CBS evening news was to the 1950s. The cultural sameness and conformity that prevailed after World War II—the era of *Father Knows Best* and Betty Crocker—have been replaced by a popular pursuit of difference and self-expression. In explaining why McDonald's has shifted a significant portion of its advertising into niches, an executive of the company told *BusinessWeek*, "From the consumer point of view, we've had a change from 'I want to be normal' to 'I want to be special.'" In a mass-media world it's hard to be special. But in the land of niches it's easy. What is blogging if not a celebration of the self?

The "Trust us, we know better" ethos that undergirded the broadcast era today seems increasingly antique. If red and blue America agree on anything, it's that they don't believe the media. To traditionalists worried about the future of news, this attitude reflects a corrosive cynicism. But in another way it's much like the skepticism that animates great journalism. As the media have become more transparent, and suffered their own scandals, the public has learned to think about the news the same way a good journalist would—that is, to doubt everything it's told.

Although network ratings continue to plummet, there's still evidence elsewhere of an enduring demand for the sort of connectedness that only broad-based media can offer. For the six months that ended last September 30 many of America's largest newspapers saw the now customary declines in circulation. But among those that saw increases were the only three with a national subscriber base: *The New York Times*, *The Wall Street Journal*, and *USA Today*. The presidential debates last year drew impressive audiences to the broadcast networks, suggesting that although Americans no longer go to mass outlets out of habit, they will go by choice when there's good reason. In one of those debates Senator John Kerry cracked a Tony Soprano joke, and it was safe to assume that most viewers got the allusion. When we rue the passing of mass togetherness, we often forget that the strongest connective tissue in modern culture is entertainment—a mass medium if ever there was one.

Moreover, for all the pointed criticism and dismissive eye-rolling that niche and mass outlets direct each other's way, the two are becoming more and more symbiotic. Where would the *Drudge Report* and the blogging horde be without *The New York Times*, CBS News, and *The Washington Post*? Were it not for the firsthand reporting offered by those media dinosaurs, the Internet crowd would have nothing to talk about. Conversely, where would the Web versions of mass outlets be without the traffic that is directed their way by the smaller players? If there's a new media establishment taking form, it's shaped like a pyramid, with a handful of mass outlets at the top and innumerable niches supporting them from below, barking upward.

Whenever critics of the new media worry about the public's clustering in niches, there's an unspoken assumption that viewers watch only one outlet, as was common thirty years ago—that is, that there are Fox people and CNN people, and never the twain shall meet. But the same Pew poll that showed the increasingly ideological grouping of cable audiences revealed that most Americans watch the news with remote at the ready, poised to dart away at any moment. Pew also detected an enormous affinity for "inadvertent" news consumption: a large majority of Internet users from almost all demographic groups say that while online they encounter news unexpectedly, when they aren't even looking for it. "Fully 73% of Internet users come across the news this way," Pew reported, "up from 65%

two years ago, and 55% as recently as 1999." Thus it appears that one of the great joys of newspaper reading—serendipitous discovery—lives on.

And although much changes in the media over time, there are some eternal truths. Most outlets crave two things, money and impact, and the easiest path to both is the old-fashioned one: grow your audience. Ambitious niches will always seek to become larger, and in so doing to attract a more diverse audience. It's only a matter of time before the first mass blog is identified, celebrated, and showered with minivan ads.

Finally, there's no substantive evidence yet that the rise of the niches is bad for democracy. The fractious, disunited, politically partisan media of the nineteenth century heightened public awareness of politics, and taught the denizens of a new democracy how to be citizens. Fast forward to the present. The United States just held an election that was covered by noisy, divisive, often thoroughly disreputable post-broadcast-era media. And 120 million people, 60 percent of eligible voters, showed up to cast their ballots—-a higher percentage than have voted in any election since 1968. Maybe we're on to something.

WILLIAM POWERS is a columnist for *National Journal* and a former reporter for *The Washington Post*. He writes frequently about the media, politics, and culture.

Test-Your-Knowledge Form

We encourage you to photocopy and use this page as a tool to assess how the articles in *Annual Editions* expand on the information in your textbook. By reflecting on the articles you will gain enhanced text information. You can also access this useful form on a product's book support website at *http://www.mhhe.com/cls*.

NAME: _____   DATE: _____

TITLE AND NUMBER OF ARTICLE:
_____

BRIEFLY STATE THE MAIN IDEA OF THIS ARTICLE:
_____

LIST THREE IMPORTANT FACTS THAT THE AUTHOR USES TO SUPPORT THE MAIN IDEA:
_____

WHAT INFORMATION OR IDEAS DISCUSSED IN THIS ARTICLE ARE ALSO DISCUSSED IN YOUR TEXTBOOK OR OTHER READINGS THAT YOU HAVE DONE? LIST THE TEXTBOOK CHAPTERS AND PAGE NUMBERS:
_____

LIST ANY EXAMPLES OF BIAS OR FAULTY REASONING THAT YOU FOUND IN THE ARTICLE:
_____

LIST ANY NEW TERMS/CONCEPTS THAT WERE DISCUSSED IN THE ARTICLE, AND WRITE A SHORT DEFINITION:

We Want Your Advice

ANNUAL EDITIONS revisions depend on two major opinion sources: one is our Advisory Board, listed in the front of this volume, which works with us in scanning the thousands of articles published in the public press each year; the other is you—the person actually using the book. Please help us and the users of the next edition by completing the prepaid article rating form on this page and returning it to us. Thank you for your help!

ANNUAL EDITIONS: Mass Media 10/11

ARTICLE RATING FORM

Here is an opportunity for you to have direct input into the next revision of this volume.
We would like you to rate each of the articles listed below, using the following scale:

1. **Excellent: should definitely be retained**
2. **Above average: should probably be retained**
3. **Below average: should probably be deleted**
4. **Poor: should definitely be deleted**

Your ratings will play a vital part in the next revision.
Please mail this prepaid form to us as soon as possible.
Thanks for your help!

RATING	ARTICLE	RATING	ARTICLE
	1. Off Course		20. Maybe It *Is* Time to Panic
	2. Tele[re]vision		21. What's a Fair Share in the Age of Google?: How to Think about News in the Link Economy
	3. Research on the Effects of Media Violence		
	4. True Crime: The Roots of an American Obsession		22. Ideastream: *The New* "Public Media"
	5. Wikipedia in the Newsroom		23. The Shame Game: 'To Catch a Predator' Gets the Ratings, but at What Cost?
	6. Journalist Bites Reality!		
	7. The Future of Reading		24. The Battle over the Battle of Fallujah: A Videogame So Real It Hurts
	8. Are Newspapers Doomed?		
	9. The Great Wall of Facebook		25. Distorted Picture
	10. The News Mausoleum		26. The Quality-Control Quandary
	11. Overload!: Journalism's Battle for Relevance in an Age of Too Much Information		27. Why Journalists Are Not Above the Law
			28. What Would You Do?: The Journalism That Tweaks Reality, Then Reports What Happens
	12. Don't Blame the Journalism: The Economic and Technological Forces behind the Collapse of Newspapers		
			29. The Lives of Others: What Does It Mean to 'Tell Someone's Story'?
	13. Climate Change: Now What?		30. A Porous Wall
	14. Whatever Happened to Iraq?: How the Media Lost Interest in a Long-Running War with No End in Sight		31. How Can YouTube Survive?
			32. Online Salvation?
			33. The Secrets of Googlenomics
	15. Myth-Making in New Orleans		34. But Who's Counting?
	16. What the Mainstream Media Can Learn from Jon Stewart		35. Old Media Strikes Back
			36. A Fading Taboo
	17. Double Whammy		37. Nonprofit News
	18. Charticle Fever		38. Open for Business
	19. Beyond News		39. The Massless Media

BUSINESS REPLY MAIL
FIRST CLASS MAIL PERMIT NO. 551 DUBUQUE IA

POSTAGE WILL BE PAID BY ADDRESSEE

McGraw-Hill Contemporary Learning Series
501 BELL STREET
DUBUQUE, IA 52001

ABOUT YOU

Name   Date
_____

Are you a teacher? ❑ A student? ❑
Your school's name
_____

Department
_____

Address   City   State   Zip
_____

School telephone #
_____

YOUR COMMENTS ARE IMPORTANT TO US!

Please fill in the following information:
For which course did you use this book?
_____

Did you use a text with this ANNUAL EDITION? ❑ yes ❑ no
What was the title of the text?
_____

What are your general reactions to the Annual Editions concept?
_____

Have you read any pertinent articles recently that you think should be included in the next edition? Explain.
_____

Are there any articles that you feel should be replaced in the next edition? Why?
_____

Are there any World Wide Websites that you feel should be included in the next edition? Please annotate.
_____

May we contact you for editorial input? ❑ yes ❑ no
May we quote your comments? ❑ yes ❑ no